Leveraging AI for Inclusive and Equitable Development

Swati Chakraborty
Concordia University, Canada

IGI Global
Scientific Publishing
Publishing Tomorrow's Research Today

Vice President of Editorial — Melissa Wagner
Director of Acquisitions — Mikaela Felty
Director of Book Development — Jocelynn Hessler
Production Manager — Mike Brehm
Cover Design — Jose Rosado

Published in the United States of America by
IGI Global Scientific Publishing
701 East Chocolate Avenue
Hershey, PA, 17033, USA
Tel: 717-533-8845 | Fax: 717-533-7115
Website: https://www.igi-global.com E-mail: cust@igi-global.com

Library of Congress Cataloging-in-Publication Data

Names: Chakraborty, Swati, 1985- editor
Title: Leveraging AI for inclusive and equitable development / edited by: Swati Chakraborty.
Other titles: Leveraging artificial intelligence for inclusive and equitable development
Description: Hershey, PA : IGI Global Scientific Publishing, [2026] | Includes bibliographical references and index. | Summary: "This book aims to provide the research community with an interdisciplinary platform to examine AI's impact on society critically"-- Provided by publisher.
Identifiers: LCCN 2025011132 (print) | LCCN 2025011133 (ebook) | ISBN 9798337323879 hardback | ISBN 9798337323886 paperback | ISBN 9798337323893 ebook
Subjects: LCSH: Artificial intelligence--Social aspects | Technology--Social aspects | Equality--Technological innovations
Classification: LCC HM851 .L467 2025 (print) | LCC HM851 (ebook) | DDC 303.48/33--dc23/eng/20250822
LC record available at https://lccn.loc.gov/2025011132
LC ebook record available at https://lccn.loc.gov/2025011133

British Cataloguing in Publication Data
A Cataloguing in Publication record for this book is available from the British Library.

Table of Contents

Detailed Table of Contents

"From Colonization to Automation: AI's Role in Indigenous Lives in Canada" examines the profound impact of artificial intelligence (AI) on Indigenous communities, highlighting its potential to both challenge and empower these populations. By drawing historical parallels between colonization and the rapid rise of automation, this book explores how AI systems can reinforce systemic inequalities or serve as tools for decolonization and cultural preservation.Key themes include data sovereignty, ethical AI practices, and the representation of Indigenous knowledge within technological systems. The book critically assesses how automation affects traditional livelihoods, education, and economic opportunities in Indigenous communities, often exacerbating existing digital divides. At the same time, it highlights Indigenous-led initiatives that harness AI to promote self-determination, resilience, and the revitalization of languages and traditions.

Artificial Intelligence is reshaping industries and societies, offering unprecedented opportunities to foster inclusive and equitable growth. This study explores the transformative potential of AI in addressing systemic inequalities, enhancing accessibility, and promoting socio-economic development. It highlights AI-driven innovations in education, healthcare, agriculture, and finance, emphasizing their role in bridging gaps for marginalized communities. The chapter illustrates how AI can empower underserved populations, improve decision-making, and enable tailored solutions for diverse needs. It discusses ethical considerations, such as mitigating biases, ensuring transparency, and safeguarding data privacy, essential for equitable AI deployment. The study underscores the importance of inclusive AI policies, stakeholder collaboration, and capacity-building initiatives to harness AI's benefits while minimizing risks. Ultimately, this research advocates for leveraging AI as a catalyst for a sustainable future, ensuring no one is left behind in the digital transformation journey.

Many inventions are being used in the health industry every day. Human life is increasing rapidly and with the use of new technology, the health industry can reach out to more and more people by giving better and more accurate results. Advanced technologies like AI, Augmented Reality, etc. have influenced and defined the health industry in a new way. Mobile phones, wearables, wristbands, and head-mounted displays provide new opportunities for information exchange between real-world and virtual objects, enabling healthcare delivery. The way it is delivered is changing and the overall quality of patient care is improving. For example, by wearing an AR-enabled head-mounted device, surgeons can now see a patient's vital organs during a procedure and consult with a remote colleague, without needing to look away and gather data from multiple displays. Comparative study also has been done. In the end, light has also been thrown on the topic that what are the shortcomings of these applications from the virtual health point of view and which shortcomings should be addressed to improve them.

The banking and financial industry is currently undergoing radical changes induced by the latest technologies of blockchain, AI, and big data analytics. These innovations are overturning the classical methods of lending, investing, and insuring and are providing unprecedented opportunities for financial institutions across the globe. On the other hand, these metamorphoses also pose new challenges in terms of regulatory difficulties, cybersecurity threats, and the shouldering of upskilling professionals in a fast-paced technological environment. Hence, this research is significant given that in a socio-economic and political sense, it addresses how technological advancements that are given additional meaning through education will hence forth define the future of banking and finance, targeting emerging challenges in the industry.

Artificial Intelligence (AI) enables vast governance reform by building smart cities followed by distributing digital governance for official services as it delivers services efficiently and transparently and enhances citizen engagement. Smart cities use big data and IoT technology to achieve their maximum traffic management and waste disposal operations while protecting public security protection levels. E-governance employs AI-driven chatbots, automation, and blockchain for improved service accessibility and reduced bureaucratic delays. The introduction of artificial intelligence systems enhances both the public healthcare service delivery and tax regulatory functions as well as social security program delivery. For the successful adoption of AI systems it needs ethical regulations to resolve three key problems ranging from data protection concerns to algorithm-related biases and computing device inequalities.

Accurate rainfall prediction is essential for agricultural planning and water resource management, particularly in regions like Andhra Pradesh, where the economy relies heavily on monsoon-dependent agriculture. Traditional statistical and empirical models, such as linear regression and ARIMA, have been commonly employed for rainfall forecasting in the region. However, these models often fail to account for the complex, non-linear relationships between variables that influence rainfall, resulting in inaccurate predictions, especially during extreme weather events. This study proposes a hybrid deep learning model combining Bi-LSTM (Bidirectional Long Short-Term Memory) and GRU (Gated Recurrent Unit) to improve rainfall prediction accuracy. The model leverages the strengths of both Bi-LSTM and GRU networks to capture both short- and long-term dependencies in historical rainfall data.

Air pollution prediction plays a critical role in managing public health and environmental policies, especially in regions like India, where air quality is rapidly deteriorating due to urbanization, industrialization, and other anthropogenic activities. This study aims to predict air pollution levels, specifically PM2.5 concentrations, using a deep learning approach—stacked Bidirectional Gated Recurrent Units (BiGRU). The proposed model leverages the advantages of BiGRU to capture both temporal dependencies and complex, non-linear relationships in air pollution data. The study compares the performance of the stacked BiGRU model with traditional statistical and machine learning models, such as Linear Regression, ARIMA, and Support Vector Machines (SVM).

Artificial Intelligence (AI) is revolutionizing sustainable innovation and policymaking by optimizing resource management, enhancing environmental monitoring, and fostering circular economies. This chapter explores Eco-Intelligence—the integration of AI-driven analytics, predictive modeling, and automation in addressing environmental challenges. By leveraging machine learning, and digital twins, AI enables real-time decision-making for climate adaptation, carbon footprint reduction, and green supply chains. Also, AI-driven regulatory frameworks enhance compliance with sustainability standards, bridging the gap between technological advancement and environmental governance. However, ethical concerns, algorithmic biases, and data privacy issues pose challenges to AI's effective deployment in sustainability policy. This chapter critically examines the intersection of AI, environmental stewardship, and regulatory landscapes, proposing a balanced approach to harness AI's potential for long-term ecological and economic resilience.

Hate speech remains a pervasive issue in contemporary society, exacerbated by the rapid expansion of digital communication platforms. This article explores the use of Artificial Intelligence (AI) in combating hate speech, focusing on its detection, classification, and moderation capabilities. It explores how AI can be integrated into legal structures, ethical considerations, and the interplay between AI-driven hate speech detection and freedom of expression. The study provides a comprehensive overview of AI's role in mitigating hate speech, offering recommendations for policymakers and technology developers.

This chapter explores the transformative role of artificial intelligence in advancing environmental sustainability amid escalating climate challenges. It examines how AI-driven technologies optimize resource management, enhance climate monitoring, and promote green innovations across sectors such as energy, agriculture, and waste management. Through predictive analytics, machine learning, and real-time data integration, AI supports more precise climate modeling, disaster early warning systems, and efficient energy use. The chapter also addresses ethical and practical concerns, including algorithmic bias, data privacy, and the digital divide, emphasizing the need for inclusive and responsible AI deployment. By highlighting real-world applications and offering policy recommendations, it underscores the potential of AI to balance technological progress with ecological stewardship. Finally, this work advocates for interdisciplinary collaboration and equitable governance to ensure AI contributes meaningfully to a sustainable and just environmental future.

As artificial intelligence (AI) systems increasingly make decisions in areas such as justice, health, and finance, issues related to algorithmic biases have risen to prominence when discussing equity and inclusion. This chapter investigates how prejudices are built into data and model specifications, and how they can contribute to further entrenching social disparities. From a legal and ethical perspective, it examines the shortcoming that current anti-discrimination laws face when confronted with AI-generated harm. The chapter provides examples of actual cases, such as COMPAS risk assessment tool, to illustrate the real-life implications of biased algorithms. It calls for holistic approaches that include legal remedies, algorithmic transparency, participatory governance, and anti-discrimination data practices. By integrating the development of AI into fair, accountable, and human rights respecting principles, the chapter emphasize the immediate necessity of ensuring that technological development is aligned with just and inclusive development.

Artificial intelligence is disrupting the financial sector globally. Artificial intelligence will also affect financial regulation and financial system stability in several ways. Little is known about how artificial intelligence might affect the stability of the financial system. Using a contextual framework and discourse analysis methodology, this article identifies some risks that artificial intelligence could pose to financial system stability in Nigeria. The study focused on how AI risks affect those directly involved in financial stability work in Nigeria. If these risks are mitigated, the adoption of AI for financial stability work will yield positive benefits for financial stability in Nigeria.

This chapter highlights the conflict between technical advancement and socioeconomic inequality by examining the complex relationship between biotechnology, farmers' rights, and human rights. Although biotechnology has the potential to improve food security, sustainability, and agricultural production, its use frequently marginalizes smallholder farmers due to seed monopolies and stringent intellectual property laws. The chapter looks critically at how national patent laws, TRIPS, UPOV, and other international legal frameworks disproportionately favor agribusinesses at the expense of traditional knowledge, seed sovereignty, and the right to survive. A more inclusive and equitable governance model that empowers farmers as stewards of food systems and biodiversity is advocated in this chapter by contrasting the techno-economic agenda of agricultural biotechnology with the human rights imperative.

The digital divide continues to be a significant barrier to education, disproportionately affecting students with disabilities. This chapter explores the challenges these students face in accessing digital resources and the strategies necessary to create a more inclusive digital learning environment. Key areas of focus include accessible technology, assistive devices, inclusive design principles, and policy frameworks that support equitable access. By integrating universal learning design (UDL) and leveraging advances in assistive technologies, educational institutions can bridge the digital divide and foster a more inclusive learning experience. The chapter highlights best practices, case studies, and recommendations for policymakers, educators, and technology developers to enhance accessibility and ensure that all students, regardless of ability, have equal opportunities to succeed in a digital world.

Preface

INTRODUCTION

In an era marked by rapid technological advancement, artificial intelligence (AI) has emerged as a transformative force that is not only reshaping the global economy, but also redefining the contours of human society. From reimagining healthcare delivery to altering the future of work, from disrupting traditional education models to influencing governance systems, AI is now intricately woven into the fabric of our everyday lives. Yet, with this tremendous potential comes profound responsibility. The central question we must ask is not merely what AI *can* do, but for *whom* it does it—and at what cost.

Leveraging AI for Inclusive and Equitable Development was conceived out of the urgent need to address this critical inflection point. This volume seeks to move beyond utopian visions or dystopian fears, offering instead a grounded, interdisciplinary exploration of how AI can serve as a catalyst for inclusive growth and equitable opportunity—if deployed thoughtfully and ethically.

The chapters within this book reflect a rich tapestry of perspectives, ranging from academic inquiry and empirical research to case studies and policy analysis. Collectively, they interrogate the ways AI intersects with enduring issues of access, representation, and justice. The goal is not only to document how AI is being used, but also to question the systems, assumptions, and values that shape its development and deployment.

At the heart of this volume is a commitment to highlighting both the promise and the peril of AI. On one hand, AI technologies offer unprecedented tools for bridging long-standing social divides—through personalized learning for underserved students, AI-powered diagnostics in remote healthcare systems, or scalable solutions for sustainable development. On the other, there is a very real risk that these same tools can reinforce structural inequalities, amplify bias, and widen the digital divide if left unchecked.

In compiling this work, I was continually struck by the duality of AI's impact: its capacity to both empower and marginalize. This recognition shaped the editorial vision of the book—to serve not only as a scholarly resource but also as a call to action. To developers, it offers insights into responsible innovation. To policymakers, it presents frameworks for equitable governance. To educators and civil society, it provides critical tools to engage with AI's broader societal implications.

The book is particularly intended for:

- Researchers and academics in AI ethics, sociology, political science, and technology studies,
- Policymakers and organizations focused on the intersection of technology and social equity,
- Developers and practitioners working in AI, content moderation, and digital inclusion,
- And graduate and postgraduate students seeking to explore the social dimensions of AI.

As editor, my hope is that this collection will contribute meaningfully to the global discourse on AI by fostering collaboration across disciplines, sectors, and geographies. By centering the principles of equity, inclusion, and justice, we can help ensure that AI becomes not a divider, but a unifier—a technology that works *for* all of humanity, not just a privileged few.

Let this volume be a step toward that vision.

ORGANIZATION OF THE BOOK

The volume opens with **Chapter 1: From Colonization to Automation: AI's Role in Indigenous Lives in Canada**, a critical exploration of how artificial intelligence intersects with the historical and ongoing realities of colonization. Drawing on the lived experiences of Indigenous communities, the chapter reveals how AI systems—if unchecked—can replicate systemic injustices. Yet it also brings forward stories of Indigenous innovation, where AI is being harnessed for language revitalization, data sovereignty, and cultural resilience. This chapter sets a powerful foundation by urging readers to view technology through the lens of historical context, power dynamics, and self-determination.

Chapter 2: AI as a Catalyst for Inclusive and Equitable Growth offers a broad yet deeply insightful perspective on how AI can serve as a transformative engine for social inclusion and economic advancement. The chapter surveys real-world applications of AI in sectors such as healthcare, education, and agriculture, emphasizing how technology can be tailored to meet the needs of marginalized communities. It also lays out crucial ethical considerations—transparency, accountability, and bias mitigation—while advocating for inclusive AI policies that prioritize human development and sustainability.

Turning to healthcare innovation, **Chapter 3: Virtual Healthcare Using AI and Cyber Security Challenges** delves into the transformative role of AI-powered tools in medical diagnostics, treatment delivery, and surgical procedures. It explores how augmented reality, wearables, and mobile technologies are redefining patient care, especially in remote and underserved areas. However, the chapter does not shy away from examining the limitations of these technologies, particularly in terms of cybersecurity and data protection—areas that must be addressed to ensure equitable access and trust.

Chapter 4: Analysis on AI and Data Privacy Concerns in Business Analytics brings to the fore the tension between innovation and privacy in the financial sector. As AI and big data analytics revolutionize banking, lending, and investment strategies, they also introduce new vulnerabilities around personal data and algorithmic transparency. This chapter explores how the financial industry must balance technological progress with regulatory compliance, ethical data governance, and workforce readiness to navigate the challenges of digital transformation responsibly.

With **Chapter 5: AI and Governance: Smart Cities, E-Governance, and Public Service Delivery**, the book addresses how AI is transforming public administration and urban life. Through case studies of smart city initiatives and AI-driven governance models, the chapter showcases how automation, chatbots, and predictive analytics can improve public services—from traffic management to social security programs. Importantly, it highlights the risks of data bias, surveillance, and digital inequality, underscoring the need for ethical frameworks and inclusive policy design to prevent a techno-centric governance model that marginalizes vulnerable populations.

Shifting to environmental and agricultural concerns, **Chapter 6: Accurate Rainfall Prediction with Integrated BI LSTM in Deep Learning** presents a compelling application of AI in climate resilience. Focused on the Indian state of Andhra Pradesh, the chapter introduces a hybrid deep learning model that enhances the accuracy of rainfall forecasting. By combining Bi-LSTM and GRU networks, this approach enables more reliable agricultural planning and disaster preparedness, particularly for communities dependent on monsoon patterns. It exemplifies how AI can address real-world challenges in regions most vulnerable to climate change.

Finally, **Chapter 7: Air Pollution Prediction Using the Deep Learning Stacked Approach** addresses another pressing global issue—air quality. The chapter introduces a stacked BiGRU deep learning model capable of predicting PM2.5

concentrations with higher accuracy than traditional models. Focusing on urban centers in India, it highlights how AI can be instrumental in shaping public health policy and environmental regulation. This work not only advances the technical field but also contributes to a broader conversation about environmental justice and sustainable development.

Continuing the conversation on sustainability and innovation, **Chapter 8: Harnessing Artificial Intelligence for Sustainable Innovation and Policy: The Eco-Intelligence** explores how AI is increasingly at the core of environmental policy and sustainable design. The chapter introduces the concept of "Eco-Intelligence"—the strategic use of AI for optimizing resource efficiency, modeling climate scenarios, and supporting circular economies. It thoughtfully balances AI's potential for real-time environmental decision-making with the ethical dilemmas of data use, algorithmic bias, and ecological governance. By proposing actionable frameworks for integrating AI into environmental policy, this chapter reinforces the book's broader commitment to technology in service of planetary health and equitable futures.

In **Chapter 9: Hate Speech: Scope of AI for its Legal Solution Through Real-Time Detection**, the volume turns to a growing concern in digital societies: the proliferation of hate speech online. This chapter examines the potential of AI to detect and moderate harmful content in real time, while also navigating the complex intersections of legality, ethics, and free expression. It addresses how AI can support legislative efforts without overreaching or enabling censorship, offering a nuanced perspective that is especially relevant for policymakers, platform developers, and human rights advocates. The chapter underscores the need for AI tools that are not only technically sophisticated but also grounded in principles of justice and democratic accountability.

Chapter 10: AI for a Greener Tomorrow: Harnessing Artificial Intelligence for Environmental Sustainability expands upon the theme of climate resilience, showing how AI can be leveraged to support green technologies and sustainable development goals. The chapter presents applications ranging from smart agriculture and waste management to climate modeling and renewable energy optimization. It also confronts the ethical considerations of deploying AI in resource-constrained settings, emphasizing inclusivity, data justice, and cross-sector collaboration. This chapter contributes a comprehensive vision for how AI can help transition toward ecologically sound and socially inclusive futures.

With **Chapter 11: Addressing Algorithmic Bias: Legal Challenges and Solutions**, the book dives deeply into one of the most urgent challenges in AI development today: systemic bias embedded in algorithms. This chapter investigates how AI tools—particularly in high-stakes domains like criminal justice, finance, and healthcare—can perpetuate discrimination and inequity. Through case studies like the controversial COMPAS risk assessment system, the chapter critically evaluates existing legal remedies and argues for new frameworks that prioritize transparency, participatory governance, and algorithmic accountability. It is a call to integrate human rights into the very foundations of AI systems.

Chapter 12: Artificial Intelligence and Financial Stability Risks in Nigeria examines the impact of AI on national financial systems, using Nigeria as a case study. As AI adoption accelerates across banking, fintech, and regulatory landscapes, this chapter identifies emerging risks related to cybersecurity, regulatory oversight, and economic inequality. It also highlights the potential for AI to support macroeconomic resilience—provided that localized risks are acknowledged and mitigated. This contribution offers a rare and vital perspective from the Global South, situating AI within a broader discourse on equitable economic development and financial inclusion.

In **Chapter 13: Farmers' Rights vis-à-vis Plant Breeders' Privilege: Exploring the Issues and Challenges**, the tension between technological innovation and agrarian justice comes into sharp focus. The chapter examines how AI-enabled biotechnology, alongside intellectual property regimes, often disadvantages smallholder farmers by privileging corporate breeders. It critiques global frameworks such as TRIPS and UPOV and makes a compelling case for protecting traditional knowledge, seed sovereignty, and food justice. By highlighting the voices of farmers and advocating for rights-based governance, this chapter speaks directly to the human dimensions of agricultural innovation and digital equity.

Chapter 14: Bridging the Digital Divide and Improving Access for Students with Disabilities in Higher Education addresses one of the most persistent inequalities in the digital age: accessibility in education. This chapter explores how AI, universal design, and assistive technologies can close access gaps for students with disabilities in higher education. Through detailed analysis of inclusive pedagogies, institutional policy frameworks, and real-world case studies, it presents a roadmap for building more equitable digital learning environments. It also reminds us that accessibility is not a peripheral concern—it is central to the mission of inclusive technological development.

Concluding the volume, **Chapter 15: Cogs and Code: Understanding AI's Societal Impact in the Digital Era** offers a reflective and critical synthesis of AI's broader role in shaping institutions, power dynamics, and public life. Moving beyond the technical, this chapter investigates how AI is transforming how decisions are made, how services are delivered, and how societies envision progress. It raises pressing questions around transparency, accountability, and civic responsibility, and proposes ethical frameworks to ensure AI development aligns with democratic values. As a closing chapter, it invites readers to consider not just what AI does, but what kind of future it helps to build—and for whom.

CONCLUSION

As we stand at the intersection of unprecedented technological advancement and persistent global inequities, the urgency of steering artificial intelligence toward inclusive and equitable ends has never been greater. This volume, *Leveraging AI for Inclusive and Equitable Development*, emerges from that urgency—an invitation to rethink not only how we innovate, but *why*, *for whom*, and *at what cost*.

Across the chapters presented in this collection, scholars, practitioners, and advocates have examined the multifaceted role of AI through the lenses of justice, sustainability, governance, and human rights. Their contributions underscore a common truth: that technology, no matter how sophisticated, is never neutral. It reflects and reproduces the values of its designers, the biases of its data, and the structures of the societies into which it is deployed. If left unchecked, AI can exacerbate the very disparities it claims to solve. But if intentionally shaped by inclusive design, ethical frameworks, and participatory governance, it can also be a powerful tool for transformation.

This book does not offer easy answers. Instead, it asks hard questions and provides interdisciplinary insights that challenge us to look beyond the surface of technological solutions. It reminds us that the true measure of innovation lies not in efficiency or profitability alone, but in whether it uplifts the most marginalized, protects our planet, and preserves our shared humanity.

As the editor of this volume, my hope is that the work collected here serves as both a resource and a catalyst—a foundation for future scholarship, policymaking, and public dialogue on the social implications of AI. May it inspire a new generation of technologists, researchers, and decision-makers to pursue a path where artificial intelligence becomes not merely smart, but *just*.

The future of AI is still being written. Let us ensure that it is authored collectively, guided by equity, and informed by the diverse voices and lived experiences of all people.

Chapter 1
From Colonization to Automation: AI's Role in Indigenous Lives in Canada

Swati Chakraborty
https://orcid.org/0000-0003-0799-1954
Concordia University, Canada

ABSTRACT

"From Colonization to Automation: AI's Role in Indigenous Lives in Canada" examines the profound impact of artificial intelligence (AI) on Indigenous communities, highlighting its potential to both challenge and empower these populations. By drawing historical parallels between colonization and the rapid rise of automation, this book explores how AI systems can reinforce systemic inequalities or serve as tools for decolonization and cultural preservation.Key themes include data sovereignty, ethical AI practices, and the representation of Indigenous knowledge within technological systems. The book critically assesses how automation affects traditional livelihoods, education, and economic opportunities in Indigenous communities, often exacerbating existing digital divides. At the same time, it highlights Indigenous-led initiatives that harness AI to promote self-determination, resilience, and the revitalization of languages and traditions.

1. INTRODUCTION

The dawn of the artificial intelligence era presents humanity with unprecedented opportunities and profound challenges. For Indigenous communities in Canada, the advent of AI is not merely a technological shift but a new frontier in a long histo-

DOI: 10.4018/979-8-3373-2387-9.ch001

ry of engagement with external systems that have profoundly shaped their lives. From the devastating impacts of European colonization to the rapid advancements of automation, Indigenous peoples have consistently navigated forces that often threaten their sovereignty, cultures, and ways of life. This paper posits that AI, much like historical colonial mechanisms, possesses a dual capacity: to either reinforce entrenched systemic inequalities and marginalization or to serve as a transformative tool for decolonization, cultural revitalization, and empowerment.

Understanding AI's role in Indigenous lives necessitates a critical historical lens. The legacy of colonization – including forced assimilation, land dispossession, and the suppression of Indigenous languages and governance systems – has created enduring disparities in health, education, and economic opportunity. As AI permeates various sectors, from resource management to healthcare and education, it carries the potential to either amplify these existing divides, creating a "digital colonialism," or to offer innovative pathways toward genuine self-determination. This research delves into how AI impacts traditional livelihoods, exacerbates or mitigates digital divides, and explores the critical imperatives of data sovereignty, ethical AI development, and the authentic representation of Indigenous knowledge within technological frameworks. Ultimately, it seeks to illuminate the pathways through which Indigenous communities are actively shaping AI to serve their unique visions of a self-determined future (Smith, L. T. 1999).

Digital colonialism refers to a new form of colonial dominance and exploitation that occurs through the control of digital infrastructure, data, and technologies by powerful global actors—usually multinational corporations or governments in the Global North. While traditional colonialism involved the conquest of land and the exploitation of natural resources, digital colonialism operates in the virtual realm, where data becomes the new commodity and technological control equates to power (Walter, M., & Suina, M. 2019).

At the heart of digital colonialism is the extraction and appropriation of data from individuals, communities, and entire nations—especially from the Global South and Indigenous populations—without adequate consent, representation, or benefit-sharing. Tech giants often offer free services or infrastructure, such as internet access, cloud storage, or AI tools, but in exchange, they harvest massive amounts of personal and community-level data. This data is then used to generate profit, influence behavior, and even shape policies, all without accountability to the people being surveilled or mined.

i. Historical Continuities and New Power Structures

Digital colonialism is not entirely new—it echoes the colonial logic of extraction, domination, and dependency. Historically, colonial powers imposed economic systems, languages, and technologies that replaced Indigenous systems. Similarly, today's digital powers often displace local knowledge systems, languages, and digital ecosystems by imposing dominant algorithms, AI models, and global platforms (e.g., Facebook, Google, Microsoft), which may not align with local cultures, governance, or needs.

This results in a monopoly of digital infrastructures, where a few corporations from the U.S. or China control cloud services, social media platforms, and AI technologies globally. For many countries and communities, especially Indigenous ones, there is limited digital sovereignty—they don't own the data collected on their lands, nor do they have the tools or laws to govern how that data is used.

ii. Impacts on Indigenous and Marginalized Communities

Indigenous communities are especially vulnerable to digital colonialism. Their oral traditions, sacred knowledge, and cultural expressions are often digitized without proper consent or protection. For example, AI models trained on large language corpora or cultural data might include Indigenous languages, chants, or stories, but without acknowledging or benefiting those communities. This undermines Indigenous sovereignty and can perpetuate harmful stereotypes or extractive practices under the guise of innovation.

Furthermore, access to technology is uneven. While wealthy nations build smart cities and invest in AI-driven health or education, many rural and Indigenous areas lack even basic internet connectivity. This digital divide reinforces existing inequalities and keeps marginalized communities on the periphery of the digital revolution, making them passive users rather than active participants or innovators (Lewis, 2020).

iii. Towards Digital Decolonization

Digital decolonization is the effort to reclaim digital spaces, data, and tools in ways that respect Indigenous rights, promote self-determination, and challenge global hierarchies of power. It involves developing Indigenous data governance frameworks, such as OCAP® (Ownership, Control, Access, and Possession) in Canada, and promoting digital sovereignty, where communities control their own digital infrastructure and how their data is collected, stored, and used.

It also requires critically examining the ethics of AI, platform algorithms, and big data projects. Who designs these systems? Whose values do they encode? Decolonizing digital spaces means reimagining technology as a tool for liberation—not just efficiency—and building systems rooted in respect, consent, and cultural relevance. Indigenous-led technology initiatives, language revitalization apps, and

AI projects guided by traditional knowledge holders offer promising alternatives to the dominant tech paradigm (Whitt, L. A. 2009).

2. HISTORICAL CONTEXT: FROM COLONIZATION TO DIGITAL COLONIALISM

The historical relationship between Indigenous peoples and external powers in Canada is defined by colonization, a process characterized by land seizure, the imposition of foreign governance structures, and concerted efforts to assimilate Indigenous cultures. Policies such as the Indian Act and the residential school system inflicted intergenerational trauma, leading to widespread loss of language, culture, and economic independence. This legacy continues to manifest in systemic inequities, including disparities in access to education, healthcare, infrastructure, and economic opportunities, particularly within remote and rural Indigenous communities. (First Nations Information Governance Centre, 2014).

In the contemporary era, the rapid proliferation of digital technologies, including AI, introduces a new dimension to this historical power dynamic. The concept of "digital colonialism" emerges when dominant technological powers or systems replicate colonial patterns of extraction, control, and exploitation within the digital realm. This can involve the appropriation of Indigenous data without consent, the deployment of AI systems that reflect and embed colonial biases, or the imposition of technological solutions that disregard Indigenous epistemologies and needs. Just as resource extraction historically exploited Indigenous lands, data extraction in the digital age can exploit Indigenous knowledge and identities, often without equitable benefit or control.

Moreover, the significant "digital divide" within Canada disproportionately affects Indigenous communities, particularly those in remote areas. Lack of access to reliable internet infrastructure, affordable devices, and digital literacy skills creates a fundamental barrier to engaging with and benefiting from AI advancements. This digital exclusion risks widening the socio-economic gaps created by historical colonization, making it harder for Indigenous communities to participate in the digital economy, access essential services, or leverage technology for their own development. Understanding this historical continuum is crucial for analyzing AI's potential to either perpetuate or disrupt these enduring colonial legacies.

3. AI AS A REINFORCER OF SYSTEMIC INEQUALITIES

Despite its purported neutrality, AI systems are developed within existing societal structures and, as such, can inadvertently or explicitly embed and exacerbate systemic inequalities. For Indigenous communities, this risk is particularly acute, manifesting in several critical areas. Firstly, algorithmic bias, stemming from unrepresentative or historically skewed datasets, can lead to discriminatory outcomes. If AI systems are trained on data predominantly reflecting non-Indigenous populations or historical records imbued with colonial perspectives, they may misinterpret Indigenous cultural nuances, inaccurately assess risks, or unfairly allocate resources in sectors like justice, healthcare, or social services, perpetuating a cycle of disadvantage.

Secondly, the impact of automation on traditional livelihoods poses a significant threat. Many Indigenous economies are deeply connected to land-based activities, including fishing, hunting, trapping, and traditional resource management. While AI could potentially optimize some of these practices, it also presents risks of displacement, deskilling, or the imposition of industrial models that conflict with Indigenous sustainable practices and spiritual connections to the land. For instance, AI-driven surveillance or resource extraction technologies, if not governed by Indigenous consent and oversight, could further dispossess communities from their traditional territories and knowledge.

Thirdly, AI's integration into education and economic opportunities can exacerbate existing digital divides. Indigenous communities often face significant barriers to digital access, including limited broadband infrastructure, high costs, and a lack of culturally relevant digital literacy programs. Without equitable access and training, AI-driven educational tools or employment platforms can further marginalize Indigenous youth and workers, limiting their participation in the growing digital economy. This creates a two-tiered society where those without access to AI literacy and infrastructure are left behind, deepening socio-economic disparities inherited from colonial policies.

Finally, the lack of Indigenous representation in AI development and governance structures means that AI systems are often designed without consideration for Indigenous worldviews, values, or priorities. This oversight can lead to the creation of technologies that are culturally irrelevant, harmful, or that perpetuate the erasure of Indigenous identities and knowledge systems. The failure to include Indigenous voices at every stage of AI development risks replicating the top-down, extractive models that characterized historical colonization, solidifying a new form of digital marginalization.

4. AI AS A TOOL FOR DECOLONIZATION AND EMPOWERMENT

Despite the significant risks, AI also holds immense potential as a transformative tool for decolonization, cultural preservation, and self-determination within Indigenous communities. This transformative capacity hinges on Indigenous agency and control over technology's design and deployment. A foundational principle in this context is data sovereignty, asserting Indigenous peoples' inherent right to own, control, access, and possess their own data. By establishing Indigenous data governance frameworks and building community-controlled data infrastructure, AI can be leveraged in ways that benefit, rather than harm, Indigenous communities, ensuring that algorithms are trained on culturally relevant and ethical datasets.

Indigenous-led initiatives are increasingly demonstrating AI's capacity to promote self-determination and resilience. For instance, AI-powered tools are being developed to support land management based on traditional ecological knowledge, facilitating more sustainable resource practices and strengthening connections to ancestral territories. In healthcare, AI can assist in developing culturally appropriate health interventions, improving access to services in remote communities, and analyzing health data to address specific Indigenous health disparities, all while prioritizing data privacy and community control.

One of the most profound applications of AI for decolonization lies in language revitalization and cultural preservation. Many Indigenous languages in Canada are critically endangered due to colonial policies. AI, through natural language processing (NLP), machine learning, and speech recognition, offers innovative avenues to document, teach, and revitalize these languages. Projects developing AI-powered dictionaries, language learning apps, and virtual reality experiences that immerse users in traditional stories and ceremonies are powerful examples of technology serving cultural continuity. These tools can help bridge intergenerational gaps, empower fluent speakers, and make language learning more accessible to younger generations, directly countering the cultural erosion caused by colonization (Hudson, M., et al. 2020).

Furthermore, AI can empower Indigenous communities economically by creating new opportunities rooted in traditional knowledge and contemporary innovation. AI can support Indigenous entrepreneurship, e-commerce, and the development of sustainable industries that align with Indigenous values. By enabling communities to harness their own data and build their own technological solutions, AI can foster economic self-sufficiency and reduce reliance on external systems, thereby contributing to broader self-determination goals and fostering vibrant, resilient futures for Indigenous peoples in Canada.

5. ETHICAL AI PRACTICES AND INDIGENOUS KNOWLEDGE SYSTEMS

The successful and beneficial integration of AI into Indigenous lives necessitates a fundamental shift towards ethical AI practices that are rooted in Indigenous worldviews and principles. This requires moving beyond mere consultation to genuine co-design and co-governance of AI systems. Ethical AI, in this context, means ensuring that AI development is transparent, accountable, fair, and respectful of Indigenous rights, sovereignty, and cultural protocols. It demands that AI not only avoids harm but actively contributes to the well-being and flourishing of Indigenous communities (McMahon, R., & Smith, M. 2021).

A critical component of ethical AI is the robust representation and integration of Indigenous knowledge systems within technological development. Indigenous knowledge, often holistic, relational, and transmitted through generations, offers invaluable insights into sustainable living, ecological balance, and community well-being that are frequently overlooked by Western scientific paradigms. AI systems designed with Indigenous epistemologies can lead to more nuanced, culturally appropriate, and effective solutions in areas such as environmental monitoring, healthcare, and education. This involves decolonizing the data itself, ensuring that datasets reflect Indigenous perspectives and are collected and curated in ways that respect Indigenous protocols and intellectual property rights.

Developing Indigenous-specific ethical AI frameworks is paramount. These frameworks would prioritize principles such as OCAP® (Ownership, Control, Access, Possession) for data governance, community consent, benefit sharing, and the right to self-determination in technological choices. They would also emphasize the responsibility of AI developers and users to understand and respect Indigenous cultural contexts, ensuring that AI tools align with community values rather than imposing external norms. This includes addressing algorithmic fairness from an Indigenous perspective, recognizing that fairness can mean different things across diverse cultural groups.

Ultimately, fostering an environment where Indigenous peoples are not merely consumers or subjects of AI but active designers, innovators, and governors is crucial. This requires significant investment in Indigenous-led research, training, and infrastructure development, ensuring that Indigenous communities have the capacity and resources to shape AI in ways that serve their unique needs and aspirations. By embedding Indigenous knowledge and ethical frameworks at the core of AI development, technology can become a genuine ally in the ongoing journey of decolonization and the assertion of Indigenous sovereignty (Yellowhead Institute. 2021).

6. CHALLENGES AND OPPORTUNITIES

The journey from colonization to automation for Indigenous peoples in Canada is fraught with significant challenges but also presents transformative opportunities. The primary challenge remains the persistent digital divide, which limits access to the foundational infrastructure necessary for engaging with AI. This includes inadequate broadband connectivity, high costs of technology, and a lack of digital literacy programs tailored to Indigenous contexts. Without addressing these fundamental barriers, the benefits of AI will remain largely inaccessible to many Indigenous communities, further entrenching existing inequalities.

Another critical challenge lies in mitigating the risks of algorithmic bias and data exploitation. Ensuring that AI systems do not perpetuate or amplify historical injustices requires vigilance, robust Indigenous data governance, and active participation of Indigenous experts in every stage of AI development. There is also the challenge of integrating complex Indigenous knowledge systems into technological frameworks in a respectful and authentic manner, avoiding tokenism or misrepresentation.

However, the opportunities are equally profound. AI can be a powerful catalyst for decolonization by empowering Indigenous communities to reclaim control over their data, languages, and cultural narratives. It offers unprecedented tools for revitalizing endangered languages, preserving oral histories, and documenting traditional ecological knowledge. AI can also drive economic self-sufficiency through innovative Indigenous-led enterprises, improving access to education and healthcare, and enhancing governance capacities. By focusing on Indigenous-led solutions that prioritize self-determination and cultural integrity, AI can become a vital instrument in building resilient, thriving Indigenous futures, transforming a legacy of external imposition into a future of Indigenous-driven innovation and empowerment.

7. CONCLUSION

Digital colonialism is a pressing issue in our interconnected world. While the tools and mechanisms may differ from historical colonialism, the consequences—loss of autonomy, cultural erosion, and economic dependency—remain strikingly similar. Recognizing this phenomenon is the first step toward creating more just, inclusive, and accountable digital futures. For true decolonization to occur, digital development must prioritize equity, Indigenous leadership, and ethical design, challenge the centralization of power and return agency to communities long pushed to the margins.

The relationship between artificial intelligence and Indigenous lives in Canada is a complex tapestry woven from threads of historical trauma, ongoing systemic inequalities, and immense potential for decolonization and empowerment. Just as colonization fundamentally reshaped Indigenous societies, the rapid advancement of automation today presents a critical juncture, capable of either perpetuating harmful patterns of digital colonialism or catalyzing profound transformations towards self-determination.

This paper has highlighted the dual nature of AI: its capacity to exacerbate existing digital divides, reinforce algorithmic biases, and threaten traditional livelihoods, yet also its potential as an unparalleled tool for cultural preservation, language revitalization, and economic resilience. The key to unlocking AI's benevolent potential lies in upholding principles of Indigenous data sovereignty, fostering ethical AI practices grounded in Indigenous knowledge systems, and ensuring authentic Indigenous leadership in the design, development, and governance of these powerful technologies. The imperative is not merely to mitigate harm but to actively harness AI for the advancement of Indigenous rights, the revitalization of cultures, and the establishment of truly self-determined futures. By prioritizing Indigenous voices and visions, AI can transition from a potential instrument of control to a powerful ally in the ongoing journey of decolonization, paving the way for a future where technology serves Indigenous flourishing.

REFERENCES

First Nations Information Governance Centre (2014). Ownership, Control, Access and Possession (OCAP™): The Path to First Nations Information Governance.

Hudson, M., et al. (2020)."Te Ara Tika Guidelines for Māori Research Ethics: A Framework for Researchers and Ethics Committee Members.

McMahon, R., & Smith, M. (2021). *Digital Self-Determination and the 'Data Revolution' in Canada's North*. Northern Public Affairs Journal.

Lewis, J. E. (Sxwpilemaát). (2020). Indigenous Protocol and Artificial Intelligence Position Paper.

Smith, L. T. (1999). Decolonizing Methodologies: Research and Indigenous Peoples. Zed Books.

Walter, M., & Suina, M. (2019). Indigenous Data, Indigenous Methodologies and Indigenous Data Sovereignty. International Journal of Social Research Methodology.

Whitt, L. A. (2009). Science, Colonialism, and Indigenous Peoples: The Cultural Politics of Law and Knowledge. Cambridge University Press.

Yellowhead Institute. (2021). Cash Back: A Yellowhead Institute Red Paper. Toronto Metropolitan University. https://yellowheadinstitute.org

Chapter 2
AI as a Catalyst for Inclusive and Equitable Growth

Wasswa Shafik
https://orcid.org/0000-0002-9320-3186
Dig Connectivity Research Laboratory (DCRLab), Uganda

ABSTRACT

Artificial Intelligence is reshaping industries and societies, offering unprecedented opportunities to foster inclusive and equitable growth. This study explores the transformative potential of AI in addressing systemic inequalities, enhancing accessibility, and promoting socio-economic development. It highlights AI-driven innovations in education, healthcare, agriculture, and finance, emphasizing their role in bridging gaps for marginalized communities. The chapter illustrates how AI can empower underserved populations, improve decision-making, and enable tailored solutions for diverse needs. It discusses ethical considerations, such as mitigating biases, ensuring transparency, and safeguarding data privacy, essential for equitable AI deployment. The study underscores the importance of inclusive AI policies, stakeholder collaboration, and capacity-building initiatives to harness AI's benefits while minimizing risks. Ultimately, this research advocates for leveraging AI as a catalyst for a sustainable future, ensuring no one is left behind in the digital transformation journey.

INTRODUCTION

In the current hyper-competitive global market, many economies have positioned artificial intelligence (AI) to be a key transformative technology that will drive

DOI: 10.4018/979-8-3373-2387-9.ch002

not only economic but also employment, social, ethical, and civilizational change. Convergences in technology will leverage new outcomes. For example, AI with 5G can provide digital education and health to the outback in remote locations. As a technological enabler, AI has the potential to transform economies and level the growth playing field by allowing developing economies to tap new articulation opportunities (Kaur, 2024). AI tools may also work to reduce disparities associated with infrastructure deficiencies, differential social endowments, and government capacity limitations by aiding better targeting of beneficiaries of governments' social insurance and human development initiatives. One opportunity is the potential for using AI to leverage already accumulated (though not equally) human capital. AI is also capable of augmenting human potential by providing better-personalized health, education, and even mental rejuvenation plans (Gondwe, 2024). This could give lagging economies or lagging regions within economies a chance to leapfrog in human development rankings. The ease of use of such applications provides a further opportunity for empowerment for groups currently not serviced, such as parents, disabled persons, and older people. Such tools could also be used in areas of law, such as improving police community judgments, in the area of precision agriculture, etc., to reduce social inequality. Another major, predominantly market-driven use case of AI is for improving advertising and the targeting of goods and services that are better suited to the proclivities of a wide array of consumers and citizens. AI may also be used to assist us in making moral choices, widening the availability of such systems to more people (Shafik, 2024e). However, all these points have to be flagged as initial opportunities for using AI do not necessarily lead to equity-enhancing outcomes.

A new generation of technologies enabled by artificial intelligence holds the potential to unlock wide-reaching social and economic benefits but will need greater research and careful stewardship. When directed without regard for issues of distribution, governance, and externalities, new technologies can exacerbate long-standing challenges facing many global regions, including job dislocation, wage inequality, and skill gaps, as well as demographic and income disparities, species destabilization, social unrest, cyber risks, and power concentration (Habibipour, 2024). Indeed, these challenges can also exacerbate governance and other social inequalities and compound these challenges, creating difficult feedback loops. In all regions and geographies, unless active countervailing policies are enacted, such societal problems could skew benefit accrual and wealth accumulation, potentially leading to large-scale social and global political-economy destabilization. The consequences of an unmitigated inequitable impact can slow the adoption curve of AI technologies and suppress research and investment in areas where AI can be deployed to solve important problems. The AI community should proactively and thoughtfully consider these matters (Rane & Choudhary, 2024). The promise of

AI is furthered by the wider involvement of experts and dialogue among sectors and regions on the opportunities and challenges. Although scientists, professionals, and political communities are increasingly engaging in dialogue on addressing these challenges in scientific, engineering, and governance domains, the AI policy community can play an important global role in identifying, communicating, and marshaling resources for advancing beneficial AI development. Several international AI research and policy organizations have emerged and have begun to consider the multifaceted challenges with which the research community is grappling, each through their regional or functional lenses (Dirgová Luptáková et al., 2024). Some engaged stakeholders have frameworks for AI research, documentation, and assessment. We believe there is a common set of grand challenges and opportunities that warrants increased coordination among research institutions and a focused critical mass of experts. We should seek to highlight opportunities and address challenges related to these issues, spanning global cooperation and coordination, interdisciplinary research, and international development using different expert systems, as illustrated in Figure 1 (Olabisi Oluwakemi Adeleye et al., 2024).

Figure 1. Types of expert systems

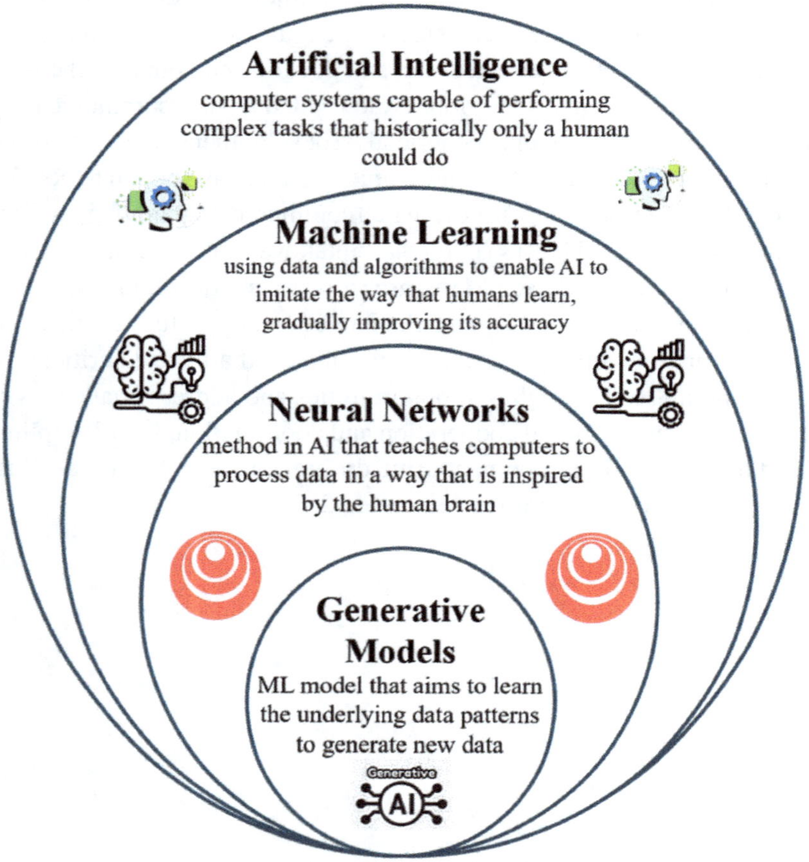

Chapter Background and Significance

The impact of AI and its trade and investment aspects has become a critical issue in the discourse on international economic relations. In this context, defining AI is a complex and nuanced process and should not be understood in the context of current digital technologies, including artificial intelligence or AI-based products or services, in isolation from the broader value creation systems in which those technologies are employed, and the significant existing scientific research designed to push forward the boundaries of AI's capabilities (Dutta, 2024). Concern over the impact of AI also leads to questions about whether AI is an evolutionary or revolutionary technological development and how the international economic community could channel AI to help meet the most pressing global challenges rather than entail mounting trade tensions and contribute to economic inequality around the world. The impact of AI on labor markets is one of the most compelling and controversial concerns associated with the AI-enabled Fourth Industrial Revolution. The impact of AI on jobs touches on several human and labor rights as well as an array of public policies that underpin economic growth and societal balance (Shafik, Kalinaki, Fahim, et al., 2024). Discussions on the consequences for employment from the Fourth Industrial Revolution are taking place in a political backdrop of significant social and economic challenges, including increasing income and wealth inequality, widening digital divides, and rising distrust in the state and global governance institutions to foster robust, inclusive, and equitable growth. At the same time, the development of AI worldwide reinforces the emerging consensus about the interconnected and transboundary nature of global problems as a scientific and innovation breakthrough collaboration, as well as the need for multi-stakeholder governance mechanisms to harness its benefits for individuals, communities, and nations building an equitable and inclusive AI ecosystem (Cobanaj et al., 2024).

Purpose of the Study

This study aims to help the AI industry, governments, international organizations, civil society, and academics make progress in leveraging AI to build a more inclusive and equitable global society. The private sector is the primary driver of AI technologies and their application. Many companies place significant emphasis on the 'social good' aspects of AI, but activities so far have been relatively fragmented (Bakkum et al., 2024). It is clear that if by 2030, AI technologies and applications have mainly been used to drive economic growth, compete with each other, benefit mainly the wealthiest and most advanced countries, and increase global inequality, it will be too late to change it. It is essential to increase the number, diversity, and effectiveness of good here-and-now activities that will build the foundations for future global use of AI to strive for shared human values like dignity, talent, and compassion (Bressane et al., 2024). How are countries leveraging AI for equitable growth, what specifically are they doing that is not happening in all other countries, and what are the initial 'first movers' experiences? These are critical to understanding to make recommendations to all the players embarking on the difficult but necessary journey of 'systematizing the messes of democracy' and helping societies build a future that we all want, prefer, and are ready to pay for (Delgado Algarra et al., 2024). These and much more are the broad but essential and non-trivial range of phenomena that this study aims to map and understand.

Scope and Limitations

While AI has the potential to be a transformative force and catalyst for driving inclusive and equitable growth, it has limitations. AI is not a panacea—deep inequalities have built up in a variety of areas as a result of long-established social and structural issues. The application and proliferation of AI tools may well strengthen and perpetuate these disparities if successful projects are scaled prematurely or without consideration for the underlying disparities that might affect the design and eventual deployment of the tool or technology. Moreover, the more solutions using AI that are deployed, the more models and systems are developed, and the more these models and systems are used, the more likely these technologies are to benefit those with existing power and privilege. These disparities are not just social; long-time market players have a competitive advantage no rational startup could easily replicate. While AI has utility across a wide range of domains and applications, we also note its limitations. AI-based decision-making can be difficult to understand and explain, which may erode trust in the technology. Moreover, overreliance on algorithmic decision-making in sensitive or consequential decision domains poses risks. Transparent and equitable decision-making institutions foster trust and cooperation and enable people to understand why decisions are made. AI applications can predict, segment, and score quite accurately as long as the world seen by the AI model does not change significantly. The rapid change in behaviors in such a case can lead to model inaccuracy and biases in AI tools, and if not, the tool will not account for a range of other potential strategic behaviors that might arise.

UNDERSTANDING AI AND ITS IMPACT ON SOCIETY

Artificial intelligence (AI) is the field of computer science that seeks to create, develop, and understand systems that exhibit or mimic human-like forms of intelligence and thought. Narrow AI refers to a machine that has been developed to perform a single task, while general AI, which is not yet in existence, would outperform humans in capabilities across a wide range of hypothetical tasks. AI has a relatively long history, with the cybernetics movement of the 1940s and 1950s providing critical inspiration (Liew, 2024). The "fourth revolution" centers around autonomous systems and their application in various fields such as e-commerce, medicine, finance, and transportation, among others. In healthcare, AI applications include diagnostic tools and the use of AI as a clinical decision support tool. In finance, AI can be used to identify risks, fraud, and regulatory compliance and to automate large amounts of data to facilitate trading. AI can also be used in education to enable adaptable learning objects that respond to the learning progress. AI has inherent dual-use capabilities that can be used for evil or for good. This has led to concern from political scientists and technologists alike (Sanghvi et al., 2024). There is a danger that the AI research community may produce applications that reduce overall human autonomy, especially for society's more vulnerable members who do not have access to these advanced capabilities themselves. It may also be the case that the economic inequality that already exists within society is further exacerbated by the unequal access to the positive effects AI is likely to bring, while at the same time, the negative outcomes will add to the existing societal strains. Nevertheless, it is important to bear in mind that the utility of AI is largely determined by the use to which it is put. Hence, interest must be focused on strategy, as well as ethics, in order to maintain and develop equitability (Osama, 2024). Therefore, it is important to ensure the public does not have access to unbalanced coverage of AI.

Definition and Scope of AI

A full definition of AI identifies three principal components: AI is a computational agents that perform functions typical of human intelligence, such as perception, action, and cognitive coordination. It is a field of study that encompasses 'intelligent systems': technologies that harness informed, computational strategies to reach complex, interrelated objectives. It is a field that approximates, when possible, the rationality, autonomy, and articulation in human or other animal systems required to reach its objectives (Fundira et al., 2024). There are a myriad of ways AI has been implemented in societal contexts, including supervised learning, unsupervised learning, and reinforced learning, which is commonly referred to as 'Machine Learning' (ML). Deep Learning (DL), which operates on layered, multi-perceptron neural networks, is a subset of ML. Much AI system design uses ML; other AI technologies include natural language processing (NLP), robotics, expert systems, and well-established rules-based systems such as decision trees and databases designed to harness large data sets quickly and effectively (Shafik, 2025a). AI technologies such as DL can transfigure or deliver significant change in the global and national economy. DL in drug discovery, for instance, can reduce the time it takes to discover a blockbuster drug by more than half, for a total cost saving estimated at $323 million. AI can address complex sociotechnical problems – such as urban traffic congestion in connected 'smart cities' or the management and control of urban air quality in the time of 'mega fires' and a global pandemic – where it is necessary to interpret and manage simultaneously (Shafik, 2024h):

(i) Economic policy for the public good and profit-oriented entities;
(ii) Societal and situational uncertainty;
(iii) Rapid, irregular, and complex change.

While AI is capable of assessing these problems from different perspectives, diverse quarters expect AI to contribute to society and feed profits, thereby illustrating the equivocal nature of the technology. Even so, a shared understanding of AI is imperative to allow for informed and responsible usage of AI in the broader society.

Historical Development of AI

In a seminal paper in the mid-last century, Alan Turing suggested a simple philosophical test for machine intelligence. In the Turing Test, Turing proposed that a person ask questions of two individuals, one human, and one machine, without being able to see them. The machine can be thought of as being intelligent or as having cognition if its responses are indistinguishable from those of the human. While it is not certain if certain AI systems in a few years will pass the Turing Test as described, the emergence of machine learning, neural networks, and successful AI examples and stories is hard to deny (Olabisi Oluwakemi Adeleye et al., 2024). In brief, this section will cover historical research, including Turing, Rosenblatt, and a progression of the AI winter to the developments of the last few years in face recognition and already realized applications of autonomy and AI. AI has been defined in this paper by the high-level results that AI can aim for, such as reasoning, natural language processing, problem-solving, perception, and learning. For much of AI's history, the development of technology has had an impact on the results of AI (Antony et al., 2024). There have been periods of AI history where the industry has been dominant in generating new insights and has driven the center of AI research focus. In the 1970s and 1980s, companies with problems in unstructured data like natural language also held the majority of AI funding and effort. In the 2010s and 2020s, much of the focus has been on various companies, sampled as illustrated in Figure 2 (Kelkar et al., 2024). The internal and external documents of these organizations, as well as the AI literature, all informed the developments of AI, and there were key technology strides that dictated the direction of subsequent research, as we covered in the next section.

Figure 2. Economic and environmental protection approaches

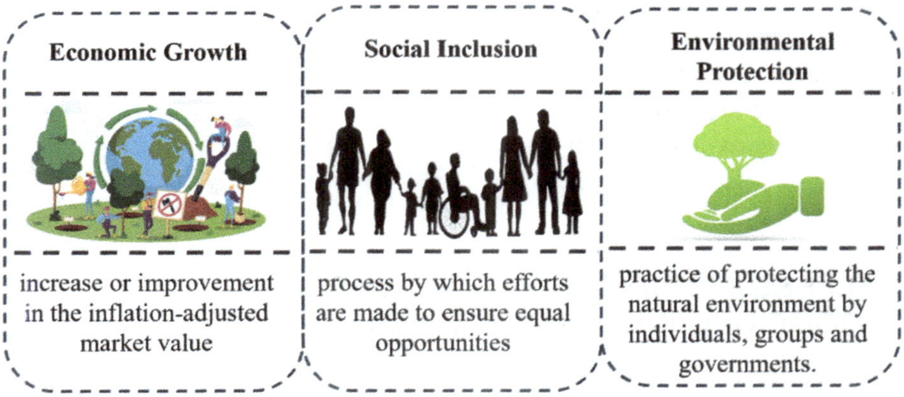

AI Applications in Various Sectors

AI is multifaceted, and solutions can be widely applied across different sectors to solve real-world problems. Five percent additional investment in AI potentially raises the rate of output growth by 1 to 1.5 percentage points over a 10-year horizon. In healthcare and diagnostics, AI applications have enhanced the accuracy of readings and offer benefits such as reductions in the cost of time, human errors, and loss in operations (Osama, 2024). AI has been used to review MRI images to assess the stage of cancer and carries the equal potential to identify large blood pressure risks with enhanced efficacy. In education, AI offers personalized learning processes, provides suggestions for students, offers changed lesson plans, and suggests videos, text material, or websites that are beneficial for a specific task. Moreover, it identifies students at risk of failing or dropping out of a course before such a situation arises. In the field of agriculture, AI applications in robotics potentially increase efficiency and consistency (Patel et al., 2024). AI weather and soil-prediction models predict local weather and crop health and provide early warnings of disease targeting, pests, and floods, which may result in reduced crop productivity. Drones with machine learning are used for precision agriculture, for instance, to determine the volume of irrigation water needed. AI applications in the financial sector suggest plans to eliminate regulatory barriers, likely leading to the lowering of costs and an offer of customized services to banking and finance. AI lends assistive technologies to break down language barriers and provides help to physically challenged people (Adekunle, 2024). AI is capable of translating text and sound from one language to another and adapting website navigation for people with disabilities. There are, however, potential downsides to consider: AI's reliance on data might raise data protection and privacy, trustworthiness, and transparency issues. AI applications can widen barriers or inequalities due to inherent cultural biases present in training data, ethics, and rights. Moreover, a pacing worry is task displacement and possibly unemployment from the use of automation or AI (Kaur, 2024). There may also be problems and policy implications associated with legal accountability and moral agency.

CHALLENGES AND OPPORTUNITIES OF AI IN PROMOTING INCLUSIVE GROWTH

Ethical considerations are essential when it comes to the development and implementation of artificial intelligence technologies. Without these, there will be no legitimacy or social license, hence no innovation. The accessibility and affordability of AI are concern areas in this regard, with the technologies being largely inaccessible to large segments of the population, especially the underserved and less represented in the global South. The socio-economic drivers shaping an AI-driven future, inclusive of enhancing education and, thus, skills, are also an obstacle that needs to be addressed (Habibipour, 2024). Furthermore, there are potential challenges resulting from the increasing polarization within societies, primarily in terms of gender, income, or rural and urban divides. There are significant opportunities that AI can offer. The technologies are cost-efficient and scalable, enabling a large number of people to benefit from them. In addition, AI technologies are significantly decentralized, and smaller societies have it within their immediate capacity to take the lead and foster inclusive and equitable growth. Not only can such technologies promote innovation, especially in the realm of such states' competitive advantage, but they offer immediate benefits in terms of automation and enhanced administrative efficiency (Dirgová Luptáková et al., 2024). In these situations, AI can not only compete with the global superpowers, but it can offer these small states an opportunity that the great technological powers cannot: an immediate impact on their day-to-day socioeconomic operations and enhanced efficiency and development.

Ethical Considerations in Artificial Intelligence Development

The introduction of AI technologies develops ethical tensions that must be addressed. Recent reports suggest that AI technologies harbor race and gender biases, contribute to prejudiced decisions that selectively target students in Black or Brown schools, create women as backup drivers for mostly white autonomous vehicles, incarcerate 'undesirable' individuals in racially unequal prisons, and treat all global citizens as less than human (Adu-Gyamfi et al., 2024). In this way, deontological ethics are of particular interest in considering the ethics of technological innovation. Kant's stance on human exceptionalism and his belief in pure practical reason make the autonomy and dignity of humanity his categorical imperative. With Kant, we have the grounds that for AI or any information systems to maintain ethical obligations and responsibilities, human dignity and the potential for reciprocity of all information systems' users (be they human or machine) must be maintained. This includes a strong sense of the necessity for honesty (Fan et al., 2024). The 20th-century philosopher Carole Pateman and her contemporaries pull at this thread, noting that a space for the other hypostasizes a space for a just society. Identifying the ethical dilemmas in a pre-reflective technological landscape should drive a commitment to transparent, accountable, and fair systems. It is true that biases already perpetuated actively or passively form the basis for our machine learning datasets. A failure to develop guidelines or frameworks for which unintended consequences of AI design are made known, however, implicates these AI developers (Shafik, 2024e). It is for this reason that a plurality of voices with a stake in the development of our digital future must reflect on how to govern AI as a foundational technology to our inclusive growth. Policymakers and stakeholders in this process must establish mechanisms for a redistribution of much more than knowledge. Wealth, sure: there is now a stronger connection between the nation's AI leadership and the wealth share of its top one percent. In addition to the economic disparities AI fosters, ethical lapses can also perpetuate existing injustices while also erecting new imbalances, thereby turning off any gains in inclusive prosperity realized through technology (Kaur, 2024). Requiring the acceleration of ethical AI principles, the ascension of a responsible AI landscape is a matter of both equilibrium and justice though AI comes with some levels of marginalization, as demonstrated in Figure 3.

Figure 3. Causes of marginalization

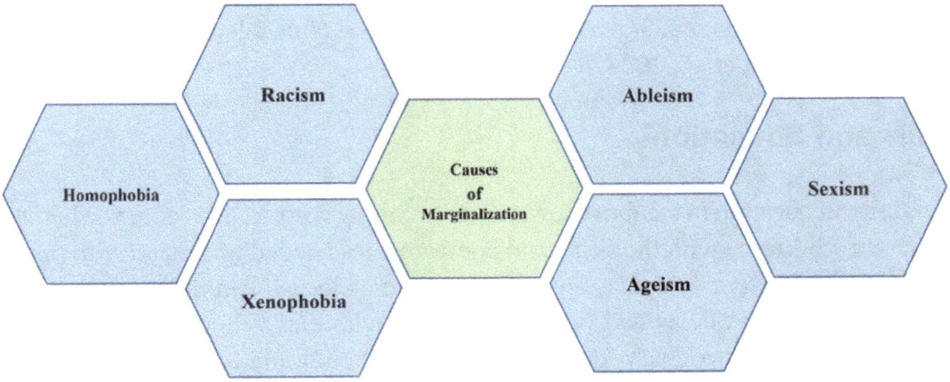

Accessibility and Affordability

Accessibility is seen as one of the most critical and thorny issues accompanying the global AI revolution. In fact, affiliated with a world where AI is widely incorporated and a wide variety of problems is "solved now by machines," the normal population cannot enjoy the facilities that AI applications might bring about. The world is split into two: one where large groups always struggle to survive from poverty, while the other is on the track of realizing dreams and aspirations (Rane & Choudhary, 2024). Particularly, AI technologies are not equally available or popularized among the workforce of different demographic groups. Women, people with disabilities, and the aging population encounter significant barriers to accessing information about AI vacancies, networks, training materials, and social or language skills to help them gain opportunities in AI. Barriers to accessibility can exacerbate existing inequalities in other ways as well. For example, AI-driven technologies often rely on data, and systematic exclusion can mean that not all communities' experiences are accurately represented (Antony et al., 2024). It is important that AI infrastructure is enhanced, and the technology space is ready for all so that the societal progress AI can bring is inclusive for everyone. Another point concerning "accessibility" that is often considered, is about the "affordability" of AI solutions. Suppose it is not possible on economic grounds resulting from the cost and resources invested in creating the product. In that case, it should be at such a price that the people involved in AI work can still afford access to such a luxury (Tang, 2024). Affordability has a direct bearing on accessibility. Affordability is not confined to the purchase value alone; it also includes maintenance and access costs, particularly when it comes to new and disruptive products claiming to produce societal good. Air transportation is overwhelmingly affordable today because of its vast need. Public investment has been shown to be feasible, but this should be alongside effective development and implementation of technology for all. In addition, public partnership with the private sector may maximize the accessibility of supportive, just, and synergistic services, enabling a model for stakeholders to build available, fault-tolerant AI systems of their own (Iacoban et al., 2024).

Skills and Education

A critical question in the move towards an economy with AI at its core is whether we have a workforce with the skills and competencies needed to engage with these technologies. Current evidence suggests there are major gaps in the skills that the industry requires. Policies and practices dealing with early childhood education, primary education, secondary education, higher education, and vocational education and training have to be realigned to address these gaps (Wang'ang'a, 2024). Lifelong learning policies will also be crucial. Digital skills, including computational thinking and digital competencies, have been increasingly integrated into national curricula, particularly in primary and secondary schools. This is a positive initial step towards ensuring AI literacy is a core focus of early education. However, a greater focus is needed on digital competencies that emphasize the understanding of AI as a technological tool and how it can be incorporated into a wide range of sectors rather than a siloed skill focusing on technology development (Adekunle, 2024). Global initiatives that focus on improving digital and AI skills among underrepresented groups should be considered a model for how to address gaps in advancement opportunities in the early-stage industry workforce. They can serve as successful policy blueprints for growth sectors in a variety of countries. Educational institutions and individuals taking social studies, cognitive psychology, or political science classes are being inundated with information about the changes in workforce and labor markets that will occur due to artificial intelligence (Chauncey & McKenna, 2024). This knowledge is not necessarily negative; it may empower individuals and organizations to adapt earlier to these changes to foster the growth of AI more inclusively. From a public policy perspective, embedding these points into educational initiatives may be a way to encourage an understanding of the broader environment within which these technologies develop rather than seeing them as siloed forces leading to global economic changes. This association with broader workforce development initiatives ensures that these students understand the relevance of these topics to society at large and may encourage them to get involved in workforce development initiatives (Mishra, 2024).

POLICY FRAMEWORKS AND REGULATIONS FOR INCLUSIVE AI

Policies and regulations are crucial for AI's contribution to inclusive growth. Global initiatives and agreements relating to AI and emerging technologies are working on laws, guidelines, and frameworks centered on values such as democracy, transparency, fairness, cooperation, human rights, multistakeholder engagement, and social utility. It is important to note that various uses of AI are pertinent to these values, particularly those that impact social groups who have historically been marginalized or persecuted (Ahmad et al., 2024). The approaches countries have taken toward national policies depict how institutions of governance have recognized the requirement for government oversight or regulation of AI governance processes and AI product or development priorities. Different countries are using their positioning through national AI policies and strategies to promote the synchronized development of AI with values like social oversight, economic innovation, enjoyment, and acknowledgment of humans (Salajan et al., 2024). While the specifics of what is included in such documents diversify greatly from country to country, it is crucial to notice that leading among the principles or high-level guidance appears to be efforts to prioritize themselves, the applied regulatory or norm-reinforcement measures. Current AI development and future criticism are deploying these efforts as reflective of their values. Providing critical discussion of the national AI policy or strategy with a focus on national AI governance or AI development that contributes to inclusive growth, we provide examples below to document elements of AI's application, systems, and policies that may be resistant. We, therefore, need to redirect policy and regulation rapidly (Bulutoding et al., 2024). The policy requires proper attentiveness to the specific traits that AI includes in its regulation, which is the objective of this article. Many existing policies and policy suggestions, in basically mentioning AI, give little clarification of what the AI extension involves. AI is thought of more and more by history and civil society as a set of software projects, with assumptions and suggestions developed on collective experience (Chima Abimbola Edeni et al., 2024). AI has particular features of social significance in addition to being software. Providing guidance suitable to AI requires that the two kinds of forms be connected to some causes of disparities as illustrated in Figure 4.

Figure 4. Causes of marginalization among the sick (disabled)

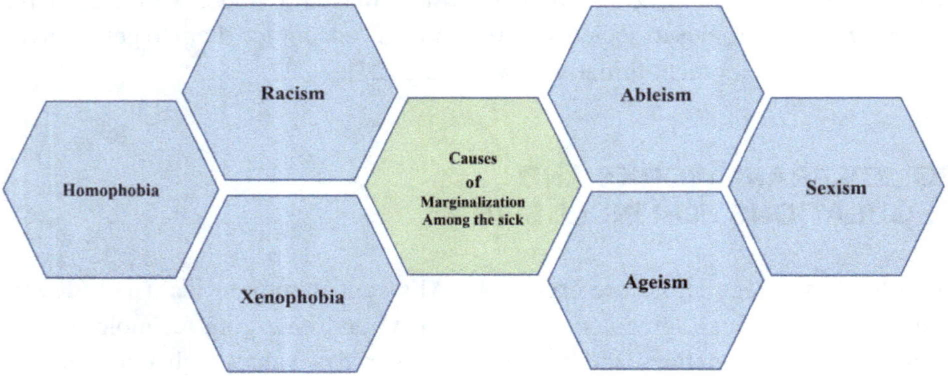

Global Initiatives and Agreements

In the wake of widespread interest and concerns about the exponential progress of AI, a number of global initiatives and agreements have been established to help foster the development of AI to support inclusive growth. Many were created through a partnership of various organizations, institutions, and industries, bringing together governments to identify shared values, principles, and good practices. An effort has been led by partnering with many other institutions (Shafik, 2024a). They released two agreements: "The Ethics of Artificial Intelligence" and "The Recommendations for the Ethics of AI." Similar initiatives include principles on Artificial Intelligence and other organizations. These initiatives usually concentrate on key sectors, including those promoting cross-border trust in AI through international standardization. The different international initiatives and agreements are often positioned as addressing disparities in the governance of AI, ensuring that no country, industry, or group is left behind. Because the development and deployment of AI in one jurisdiction can positively or negatively impact other countries and citizens of the world, such efforts offer a process across borders where countries, multilateral organizations, and others can share best practices, risk assessments, and thought leadership (Patel et al., 2024). The collaborations also can create positive development at home, with the shared knowledge in pilot programs enhancing education, research, and other sectors. The approaches also aim to enhance public accountability and address a wide range of AI ethical issues where the impact of AI has been felt. Given the scale and scope of AI, they bring in multidisciplinary input and are open to the creation of partnerships and written documents. As more countries become involved in creating national plans for such research, AI-focused multilateral organizations will be critical to the international sharing of information, expertise, and training on the production side (Bakkum et al., 2024). It is widely expected that the international sharing of research programs will enhance the overall global efforts at AI to ensure that AI is more inclusive.

National Policy Approaches

Several policy approaches have been developed at the national level that are focused on ensuring the promises of AI are broadly shared across society. Some national policies comprise comprehensive, system-wide strategies for developing and promoting AI, as well as specific policies to ensure AI benefit all. A series of elements have been repeated across national policy efforts, with a focus on data regulation, training, algorithmic accountability, and market innovation. A subtheme in several of these approaches is economic and regional development (Bakkum et al., 2024). For example, one strategy has a strong focus on robotics and those who are at a competitive disadvantage; another country likewise hopes to use AI to transform its agricultural sector and is conducting pilot AI projects targeted at manufacturing, the medical sector, agriculture, trade, creative economy, and services. Case studies show that in addition to the establishment of a particular institution to deal with AI, the implementation of a national AI strategy comprises a range of instruments: companies are supported to innovate and invest in AI. A few case study countries also have programs to facilitate enhanced SME access to data or infrastructure with data management initiatives, the publication of open-source data, and supporting data-led start-ups (Antony et al., 2024). Based on the case studies and other research conducted, we find that there is no uniform strategy that can be pursued in order to forge inclusive AI systems. Instead of a one-size-fits-all solution being applicable to all forms of AI policy and action, national strategies are tailored to the specific socio-economic context in which they are to be applied. This also suggests another implication: national initiatives are subject to failure in terms of inclusive growth; in the end, the strategy's effectiveness is the most important (Tang, 2024). Countries should, therefore, develop a framework for impact assessment and, as necessary, alter incentives and structures to enable inclusive growth to flourish with inclusion as illustrated in Figure 5.

Figure 5. Sampled cases of disabilities

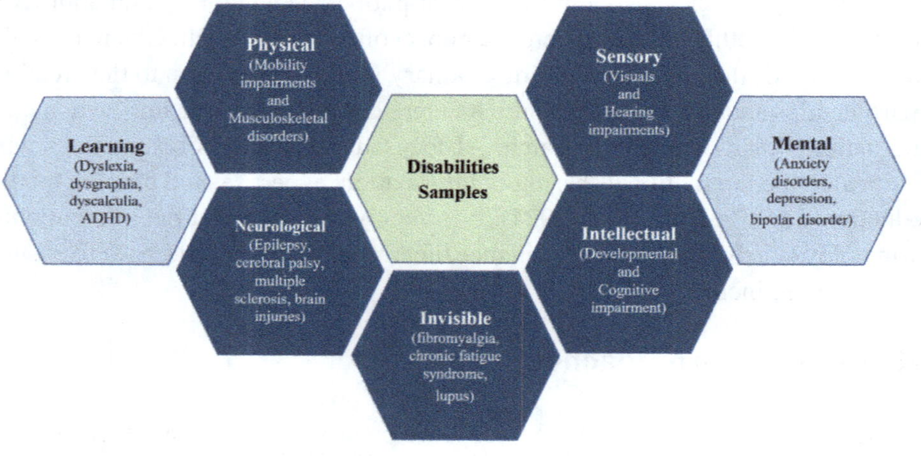

CASE STUDIES OF AI INITIATIVES FOR INCLUSIVE GROWTH

Several case studies display how AI can contribute to creating new, inclusive growth that directly benefits marginalized populations. A number of such initiatives have targeted problems faced by small towns and marginal communities. For example, they have sought to find out if a child has a serious heart disease by using AI algorithms to make rapid analyses of heart sounds, gather field data on poor farmers' income sources, their health cost expenditure, and health-seeking behavior, and to use multilingual voice interface technologies to help semi-literate tribal and

Adivasi citizens access services (Ahmad et al., 2024). AI technologies can increase versatility and resilience by complementing labor and capital, enhancing human capacities, and increasing economic and power correlations, especially through access to information. However, to ensure technological change is socially robust, these cases also point to the necessity of addressing the power asymmetries that bolster accumulated disadvantages and exclusion, limiting individual and social capabilities. In conclusion, the case studies collected in this report offer some insight into the kinds of solutions being pursued by stakeholders interested in bringing greater equity to AI applications, what they have learned, and how they hope the results can be taken to scale (Chima Abimbola Edeni et al., 2024). Themes include questions of definition and measurement, the role of power in shaping who benefits and who is harmed, and the crucial conditions that make an initiative to take advantage of AI to bolster inclusive growth effectively.

Each of the case studies included in this report describes an initiative intended to use AI to drive new economic growth that is inclusive and accessible to marginalized and underserved communities. While all of these case studies are difficult to compare, they have provided results, some of which can be scaled up for wider impact. The hope is that the results described here can inspire or inform similar initiatives that prime the ground for services that fit within the constraints of human, financial, and other fundamental and practical constraints, as well as the motivating forces of market demand. Each of the initiatives described in the case studies has been successful in creating value, and they also illustrate some of the key factors that need to be in place to create that value (Sanghvi et al., 2024). They illustrate initiatives to make cultural materials and knowledge more accessible as a source of innovation, to amplify voices from beyond the global economic centers, and to assuage – and in some cases quantify – safety and other grounded fears in order to engage people with technologies that promise greater efficiency, meaning, and purpose, or to reveal new opportunities or solutions. Finally, these case studies highlight the crucial role of trade policies, including regulation and data laws, government spending choices, and other regulatory tools, in ensuring positive spillovers, complementary spillovers, and shared welfare (Adekunle, 2024; Tang, 2024).

Healthcare

The AI revolution drives radical improvements to a range of activities. A number of these have the power to push against the power-law distribution. Fewer than 10 percent of the world's people, and about half of all Americans, have access to state-of-the-art healthcare. The diagnosis you receive depends on where and from whom you seek care. One way to ameliorate disparities in access to and effectiveness of healthcare would be to ensure that more people have a wider range of healthcare options. Because AI delivers amazing diagnostic insights to nurses, doctors, and other healthcare workers, it can make it possible for many more kinds of professionals to offer specialized healthcare (Shafik, 2024d). For example, certain hospitals managed to scale up their ability to diagnose and treat retinopathy, thus ensuring early intervention for most poor and diabetic patients. AI can improve the time and methods of diagnostics and make the work of nurse practitioners, physical therapists, epidemiologists, health educators, fitness instructors, informal caregivers, social workers, and community health workers more reliable, all of whom already figure in healthcare delivery in much greater numbers than doctors do (Shafik, 2024j). AI can complement the existing skills of human professionals and change healthcare delivery from being centered on helping public health professionals manage an aggregate health outcome to ensuring that every person has the best chance at living the healthiest life possible. As such, it would be aligned with taking a Black Lives Matter approach to public health—something that many personal health efforts consistently fail to do (Kelkar et al., 2024; Shafik, 2024g).

Education

AI's influence on education could be transformative. For example, an AI tool provides educators with instructional guidance and resources for main module and sub-module development. Through AI, educational programs can collect near-continuous data streams on students, learning tasks, and goals, mapping competencies through learning resources to psychometrics or performance indicators. Likewise, a personal learning coach for computer science courses gives each student tailored educational resources, tutoring, feedback, and support. The software has been piloted in low education attainment and low socioeconomic status groups, where participants also reported benefits in terms of decreased feelings of inferiority and embarrassment and increased enjoyment (Shafik, 2024k). An AI platform uses licensed early education content to deliver personalized curriculums for young children. Some worry that AI use might overlook the needs of some learners. As an example, one of the biggest interventions to date is in vocational career support as part of a national service. Currently, all universities face a legal requirement to use algorithms to assess applications to be fairer to all groups of students (Shafik, 2024i). This has prompted serious debate about the fairness of relying on protected characteristic data to train algorithms and a belief that this could lead to discrimination in applications or offers. Recently, a hackathon challenge competition was hosted in order to garner proposals for edtech tools and approaches from some of the top tech companies. This resulted in parties from across edtech and IT formulating programs together with some local education support institutions or bodies. An innovation program has been launched in partnership with a consulting firm. Because of this potentially significant impact, inclusive AI projects need to be created ethically (Salajan et al., 2024). In a critical step, the data handling of AI was designed to be consistent with the more extensive program governance protocols. The program is gathering data on the AI tools' impacts and acceptance as well as refining the tools. There is a clear opportunity to develop parallel AI for labs. This would involve various partnerships between education providers, AI tech delivery, and researchers.

Agriculture

Agriculture is the largest economic sector in developing countries and a critical pathway for countries to diversify and enhance local, regional, and global trade and investment. The application of AI in agriculture has the potential to make growth in this sector more inclusive. In recent years, we have seen innovative AI applications for a wide range of farming practices, from plant and soil health prediction to smart farm machinery and drones and satellites that provide near real-time measurements of crop health, vegetation volatility, water usage, and soil properties (Shafik, 2024b). AI-powered tools can be used to analyze data on, for example, weather trends, temperature, humidity, and wind speed to deliver localized forecasts and advice. By learning local and regional language models, these tools can deliver more accurate insights to address the unique challenges faced by farmers. These applications are especially beneficial for smallholders who depend on agriculture as their primary source of income, yet they have often been overlooked when it comes to receiving the benefits of better inputs and extension services that can result in increased productivity (Shafik, 2024c). Smallholder farmers—those growing smaller plots of land—often face challenges relating to agriculture and often bear the brunt of unsustainable practices such as overuse of water and chemical fertilizers. They are also vulnerable to the effects of climate change. AI-powered insights can help to mitigate some of these risks, such as by improving soil fertility and efficient water use. This is being demonstrated in the field: a startup has created a voice-based farmer support system to deliver agricultural information and services to smallholders, while another uses a backpack-sized instrument powered by AI to help smallholders optimize the use of seeds and fertilizers. AI insights also deliver better harvest predictions to rural communities, helping to reduce food waste and preserve rural livelihoods (Shafik, 2025b). The challenges faced by farmers, however, are their ability to access these AI tools and resources. Given these opportunities, efforts are being made to democratize access and availability.

Finance

The newest AI technologies can be applied in the very large financial sector to improve its operation for financing community development and business formation by many groups. The community investment activities of banks and other financial institutions provide some human aid locally and act as catalysts to development but are now directed mostly to simple investments in longer-dated financial assets, which provide little actual assistance to human development. To finance business formation for all who desire and are capable of creating small businesses, much more sophisticated financial software and services are required (Gondwe, 2024). The former application of AI technology can be focused on obstacles to workforce development and employment that are often found to be greater in areas of very low median incomes. Microfinance for business development currently suffers from prohibitively high transaction costs because of the small-dollar sizes of credits. Twice the minimum efficient size reduces the caretaking costs and makes community-based microfinance possible. When longer-term investment is combined for developed business, three important components are joined: each amount of money in wealthy savings banks and money market accounts; each amount in insured branches and agencies of foreign banks receiving their money from deposits of the wealthy escaping tax; and all existing and perhaps additional new microfinance Community Development Banks at twice the minimum efficient size with insured deposits that are reported federally (Rane & Choudhary, 2024). An upper Cretaceous evolution of community-based microfinance 50 years ago in Morocco occurred with a joint spurt of development assistance and federal deposit insurance for village post offices. The cost and obstacles of extending federal deposit insurance to bank CDs for community CDBs and MFIs are small relative to the mission impact; all current federal deposit insurance programs combined total just a small percentage of the Ceiling Obligation for their private counterpart. Extensions with bank CDs can support the transaction costs of community investment institutions and provide the clientele of the wealthy with diversification benefits inside the threshold (Dirgová Luptáková et al., 2024). The addition of recourse to Shelter Banks and other money market mutual funds varying other than proportional to the period to maturity is predicted to contribute an additional premium on bank capital. In addition to the positive development impetus of longer-term capital, additional federal guarantees and lines of capital are assumed to be added to the whole private banking industry. These additions can be secured through higher guarantees and capital requirements for all federally insured banks, domestically chartered or branches of foreign banks (Adu-Gyamfi et al., 2024; Shafik, 2024f).

Transportation

Transportation has a channeling effect on the distribution of economic advantages. More productive cities have higher transportation costs, and public transportation investment should be proportionally focused on these cities. Here, an advanced data-driven approach can greatly amplify the equity effects of transportation investment. First, an intelligent and cooperative mobility system can effectively improve accessibility for the elderly and disabled population. Second, data-driven approaches can help in prioritizing first-mile and last-mile services and shared solutions that disproportionately help lower-income residents (Gondwe, 2024). Moreover, Mobility as a Service can liberate lower-income families from the burden of car ownership and provide a cheaper transport alternative for people who cannot or do not want to drive mid- to long distances. Furthermore, the improved efficiency of autonomous vehicles can effectively lower the cost of public transportation. Recent research revealed that a single self-driving shuttle bus could replace approximately 11 cars—around 0.3 to 0.69 times the average daily car trips in Ontario (Olabisi Oluwakemi Adeleye et al., 2024). Several studies reported an average of 25 to 30% of Americans and nearly 40% of Europeans choosing AV self-driving commuter buses as their preferred tool for daily commutes, with the cost of using those self-driving commuter buses being $84 to $132.50. This kind of rapid transformation in public transportation greatly benefits social equity since a larger number of citizens could thus hold a driving license. The improvement in accessibility, when licensing policies are rather strict, has a hedonistic aspect of the driving experience for those taking full advantage of it, using the vehicle for entertainment and leisure, possibly for more profitable and sustainable uses (Dutta, 2024). The future wide availability of AVs will then cause potential loss when depriving these resourceful citizens of the benefits they are used to.

MEASURING IMPACT AND EFFECTIVENESS OF AI IN INCLUSIVE GROWTH

The previous paper delved into the why and what of measuring AI's role in inclusive growth. Conversely, this paper explores how. Methodologies, tools, and practices are frequently changing; several options are outlined but not constituted here. Changing political circumstances and varied global regions can provide a variety of options again. Practice may range from testing existing programs designed to support inclusive and growth-friendly AI to new programs and decision-making methods (Adu-Gyamfi et al., 2024). The choice may be affected by factors such as current AI market concentration, significant potential data analysis, and collection challenges, and create additional need for consideration of diverse community needs and viewpoints. Panelists and questionnaires have presented a variety of tools and methodologies that have been used for the value for money, evaluation, and impact of AI projects (Fan et al., 2024; Iacoban et al., 2024):

(i) The "Theory of Change" method, which conceptualizes the transformation process from inputs to outcomes and impacts; and the ways in which enterprises and/or businesses and beneficiaries contribute to the change in the long term, ensuring that the results of these studies are as practical as possible and incorporate innovative and inclusive growth provisions.
(ii) conventional project benefits evaluations such as cost-benefit and cost-consequences. Task lists of values for money and options research are carried out at project design time or during project module development and feasibility assessment, while effect assessments and economic expressions of options are necessary to view the results on the ground to assess success.

Interviews can, for example, determine how well a planned project is expected to have any of its projected beneficial impacts, and this will be clearly necessary. To measure the effectiveness of effect measurements, sufficiently long-term evaluations are needed. Panelists reiterated these cultural considerations. The resulting measurement as the responsibility of funding organizations was characterized by its purpose to reveal the effects of AI projects rather than necessarily capture only the results of a particular outcome (Wang'ang'a, 2024). Case studies in this stream complement many of the other techniques from the 'inclusive AI' streams.

Ethical Considerations in AI

We will not create a world that works for everyone without intention, ethical thinking, and hard work. In addition to these two foundational concepts, a third came to us in the form of a work that asks us to act on questions grouped as made up of Action and Ethics. It is noted that we do not always use the guardrails AI can provide. However, technology does not have to have negative impacts; AI also has the potential for good. Even in my generation, we have seen human differences based on gender and race increasingly thought of as areas in which we can do better (Adekunle, 2024). Reassured by that, I decided to use whatever skills and influence I had to work with AI in conjunction with an excellent team to make a difference. However, I have sometimes seen firsthand the negative uses of technology, so I believe that technological development, ethical development, diversity, and inclusion in technology are of the utmost urgency. We have also seen good examples of all of them. One of those positive experiences came in my interactions with a leading economist (Chauncey & McKenna, 2024). Companies, governments, and developers collectively must understand the importance of ethical considerations and accountability in AI. Some support and note the importance of ethical AI guidelines. In that vein, there are thoughtful discussions about the importance of visual ethics representation in AI. We believe that conversations emphasize that transparency and good use of data in AI will also enable fairness. Then there are those business leaders urging action on the need for ethical guidelines and valuing ethical considerations and the power and influence they wield for good (Kaur, 2024; Rane & Choudhary, 2024).

Addressing Bias in AI Systems

In this section, we discuss a number of approaches to address bias, also known as unfairness, in AI. While we primarily focus on these within the context of deploying AI for public policy—highlighting the concerns particular to this domain—we note that many of these methods have more general applicability to other settings, too. Indeed, AI is being deployed in various contexts where fairness is a value of interest, for example, in credit scoring, hiring, and admission processes, and many companies are working hard to address these issues (Olabisi Oluwakemi Adeleye et al., 2024). In essence, we are posing a slightly different question here: how do we construct AI systems that are inherently trustworthy because they are being used for the public good? Definitions matter, and naturally, there are a number that pertain to fairness. A widely used definition considers the base rate as a natural benchmark and aims to assure that the probability of a positive outcome exceeds the base rate when the attribute has a positive value, while the probability of a positive outcome is less than or equal to the base rate when the attribute has a negative value (Adu-Gyamfi et al., 2024). This condition effectively imposes equalizing odds on the model's outputs. Such conditions ensure that the procedure applied to the total population of individuals results in a positive outcome for the same fraction of individuals within each class. This is similar to what has in the past been referred to as a disparate impact in other fair lending laws or affirmative action. Other similar models and collaterals have been developed with the aim of generating other socially acceptable solutions (Kelkar et al., 2024).

FUTURE TRENDS AND INNOVATIONS IN AI FOR INCLUSIVE GROWTH

The future of AI is likely to be reshaped by many new developments that are on the horizon. Vision exercises are limited by current technologies. As AI researchers, technologists, and policymakers become more aware of potential societal implications from this technology, we are likely to see an increased focus on the development of technologies and operational frameworks that promote greater economic inclusion. Partnerships: A growing collaboration between AI researchers, policymakers, and affected communities could become one of the key drivers of future AI innovations. International Humanitarian Aid Scene: AI for Good initiatives and innovations that could reshape certain sectors. Collaboration in the Basque Country (Ahmad et al., 2024). We envisage this list – and many of the other scenarios – will be deeply informed by engagement with communities. They outline valuable entry points for the technology to become more inclusive, equitable, and sensitive to societal needs. Explainable and Ethical AI Frameworks: The increasing possibility of mass unemployment and demands from stakeholders for answers is likely to lead to a new round of thinking around explainable AI that goes beyond technical considerations. Expensive AI Talent: Economies equipped with a large pool of AI experts will have a competitive advantage over those that do not. Despite inclusivity being a corporate value, less scrupulous companies could actively exploit AI systems for profit, regardless of their effect on society. AI Diplomacy and Soft Power: Countries that shape global governance norms around AI will possess significant leverage on a global stage (Chima Abimbola Edeni et al., 2024; Fundira et al., 2024). AI policies will therefore be borne from a position of self-interest. By planning for such an AI-enhanced future, we can actively work toward making technology work for us all.

AI and Inclusive Growth

As with digital technologies more generally, AI is a tool and can be used to promote growth that is both equitable and inclusive. Indeed, the history of major technical progress suggests that the initial impact is to exacerbate inequality and to result in growth that is not inclusive. However, the evidence also suggests that, in the long run, as societies adjust, these do not have to be the consequences of technical progress. The channels through which AI could cause growth that is not inclusive and exacerbate inequality are straightforward (Delgado Algarra et al., 2024; Liew, 2024). They arise from the nature of labor-augmenting technological change and from the fact that AI-driven technical progress in the near and medium term is likely to supplement, and even replace, predominantly, high-income workers, and to complement and even converge with low-income workers; sometimes, however, also to replace them. On the other hand, the channels through which AI can promote inclusive growth also become apparent upon reflection. After all, the extent to which technical progress impinges upon income and wealth distribution depends on how its causes and consequences are managed; that itself is endogenous to institutions, policies, and regulations (Bressane et al., 2024). Some of the main channels through which AI can be used to mitigate the potential downsides of promoting growth through AI, and to promote a more inclusive growth path, are straightforward. The primary policy lever through which countries can hope to achieve these objectives is education and skills training, particularly for those who might be replaced by AI technologies and much more for adults than has hitherto been the practice. While most estimates suggest that AI effects on employment can be expected to be small, considerable occupational reallocation seems likely; and this is especially true where opportunities created for wage earners by AI would be low, and retraining schemes rare (Gondwe, 2024; Olabisi Oluwakemi Adeleye et al., 2024).

AI and Equitable Growth

Many countries have experienced a decrease in labor's share of national income, an increase in wage inequality between high- and low-skilled workers, and aging populations with a reduced share of the population in the workforce. In the future, more inclusive and equitable growth will require innovations in the workforce, including lifelong learning, registration strategies for AI, and new worker benefit packages, to ensure that AI expands the workforce, creates new high-skill job opportunities, promotes wage growth and equality, and facilitates landing for people whose jobs may require restructuring (Adu-Gyamfi et al., 2024; Antony et al., 2024). There are several considerations that illustrate the rules of labor policy influenced by the incentives between digital technology and low wages that allow workers to navigate the labor market while AI technologies provide efficient and effective services for companies. The time period during which AI pays will depend on the number of workers needed and the needs of workers in various forms of businesses and industries, the relative yield of capital, and policy options. In many cases, these workers are expected to increase in productivity, but this has not always applied to AI or previous breakthroughs in artificial intelligence (Fan et al., 2024; Tang, 2024). Policymakers have learned more about how to adapt policy and regulatory channels to key channels in world markets, institute mechanisms for moving workers into new job demands and investment measures, including changes in formal learning and investments to enable managers to strengthen social services and support organizations to provide equitable adjustments to the pressures and opportunities presented by AI. Companies worldwide also need to increase employee training and education in line with the growing focus on AI. Needed levels of policy change for social purposes, including training and transition sharing, can be influenced by a number of parameters (Mishra, 2024).

Emerging Technologies

Artificial intelligence has the potential to promote higher growth in the U.S. and could also generate greater inclusion—rising living standards broadly for non-college-educated workers and for the areas that are currently lagging in innovation. Meeting these objectives, however, will depend on policies around tax reform, education and workforce development, and innovation. The United States must also stay true to its values around maintaining the rule of law, free speech, privacy, and free enterprise (Shafik, Kalinaki, & Zakari, 2024). We offer five principles to consider as the nation addresses the policy implications of AI and these profound economic opportunities. Tools of artificial intelligence are becoming more and more accessible, within reach not just of computer scientists and trained professionals but also of workers, managers, and firms from a wide range of industries. It has arrived at a moment when our world is generating more data than ever, computing tools are getting more powerful, and high-quality collaboration between humans and machines is increasingly feasible. Ideas and products that rely on AI techniques are in development in laboratories around the world (Sanghvi et al., 2024). The emerging technologies include broad areas of machine learning, such as neural networks, data labeling tools, methods for interpreting and validating AI decisions, unsupervised learning, natural language processing techniques, and reinforcement learning. Tailoring the benefits of AI to an inclusive audience will require a deep set of principles guiding research, development, and policy (Adu-Gyamfi et al., 2024). Then, AI could deliver not just rapid growth, but growth diffused more widely, creating a broader increase in opportunities and rising living standards not just for a few, but for everyone.

Impact on Employment

In conclusion, AI will be the engine for growth and development in the twenty-first century. It will transform sectors that are vital to economic growth, such as healthcare, financial services, government, materials and manufacturing, mobility and transportation, and energy and environmental resources. AI has already begun to revolutionize these sectors, and there is a growing body of evidence suggesting AI will deliver productivity enhancements and potentially be a long-term catalyst for growth. Employment is the key to the global economy's future. AI poses two employment challenges (Rane & Choudhary, 2024). The first is job displacement. It is estimated that up to 30% of global workers could have their jobs automated by 2030. Unlike in previous technological transformations, when rural workers moved to cities and unskilled workers moved into factories and found employment, the AI-driven transformation suggests that job loss will be worse in urban areas than rural ones and may increase income inequality. High-paying occupations and the most education-intensive low-paying occupations are to experience little losses, or even net job gains by 2030 (Olabisi Oluwakemi Adeleye et al., 2024). On the other hand, low-paying jobs of middle-skill and low-skilled workers are to be the most affected. Workplace dynamism was high in the earliest AI era, the Industrial Revolution. We believe that similar growth lies ahead if we learn from but do not repeat the policy mistakes of past eras. What new firms, industries, and job requirements are created determines what workers learn and what they earn. The benefits of workplace dynamism in practice are not merely anemic. Jobs chosen by software are often self-appointed (Adu-Gyamfi et al., 2024). Marketplace exchange depends upon workers wanting the new job requirements. Markets quickly reorganize with lower skill barriers and costs enough to make them viable. The current disruption from so-called digital labor platforms exemplifies these dynamics. It has been ad hoc, as rapid change often is. These platforms are cobbled together by creative entrepreneurs. Their operations and regulations are industry-specific due to the federalist overlay of regulations that shifts hiring costs to potential employers rather than workers. These platforms offer potential on-ramps to an economy like the dynamism driven by the earliest AI, the mechanization era (Kelkar et al., 2024).

SUMMARY OF KEY FINDINGS

The benefits of AI need to be realized. To benefit from AI, governments recognize the need to undertake economic, labor, and social policies to proactively adapt to the opportunities that come with it.

(i) Addressing issues of corporate culture, as well as consumer and citizen biases, is important for effective societal understanding and adoption of AI. This includes the setting of AI ethical guidelines, the establishment of public-private partnerships, and the responsible reporting of AI use.
(ii) Industry organizations and governments must work together to provide a comprehensive framework to address the ethical implications and efficient regulation of AI, which will lead to faster adoption and fuller utilization. Public-private partnerships, leveraging cooperation between industry partners, service providers, and the government, can also be very important to success in leveraging AI.
(iii) Despite the transformative potential for economies, AI, like any new technology, offers both opportunity and challenge. The challenge lies in how businesses and societies manage within the constraints imposed by the transition process. The real danger comes from inaction.

(iv) Through greater collaboration across industries and by informing public policy discussions, this report hopes to address stakeholders' concerns and create a positive message about the potential improvements that will derive from implementing AI.
(v) The success of AI will depend on comprehensive understanding and engagement from many different stakeholder actors, including global leaders, policymakers, social influencers, business leaders, and experts in machine learning and other AI techniques from diverse backgrounds.
(vi) After receiving unique and diverse viewpoints, this report aims to emphasize the necessity of an inclusive effort that brings multiple voices into the international AI dialogue. Incentives should be directed to making society prepared and inclusive of this revolutionary development. Close collaboration will lead to success.

Some academics and research organizations have already begun to help address these challenges. Still, more work can be done to identify practical approaches to ensure the benefits of AI, build inclusive growth, and scale these approaches to impact. The discussion around how to create a future where all people can share economic growth made possible by AI is still at a very formative stage. While the elements of the challenge are clear, solutions are still a work in progress (Iacoban et al., 2024). This must change.

Future research could help to answer a number of core questions about the impact of AI on economic growth. Research can be divided into three bodies of work: measuring the impact of AI and other advanced technologies on aggregate economic growth and productivity; understanding the implications of integrating workers and preventing labor market disparities; and applying AI to help address societal challenges (Ahmad et al., 2024; Salajan et al., 2024). First, regarding the impact of AI on economic growth and productivity, how quickly will AI be integrated into productive processes, and how quickly will those new processes be adopted across the economy? These questions are key to determining the ultimate impact of AI on aggregate growth, stratification across different regions, and the degree to which different labor market outcomes will materialize simultaneously versus over time. The answers to these questions will depend crucially on how industries adopt and integrate AI, as well as aggregate cyclical conditions interacting with adoption and labor market outcomes (Osama, 2024).

CONCLUSION

This chapter has sought to make the case for addressing AI as a catalytic technology for inclusive growth. Throughout this essay, we have highlighted some of the prevailing obstacles to promoting and achieving inclusive economic growth. Chief among these is the failure to democratize access to foundational opportunities for meaningful connection, learning, labor, and leisure. AI can help to address these and other fundamental human needs. We are, therefore, hopeful that AI can be the technological lynchpin we need to redouble our efforts to create an inclusive digital age and society. Where some see the automation of jobs, we see the automation of drudgery and a corresponding liberation from toil. Where some see an over-empowered, centralized digital infrastructure, we see an opportunity to build a more human-centric computing era, one in which the World Wide Web becomes a truly global utility platform for safe, distributed, decent-linked intelligence and collaboration. These are the possibilities of an era of inclusive AI that we want to further. It is important, however, to register the many hazards and obstacles in our path. AI is not a panacea, nor will it reduce inequalities by itself. We have cataloged many of the challenges before us here, from technological dismay and the inevitable path dependence of fixated policymakers to the fragmentation and corporate capture that could stymie projects seeking to align the values of AI producers, capital holders, and users to the achievement of a more equitable future. We unite, however, with the many others committed to this cause, who have set about actionable agendas designed to meet these and other concerns. We close this essay with some of our own recommendations for these collectives of committed actors—chief among them, we hope, you.

REFERENCES

Adekunle, A. (2024). Application of Artificial Intelligence and Digital Technologies in Fashion Design and Innovation in Nigeria. *International Journal of Fashion and Design*, *3*(1). Advance online publication. DOI: 10.47604/ijfd.2389

Adeleye, O. O., Eden, C. A., & Adeniyi, I. S. (2024). Innovative teaching methodologies in the era of artificial intelligence: A review of inclusive educational practices. *World Journal of Advanced Engineering Technology and Sciences*, *11*(2). Advance online publication. DOI: 10.30574/wjaets.2024.11.2.0091

Adu-Gyamfi, B., Ariyaningsih, A., Zuquan, H., Yamazawa, N., Kato, A., & Shaw, R. (2024). Reflections on science, technology and innovation on the aspirations of the Sendai framework for disaster risk reduction. *International Journal of Disaster Resilience in the Built Environment*, *15*(2). Advance online publication. DOI: 10.1108/IJDRBE-06-2022-0062

Ahmad, I., Sharma, S., Singh, R., Gehlot, A., Gupta, L. R., Thakur, A. K., Priyadarshi, N., & Twala, B. (2024). Inclusive learning using industry 4.0 technologies: addressing student diversity in modern education. In *Cogent Education* (Vol. 11, Issue 1). https://doi.org/DOI: 10.1080/2331186X.2024.2330235

Antony, P. J., Kannan, R., & Professor, A. (2024). Revolutionizing the Tourism Industry through Artificial Intelligence: A Comprehensive Review of AI Integration, Impact on Customer Experience, Operational Efficiency, and Future Trends. In www.chandigarhphilosophers.com *International Journal for Multidimensional Research Perspectives (IJMRP: Vol. ISSN* (Issue 1).

Bakkum, M. J., Hartjes, M. G., Piët, J. D., Donker, E. M., Likic, R., Sanz, E., de Ponti, F., Verdonk, P., Richir, M. C., van Agtmael, M. A., & Tichelaar, J. (2024). Using artificial intelligence to create diverse and inclusive medical case vignettes for education. *British Journal of Clinical Pharmacology*, *90*(3). Advance online publication. DOI: 10.1111/bcp.15977 PMID: 38016816

Bressane, A., Zwirn, D., Essiptchouk, A., Saraiva, A. C. V., Carvalho, F. L. de C., Formiga, J. K. S., Medeiros, L. C. de C., & Negri, R. G. (2024). Understanding the role of study strategies and learning disabilities on student academic performance to enhance educational approaches: A proposal using artificial intelligence. *Computers and Education: Artificial Intelligence*, *6*. Advance online publication. DOI: 10.1016/j.caeai.2023.100196

Bulutoding, L., Rahmah Sari, N., Yulia, R., & Manoppo, V. P. (2024). Ethical Implications Of Human Resource Development And Application Of Artificial General Intelligence (AGI) In The Context Of Global Business Governance. *International Journal of Humanities, Social Sciences and Business (INJOSS), 3*(1).

Chauncey, S. A., & McKenna, H. P. (2024). Creativity and Innovation in Civic Spaces Supported by Cognitive Flexibility When Learning with AI Chatbots in Smart Cities. *Urban Science (Basel, Switzerland), 8*(1). Advance online publication. DOI: 10.3390/urbansci8010016

Cobanaj, M., Corti, C., Dee, E. C., McCullum, L., Boldrini, L., Schlam, I., Tolaney, S. M., Celi, L. A., Curigliano, G., & Criscitiello, C. (2024). Advancing equitable and personalized cancer care: Novel applications and priorities of artificial intelligence for fairness and inclusivity in the patient care workflow. In *European Journal of Cancer* (Vol. 198). https://doi.org/DOI: 10.1016/j.ejca.2023.113504

Delgado Algarra, E. J., Bernal Bravo, C., Morales Cevallos, M. B., & López Meneses, E. (2024). Pedagogical and Technical Analyses of Massive Open Online Courses on Artificial Intelligence. *Applied Sciences (Switzerland), 14*(3). Advance online publication. DOI: 10.3390/app14031051

Dirgová Luptáková, I., Pospíchal, J., & Huraj, L. (2024). Beyond Code and Algorithms: Navigating Ethical Complexities in Artificial Intelligence. *Lecture Notes in Networks and Systems, 934 LNNS*. https://doi.org/DOI: 10.1007/978-3-031-54813-0_30

Dutta, S. (2024). Framing the Landscape of Technological Enhancements: Artificial Intelligence, Gender Issues, and Ethical Dilemmas. In *Signals and Communication Technology: Vol. Part F1803*. https://doi.org/DOI: 10.1007/978-3-031-45237-6_10

Edeni, C. A., Adeleye, O. O., & Adeniyi, I. S. (2024). The role of AI-enhanced tools in overcoming socioeconomic barriers in education: A conceptual analysis. *World Journal of Advanced Research and Reviews, 21*(3). Advance online publication. DOI: 10.30574/wjarr.2024.21.3.0780

Fan, B. E., Chow, M., & Winkler, S. (2024). Artificial Intelligence-Generated Facial Images for Medical Education. *Medical Science Educator, 34*(1). Advance online publication. DOI: 10.1007/s40670-023-01942-5 PMID: 38510393

Fundira, M., Edoun, E. I., & Pradhan, A. (2024). Evaluating end-users' digital competencies and ethical perceptions of AI systems in the context of sustainable digital banking. *Sustainable Development*. Advance online publication. DOI: 10.1002/sd.2945

Gondwe, G. (2024). Artificial Intelligence, Journalism, and the Ubuntu Robot in Sub-Saharan Africa: Towards a Normative Framework. *Digital Journalism (Abingdon, England)*. Advance online publication. DOI: 10.1080/21670811.2024.2311258

Habibipour, A. (2024). Responsible living labs: What can go wrong? *Journal of Information. Communication and Ethics in Society*, *22*(2). Advance online publication. DOI: 10.1108/JICES-11-2023-0137

Iacoban, S. R., Piron-Dumitrascu, M., Suciu, I. D., Cretoiu, D., & Suciu, N. (2024). Innovative Models for Integrative Prenatal Care. *BRAIN. Broad Research in Artificial Intelligence and Neuroscience*, *15*(1). Advance online publication. DOI: 10.18662/brain/15.1/532

Kaur, T. (2024). AI Architectures and Technologies for Raising Society 5.0. In *Artificial Intelligence and Society 5.0: Issues, Opportunities, and Challenges*. https://doi.org/DOI: 10.1201/9781003397052-2

Kelkar, A. H., Hantel, A., Koranteng, E., Cutler, C. S., Hammer, M. J., & Abel, G. A. (2024). Digital Health to Patient-Facing Artificial Intelligence: Ethical Implications and Threats to Dignity for Patients With Cancer. *JCO Oncology Practice*, *20*(3). Advance online publication. DOI: 10.1200/op.23.00412 PMID: 37922435

Liew, J. (2024). Translating Vision into Reality for Early Education & Development. *Early Education and Development*, *35*(1). Advance online publication. DOI: 10.1080/10409289.2024.2287684

Mishra, S. (2024). Classification Based on Ethnicity and Race: A Comprehensive Review. *International Journal for Research in Applied Science and Engineering Technology*, *12*(3). Advance online publication. DOI: 10.22214/ijraset.2024.57989

Osama, M. (2024). Artificial Intelligence in scientific writing and research publication: A paradigm shift in language inclusivity. In *Journal of Back and Musculoskeletal Rehabilitation* (Vol. 37, Issue 2). https://doi.org/DOI: 10.3233/BMR-245001

Patel, P., Moz-Ruiz, D., Garcia, R., Chatterjee, A., Morreale, P., & Burnett, M. (2024). From Workshops to Classrooms: Faculty Experiences with Implementing Inclusive Design Principles. *SIGCSE 2024 - Proceedings of the 55th ACM Technical Symposium on Computer Science Education, 1*. https://doi.org/DOI: 10.1145/3626252.3630861

Rane, N., & Choudhary, S. (2024). Role and challenges of ChatGPT and similar generative artificial intelligence in arts and humanities. *Studies in Humanities and Education*, *5*(1). Advance online publication. DOI: 10.48185/she.v5i1.999

Salajan, F. D., Barnes, T. L., & Becker, A. (2024). Comparative regionalism cases of artificial intelligence governance in education: The Caribbean Community and the European Union. *The Round Table*, *113*(1). Advance online publication. DOI: 10.1080/00358533.2024.2307793

Sanghvi, H., Bhavsar, R., Hundlani, V., Gohil, L., Vyas, T., Nair, A., Desai, S., Jadav, N. K., Tanwar, S., Sharma, R., & Yamsani, N. (2024). MetaHate : AI-based hate speech detection for secured online gaming in metaverse using blockchain. *Security and Privacy*, *7*(2). Advance online publication. DOI: 10.1002/spy2.343

Shafik, W. (2024a). An Overview of Computational Modeling and Simulations in Wireless Communication Systems. *Computational Modeling and Simulation of Advanced Wireless Communication Systems*, 8–40.

Shafik, W. (2024b). Barriers to Implementing Computational Intelligence-Based Agriculture System. In *Computational Intelligence in Internet of Agricultural Things* (pp. 193–219). Springer., DOI: 10.1007/978-3-031-67450-1_8

Shafik, W. (2024c). Biosensor-Based Drones Anomaly Detection Integration for Sustainable Agriculture Development. In *Achieving Food Security Through Sustainable Agriculture* (pp. 283–316). IGI Global., DOI: 10.4018/979-8-3693-4240-4.ch012

Shafik, W. (2024d). Connected healthcare—the impact of Internet of Things on medical services. In *Artificial Intelligence and Internet of Things based Augmented Trends for Data Driven Systems* (pp. 181–217). CRC Press., DOI: 10.1201/9781003497318-10

Shafik, W. (2024e). Deep Learning Impacts in the Field of Artificial Intelligence. In *Deep Learning Concepts in Operations Research* (pp. 9–26). Auerbach Publications., DOI: 10.1201/9781003433309-2

Shafik, W. (2024f). Factors Affecting Green Purchase Behaviors for Small and Medium Enterprises (SMEs) in Uganda. In *Entrepreneurial Strategies for the Internationalization and Digitalization of SMEs* (pp. 198–224). IGI Global. https://doi.org/DOI: 10.4018/979-8-3693-3518-5.ch009

Shafik, W. (2024g). IoT-Enabled Secure and Intelligent Smart Healthcare: Beyond 5G in Enabling Smart Cities. In *Secure and Intelligent IoT-Enabled Smart Cities* (pp. 308–333). IGI Global.

Shafik, W. (2024h). Machine Learning for Advanced Wireless Communication. In *Microwave Devices and Circuits for Advanced Wireless Communication* (pp. 252–278). CRC Press., DOI: 10.1201/9781032656021-13

Shafik, W. (2024i). Mobile Learning and Bring Your Own Device (BYOD): Enhancing Education in the Digital Age. In *Integrating Cutting-Edge Technology Into the Classroom* (pp. 240–267). IGI Global.

Shafik, W. (2024j). The Future of Healthcare: AIoMT—Redefining Healthcare with Advanced Artificial Intelligence and Machine Learning Techniques. In *Artificial Intelligence and Machine Learning in Drug Design and Development* (pp. 605–634). Wiley., DOI: 10.1002/9781394234196.ch19

Shafik, W. (2024k). Towards Trustworthy and Explainable AI Educational Systems. In *Explainable AI for Education: Recent Trends and Challenges* (pp. 17–41). Springer.

Shafik, W. (2025a). Machine Learning Techniques for Multicriteria Decision-Making. In *Multi-Criteria Decision-Making and Optimum Design with Machine Learning* (pp. 165–194). CRC Press.

Shafik, W. (2025b). Sustainable Agriculture and Diet for Urban Development. In *Sustainable Smart Cities and the Future of Urban Development* (pp. 165–192). IGI Global Scientific Publishing.

Shafik, W., Kalinaki, K., Fahim, K. E., & Adam, M. (2024). Safeguarding Data Privacy and Security in Federated Learning Systems. In *Federated Deep Learning for Healthcare* (pp. 170–190). CRC Press., DOI: 10.1201/9781032694870-13

Shafik, W., Kalinaki, K., & Zakari, R. Y. (2024). Blockchain's Motivation for IoT-Enabled Smart City. In *Secure and Intelligent IoT-Enabled Smart Cities* (pp. 195–221). IGI Global., DOI: 10.4018/979-8-3693-2373-1.ch010

Tang, K. H. D. (2024). Implications of Artificial Intelligence for Teaching and Learning. *Acta Pedagogia Asiana*, *3*(2). Advance online publication. DOI: 10.53623/apga.v3i2.404

Wang'ang'a, A. W. (2024). Consequences of Artificial Intelligence on Teaching and Learning in Higher Education in Kenya: Literature Review. *East African Journal of Education Studies*, *7*(1). Advance online publication. DOI: 10.37284/eajes.7.1.1718

Chapter 3
Virtual Healthcare Using AI and Cyber Security Challenges

Nitish Kumar Ojha
https://orcid.org/0000-0002-2236-0766
Amity Universaity, Noida, India

Kire Jakimoski
https://orcid.org/0000-0002-4969-8054
Military Academy "General Mihailo Apostolski", Skopje, North Macedonia

ABSTRACT

Many inventions are being used in the health industry every day. Human life is increasing rapidly and with the use of new technology, the health industry can reach out to more and more people by giving better and more accurate results. Advanced technologies like AI, Augmented Reality, etc. have influenced and defined the health industry in a new way. Mobile phones, wearables, wristbands, and head-mounted displays provide new opportunities for information exchange between real-world and virtual objects, enabling healthcare delivery. The way it is delivered is changing and the overall quality of patient care is improving. For example, by wearing an AR-enabled head-mounted device, surgeons can now see a patient's vital organs during a procedure and consult with a remote colleague, without needing to look away and gather data from multiple displays. Comparative study also has been done. In the end, light has also been thrown on the topic that what are the shortcomings of these applications from the virtual health point of view and which shortcomings should be addressed to improve them.

DOI: 10.4018/979-8-3373-2387-9.ch003

INTRODUCTION

Goldman Sachs in one of its reports predicts that the future belongs to AI and the involvement of AI is going to be high annually as the use of AR and VR in the healthcare industry will reach $6 billion by 2026 globally. Based on several reports, this is predicted that if its growth continues to increase in this manner, then it is going to be a separate dedicated industry and surely it will take its definite form. If we look carefully, when the healthcare industry was equipped with virtual technology, the healthcare industry influenced many segments of the medical sector mainly robotic surgery, patient care management, therapy, telemedicine, rehabilitation, hospital navigation, nursing management, employee management, etc. Many applications have been created according to all these segments which provide high-quality services in these fields. Some applications are designed directly to solve the problems they can solve, such as robotic surgery or nursing timetable management, and other types of applications include those that allow doctors and other medical professionals to specialize in a particular discipline of virtual health. These are used to train people, which can also be called educational apps. Many applications are used for 3D visuals of surgical set-up, interactive simulations, and knowledge checks. In the third category, there are apps for use by the general app, which the public uses for general information about their health (Kong et al., 2020).

LITERATURE REVIEW

Various health applications have been designed to use healthcare data in a segmented and processed manner according to the needs of industry, environment, and regulations. Several surveys exist in this field however they don't deal with the approach of analyzing all of them on a bigger canvas including several parameters. Most of the works deal with the security concerns posed by Android apps and privacy issues of health care data if data is stored at cloud storage or a local level. A detailed survey is needed to cover the different varieties of mobile apps and their usability in different aspects of virtual healthcare. After the pandemic, a quantum jump has been seen in this segment, and not only has the number of users increased but the apps in many fields also. Many surveys have reported that this figure will change, and the advancement of mobile devices will change the scenario in the long term. Many studies report that the change in the positive direction is certain. There are more than 55000 apps on the Google mobile store that are related to health and medical sciences directly and indirectly. Category-wise highest downloading apps on the Google platform are mostly fitness apps and those are products of specialized companies i.e., MyFitnessPal, and Calm App, which means the growth in the hardware segment is also increasing which is a positive sign. The papers and surveys also reported that the scenarios and objectives of mobile apps in this field are changing. A Paper by Khasawneh (Al-Khasawneh, 2015) paper provides a broad overview of the role of mobile applications in healthcare, covering various aspects and types of apps. Rajput et al. (2014) (Rajput et al., 2023) in their survey paper focus on the use of mobile health technology in developing countries and assess its impact and challenges. Moving further, Lagan et al. (2017) reviewed and analyzed mobile health applications specifically designed for prenatal care. These papers can provide comprehensive insights into the various facets of mobile health apps, ranging from their applications in specific health domains to their impact in different geographic and demographic contexts(Lagan et al., 2021) .

During the years 2019 to 2024, many medical apps arose in the market because of Covid-19 and virtual medical technology improved in many segments of disease identification or prognosis. The COVID-19 pandemic has significantly accelerated the growth of the virtual medical applications industry. Before the pandemic, telehealth and other virtual health services were gradually gaining traction, but the necessity for remote healthcare solutions during lockdowns and social distancing measures led to an unprecedented surge in their adoption. During the peak of the pandemic, telehealth usage increased dramatically, with some reports indicating a rise in telehealth utilization for office visits and outpatient care compared to pre-pandemic levels. This rapid adoption was driven by several factors, including increased consumer and provider willingness to use telehealth, regulatory changes that expanded access and reimbursement, and the urgent need to minimize in-person interactions to reduce the spread of the virus. The boom in virtual medical applications has not only been limited to telehealth consultations. The industry has seen significant advancements in digital therapeutics, remote patient monitoring, and AI-driven diagnostic tools. These technologies have enabled healthcare providers to offer comprehensive care remotely, improving access to healthcare services, especially in underserved and rural areas, (Mejía-Granda et al., 2023).

Investment in virtual healthcare has also skyrocketed, with venture capital funding for digital health tripling in 2020 compared to 20171. This influx of capital has fueled innovation, leading to the development of more sophisticated and user-friendly virtual health solutions. Additionally, the integration of AI and machine learning has enhanced the accuracy and efficiency of virtual diagnostics and treatment plans. Despite the rapid growth, the industry faces challenges such as ensuring data security, maintaining patient privacy, and addressing the digital divide that limits access for some populations. However, the continued evolution of virtual medical applications promises to transform healthcare delivery, making it more accessible, efficient, and patient-centered. An exploration kind of work was performed by Khasawneh et al.in year 2023 for virtual healthcare which focuses on the privacy and security risks associated with mHealth applications. It highlights the lack of encryption in many apps and proposes a framework to enhance data confidentiality, integrity, and availability. The study uses a tool to evaluate the security protocols of various Android and iOS health apps. Apps may have vulnerabilities, so a similar study was performed in European countries especially targeting those virtual health based app which are working in those EU (European countries). The work reported by Rajput et al. (2023) concludes almost each apps of medical science and categorizes them on several parameters. This paper reviews existing frameworks for evaluating mobile health apps, emphasizing the importance of privacy and clinical foundation. It introduces the MIND (Mhealth Index and Navigation Database) framework, which includes comprehensive and auditable questions to help users select safe and effective health apps.

Another work reported by the author in 2023 (Mejía-Granda et al., 2023) analyzes security vulnerabilities in healthcare, focusing on medical devices and software from 2001 to 2022. It projects future security issues and suggests mitigation mechanisms to address the rising cybercriminal tendencies.

In some recent work, the work reported by is worthy to cite which was published in a Journal which examines the integration of IoT in healthcare and its associated vulnerabilities. The research highlights critical vulnerabilities in electronic health records, wireless infusion pumps, endoscope cameras, and radiology information systems (Ewoh & Vartiainen, 2024). Key issues identified include poor credential management and hard-coded credentials. The paper provides insights into the consequences of these vulnerabilities and offers mitigation strategies. It emphasizes the need for robust security measures, continuous monitoring, and regulatory adherence to protect patient safety and system integrity. Vulnerability assessment has been a major area of concern in many medical apps where the stealing of sensitive patient data are the main objective. One work reported and published in the Journal of Medical Internet Research, this review article focuses on the cybersecurity challenges faced by medical apps. It analyzes various reports, review articles, and industry white papers to identify common vulnerabilities and potential solutions. The study highlights the importance of secure software development practices, regular security assessments, and user education to mitigate risks. It also discusses the role of regulatory frameworks in ensuring the security of medical apps (Islam et al., 2015).

As the world adapts to a post-pandemic reality, the virtual medical applications industry is poised to play a crucial role in the future of healthcare so in the coming future, more research papers are set to come.

History

The history of medical mobile apps is closely tied to the evolution of smartphones and the increasing demand for accessible healthcare solutions. The journey began in the early 2000s with the advent of smartphones, which provided a platform for developing various applications, including those for health and wellness.

The first wave of medical apps focused on general health tracking, such as fitness and diet monitoring. These apps allow users to log their daily activities, track their calorie intake, and monitor their physical activity. As technology advanced, so did the capabilities of these apps. By the late 2000s, more sophisticated apps emerged, offering features like heart rate monitoring, sleep tracking, and even basic diagnostic tools, ("14 Biggest Healthcare Data Breaches," n.d.).

A significant milestone in the development of medical mobile apps was the introduction of the Apple App Store in 2008 and the Google Play Store in 2012. These platforms provided a centralized location for users to download and access a wide range of health-related apps. This period saw a surge in the development of condition-specific apps, such as those for diabetes management, mental health support, and pregnancy tracking. The integration of wearable technology further propelled the growth of medical apps. Devices like smartwatches and fitness bands could sync with mobile apps, providing real-time health data and personalized insights. This integration allowed for continuous monitoring of vital signs and more accurate health assessments.

In these recent years, the focus has shifted toward telemedicine and remote patient monitoring. Medical apps now enable virtual consultations, allowing patients to connect with healthcare providers from the comfort of their homes. This has been particularly beneficial during the COVID-19 pandemic, where in-person visits were limited. Despite the rapid advancements, challenges such as data privacy, regulatory compliance, and accessibility remain. However, the potential of medical mobile apps to revolutionize healthcare delivery and improve patient outcomes continues to drive innovation in this field (Crawford et al., 2024).

Category of Apps

Different categories of applications have evolved for a long time. These apps can be categorized into three categories.

Figure 1 describes the categories of applications which are used in virtual healthcare for diagnostic purpose -

Figure 1. Categories of virtual health apps as depicted in this chapter

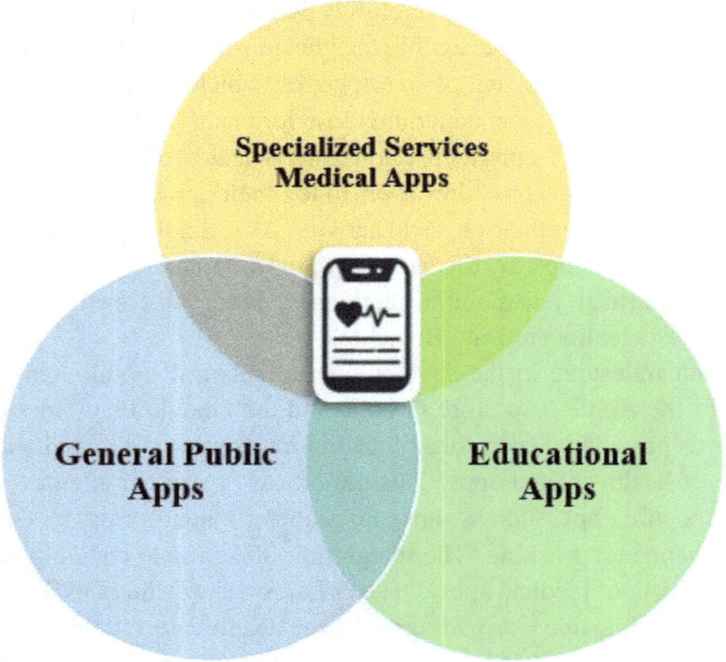

Specialized Services Medical Apps

Some work-specific applications have been used i.e. -

Robot-Assisted Surgery Apps

Robot-assisted surgery apps represent a significant advancement in medical technology, enhancing the precision and efficiency of surgical procedures. These apps are integral to robotic surgical systems, which use robotic arms controlled by surgeons to perform complex surgeries with high accuracy. The introduction of these systems dates back to the late 20th century, with the da Vinci Surgical System being one of the most notable early examples.

These apps provide surgeons with real-time data, 3D visualizations, and enhanced control over surgical instruments. They also facilitate minimally invasive procedures, reducing patient recovery times and minimizing surgical risks. For instance, the **da Vinci Surgical System app** allows surgeons to perform delicate operations through small incisions, offering greater dexterity and control than traditional methods. Another example is the **Mako Robotic-Arm Assisted Surgery app**, used primarily in orthopedic surgeries. This app helps in pre-surgical planning and provides real-time feedback during procedures, ensuring precise placement of implants. Additionally, the **ROSA Knee System app** assists in knee replacement surgeries by offering detailed anatomical mapping and precise alignment of surgical tools, (Bonaiuti et al., 2024).

Wound Care Management Apps

Wound care management mobile apps have revolutionized the way healthcare providers assess, monitor, and treat wounds. These apps offer a range of features that enhance the accuracy and efficiency of wound care, making it easier for clinicians to provide high-quality care.

A prominent example is the **Swift Skin and Wound app**, which digitizes wound measurement, imaging, and tracking. This app uses a smartphone to capture wound images and measurements without direct contact, ensuring precision and reducing the risk of infection. Another notable app is **WoundMatrix**, which offers comprehensive wound assessment and documentation tools. This is especially valuable in rural or underserved areas where access to specialized wound care may be limited (Sarlon et al., 2024).

Physical Therapy and Rehabilitation Supporting Apps

Physical therapy and rehabilitation supporting mobile apps have transformed patient care by making therapy more accessible and engaging. These apps offer features like exercise tutorials, progress tracking, and virtual consultations, enhancing the overall rehabilitation experience.

One notable example is **Exer Health**, which uses a smartphone's camera and motion AI to measure a patient's range of motion and ensure proper exercise form. This app provides real-time feedback and detailed reports for physical therapists to review, making it easier to monitor patient progress remotely.

Another popular app is **PT Decide by Orca Health**, which serves as an educational tool for patients. It includes interactive 3D anatomical models and videos of exercises, helping patients understand their conditions and follow their home exercise programs accurately.

PhysiApp is another excellent example, offering video-guided exercises prescribed by therapists. Patients can follow these exercises at home, and therapists can track their adherence and progress through the app. This ensures continuous engagement and better outcomes.

These apps not only improve patient compliance but also allow for personalized care plans and remote monitoring, making physical therapy more efficient and effective, (“14 Biggest Healthcare Data Breaches,” n.d.).

Patient Record-Keeping Apps

Patient record-keeping mobile apps have become essential tools for managing personal health information efficiently. These apps allow users to store, organize, and access their medical records digitally, ensuring that critical health data is always at their fingertips.

One prominent example is **Apple Health**, which comes pre-installed on all iPhones. This app integrates with various health devices and apps to collect and store data such as medical conditions, medications, lab results, and vital signs. It also features a Medical ID that can be accessed from the lock screen in emergencies, providing crucial information to healthcare providers.

Another notable app is **GenieMD**, available on both Android and iOS. GenieMD is HIPAA compliant, ensuring the privacy and security of patient data. It allows users to record their medical history, track vital signs, and manage medications. The app also supports telehealth consultations, making it easier for patients to connect with healthcare providers remotely.

Hospital Staff Management Apps

Hospital staff management apps are essential tools for efficiently managing healthcare personnel. These apps streamline scheduling, attendance tracking, and communication, ensuring optimal staffing and reducing administrative burdens.

One notable example is **When I Work**, which simplifies shift management across multiple locations. It allows administrators to create and adjust schedules easily, track time and attendance, and manage shift swaps. The app also features real-time notifications, ensuring staff are always informed about their schedules.

Another example is **QGenda**, known for its robust reporting capabilities and nurse scheduling features. It helps in managing staff availability, automating shift assignments, and ensuring compliance with labor regulations. QGenda also integrates with other hospital systems, providing a seamless workflow (Hayes & Fitzpatrick, 2024).

Challenges in this Category

Specialized medical apps face several security challenges that can impact patient data privacy and the overall integrity of healthcare systems. Here are some key challenges:

1. **Data Breaches:** Medical apps often store sensitive patient information, making them prime targets for cyberattacks. Breaches can lead to unauthorized access to personal health data, which can be exploited for identity theft or insurance fraud.
2. **Lack of Encryption:** Inadequate encryption of data during storage and transmission can expose sensitive information to interception and unauthorized access. Ensuring robust encryption protocols is essential to protect patient data.
3. **Phishing and Malware:** Healthcare professionals and patients using these apps are vulnerable to phishing attacks and malware. These threats can compromise login credentials and other sensitive information, leading to unauthorized access.
4. **Regulatory Compliance:** Medical apps must comply with various regulations like HIPAA (Health Insurance Portability and Accountability Act) in the U.S. and GDPR (General Data Protection Regulation) in Europe. Ensuring compliance can be complex and challenging, especially for apps operating across multiple regions (Rawabdeh, 2024).
5. **User Authentication:** Weak authentication mechanisms can make it easier for unauthorized users to access sensitive data. Implementing strong, multi-factor authentication is crucial to enhance security.
6. **Interoperability Issues:** Integrating medical apps with other healthcare systems can introduce vulnerabilities if not done securely. Ensuring secure data exchange between systems is vital to maintaining data integrity and confidentiality.

Educational Apps

Educational apps in medical sciences have revolutionized learning by providing interactive and accessible resources. Apps like **Anatomy Learning** and **Complete Anatomy** offer detailed 3D models, enhancing the understanding of human anatomy. **Medscape** and **UpToDate** provide up-to-date medical information and research, aiding in clinical decision-making. **Quizlet** and **Osmosis** offer flashcards and video tutorials, making complex topics easier to grasp. There are many categories to it -

Medical Professional Training Apps

Medical training mobile apps are designed to enhance healthcare professionals' and students' education and skills. These apps provide interactive learning experiences, access to vast medical resources, and tools for practical training. One notable example is Complete Anatomy, which offers detailed 3D human body models. This app allows users to explore anatomical structures, simulate dissections, and understand complex physiological processes. It is widely used by medical students and professionals for its comprehensive and interactive content (Bohr & Memarzadeh, 2020).

Another example is Touch Surgery, an app that provides surgical simulations and step-by-step guides for various procedures. It allows users to practice surgeries in a virtual environment, improving their skills and confidence before performing real-life operations. The app covers various specialties, including general surgery, orthopedics, and neurosurgery.

Medscape is also a valuable resource, offering a vast library of medical information, including drug references, disease overviews, and clinical guidelines. It helps medical professionals stay updated with the latest research and best practices.

Physician Training Apps

Physician training apps are designed to enhance medical education and clinical skills. **Medscape** is a popular app offering a vast library of medical references, drug information, and clinical guidelines, aiding in continuous learning Surgery provides interactive surgical simulations, allowing physicians to practice procedures virtually. There are many other Apps which detailed 3D models for in-depth anatomical study, enhancing understanding of complex structures.

Medical Reference Apps

Medicine reference apps provide healthcare professionals with quick access to comprehensive drug information is a widely used app that offers detailed drug interactions, dosing guidelines, and pill identification features. Another example is Micromedex, which provides evidence-based drug information, including proper dosages and potential side effects. These apps enhance clinical decision-making by ensuring that accurate and up-to-date information is readily available, improving patient safety and care quality (Fiore, 2017).

Drug Interaction Checker Apps

Drug interaction checker apps are tools designed to help healthcare professionals and patients identify potential interactions between different medications, foods, supplements, and medical conditions. These apps are crucial for ensuring patient safety by preventing adverse drug reactions.

Examples of drug interaction checker apps include:

1. **Drugs.com Medication Guide App:** This app provides a comprehensive drug interaction checker, allowing users to input multiple medications and receive detailed information about potential interactions.
2. **Medscape:** Known for its extensive medical resources, Medscape includes a drug interaction checker that helps healthcare providers quickly identify and manage potential drug interactions.
3. **Micromedex Drug Interactions App:** This app offers evidence-based information on drug interactions, including severity levels and clinical management recommendations.

These apps enhance clinical decision-making by providing reliable, up-to-date information, helping to prevent harmful interactions and improve patient care.

Clinical Trial Apps

Clinical trial apps facilitate the management and participation in medical research studies. Be Part of Research, integrated into the medical trial research app i.e. NHS App, allows users to find and join clinical trials relevant to their health conditions (Akindele et al., 2024).

Patient Communication Apps

Patient monitoring apps enable continuous tracking of vital signs and health metrics, enhancing remote healthcare management. **MyChart** by Epic Systems is a prime example, allowing patients to monitor their health data, communicate with healthcare providers, and access their medical records. Another example is **HealthTap**, which offers real-time monitoring and virtual consultations, ensuring timely medical intervention. These apps improve patient outcomes by facilitating proactive care and timely medical responses.

Dosage Calculator Apps

Dosage calculator apps help healthcare professionals determine the correct medication dosage based on various factors like patient weight, age, and medical condition. MDApp's Pediatric Dose Calculator is a prime example, allowing users to calculate infant and child doses from adult doses using weight, body surface area (BSA), or age. Another example is the Dosage Calculator by MDApp, which estimates daily doses and breaks them into safe amounts based on administration frequency. These apps enhance accuracy and safety in medication administration, reducing the risk of dosing errors.

Electronic Health Record (EHR) Apps

Electronic Health Record (EHR) apps digitize patient medical records, making them easily accessible and manageable. Epic's MyChart is a leading example, allowing patients to view their health records, schedule appointments, and communicate with healthcare providers. It integrates seamlessly with hospital systems, ensuring real-time updates and comprehensive patient care. Another example is Cerner PowerChart, which offers robust features for clinical documentation, order entry, and patient monitoring. These apps enhance healthcare efficiency, improve patient engagement, and ensure accurate record-keeping.

Challenges in this Category

Clinical trial apps face several challenges that can impact their effectiveness and reliability. One major challenge is participant engagement. Ensuring that participants remain active and consistently provide data throughout the trial is crucial, yet difficult to achieve.

Data accuracy and completeness are also significant concerns. Remote data collection can lead to data artifacts and incomplete datasets, which can compromise the integrity of the trial results1. Additionally, participant authentication is critical to ensure that the data collected is from the intended individuals, preventing fraudulent entries.

Regulatory Compliance Poses Another Challenge

Clinical trial apps must adhere to stringent regulations like GDPR and HIPAA, which govern data privacy and security. Navigating these regulations can be complex and time-consuming.

Technical issues such as app usability, compatibility with various devices, and ensuring seamless integration with other healthcare systems can also hinder the effectiveness of clinical trial apps. Moreover, the high cost of developing and maintaining these apps can be a barrier, especially for smaller research organizations.

General Public Apps

Women's Healthcare App

Women's health care apps, often referred to as femtech, are designed to address various health needs specific to women. These apps provide tools for tracking menstrual cycles, managing pregnancy, monitoring fertility, and supporting overall wellness.

Examples of women's health care apps include:

1. **Flo:** This period and ovulation tracker helps women monitor their menstrual cycles, predict ovulation, and track symptoms. It also offers insights into reproductive health and wellness.
2. **Clue:** Another popular period and ovulation tracker, Clue helps users understand their cycles, predict fertile windows, and manage PMS symptoms. It also provides educational content on reproductive health.
3. **Maven Clinic**: This app offers virtual care for women, including access to gynecologists, mental health professionals, and nutritionists. It supports women through various stages of life, from fertility and pregnancy to menopause.
4. **Eve by Glow:** Focused on sexual health and wellness, Eve helps users track their periods, understand their sexual health, and connect with a community for support and advice (Akindele et al., 2024).

These apps enhance women's health by providing personalized insights, facilitating access to healthcare professionals, and promoting proactive health management.

Doctor Search Apps

Doctor search apps are designed to help patients find and connect with healthcare providers quickly and efficiently. These apps offer features such as doctor profiles, patient reviews, appointment scheduling, and telemedicine options, making it easier for users to access medical care.

Examples of doctor search apps include:

1. **Zocdoc:** This app allows users to search for doctors by specialty, location, and insurance. It provides detailed profiles, patient reviews, and the ability to book appointments online. Zocdoc also offers telehealth services, enabling virtual consultations.
2. **Practo:** Popular in India, Practo helps users find doctors, book appointments, and access telemedicine services. It also offers features like online consultations, digital prescriptions, and health records management.
3. **HealthTap:** This app connects users with a network of doctors for virtual consultations. It provides personalized health advice, symptom checkers, and the ability to book in-person appointments if needed.

These apps enhance healthcare accessibility by providing a convenient platform for patients to find and connect with healthcare providers, ensuring timely and efficient medical care.

Appointment Scheduling App

Appointment scheduling apps streamline the process of booking and managing appointments, reducing administrative burdens and improving efficiency. These apps allow users to schedule, reschedule, and cancel appointments online, often integrating with calendars and sending reminders to both parties.

Examples of appointment scheduling apps include:

1. **Calendly:** Known for its ease of use and customization options.
2. **Acuity Scheduling:** Offers robust features for managing client bookings and payments.
3. **Setmore:** Provides free booking software with features like staff scheduling and customer management.

These apps enhance productivity and ensure seamless appointment management.

Medical Prescription Reading App

Medical prescription reading apps are designed to help users decipher and understand handwritten or digital prescriptions, ensuring accurate medication management.

These apps use advanced technologies like optical character recognition (OCR) and artificial intelligence (AI) to read and interpret prescription details.

One notable example is the **Medscape app,** which includes a feature for reading and understanding prescriptions. It provides detailed information about prescribed medications, including dosage, potential side effects, and drug interactions1. This helps patients and healthcare providers ensure that medications are taken correctly and safely.

Another example is the **GoodRx app,** which not only helps users read prescriptions but also compares drug prices at different pharmacies. This app provides information on generic alternatives and potential savings, making it easier for patients to manage their medication costs.

These apps enhance patient safety by reducing the risk of medication errors and improving adherence to prescribed treatments. They also empower patients with knowledge about their medications, fostering better communication with healthcare providers.

Challenges in this Category

These mobile applications face lots of issues at many stages either at the execution level at the installation level or at the integration level. These all challenges can be summarized in the following categories –

1. **Data Privacy**: Protecting sensitive patient information, such as medical history and personal details, from unauthorized access and breaches.
2. **Authentication and Authorization**: Ensuring that only authorized users (patients and doctors) can access the app and its features, preventing unauthorized access.
3. **Data Encryption**: Encrypting data both in transit and at rest to safeguard it from interception and unauthorized access.
4. **Compliance with Regulations**: Adhering to healthcare regulations like HIPAA (in the US) or GDPR (in the EU) to ensure data protection and privacy.
5. **Secure Communication**: Implementing secure communication channels between patients and doctors to prevent eavesdropping and data leaks.
6. **Vulnerability Management**: Regularly updating the app to patch vulnerabilities and protect against new threats.
7. **User Education**: Educating users about security best practices, such as using strong passwords and recognizing phishing attempts.
8. **Third-Party Integrations**: Ensuring that any third-party services integrated with the app comply with security standards and do not introduce vulnerabilities.

These challenges require continuous attention and robust security measures to ensure the safety and privacy of users' data.

SOME COMMON VULNERABILITIES REPORTED IN MEDICAL MOBILE APPS

Medical mobile apps often face several common security vulnerabilities, including:

Data Leakage

Many apps improperly handle sensitive data, leading to potential leaks. This is a significant issue, especially for COVID-tracking apps.

One notable example of data leakage in a medical app involved multiple mobile health apps that were found to be leaking sensitive data through their APIs. A cybersecurity report highlighted that 30 mobile health apps collectively exposed 23 million users to potential attacks. The vulnerabilities included hardcoded API keys and usernames/passwords, which could be exploited to access electronic health records (EHRs) and other sensitive information.

The following Figure 2 from the report reveals the way of data leakage issues –

Figure 2. Data Leakage Issue in mobile apps

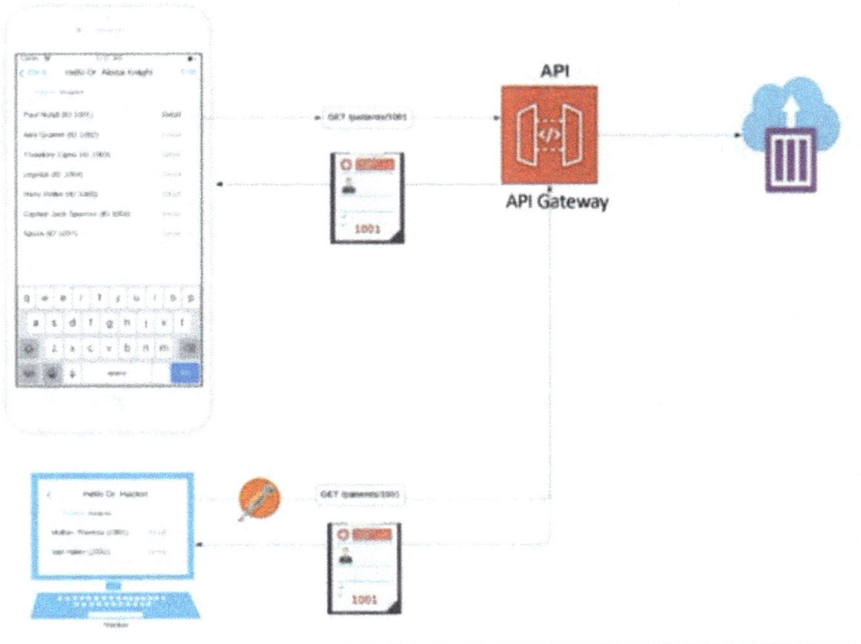

Source: Knight Ink

(Fiore, 2017)

This incident underscores the importance of robust security measures in medical apps to protect user data.

Improper Encryption

A large percentage of healthcare apps do not use proper encryption methods, making data susceptible to interception. One example of improper encryption in health apps involves a study that found up to 23% of mobile health (mHealth) apps transmitted user data unencrypted over HTTP traffic. This made sensitive information like device IDs, GPS data, and contact details vulnerable to hackers (Akindele et al., 2024).

Unauthorized Access

Weak authentication mechanisms can allow unauthorized users to access protected health information (PHI). One notable example of unauthorized access in a health mobile application occurred with the app "MyFitnessPal." In 2018, the app experienced a significant data breach where unauthorized individuals accessed usernames, email addresses, and hashed passwords of approximately 150 million users. This breach highlighted the importance of robust security measures to protect sensitive health data, (Akindele et al., 2024).

Reverse Engineering

Attackers can reverse-engineer apps to discover vulnerabilities or extract sensitive information.

Backend Server Attacks

Vulnerabilities in backend servers can be exploited to gain access to the app's data and functionality. A study by Knight Ink and Approov revealed that 30 popular mobile health apps were vulnerable to API attacks. These vulnerabilities exposed sensitive patient information, including electronic health records (EHRs) and personal health information (PHI). The study found that 77% of the apps contained hardcoded API keys, and some even had hardcoded usernames and passwords.

Ransomware

Medical apps can be targeted by ransomware, which can lock users out of their data until a ransom is paid.

Rooting and Jailbreaking

Apps running on rooted or jailbroken devices are more vulnerable to attacks, as these devices bypass many built-in security measures.

Hard-Coded Credentials

Some apps use hard-coded credentials, which can be easily discovered and exploited by attackers.

API Level Vulnerabilities

Many vulnerabilities have been observed at the native API level. Some of them can be counted as –

1. **Broken Object Level Authorization:** This kind of vulnerability occurs when an app fails to properly enforce access controls, allowing attackers to manipulate object IDs to access unauthorized data.
2. **Broken User Authentication:** Weak authentication mechanisms can allow attackers to impersonate users and gain unauthorized access.
3. **Excessive Data Exposure:** APIs that return more data than necessary can expose sensitive information to attackers.
4. **Lack of Resources & Rate Limiting:** APIs that do not implement rate limiting can be susceptible to denial-of-service (DoS) attacks.

Addressing these vulnerabilities requires a combination of robust security practices, regular updates, and user education.

CONCLUSION

Designing a secure health mobile app involves several key practices to minimize vulnerabilities. Considering the most prominent is data encryption. Ensure all sensitive data is encrypted both in transit and at rest. Use strong encryption protocols like AES-256 to protect user data from unauthorized access. Implement robust authentication mechanisms, such as multi-factor authentication (MFA) and OAuth (Open Authentication), to verify user identities. Avoid using hardcoded credentials and ensure password policies are strong. Implementing proper authentication, authorization, and input validation is another way to eliminate the chances of native vulnerabilities in apps. Use rate limiting to prevent abuse and ensure APIs do not expose more data than necessary. Adhere to relevant healthcare regulations like HIPAA, GDPR, and CCPA. Ensure that the app's data handling practices comply with these regulations to protect user privacy. Using secure communication protocols like HTTPS to protect data transmitted between the app and servers. Implement certificate pinning to prevent man-in-the-middle attacks are few ways to counter the attacks and vulnerabilities in virtual mobile-based application. Following secure coding practices and use secure development frameworks. Conduct code reviews and use static and dynamic analysis tools to identify and fix security issues early in the development process.

By implementing these practices, you can significantly reduce the risk of vulnerabilities in your health mobile app, ensuring a safer experience for users. The future of mobile health apps looks promising, driven by advancements in technology and increasing demand for accessible healthcare. These apps will likely integrate more with wearable devices, providing real-time health monitoring and personalized insights. Artificial intelligence (AI) and machine learning (ML) will play a significant role in predictive analytics, helping to identify potential health issues before they become critical.

Telemedicine will continue to grow, offering remote consultations and reducing the need for in-person visits. Enhanced data security measures will be crucial to protect sensitive health information, ensuring user trust. Additionally, mobile health apps will become more user-friendly, with intuitive interfaces and better accessibility features.

Overall, mobile health apps will empower individuals to take control of their health, improve patient outcomes, and make healthcare more efficient and personalized.

REFERENCES

14 biggest healthcare data breaches [Updated 2024] | UpGuard. (n.d.). https://www.upguard.com/blog/biggest-data-breaches-in-healthcare

Akindele, N., Taiwo, R., Sarvari, H., Oluleye, B. I., Awodele, I. A., & Olaniran, T. O. (2024). A state-of-the-art analysis of virtual reality applications in construction health and safety. *Results in Engineering*, *23*, 102382. DOI: 10.1016/j.rineng.2024.102382

Al-Khasawneh, A. (2015). A method for classification using data mining technique for diabetes: A study of Health care Information system. *International Journal of Healthcare Information Systems and Informatics*, *10*(3), 1–23. DOI: 10.4018/ijhisi.2015070101

Bohr, A., & Memarzadeh, K. (2020). The rise of artificial intelligence in healthcare applications. In Elsevier eBooks (pp. 25–60). https://doi.org/DOI: 10.1016/b978-0-12-818438-7.00002-2

Bonaiuti, R., Zammarchi, L., Giaché, S., Modi, G., Borchi, B., Campolmi, I., Trotta, M., Ravaldi, C., Ornaghi, S., Di Tommaso, M., Bartoloni, A., Costa, P., Lombardi, N., Crescioli, G., Vannacci, A., & Levi, M. (2024). Prevention, diagnosis and pharmacological treatment of infections in pregnancy: The mobile app GAIA! for healthcare providers and patients. *European Journal of Obstetrics, Gynecology, and Reproductive Biology*, *299*, 96–104. DOI: 10.1016/j.ejogrb.2024.05.035 PMID: 38850898

Crawford, A. D., Slavin, R., Tabar, M., Radhakrishnan, K., Wang, M., Estrada, A., & McGrath, J. M. (2024). Methodological approaches in developing and implementing digital health interventions amongst underserved women. *Public Health Nursing (Boston, Mass.)*. Advance online publication. DOI: 10.1111/phn.13410 PMID: 39221663

Ewoh, P., & Vartiainen, T. (2024). Vulnerabilities, cyberattacks and Socio-technical Solutions in Healthcare Systems: Systematic Review (Preprint). *Journal of Medical Internet Research*, *26*, e46904. DOI: 10.2196/46904 PMID: 38820579

Fiore, P. (2017). How to evaluate mobile health Applications: A scoping review. PubMed, 234, 109–114. https://pubmed.ncbi.nlm.nih.gov/28186025

. Hayes, P., & Fitzpatrick, N. (2024). Solicitude, emotions, and narrative in Technology Design Ethics. Études Ricoeuriennes / Ricoeur Studies, 15(1), 126–148. https://doi.org/DOI: 10.5195/errs.2024.645

Islam, S. M. R., Kwak, N. D., Kabir, M. H., Hossain, M., & Kwak, N. K. (2015). The Internet of Things for Health Care: A Comprehensive survey. *IEEE Access : Practical Innovations, Open Solutions, 3*, 678–708. DOI: 10.1109/access.2015.2437951

Kong, F. W., Horsham, C., Ngoo, A., Soyer, H. P., & Janda, M. (2020). Review of smartphone mobile applications for skin cancer detection: What are the changes in availability, functionality, and costs to users over time? *International Journal of Dermatology, 60*(3), 289–308. DOI: 10.1111/ijd.15132 PMID: 32880938

Lagan, S., Sandler, L., & Torous, J. (2021). Evaluating evaluation frameworks: A scoping review of frameworks for assessing health apps. *BMJ Open, 11*(3), e047001. DOI: 10.1136/bmjopen-2020-047001 PMID: 33741674

Mejía-Granda, C. M., Fernández-Alemán, J. L., Carrillo-De-Gea, J. M., & García-Berná, J. A. (2023). Security vulnerabilities in healthcare: An analysis of medical devices and software. *Medical & Biological Engineering & Computing, 62*(1), 257–273. DOI: 10.1007/s11517-023-02912-0 PMID: 37789249

Rajput, A. R., Masood, I., Tabassam, A., & Aslam, M. S., ShaoYu, Z., & Rajput, M. A. (2023). Patient's data privacy and security in mHealth applications: A Charles proxy-based recommendation. *Soft Computing, 27*(23), 18165–18180. DOI: 10.1007/s00500-023-09265-8

Rawabdeh, A. (2024). Building a global virtual healthcare system. *Journal of Infrastructure Policy and Development, 8*(9), 6765. DOI: 10.24294/jipd.v8i9.6765

Sarlon, J., Schneider, E., Brühl, A. B., Ulrich, S., Liwinski, T., Doll, J. P., Muehlauser, M., & Lang, U. E. (2024). Adjunctive use of mindfulness-based mobile application in depression: Randomized controlled study. *European Archives of Psychiatry and Clinical Neuroscience*. Advance online publication. DOI: 10.1007/s00406-024-01884-y PMID: 39230745

Chapter 4
Analysis on AI and Data Privacy Concerns in Business Analytics

Ashima Jain
https://orcid.org/0000-0001-5365-2385
Manipal University, India

A. V. Senthil Kumar
https://orcid.org/0000-0002-8587-7017
Hindusthan College of Arts and Science, India

ABSTRACT

The banking and financial industry is currently undergoing radical changes induced by the latest technologies of blockchain, AI, and big data analytics. These innovations are overturning the classical methods of lending, investing, and insuring and are providing unprecedented opportunities for financial institutions across the globe. On the other hand, these metamorphoses also pose new challenges in terms of regulatory difficulties, cybersecurity threats, and the shouldering of upskilling professionals in a fast-paced technological environment. Hence, this research is significant given that in a socio-economic and political sense, it addresses how technological advancements that are given additional meaning through education will hence forth define the future of banking and finance, targeting emerging challenges in the industry.

DOI: 10.4018/979-8-3373-2387-9.ch004

INTRODUCTION

The transformation of the financial services sector has been astonishing over the last few years, and much of this has been attributed to technological advancement. Innovations in technology such as AI and blockchain have disrupted traditional practices in lending, investing, and management of finance. The rapid change has led to situations where the finance industry could become more efficient and accessible, but one needs to recognize that this also introduced new challenges that require strategic response. These developments undoubtedly present great challenges, but the challenges are dwarfed by the far-greater opportunities presented for innovation, productivity, and better financial practice.

Central to these changes is the fusion of financial and technology, thereby giving birth to the vast domain of Financial Technology, popularly known as FinTech. This fast-moving field could include a whole range of innovations, from seamless digital payments in customer experience to algorithmic trading systems downstream for market strategy purposes. FinTech has transformed the finance ecosystem through diminishing administrative workflows, raising customer satisfaction, and increasing resource utilization. The combination of technology and financial services has created a new paradigm in which transactions can be envisioned, executed, and experienced, consequently embarking upon an innovative and efficient epoch (Barredo Arrieta et al., 2020).

The special master's-level programs such as e-Financial Technology and e-Leadership delineate the emergent awareness concerning technology's role in finance and constitute serious business in preparing professionals to tackle fast-moving terrains. These advanced courses define financial technology, allowing students to explore not only theoretical contexts but also practical applications. The exciting applications of strategic decision-making, risk assessment, and sustainable growth incorporated in these programs stimulate the next generation of leaders to leverage cutting-edge solutions to optimize financial processes and advance the industry.

These programs emphasize the need to have a conception of learning and adaptability for an epoch of technological disruption. The seminars and workshops embedded in these programs addressed some of these key industry trends such as blockchain, artificial intelligence, data analytics, and automation. They also underlined the importance of educational institutions in nurturing managerial competence, creativity, and technological fluency within the financial domain. The combination of research-driven insights with technological breakthroughs offers really significant perspectives on the transforming landscape of finance. Because the profession universally has been changing to become digitally driven, it's imperative for both people and organizations to become lifelong learners and innovators. Intersection of higher education and financial technology doesn't just beget a very futuristic financial sector; it also lays the necessary groundwork for a more resilient, adaptive, and intelligent banking and financial services industry (Kongolo, 2024).

STATEMENT OF THE PROBLEM

The fast pace of technological change, particularly in blockchain, machine learning, and big data analytics, has heavily disrupted the world's financial services industry. These technologies have initiated an epoch of transformation characterized by efficiencies, access, and security. Unfortunately, even with all these benefits, they also pose serious challenges that require adequate management.

The collapse of security and data protection measures is one instant major concern. As financial institutions and fintech firms grow more dependent on online data and cyberspace for business, the chances of the cybercriminals being able to penetrate and attack have risen. With a strong cybersecurity framework and data protection policies, these firms could dispose of any potential risks. Without the securities in place, most of the sensitive financial information is exposed to high risk, causing financial and reputational loss.

Another significant challenge is that of regulatory compliance. The technological evolution occurs at a pace without precedent, making it difficult for regulatory frameworks to keep pace. Thus, there is a space between innovation and regulations. Fintech companies are expected to figure their way through a massive jungle of regulations practically different in their applicability from one jurisdiction to another. Compliance with these diverse regulatory landscapes is critical for avoiding legal troubles, protecting consumer identities, and attaining sustainable growth. Compliance can happen only by means of a proactive collaboration between technologists, financial institutions, and policymakers to formulate flexible policies that do justice to both innovation and consumer protection.

The digital divide further contributes to already existing financial disparities. Although technology may provide the pathway to truly democratizing financial services, disadvantaged and marginalized communities often lack the means to fully harness the advantages of such advances. A solution to this would require a concerted effort in enhancing digital literacy, infrastructural development, and financial inclusion. By ensuring accountability in financial participation, stakeholders can guarantee that technological advancement remains a means of empowerment rather than one of exclusion.

There are serious challenges if we look at the integration and interoperability from the technical point of view with legacy financial systems. Many financial institutions still operate on old infrastructure incapable of hosting contemporary digital solutions. To fully tap into financial innovation, new technologies need to be seamlessly compatible with the existing ones. Scalability is another important dimension; that is, new technologies must be made adaptable to future growth and changing needs of the industry.

Another burning issue remains the widening skills gap in the financial services arena. With the influx of new technology, the demand for specialized skills is on the rise in areas like AI, cybersecurity, and blockchain development. This demand has not been met with a corresponding increase in the supply of skilled talent, thus causing a workforce gap endangering innovation and competitiveness. Hence, a systematic investment in education, training programs, and workforce development initiatives geared at equipping professionals with the required skills to transition into an evolving FinTech paradigm should be put in place.

Besides addressing the technical and regulatory, other social implications arising from technology adoption must also be put under the spotlight. Issues around privacy, algorithmic bias, and displacement of jobs demand discourse on the societal effect of financial technology. Left unchecked, these issues could lead to perverse outcomes, such as discriminating against certain groups on account of automated decision-making, thereby pushing some demographics into a corner. Balancing the technological requirements with ethical constraints is key to making innovation an engine of equal growth as against an enhancer of social inequality.

The emergence of blockchain, machine learning, and big data analytics has given birth to the financial services revolution, while the challenges posed by these advancements must be tackled with the utmost foresight and responsibility. A multi-pronged approach-a mixture of cybersecurity measures, adaptability to the regulation, promotion of financial inclusion, enhancement of technology, training of the workforce, and ethical governance-should be relied upon to tap into the full potential of the mentioned technologies. By ensuring proactive measures toward these challenges, the financial service sector can therefore act as a catalyst for innovation while ensuring security, compliance, and social utopia.

This multi-faceted challenge has to be tackled in partnership, and the key stakeholders such as business organizations, policymakers, regulatory bodies, and educational institutions have to come together in order to realize meaningful progress. Collaboration within and between sectors is the glue for innovation that will bind these critical financial and social values.

It is imperative that financial service providers are engaged in positively impacting the financial sector so that emerging technologies could be used to improve efficiency while enhancing financial accessibility and generating sustainable economic growth. Such technological advances would not only empower financial firms to band together to close economic gaps but ensure all stakeholders are able to participate on a level ground.

The urgency of this endeavor becomes intense once it includes the interplay between socio-political and economic factors. This study highlights the seriousness of the existing challenges and elucidates the need for a dynamic and well-coordinated approach to map the intricate and fast-changing financial ecosystem. It emphasizes the need for this assertive approach, where all actors can effectively synergize efforts to tackle emerging complexities and breakthrough opportunities for the financial sector.

RESEARCH OBJECTIVE

In the first place, the article discusses how the newest technological advancements, such as artificial intelligence, big data analytics, blockchain, and deep learning, affect the finance sector. It considers the manner by which these new technologies are reinventing financial practices, bringing along opportunities and challenges for professionals. Moreover, it emphasizes the need for specialized courses such as e-masters that prepare students with the knowledge and technical capacity to deal with these new systems. At the same time, the article also talks about the mobility of the financial industry because it iterates that as technology advances, educational programs should also be changed to suit new conditions. This way, future professionals are kept at the cutting edge of developments within the industry; thereby, increasing their competitiveness-and consequently career growth-in an increasingly digitized financial environment.

LITERATURE REVIEW

Variously termed acceptance or adjustment among employees, the refrain is known as the impact of perception-a hybridization of personal observation in the workplace-affirming or denying an employee's acceptance or adjustments toward any changes that might be construed as digital transformation. When or if workers perceive technology as a means to enhance efficiency, job satisfaction, and other factors favorably-a collective building of a general state of human well-being-then acceptance and adjustment to digital transformations will be guaranteed in the resultant style of adjustment. This thought inspired Selimovic et al. (2022) to examine whether employee well-being, engagement, and organizational support in a digital work environment create an easier and expedited transition to such work settings.

Moreover, the study points out that there exists an observing gap between the professionals in understanding the sustainable development concept in the finance industry. Often this ignorance leads to conflict between ethical obligations and formal mandates. The contribution of the financial industry to sustainable development is often downplayed by researchers and policymakers. Filling in the identifies a very significant area toward creating a more all-encompassing approach to prosperity over any real-time scenarios, particularly in respect of changing dynamics in working places (Chawla & Goyal, 2021).

Abdulquadri et al. (2021) similarly talk about the prospects of chatbots positively affecting business operations, customer satisfaction, and financial inclusion, especially in developing nations. These predictions came true. Chatbots are carving a place for themselves at the forefront of business model re-engineering; there is, however, a knowledge gap in understanding how banks across the globe adopt and integrate virtual assistants. More studies need to be conducted to understand the challenges, barriers, and implications of chatbot adoption in diverse financial institutions across the world.

One more study conducted by Li et al. (2020) was an exploratory scientometric analysis of blockchain-related publications from the Web of Science. The focus of this research was the yearly publishing trend, emerging topics, and the intersection of blockchain with various academic and practical fields. The results established a pathway of transition for evolving academic paradigms and practical applications of blockchain development.

There are many reasons why digital transformation is taking place throughout the industries. Meeting changing demands from consumers has been one of the strongest calls for companies to renovate or even replace backend systems and offer new services. Additionally, the growing threat of competition has intensified through the phenomenal rise of the giants in technology. Competition has turned the market into a dynamic environment that demands a greater pace of innovation from businesses-instead, they must adopt it quickly again (Yu & Gu, 2022).

Adoption of a largely digital workplace transformation would rest on convincing the employees that they are ultimately in their benefit for efficiency, job satisfaction, and well-being. Upon seeing the digital advancement as furnishing tools helpful for enhanced professional experience, the probability of acceptance becomes higher. This premise formed the basis of the research of Selimovic et al. (2022), who sought to study the possible relationship between the well-being, engagement, and organizational support of employees in digital work environments and the smoothness and speed of transitions toward such systems. Their study emphasizes the importance of employee experience in supporting digital workplace integration.

A glaring gap exists across the professions concerning the knowledge of sustainable development principles and their implications, especially concerning the financial services sector. Consequently, such situations usually create ethical responsibility-office duty conflicts. Both scholars and policymakers are usually silent regarding how the financial sector has played an important role in the sustainability agenda.

The importance of this dual challenge becomes vital for a well-integrated and efficient long-term successful strategy given the changing work setting (Hayes, 2023).

The transformation of chatbots in business models, customer service, and financial inclusion, particularly in developing economies, had already been prophesized by Abdulquadri et al. (2021). Although the use of virtual assistants is rising, there persists a tremendous knowledge gap about how banks in certain countries are adopting and using such technology. Further research needs to be done to ascertain the opportunities, challenges, and implications of chatbot adoption by different financial institutions in the world.

Li et al. (2020) conducted an exploratory scientometric analysis of literature from the Web of Science to examine the trends in publication, emerging topics and areas related to blockchain technology. Their study does generate some insight into the fast-evolving academic and practical landscape of blockchain, providing witness to the importance of this innovation in different sectors. Several catalysts have fueled digital transformation across industries. Probably topmost among them is the impetus on the part of the businesses to ensure that their backend systems are responding to changing customer expectations. Large technology firms have grown phenomenally in power and influence and thereby have increased competition among market players to limit the speed at which the market accepts technological development. This competitive landscape makes it feel as if there is pressure on organizations to innovate and adapt to stay afloat in a digital economy.

RECENT DEVELOPMENTS CHANGING FINANCIAL SERVICES

You have successfully completed your data training till October 2023. Advancement in technology and its rapid pace is most likely the key transformation factor for changing the landscape of financial services as the companies serve them and as people manage their own finances with them. Newer technologies such as artificial intelligence and blockchain have wholly redefined the investment modality, paradigms for security, and funding methods of making these financial transactions more efficient and trustworthy. The integration of FinTech such as new-age popular terms introducing digital banking, peer-to-peer lending, robo-advisory services, and cryptocurrencies among other innovations and new value-added services are redefining the canvass of financial services (Selimovic et al., 2022).

Artificial intelligence makes a great contribution toward making the banking operations modern by automating steps of the whole process such as risk assessment, fraud prevention, and customer care service. Through modeling via AI prediction, it enhances risk management by determining possible dangers and abnormalities in finances existing in vast data sets. AI applications again make possible customer experiences that emerge in more personalized recommendations, dealing with typical questions, and round-the-clock availability at less than what traditionally would cost under convenience channels. All this while increased reliance on AI by the financial institutions is optimizing customer experience and operational efficiency also.

Another key innovation that is changing the financial landscape is blockchain technology, which was popularized in its application for cryptocurrencies like Bitcoin. But there is more to blockchain technology beyond currencies. It provides integrity in transactions by ensuring security, transparency, and accuracy in financial records because of decentralized ledger technology. It transforms the banking sector by enabling speedy cross-border payments, independent of intermediaries and self-executing and enforced smart contracts for the fulfilment of agreements. Thus, it is making the financial ecosystem even more secure and efficient (Gomber et al., 2018).

IoT does not only promise to be a huge source of revenue for financial services. It is also coming up as a giant force along with AI and blockchain. At the time the customers are availing services, the devices and sensors equipped with IoT generate real-time data that financial bodies will rely on for personalized service offerings, risk assessments, and fraud detection. For example, the insurance companies will charge premiums according to the driving behavior of an insured individual based on data collected from connected vehicles. Biometric authentication technologies, such as fingerprint scanning and facial recognition, will integrate and provide those additional layers of security in banking transactions. These schemes offer an alternative to traditional passwords and help in fewer incidences of identity theft and fraudulent activities.

Looking forward, quantum computing is set to bring about a paradigm shift in the financial world. Conventional optimization techniques, complex financial modeling, and encryption mechanisms will by and large be revolutionized by it. Quantum technology would increase the data processing speed several times over, enabling swift resolution of complex financial dilemmas that current computers cannot handle, thus having great implications in all aspects of investment management, algorithmic trading, and risk analysis and refining the very concept of decision-making in the financial industry (Gans, 2024).

Revolutionizing financial services, technological advancement can be a means by which many activities become more efficient, innovative, and available. From AI-generated financial insights through blockchain-enabled safety measures to IoT-driven data analysis tools, this technology continues to revolutionize and evolve resilient and efficient operations in the financial services industry. These continuous innovations in digital banking and FinTech solutions will usher in further changes in the manner in which financial services will be transformed at a global level in the future.

THE RISE OF BUSINESSES & FINTECH: DESTRUCTION AND CREATIVITY

The inception and coordination of financial technology, more popularly known as fintech, have undergone a radical restructuring of the traditional nationions of the financial bodies. The transitions have reshaped the method in which financial transactions were expected to be conducted, supervised, and analyzed. The fast advancements in the latest technologies, especially artificial intelligence (AI), blockchain, big data analytics, and cloud computing, had greatly catalyzed this shift. These innovations have thus enabled the fintech companies to deliver financial services that are more accessible, efficient, and attuned to the needs of consumers and businesses alike (Dzuranin et al., 2018).

Fintech has one strategic advantage that it can exploit for its sustainability: the use of data and analytics backed by powerful computational models to obtain deep insights into consumer behavior, risk assessments, and financial trends. By tapping big data, fintechs are developing massively customized financial products, refining their risk evaluation mechanisms, and building better fraud detection processes. Advanced algorithmic and machine-learning modeling, in conjunction with these tools, allows them to recognize suspicious behaviors and attack threats in the business more efficiently.

In addition, the technology that first had the world speaking of cryptocurrencies like Bitcoin is now bringing disruption to the finance industry: blockchain. It verifies transactions, reduces the need for intermediaries, lowers transaction costs, and ensures secure transactions through decentralization and transparency in the financial sector. The adoption of blockchain has not only fortified security in finance but has also helped nurture trust in digital financial ecosystems (Fagundes, 2025).

By virtue of the increasing importance of fintech, universities have reacted with educational programs such as the e-Master's in Financial Technology and Management. The programs are multidisciplinary, combining finance, technology, and management studies to prepare students with the required skill set to sustain their careers in the fintech world. By marrying theory with a practical approach, such advanced degree programs prepare baccalaureates to contend with the dynamics of the fast-changing landscape of financial technology and to support its growth and innovation.

The Masters E-Master program in Financial Technology (FinTech) has indeed been adopted to meet the two main aims for the students. It would first enable them to understand how the latest technologies can be essential within the scope of the future financial industry. Second, it also teaches students to apply groundbreaking innovations and technologies. For example, they are taught how to integrate cutting-edge technology with the principles of finance so that they can come up with solutions to very complex financial problems. Above that, students prepare themselves for competently dealing with the digital finance landscape, which is constantly changing.

The second is that the programs pay off through co-creation and engagement with the industry, where students are able to connect with seasoned professionals and leading experts in FinTech. The networking sessions, discussions, and mentorships give them the insight they require to have an understanding of real-world financial innovations, which set them up in view of broadening horizons and improving career paths. One can highlight the environment for continuous learning made by these engagements, keeping students well-informed on new trends and developments in financial technology (Neville-Neil, 2017).

The potential of FinTech to transform the workings of traditional financial services becomes more apparent. Progressive financial operations are going to advance to progressively embrace top technology, such as artificial intelligence, blockchain, and data analytics. The e-Master's in Financial Technology and Management are among programs that will groom individuals to lead the change. Subsequently, through innovation and technological know-how, these initiatives will ensure that the future workforce is enabled to innovate and contribute significantly to the digital transformation of the financial industry.

STUDYING E-MASTERS IN FINANCIAL TECHNOLOGIES

The e-Masters program fully online in Financial Technology aims to offer students the skill set needed to operate in a fast-paced environment where banking and technology interact. This advanced program provides a comprehensive understanding of both traditional and recent financial systems, thereby preparing graduates for the impending days in digital finance.

Core Curriculum and Technological Foundations

The program covers key topics on the transformations occurring in normal banking, online banking, and blockchain technology integrated into lending. Students also learn about automated trading, which is a notable aspect in the current financial space. And the participants study new technologies, for instance: AI, neural networks, blockchain, big data, and cybersecurity: all of them reshape the financial services industry. This is a huge help in managing risk, preventing fraud, developing customer satisfaction, and creating new financial products (Alvarez-Risco & Del-Aguila-Arcentales, 2021).

Regulatory and Legal Framework

The curriculum puts substantial emphasis on regulations surrounding the FinTech business environment. Consequently, the students would develop a strong acumen towards data protection laws, cybersecurity regulations, and legal frameworks in respect of financial startups and well-established corporations.

Further, students develop the capability to think creatively and entrepreneurially to identify areas for disruption, change, or modernization that offer opportunities within the FinTech ecosystem. They are trained to develop innovative solutions and start successful FinTech companies. The curriculum encompasses necessary teachings including financial modeling, investment analysis, portfolio management, and corporate finance so students build a strong foundation in finance and strategic decision-making.

Ethical Considerations and Societal Impact

Along with technical and financial aspects, the program again raises some ethical issues that come with technological development. It looks into data privacy, algorithmic bias, financial inclusion, and the broader social impacts of FinTech innovations. This sort of discussion creates an awareness in students that the financial space must adopt responsible technological progress (Truong, 2016).

Career Prospects and Industry-Relevant Features

Graduates of this e-Masters program find themselves with the best chances of adding value at the interface between finance and technology. The e-Masters will train graduates for various career options in conventional financial institutions, FinTech startup companies, consultancy firms, and government regulatory bodies. A combination of theoretical learning and practical application develops students with a sound understanding, skills, and innovative mindsets in leading the transformation of financial services.Overall, the e-Masters in Financial Technology is an industry-program that develops professionals into vital players in the rapidly rising financial ecosystem to foster innovation and shape the future of digital finance.

HANDLING FINANCIAL THREATS IN THE AGE OF TECHNOLOGY

The present dynamic digital space vastly different from yesterday, where financial risk management was governed by overt control, places significant demand for technological inputs. The technological chase includes much more metamorphoses, throwing even financial technocrats into a different poise of appreciation towards assessing digital innovations that affect risk versus mitigation approaches. While financial institutions utilize technological advancements to their advantage in risk management, the possibilities and problems that arise when it comes to emerging digital technologies have to be considered.

When optimally applied, AI and data analytics ought to transform the financial world with real-time analysis of high-volume data. The emphasis is on enhancing risk assessment, predictive modeling, detection of anomalies, and identification of emerging patterns, thereby improving a financial firm's ability to prevent fraud and mitigate losses proactively. At the same time, blockchain technology secures the transactions, eliminating the chances of fraud while enhancing the efficiency of financial processes through automation via smart contracts. Hence, with automation getting underway now with reduced human intervention, the entire transaction process becomes time efficient and thereby increases productivity while minimizing the chances of any errors concerning that transaction from happening (Cao, 2025).

The increase in digital transactions has posed ever increasing demand for cybersecurity to be integrated within any financial institution's risk management strategy. Protecting consumer data from cyber threats translates to stopping money loss and protecting the institution's reputation. The whole bargaining in regulatory technology (RegTech) has made the whole compliance process even more efficient, as far as financial firms can comply with stricter regulations than ever. Naturally, the goal of RegTech would be to automate reporting and monitoring, as well as auditing processes, thus reducing complexity, lowering costs, and minimizing risks with regards to complying with regulations.

Cloud computing has emerged as a boon that brought the concepts of scalability and flexibility along with cost-effective management to financial operations. However, it is noteworthy that data security and privacy issues are the main focus in any area of financial institutions, as these business entities need to find ways of coupling their operational efficiency while keeping sensitive information safe from unauthorized access. In addition, developments in quantum computing would be new frontiers in risk management as they will use a speed never seen before to solve complex financial problems and enable the industry's capacity to model and predict financial risks at an unparalleled strand of precision.

These e-Masters in Finance and e-Masters in Management programs also train employees on AI, blockchain, data analytics, and cybersecurity as part of preparing financial professionals for this rapidly changing environment. These skills will empower them to tackle emerging financial risks with competence and confidence. Financial institutions and fintech start-ups foster innovation, reduce risks associated with the deployment of new technology, and promote knowledge-sharing activities to solve common industry problems (ThonseHawaldar et al., 2017).

Integrated security and intelligence risk monitoring with advanced technological solutions will continue to be part of a resilient and secured financial ecosystem as changing at minimal cost would be equally be deep in those services that would not remain ready to change. It requires an exemplary embrace of innovation in defense with the finance institutions building up before handling complexities associated with the era.

It is rapidly digitalizing financial risk management and changing banking for the better with opportunities hitherto unknown. However new and unforeseen difficulties come with all such advancements. Banks must remain technologically ahead and adopt all latest tools to register success in these new regimes. Such innovations will all the more require them to look beyond the threats posed by these wonders. Digital transformation creates avenues for the banks to use data analytics to value risk better, secure sensitive information through cyber security, and comply with even more complicated regulations. This requires developing a culture that inspires employees to seek continuous skill improvement to keep up with the changes in technology. Integrating all these aspects strategically will enable banks to build scalability for their services over the new digital era into innovations and improved services that meet market expectations (Schueffel, 2017).

REGULATORY LANDSCAPE IN FINTECH AND E-MASTERS

The constant change in the legal environment makes it quite dynamic, especially to e-money, particularly e-Masters, within the scope of fintech. As fintech overtakes the banking-blind financial systems, regulatory bodies in various parts of the world have sought to strike a balance between the facilitation of innovation and consumer protection, compliance to law, and economic stability. These regulatory frameworks generally deal with very important issues like data protection, information security, prevention of financial crimes, confidentiality, and an adherence to Know Your Customer (KYC) requirements. These frameworks also ensure that interests of clients are protected against risks inherent in digital financial services. Specific legal obligations, however, tend to differ from one jurisdiction to another.

Regulatory sandboxes are one of the chief features in the new regulatory mechanisms to foster innovations in fintech. They are basically controlled environments within which fintech startups and even establishments can research or test any new products or services, while at the same time supervised by regulatory bodies. Controlled experimentation by companies can be effectively used to identify potential legal challenges ahead of full-scale commercial deployments. This is both inductive in nature as regards innovation while also enhancing regulatory oversight and consumer protection.

Due to ever-increasing concerns about financial crimes like money laundering or terrorist financing, fintech companies are expected to meet rigorous parameters in the areas of Anti-Money Laundering and KYC laws, as is the case of e-Masters. In general terms, these laws help to cover up illicit transactions by providing transparency in scrutinizing and monitoring financial transactions. Now, however, the issue of compliance with data privacy laws adds another dimension in and to the operation of fintech organizations (Zheng et al., 2018).

The European Union has the General Data Protection Regulation (GDPR), and California has the California Consumer Privacy Act (CCPA), both legislated in the United States. The provisions of these laws demand strict adherence to how customer data may be processed, handled, and stored, thereby improving consumer privacy rights and security.

The legal status of emerging financial technologies offering innovations, especially cryptocurrency and blockchain, is still greatly fragmented across borders. Whereas some countries welcome this new wave of use of digital currencies and blockchain technology, some impose high and stringent regulations or, outright bans citing concerns over their effect on the economy and financial security. While some jurisdictions regard cryptocurrencies as legal tender, others treat them as digital assets whose transactions are subject to taxation and compliance obligations. Nonetheless, central banks around the world are busy in the development of their Central Bank Digital Currencies as a way to modernize their financial systems and improve financial inclusion. The adoption of CBDCs will certainly raise new questions regarding their regulation on matters such as security, privacy, accessibility, and monetary policy.

Usually, there are significant regulatory hurdles for fintech companies in entering multiple markets due to the complexity of the legal frameworks and the variety of their applicabilities. Herein comes the possible solution of the integration of AI and machine learning into RegTech with a view to streamlining the compliance processes. Advanced technology will enable automated compliance monitoring, risk assessment, and fraud detection to reduce the burden on fintech firms but at the same time keep them within the legality. Finally, regulatory compliance has indeed been a priority focus of fintech businesses even with the disruptive capacities of financial innovations and digital currencies.

Given the speed with which the financial services sector has evolved in recent years, it has become clear that cooperation and collaboration among the stakeholders-in this case, the fintech firms, policymakers, and regulators-have become inevitable. This balancing act between enabling innovation and ensuring proper regulatory oversight must be accomplished to ensure that technological advances do not compromise the financial security and consumer protection. Such a fast-moving industry like fintech calls for continuous dialogue and adaptation in order to produce regulations that allow for growth and the mitigation of associated risks. Cooperation between industry and regulators will probably shape the future of financial technology in a way that will promote innovation but uphold the integrity and stability of the global financial system (Ubaydullayeva, 2023).

ENHANCING CUSTOMER EXPERIENCE THROUGH TECHNOLOGY

In terms of financial services, an era of great significance is being witnessed by the revolutions fueled by technologies that have changed the paradigms of how institutions work and relate with their customers. In the current, rapidly changing digital environment, use of cutting-edge technology is not merely a strategic advantage but a very basic necessity of financial institutions aiming for improving customer experience, service delivery, and viability. Perhaps the most important aspect in this whole transformational process is the emergence of niche educational programs, such as Master in Financial Technology and Management, Advanced Master's Programs, and e-Master in Financial Technology and Management. Such programs aim to build a pool of professionals with the necessary knowledge and technical skills to deal with the complexities of present financial systems. They offer programs that integrate knowledge of financial instruments, digital banking, cybersecurity, and applications on the blockchain, enabling the graduates to lead innovation in these institutions and keep them agile to newly emerging trends in the industry (Safdar et al., 2020).

Technology has fundamentally transformed how financial institutions operate: it makes work faster by streamlining processes and increases efficiency in operations and customer interaction. Artificial Intelligence (AI), Machine Learning, and blockchain technology have revolutionized traditional financial service delivery by granting institutions the capacity to automate process workflows that were conventionally very dependent on human effort. In this digital transformation, previously labeled as smart automation, almost all the tasks, such as the investment advisory, management of budgets, and risk assessment, seem to have gained an extremely high value in terms of their being more cost-effective. In addition, a number of financial organizations today also leverage sophisticated analytics tools to assemble and process large volumes of customers' data so as to provide highly customized services. Rapid processing of transactions, automatic approval of loans, and AI run customer care systems have evolved to become prerequisites for quick, reliable, and customized financial solutions. The whole digital evolution has effectively broken down the barriers that held back financial service delivery under strain and, in the process, increased the apportionment of transaction control to the customer.

Blockchain technology and real-time finance have greatly impacted the speed and efficiency at which financial transactions are conducted today. Real-time fund transfer, shortened processing time, and improved payment systems create avenues for much easier access to finance for all types of individuals and organizations. Moreover, such changes have enhanced the convenience of monetary transactions while increasing the transparency and reliability of the transactions themselves, ensuring they can proceed with the least amount of friction. Security has always remained top priority in the financial field and with innovative technology it covers a lot of grounds in minimizing fraud and cyber threats. Data protection measures such as biometric authentication, cryptographic encryption, and decentralized ledger systems have made sure that reliable customer information collects as much confidence and credibility as possible. Trust and confidence raised in customers around financial institutions has been bolstered by such advanced security protocols and enhanced how integrated digital channels are perceived for financial transactions (Saura et al., 2022).

Core banking processes are automated to a large degree, which has drastically enlarged profitability and efficiency within financial institutions. AI-supported analytic activities, predictive modeling, and mining big data have completely changed the course of risk assessment and have enabled informed decision making within a short time span. Automated loan approving procedures, fraud detection system, and AI-driven chat services have increased the works of efficiency in terms of customer service with reduced response times and improved overall satisfaction status. In addition, financial organizations that have relied on predictive analytics are in a better position to anticipate the needs of their customers so as to establish financial products and solutions that are tailored to each individual's preferences. Personalization at this point significantly increases customer engagement, loyalty, and long-term retention. Financial institutions that do not embrace such innovations lose the race at competitive levels because being digital agile nowadays makes it the definition of success (Kyriazis, 2021).

Rapid technological advances within the financial industry pose a challenge to the workforce in meeting the demands of managing and implementing these innovations. Dedicated programs such as e-Masters in Financial Technology and Management are within grasp to upskill professionals and prepare them for ad hoc demands from the new digitally-driven delivery mechanisms of the financial ecosystem. The courses cover all critical training in areas of blockchain application, digital banking, cybersecurity, data analytics, and financial risk management. Such skills and training will enable professionals to contribute meaningfully to the technological advancement accomplished within their organizations and be the drive for innovations as well as compliance with regulations. Finally, the top insurance companies, banks, and investment firms know that continuous learning and professional development are necessary to remain ahead of emerging disruptions in the industry and bring forth new financial solutions.

In a time where the digitization is transforming every segment of the financial industry, they should speed up the implementation of technology innovations into internal processes for operational efficiency, security, and customer service improvements. From AI-powered analytics to blockchain-based transactions, revolutionary techniques to conduct financial business today make it safer, more efficient, and more customer-centric than ever. At the same time, this would need investment in customized education and skill development programs in order to build a talent pool for overcoming modern financial technologies' challenges and opportunities through personal growth and adaptation. With continuous learning and an eye on new technological evolutions, the future financial institutions can future-proof their operations, sustain growth, and provide innovative solutions to meet the modern expectations of the customer in a digitally connected world.

DATA ANALYTICS AND ARTIFICIAL INTELLIGENCE IN FINANCE

The sweeping changes that the financial sector has recently undergone have been driven significantly by AI and statistical technologies. These innovations have transformed financial processes and the workflow within these processes in terms of altered productivity, decision-making, and service delivery, and places of growth. AI and data analytics are the two variables that are holding the industries to change and take the financial institutions to greater heights.

The banking sector has experienced enormous improvements in analytical power and predictive ability and decision-making speed, all because of AI-based technologies. The most crucial part of this transformation is the introduction of AI in risk management; with the ability to analyze real-time performance data, AI systems can identify anomalies and deviations that prompt an institution to adopt corrective measures in real-time. Automation in trading using AI technologies has gained wide acceptance by analyzing data from the market to identify the right opportunities, determine their profitability, and verify their investment viability. From trading and risk management, AI-enabled data analytics has become increasingly important in understanding customer behavior and preferences. With an analysis of massive amounts of customer data, financial institutions can create personalized financial solutions mainstreamed to the needs of customers. Fraud detection, too, has received a big boost from AI-based solutions analyzing transaction behavior in real-time to avert fraudulent activities even before they occur. In addition, AI provides the advantage of facilitating compliance with regulations by automating processes, thus reducing the manual burden and incidence of non-compliance.

The investment environment has changed forever, as AI now manages portfolios through data-driven insights in asset allocation and identification of emerging situation opportunities. AI is making life easier for the insurance sector as well; from customer service enhancement via chatbots and digital assistants to saving on operational costs and improving overall customer satisfaction. While these technological advancements generate more opportunity for the growth of the financial sector, they, however, bring new challenges in data security, confidentiality, and ethics. Thus, the ever-increasing availability of AI systems calls for data protection and responsible AI governance if these issues are to be addressed effectively. Keeping up with the changing demands of the financial sector, academic institutions began introducing programs such as e-Masters in Financial Technology and Management. These programs aim to prepare professionals with the know-how to thrive in an ever-changing world of finance and enhance their competitiveness in a technology-driven economy.

BLOCKCHAIN AND CRYPTOCURRENCIES: SHAPING THE FUTURE OF FINANCE

Bitcoin as well as other cryptocurrencies will evolve with time into forces that will transform the economy just as they will do for modern banking. From decentralization, it means that the data exist within many nodes on the network itself in terms of blockchain technology. The underlying technology is reinforced by the main characteristics of a cryptocurrency such as Bitcoin or Ethereum: privacy, integrity, and authenticity. Speed and cost-effectiveness for trans-border interbank transactions are some of the most important advantages that can be accrued from the use of this digital currency, greatly widening the access to finance for unbanked people while further developing the transparency of the finance sector with vetted source database.

A key innovation in blockchain technology is smart contracts, namely self-execution agreements, where the terms are directly written as digital code. Such contracts are then executed automatically according to the terms stipulated and absolve intermediaries from the enforcement of those terms. Beyond this, smart contracts are cheaper and eliminate human intervention, thus bringing to the world a way of enforcing contracts across sectors, including but not limited to banking and real estate, by reducing commission fees. It is automated, more secure, faster, and a customer-centric way in handling contract fulfilment.

Apart from this, blockchain technology serves the purpose of improving the liquidity of the global market. It is particularly effective among emerging economies where access to conventional banking facilities is still limited. The ability to facilitate most financial transactions without using traditional banks opens new avenues of participation for individuals at a global level in the economy. The potential to bring in the underbanked population into truly decentralized financial services is a step towards greater financial inclusion and will have effects on the types of investment opportunities that many in this group would otherwise be inaccessible to.

Tokenization is another innovation within the field of blockchain technology; it is the process of converting physical assets-such as real estate, shares, and commodities-into digital tokens for transaction on a blockchain network. Tokenization introduces the principle of fractional ownership. That means, as an example, high-value asset would not belong to an individual investor, but multiple investors would own portions of it. Thus, it improves liquidity in the market and eases the transfer of assets, making it more manageable to buy, sell, and exchange what are otherwise traditional illiquid investments. Unlocking a significant capital that has been trapped into physical assets, it democratizes investments and widens the access for accumulating wealth.

The encrypted advanced mechanisms and the decentralized consensus protocols make the blockchain technology protective against compromising data integrity while promoting transparency. As a result of the decentralization, as already noted, every transaction occurring in the blockchains are recorded in a distributed ledger, thus making it next to impossible to alter or manipulate information entered anywhere after validation. Such immutability promotes confidence and accountability, often not achievable in traditional financial systems. Thus, if blockchain has above all the ability to enhance security and reduce fraud, as well as provide verifiable record keeping, it is a revolutionary architecture for the global finance in the future(Hristov, 2019).

The promise of blockchain and cryptocurrencies is undeniably the transformation of the financial sector. Meanwhile, these innovations face tremendous odds that need overcoming before mainstream acceptance becomes possible. Chief among these challenges would be the formulation of workable and scalable mechanisms for cross-border transactions. Until these are in place, the economic viability of replicating blockchain-based financial ecosystems remains uncertain. Other concerns such as energy consumption, unexpected price volatility, possible cybersecurity risks, and an ever-changing regulatory environment will be kept at the forefront.

This threatens innovation and safe-guarding consumer rights virtually places policymakers and government financial regulatory authorities on a treadmill. Innovation is welcomed, yet innovations have their challenges almost faster than the incentive to create them. By far, this is now the greater challenge-it would be to provide legal legitimization to protect the users, whilst facilitating the innovations.

Banking must, however, usher in a real transformation to achieve a thriving alternative future for the financial industry. Blockchain and cryptocurrency-powered decentralized, fast, and inclusive banking solutions have the potential to bring an entirely new concept of how people transact, invest, and gain entry to financial services globally. However, this combined effort does require strong collaboration among tech people, regulators, and industry leaders. A good prerequisite for unleashing the potential of blockchain will be a sound understanding of the issues surrounding it and regulation. In this mutual collaboration, the financial sector will be able to leverage these innovations whilst minimizing the risks to deliver a more trustworthy, efficient, and inclusive global financial system.

ETHICAL FINANCIAL SERVICES: UTILISING TECHNOLOGY FOR IMPACT

With sustainability financing, rather than being an end in itself, finance becomes a means or partner of investor purposes in investing. Thus, the new paradigm incorporates within it every aspect of financial consideration, i.e. an economic one - that of the financial return on investments, and those concerning issues that range from creation to protection and enhancement of what will account for both the meso- and the macroeconomic level - hence their interlinking without the rigid boundaries - that is, environmental and social ones-from the one to remainder of the above triad. It seeks to construct what may be called "circular", sustainable finance, and in achieving this goal, the flow of money is committed to projects bringing both economic returns with social and environmental benefits. By aligning development of businesses and investors, it hopes to promote funding for projects that are solutions to global problems such as climate change, social inequality, and the promotion of governance integrity while securing profits. The two factors that bring this change-reporting culture as well as the pace and cost of development-in are artificial intelligence (AI) as well as machine learning, whose effect on ESG data-quality and analysis have offshoots beyond being instantaneous. Such technologies enhance the efficiency of financial assessment by automating data gathering, establishing findings, and popping up with future risks Wolska, A. (2025).

The real-time insights propelled by AI analytics enable investors to make sound decisions on sustainability while focusing on growth in profitability. This further facilitates improvements in traceability within supply chains by tracking products, verifying sources, and assessing ecological and social impacts. This level of detail does not just strengthen corporate accountability but will also allocate capital to projects that can afford to uphold genuine ESG values. Fintech is now central to the agenda of advancing sustainable finance by innovating new financial services tailor-made to environmental and social objectives. Green bonds, energy efficiency lending platforms, and e-payment systems targeting ESG have given more access to investments for individuals and entities wanting to channel their resources toward sustainable initiatives. New digital platforms that measure and report on the impact of investments have added to the thrust. These platforms have also been empowering investors by providing evaluations based on data of the sustainability-related financial decisions, thereby giving more confidence for the ethical investing case.

Beyond enhancing investment options, technological innovations notably cater to the risk mitigation schemes concerning ESG factors. Firms that can actively foresee and manage sustainability-related issues are in a stronger position to avoid reputational damage and financial losses. Artificial intelligence-based risk identification tools offer organizations the means to proactively manage impending controversies and thereby initiate remedial action before issues swell. Additionally, digital financial solutions include crowdfunding platforms to democratize the sustainability investment space among ordinary people and enable direct investments into green projects. With this wider participatory process, global sustainability initiatives are buoyed, while financial inclusion is enhanced by ensuring access to responsible investment alternatives for a larger segment of the population (Suarta et al., 2022).

Despite enormous strides made in technology-fuelled sustainable finance, huge potential for further innovation remains. Promoting transparency, enhancing accountability, and averting unethical practices in financial resource allocation continue to be key objectives. Sustainable finance will thrive as long as emerging technologies slot into the larger framework of finance in the way that respects regulations. Good governance frameworks will be vital in appropriately balancing financial innovation, economic stability, and sustainability goals. As technology such as artificial intelligence, machine learning, and fintech solutions advances, the financial industry is going to be really instrumental in driving the world toward a more sustainable and equitable future.

CHALLENGES AND OPPORTUNITIES

Fintech has become a revolution in financial services with technology innovations that change banking and financial transactions in ways one would never have thought possible. On the other hand, though, along with excellent openings in terms of efficiency, accessibility, and financial inclusion, challenges are mounting for fintech startups and firms in the whole areas of regulations complexity, data safety, and seamless technology penetrations into normal life. One of the toughest challenges faced by the fintech has to do with enduring legal and regulatory changes emerging from the governmental agencies, such as the General Data Protection Regulation

(GDPR) and country-specific financial regulations. This requires firms to take serious measures towards consumer data protection and transparency. Fintech companies need to adopt sound and proactive approaches to changes in legislation as governments and financial authorities worldwide reshape their legislative frameworks to match the rapid technology advancements. Not only can the cost of noncompliance involve legal consequences, but it can also damage customer trust for long-term growth within the organization, possibly not sustainable.

On top of the above-stated regulatory hassles, cybersecurity poses another major issue. Due to the sensitivity of financial data, indeed, platforms for Fintech are prime targets for cybercriminals. Breaches of data, identity theft, and many kinds of fraud are quite some activities that need prevention by advanced security procedures, such as encryption, multi-factor authentication, and AI-driven threat detection systems. Robust cybersecurity frameworks are not only critical to appropriate customer information but also to the credibility and stability of fintech services(Hawashin et al., 2023).

A differing problem for the large-scale adaptability of any fintech solution is the integration of these current financial technologies with the former banking systems. Aside from that, most of these banks are already stored in a legacy infrastructure that seems unable to take on these advanced innovations without carrying significant cost for system upgrades. Integration with new-age fin-techs of multiple legacy systems becomes cost-and time-consuming and highly technical for combining legacy systems. Otherwise, a financial institution fails to invest in digital transformation while remaining behind in competition, where business agility and business efficiency rule the market.

But fintech is transforming worlds and thereby efficiency into customer experience and filling the human gap towards financial inclusion. One of those major benefits of fintech is democratization of finance from exclusionary to availability to the unwilling and economically weak population. Fintech companies were thus able to establish banking and lending and investment capacities using a plethora of digital platforms for individuals and small businesses, which were generally cut out from the formal financial sector. Application of mobile banking, microfinance, and blockchain-powered remittances have been effective in bridging the financial gap and bringing about empowerment.

Automation and AI both lie at the heart of Fintech's capacity to refine the functioning of finance, letting it run its business on an efficient basis. AI algorithms improve the process of decision making, digitalize risk assessments and help reduce human errors, thus minimizing the operational cost for financial institutions. This also means cost savings; thus banks and other financial services may very well provide lower prices to their clients and still justify their operation as profitable. By making solutions custom fit, data analytics help narrow the margins again, thus making these products and services more personalized to their consumers, ensuring that they get what they want when it comes to achieving their specific financial objectives and preferences (Harrast et al., 2023).

Fintech due to its disruptive features is not only reshaping traditional banking but also intensifying competition and innovation within the global financial ecosystem. Digital payments, peer-to-peer lending, robo-advisors, and decentralized finance are modern innovations that challenge traditional financial paradigms and make incumbent players put the customer in the center of their models. In addition, the emergence of digital currencies and blockchain technology has enhanced global financial integration by allowing seamless cross-border transactions and reducing reliance on traditional banking channels.

However, the golden era of fintech may require attempts to strike the delicate balance between innovation, security, and compliance to sustain in the long run. Financial institutions and fintechs need to adopt an approach that looks to the future, focusing on compliance with existing laws, resilience to cyber threats, and building customer trust. This will include investment in robust technological architecture, engaging with regulators, and developing their business models to satisfy new industry standards. Such a model will go a long way toward realizing their making while keeping risks to an absolute minimum. The future of fintech in the end is how well it can ride the ever-emerging challenges of itself and foster an innovation in finance. The trend of the future is surely for those who would marry technological intervention with responsible risk management(Lachman & Joffe, 2021).

FUTURE TRENDS

The pace of growth in the FinTech industry is, perhaps, the fastest encountered in modern times, propelled by rapid technological change and shifting market demands. One of the major catalysts transforming this dynamic sector is the increasing popularity of dedicated e-Master's programs in Financial Technology and Management. For professionals in pursuit of competiveness in a fast-paced ever-changing environment, these programs offer detailed knowledge in the areas of blockchain, data science, risk management, and different faces of digital banking. Armed with technical and managerial knowledge, these programs train individuals for very promising careers in finance, technology, and entrepreneurship.

Moreover, Blockchain and DLT are another driving force in FinTech innovation. These two revolutionary technologies enable secure, transparent, and efficient settlement of transactions that do not require conventional intermediaries. The decentralized means of maintaining trust provided by Blockchain minimizes opportunities for data manipulation and fraud. The spectrum of applications for Blockchain covers almost every facet of finance: from payments to settlement, from smart contracts to custody of digital assets. By simplifying procedures and improving operational efficiencies, blockchain becomes an enabler and foundation for modern financial infrastructure.

The great transformation that AI and ML nurture would be held to impact the financial system in various ways-all in the process of revamping the decision processes of financial activities. AI-driven predictive analytics are shaping the investment process by allowing players in finance to make decisions grounded in data, assess risk more intelligently, and deliver personalized experiences to customers. AI-backed voice response systems and chatbots have thus far transformed pricing by providing real-time responses, eliminating long waits, and ultimately improving client satisfaction. The adoption of AI in financial services is thus enhancing operational efficiencies and allowing firms to proactively assess market changes and adapt.

Big data and analytics considerably impact financial services by yielding valuable insights into customer behavior, market development, and risk management. Ability to process immense amounts of data helps an organization build better credit scores, detect frauds, and manage investments better. Data-driven decision-making also helps assure regulatory compliance, thereby ensuring that organizations adhere to industrial standards while minimizing risks. Through the insightful application of analytics, financial organizations design innovative and customized products that align with the dynamic needs of consumers (Jain & Jain, 2023).

Another major technological breakthrough within FinTech is the introduction of robotic process automation (RPA). RPA greatly heightens efficiency, dramatically reduces operational costs, and minimizes human intervention in routine yet intricate financial functions. Transaction processing, compliance reporting, or reconciling data represent only a few of the activities possible for automation; with such automation comes greater accuracy in execution and fewer manual errors. When combined with AI, RPA becomes an intelligent automation system which learns from patterns and adapts them to complex financial workflows, providing further optimization for the business.

With the increased digital financial transactions, cybersecurity has become the prime focus for the FinTech companies and the other traditional financial institutions. The increasing cyber threats of data breaches, identity thefts, and frauds demand enforcement of firm security protocols. Organizations are now protecting sensitive financial data with advanced encryption, biometric authentication, and AI-based threat detection systems. Reinforcement of the cybersecurity frame will mark consumer trust and the integrity of digital financial ecosystems.

Regulatory Technology (RegTech) is now on the verge of changing compliance management in the financial sector. The administration of compliance monitoring in real-time remains along the same lines provided by innovative technologies like artificial intelligence (AI), blockchain, and data analytics regarding regulatory requirements. Therefore, financial institutions especially comeunder dynamic changes in legal frames that RegTech enhances transparency and, consequently, makes accountability and risk management more efficient processes. Straightening the process of compliance through automated solutions and data-driven insights is a great way for reducing operational costs while gaining better overall adherence to regulations(Bose et al., 2023).

The rapid digital transformation of financial services is propelled by the speedy acceptance of mobile banking, digital wallets, and contactless payment systems. As the consumers now depend on digital spaces for their financial needs, both nascent FinTech firms and established financial institutions are challenged to either innovate for relevancy or become obsolete in real terms. The demand for mobile accessibility is a change in consumer behavior, thereby prompting financial service providers to provide their enhanced user experience with intuitive and seamless digital solutions. Hence, the amalgamation of technology outbreaks with changing financial education demarcates the future course of the financial industry. Organizations that stress a proactive approach to changes and innovation via cutting-edge technologies keeping abreast with momentary trends will only create and continuous hold onto these competitive advantages. Traditional banking organizations must appreciate the evolving period in financial services and find a way of applying digital solutions strategically in order to stay relevant.

CONCLUSION

The financial services sector is experiencing dramatic transformations. These transformations are ushering in specialized e-master programs in Financial Technology and Management to respond to demand. Thus far, almost everything pertaining to banking, investments, or finance is being pushed beyond its traditional periphery to accommodate new-age technologies. Efficiency, security, and access are the characteristics most expected from this ecosystem, with financial services becoming more agile and consumer-centric.

The key technologies enabling a shift in financial processes include AI, blockchain, and big data analytics. For example, AI algorithms have become extremely important in automating customer service, monitoring for fraudulent transactions, and fine-tuning risk assessments. Such intelligence makes the decision process more efficient and adds to helping financial institutions navigate through new sets of challenges. Decentralized and, above all, tamper-proof, blockchain provides the transparency, security, and technical efficiency for the revolutionization of payments processing and settlements in finance. On the other hand, big data analytics enable organizations to collect vast volumes of information said to be useful that would, in turn, affect some specific big strategic decisions. Applying data-driven methods would allow financial institutions to offer customized services, predict their customers' needs, and maintain an active response to market dynamics.

With technological disruption unfolding at an unprecedented pace, e-Masters programs have become a central platform for equipping professionals with knowledge and technical skills relevant to the changing financial environment. Fintech innovations, legal regulation, economic trends, and strategic financial management provide specialized insights through these distinct programs. All these attributes foster digital literacy and analytical competency so that the program graduates work for spearheading the digital transformation and steering financial institutions toward sustainable growth and innovation.

Fintech advancements are generating opportunities in various sectors, but some challenges are being experienced and placed on the table for consideration. Cybersecurity threats lurk at all times; hence, sensitive data must be protected against threats of cyberattack and fraud by financial institutions. The regulatory environment, meanwhile, requires compliance with complicated legal frameworks around digital finance. Ethical papers like data privacy and responsible AI go into shaping the standards of practice in the industry. Furthermore, with increasing automation in financial processes, there arise concerns about displacement of workers, thus requiring ways to reskill such professionals and redefine job roles in the digital economy.

Responding to these challenges would require a collaborative effort from financial institutions and regulators with technology experts and thought leaders in the industry to balance innovation with risk mitigation. The interplay between human expertise and machine intelligence will act as a game changer for the financial industry, demanding practitioners' access to continuous learning and adaptation.

In this digital age, financial service providers must undertake strategic transformation, invest in human capital, and initiate a proactive approach toward emerging technologies to remain competitive in the market. Financial institutions can learn to navigate the complexities of modern finance through innovation and resilience and provide enhanced value to their customers and stakeholders while facilitating societal and economic growth. The future of finance lies in the dynamic amalgamation of technology and knowledge that creates an agile, secure, and inclusive financial ecosystem.

REFERENCES

Alvarez-Risco, A., & Del-Aguila-Arcentales, S. (2021). A note on changing regulation in International Business: The World Intellectual Property Organization (WIPO) and Artificial Intelligence. Progress in International Business Research, 363–371. DOI: 10.1108/s1745-886220210000015020

Barredo Arrieta, A., Díaz-Rodríguez, N., Del Ser, J., Bennetot, A., Tabik, S., Barbado, A., Garcia, S., Gil-Lopez, S., Molina, D., Benjamins, R., Chatila, R., & Herrera, F. (2020). Explainable artificial intelligence (XAI): Concepts, taxonomies, opportunities and challenges toward responsible AI. *Information Fusion*, *58*, 82–115. DOI: 10.1016/j.inffus.2019.12.012

Bose, S., Kumar Dey, S., & Bhattacharjee, S. (2023). Big Data, data analytics and Artificial Intelligence in Accounting: An overview. Handbook of Big Data Research Methods, 32–51. DOI: 10.4337/9781800888555.00007

Cao, Y. (2025). How Ai Is Shaping. *Accounting and Finance*. Advance online publication. DOI: 10.2139/ssrn.5177863

Chawla, R. N., & Goyal, P. (2021). Emerging trends in digital transformation: A bibliometric analysis. *Benchmarking*, *29*(4), 1069–1112. DOI: 10.1108/bij-01-2021-0009

Dzuranin, A. C., Jones, J. R., & Olvera, R. M. (2018). Infusing Data Analytics into the accounting curriculum: A Framework and insights from faculty. *Journal of Accounting Education*, *43*, 24–39. DOI: 10.1016/j.jaccedu.2018.03.004

Fagundes, D. (2025). Genetic property rhetoric and the public domain. Texas A&amp. *M Journal of Property Law*, *11*(1), 1–16. DOI: 10.37419/jpl.v11.i1.1

Gans, J. (2024). Copyright policy options for generative artificial intelligence. SSRN Electronic Journal. DOI: 10.2139/ssrn.4716669

Gomber, P., Kauffman, R. J., Parker, C., & Weber, B. W. (2018). On the Fintech Revolution: Interpreting the forces of innovation, Disruption, and transformation in financial services. *Journal of Management Information Systems*, *35*(1), 220–265. DOI: 10.1080/07421222.2018.1440766

Harrast, S. A., Olsen, L., & Sun, Y. (2023). Analyzing eight emerging topics and their importance to career success. *Journal of Emerging Technologies in Accounting*, *20*(1), 289–304. DOI: 10.2308/jeta-2021-047

Hawashin, B., Althunibat, A., Kanan, T., AlZu'bi, S., & Sharrab, Y. (2023). Improving Arabic fake news detection using optimized feature selection. *2023 International Conference on Information Technology (ICIT)*, 690–694. DOI: 10.1109/icit58056.2023.10225974

Hayes, C. M. (2023). Generative Artificial Intelligence and copyright: Both sides of the black box. SSRN Electronic Journal. DOI: 10.2139/ssrn.4517799

Hristov, K. (2019). Artificial Intelligence and the copyright survey. SSRN Electronic Journal. DOI: 10.2139/ssrn.3490458

Jain, R., & Jain, D. (2023). Revolutionizing Business Management: An exploration of emerging technologies. SSRN Electronic Journal. *Available at:* DOI: 10.2139/ssrn.4448305

Kongolo, T. (2024). Intellectual property and artificial intelligence. Intellectual Property and Emerging Technologies, 19–47. DOI: 10.4324/9781003309086-3

Kyriazis, N. A. (2021). A survey on volatility fluctuations in the decentralized cryptocurrency financial assets. *Journal of Risk and Financial Management, 14*(7), 293. DOI: 10.3390/jrfm14070293

Lachman, R., & Joffe, M. (2021). Applications of artificial intelligence in media and entertainment. *Advances in Computational Intelligence and Robotics*, •••, 201–220. DOI: 10.4018/978-1-7998-3499-1.ch012

Neville-Neil, G. V. (2017). The chess player who couldn't pass the salt. *Communications of the ACM, 60*(4), 24–25. DOI: 10.1145/3055277

Safdar, N. M., Banja, J. D., & Meltzer, C. C. (2020). Ethical considerations in Artificial Intelligence. *European Journal of Radiology, 122*, 108768. DOI: 10.1016/j.ejrad.2019.108768 PMID: 31786504

Saura, J. R., Ribeiro-Soriano, D., & Palacios-Marqués, D. (2022). Assessing behavioral data science privacy issues in Government Artificial Intelligence Deployment. *Government Information Quarterly, 39*(4), 101679. DOI: 10.1016/j.giq.2022.101679

Schueffel, P. (2017). Taming the beast: A scientific definition of Fintech. *Journal of Innovation Management, 4*(4), 32–54. DOI: 10.24840/2183-0606_004.004_0004

Selimovic, J., Pilav-Velic, A., &Krndzija, L. (2022). Digital Workplace Transformation and innovation in the Financial Service Sector. Lecture Notes in Networks and Systems, 375–396. Available at: DOI: 10.1007/978-3-031-16598-6_16

Suarta, I. M., Suwintana, I. K., & Sudiadnyani, I. G. (2022). Technology and information system expertise demand for accounting professionals: A requirements analysis of job advertisements. *Advances in Social Science, Education and Humanities Research.* Advance online publication. DOI: 10.2991/assehr.k.220301.046

ThonseHawaldar, I., Rohit, B., Pinto, P., & T. M., R. (2017). The impact of oil price crisis on financial performance of commercial banks in Bahrain. *Banks and Bank Systems*, *12*(4), 4–16. DOI: 10.21511/bbs.12(4).2017.01

Truong, H. M. (2016). Integrating learning styles and adaptive e-learning system: Current developments, problems and opportunities. *Computers in Human Behavior*, *55*, 1185–1193. DOI: 10.1016/j.chb.2015.02.014

Ubaydullayeva, A. (2023). Intellectual property in the era of Artificial Intelligence: Challenges and Solutions. *Uzbek Journal of Law and Digital Policy*, *1*(3). Advance online publication. DOI: 10.59022/ujldp.93

Wolska, A. (2025). *Bridging the gap: The impact of open banking on traditional banking and Fintech collaboration.* FinTech and AI in Finance., DOI: 10.7190/fintaf.v2i1.414

Yu, Q., & Gu, X. (2022). On the Digital Transformation Path of financial shared services. Lecture Notes on Data Engineering and Communications Technologies, 325–331. Available at: DOI: 10.1007/978-3-030-97874-7_41

Zheng, Z., Xie, S., Dai, H. N., Chen, X., & Wang, H. (2018). Blockchain challenges and opportunities: A survey. *International Journal of Web and Grid Services*, *14*(4), 352. DOI: 10.1504/ijwgs.2018.095647

Chapter 5
AI and Governance:
Smart Cities, E-Governance, and Public Service Delivery

R. Velmurugan
https://orcid.org/0000-0002-7925-9757
Karpagam Academy of Higher Education, Coimbatore, India

R. Bhuvaneswari
https://orcid.org/0009-0003-9396-6129
Dr. Mahalingam College of Engineering and Technology, Pollachi, India

Maksud A. Madraswale
https://orcid.org/0000-0001-9565-0775
Presidency University, Bangalore, India

Ravi Thirumalaisamy
https://orcid.org/0000-0002-5954-5940
Modern College of Business and Science, Oman

ABSTRACT

Artificial Intelligence (AI) enables vast governance reform by building smart cities followed by distributing digital governance for official services as it delivers services efficiently and transparently and enhances citizen engagement. Smart cities use big data and IoT technology to achieve their maximum traffic management and waste disposal operations while protecting public security protection levels. E-governance employs AI-driven chatbots, automation, and blockchain for improved service accessibility and reduced bureaucratic delays. The introduction of artificial intelligence systems enhances both the public healthcare service delivery and tax regulatory functions as well as social security program delivery. For the successful

DOI: 10.4018/979-8-3373-2387-9.ch005

adoption of AI systems it needs ethical regulations to resolve three key problems ranging from data protection concerns to algorithm-related biases and computing device inequalities.

INTRODUCTION

The digital transformation of governance occurs through AI technology because it brings substantial improvements to operational efficiency as well as process clarity and selection capabilities. Through governance system integration with AI artificial intelligence society has established better e-governance frameworks together with advanced public service processing and the development of smart cities. These technological advances enhance contemporary governmental service delivery by generating data-guided and citizen-oriented systems which meet the current technological demands.

The implementation of AI in governance operations leads to best results through robot automation of regular operations that both decrease errors and enhance decision speed. The deployment of AI automation in public administrations enables more effective and rapidly delivered accurate public services by optimizing bureaucratic processes management. Margetts and Dunleavy (2013) establish that public administration focuses on digital technologies and AI systems to improve operational performance with reduced costs that boosts effective governance.

Through its incorporation with Artificial Intelligence systems governments successfully enhanced transparency levels in their institutions. AI enables authorities to thoroughly examine vast information which helps them detect administrative misconduct patterns along with operational shortcomings. Real-time monitoring happens with the aid of machine learning algorithms which maintain systems that ensure both public financial accountability and policy implementation standards for developing accountability systems. The transparency systems delivered by AI let citizens view government information per Janssen and Kuk (2016 so democracy becomes stronger.

AI creates its greatest impact on governance by developing smart cities. Cities employ artificial intelligence to enhance the management of resources as well as increase safety services and enhance their urban infrastructure. Utilities achieve sustainability through AI predictive analytics by using optimized traffic patterns along with energy resource management along with waste management systems. Smart city programs gain improved services by using adaptable computer systems designed to learn from citizen needs because this method generates better life quality results according to Meijer and Bolívar (2016).

The advancements in Artificial Intelligence provide significant benefits to programs based on electronic governance. AI-based deadlock prevention tools are possible because governments create intellectual chatbots which lead to automated document workflows and personalized services for individual users. The current e-governance implementation of AI automation strengthens public-government interactions and leads to decreased paperwork and better citizen service accessibility. The implementation of e-governance through AI advancement has improved both public involvement and universal participation in decision-making according to Bertot, Jaeger, and Grimes (2010).

AI has increased population service delivery through its adoption among different service systems. The combination of healthcare providers using AI systems with educational institutions and social services organizations provides better service quality by enhancing accessibility for users. Healthcare practitioners employ AI diagnostic tools to detect diseases at early stages and fabricate individualized treatments thus alleviating healthcare personnel workload pressures. Learning programs driven by AI enable education institutions to achieve better student interest rates while producing better academic results due to personalized learning approaches. Public services equipped with AI distribution mechanisms work toward equal resource allocation which produces healthier communities as Eggers and Hamill (2017) explain.

The evaluation of evidence-based policies receives enhanced benefit from AI-based processing because AI operates on complex information to forecast upcoming policy outcomes. Through machine learning algorithms past policy data becomes assessable by trend evaluation for recommendation of optimal policy choices. Data-related methods through AI enhance both accuracy and operational efficiency of government policies. Policy decisions backed by AI remove human bias and subjectivity because they operate from proven quantitative data as reported by Chen and Hsieh (2014).

The adoption of AI for public governance creates several ethical dilemmas while requiring new and associated regulatory solutions. The need for robust regulations exists because privacy concerns and bias issues persist as well as vulnerabilities created by incorrect surveillance operation handling. According to Mittelstadt et al. (2016) governance implementation of ethical AI depends on the three elements of transparency, accountability and fairness to safeguard citizen rights with equal protection against discrimination. The beneficial attributes of AI technology demand implementation of strategies because its deployment can amplify pre-existing governance system inequalities.

AI advances governance because it improves operational efficiency and shows transparent procedures which lead to better choice directions. Artificial intelligence leads to supreme governance transformations through smart cities and upgraded e-governance and efficient public service methods. The primary step to reach responsible AI implementation involves establishing ethical protocols which accompany necessary regulatory standards. The future governance structure heavily depends on AI advancement because AI collaboration with governance will create flexible and efficient people-centered governmental institutions.

AI IN SMART CITIES

Urban development reaches the level of smart cities through Artificial Intelligence systems deployment that requires improved technology and enhanced public services to deliver better quality of life for citizens. Municipalities reach optimal operational levels for their traffic management and energy distribution systems together with waste disposal and security systems through AI integration with IoT and big data analytics systems as well as automated processes (Batty 2018). AI predictive analysis tools allow urban planners to develop sustainable urban solutions by using objective data analysis in their decision-making processes (Zhang, Zhang, & Du, 2021). Smart city implementations demand artificial intelligence technology to monitor expanding urban populations because such technology delivers operational advantages combined with sustainable services for citizens.

Optimizing Urban Infrastructure

The urban living quality of smart cities improves by implementing AI technologies which allow them to refurbish infrastructure while managing systems and receiving public involvement. .zeros supply effective automated services through their data-driven systems because of their AI-based data processing capabilities. Sustainable areas can be produced through a union of advanced urban planning techniques with enhanced traffic management and energy systems together with waste administration which leads to enhanced community quality.

AI runs traffic management operations as one of its leading applications for smart cities. Municipalities enhance their congestion management through real-time predictive analytics monitoring that uses AI together with ITS systems because these capabilities improve both road security and traffic flow performance. According to Zheng et al. (2016) the team established nine different schemes to create optimized routes through the creation of step-by-step procedures that minimized travel duration and fuel consumption. The implementation of autonomous governance in traffic control systems leads to optimal traffic flow because it adjusts signal timing to construct more efficient transit network systems.

The distribution efficiency together with operational capability of infrastructure systems in smart cities receive AI-based improvements. The assessment of AI-based algorithms for approaching power demands helps operators decrease grid energy losses and integrate renewable electricity sources into their operations. AI-enabled smart grids implement sustainable and economical energy administration through the control of supply-demand ratios as Khan et al. (2020) indicate.

Semiconductor waste disposal solutions serve as basic environmental management platforms that improve waste disposal performance. AI sensors inside automated waste sorting systems maintain operational success in waste material processing from point of collection through to processing facilities. Waste management AI systems according to Pires et al. (2019) deliver critical outcomes through two pathways: they reduce waste that ends up in landfills and create better environmental benefits through predictions that use automatic decision-making mechanisms.

AI technologies provide municipal planning organizations with the ability to perform prediction model analysis in addition to geospatial analysis functions. By coupling artificial intelligence processors to community distribution assessment alongside fundamental requirements and environmental factors city strategic development becomes reachable. Code analytics in urban spaces provide planners with tools to create framework systems while planning sustainable development paths (Batty 2018).

Smart city development depends on the operation of artificial intelligence because it improves infrastructure management systems and resource distribution as well as engages citizens. The approaching age of technological advancement will create new AI system solutions that can optimize sustainable environmental urban development.

Enhancing Public Safety

Technical implementation of IoT analytics operates in real time by using machine learning algorithms which predicts sustainable city maintenance needs to reduce environmental problems and decrease traffic jams. As part of its responsible urban operations the technology collects and analyzes perpetual data to generate important information needed to meet predefined targets.

Organizations reach predictive maintenance through real-time data analysis because this characteristic represents a major benefit of the analytical system. Sensor systems monitoring conditions in real-time enable the identification of infrastructure failures beforehand by connecting to internet systems placed across bridges and roads and public transportation. The detection of equipment wear trends becomes possible with AI prediction software that evaluates multiple sensor data which allows authorities to manage maintenance operations systematically. The implementation of predictive maintenance strategies helps lower operational costs and extends urban asset operational duration as reported by Lee et al. (2018) and decreases maintenance timeframes.

Smart cities acquire their primary advantage of reduced traffic congestion through the machine learning combination with IoT technology. Real-time traffic data processed by AI systems allows them to conduct vehicle repositioning tasks alongside traffic control methods that ultimately generate superior operational outcomes for the entire system. Tang et al. (2020) shows AI traffic management controls changes in patterns to produce lower emergency responses that maintains efficient vehicle fuel consumption and decreases travel duration.

Assessing real-time information stream brings better results to environmental sustainability operations. Monitoring systems that belong to Internet of Things enable pollution detection which allows governments to make informed policy decisions. The system analyzes existing information to generate predictions about environmental pollution patterns that drive authorities to develop management plans for industrial pollution and traffic infrastructure improvements for decreasing pollution output. AI-based environmental monitoring contributes to sustainability through its capability to build quick policy solutions and optimize resource delivery according to Ahmed et al. (2021) in their paper.

The protection of security systems in urban areas increases significantly through the connection of security infrastructure to artificial intelligence surveillance systems. Security forces can identify upcoming security threats by using facial recognition technology together with anomaly detection and behavioral examination. Public safety growth through AI platforms allows police departments to reach highest efficiency in operational budgets according to Wang et al. (2019). IoT data analyzed first hand by AI creates solutions about predictive maintenance which helps achieve environmental sustainability goals and manage traffic congestion through urban management. Technology will permanently enhance its ability to build sustainable and efficient urban development throughout its developmental period.IoT data analyzed firsthand by AI creates solutions about predictive maintenance which helps achieve environmental sustainability goals and manage traffic congestion through urban management. Technology will permanently enhance its ability to build sustainable and efficient urban development throughout its developmental period.IoT data analyzed firsthand by AI creates solutions about predictive maintenance which helps achieve environmental sustainability goals and manage traffic congestion through urban management. Technology will permanently enhance its ability to build sustainable and efficient urban development throughout its developmental period.

AI IN E-GOVERNANCE

Artificial Intelligence creates revolutionary changes for urban environments to develop smart cities through optimizing infrastructure while enhancing public services with better quality of life delivery for citizens. Narrowing integration of AI technology with IoT and big data analytics and automation allows cities to execute effective traffic management while they control energy distribution systems and waste removal operations and security systems (Batty, 2018). AI predictive systems enable urban planners to base their choices on data which leads to long-lasting city growth (Zhang, Zhang, & Du, 2021). AI serves a vital part in smart cities toward achieving maximum efficiency and sustainability as well as citizen-focused governance while urban expansion and population expansion continue to intensify.

AI has brought transformations to e-governance through administrative procedure optimization and service improvement and establishment of transparency across government systems. AI-based chatbots together with virtual assistants enable easy citizen contact which decreases official red tape and develops better access to vital government services (Janssen & van den Hoven, 2020). The application of machine learning algorithms allows governments to benefit from large data analysis that creates trend identification and future need prediction capabilities to enhance data-driven policy-making (Meijer 2019). The implementation of blockchain with AI creates transactions that remain secure by being tamper-resistant thus public officials can minimize corruption and maintain transparent public administration. Digital governance continues to expand through AI which develops operational governmental systems that yield enhanced functionality and embracement and responsible reaction to population needs.

Automating Administrative Processes

Digital communication platforms under E-governance enable public agencies to enhance their connections with citizens through transparent platforms with better operational efficiency and accessible systems.

AI automation implements digitalization to reduce administration workloads through automation of paper processes and reduction of staff involvement and improved speed for making decisions. Chatbots combined with virtual assistants that use NLP technology supply immediate citizen responses and increase both accessible services and decreased waiting times. The findings of Bertot et al. (2016) show how AI-powered e-governance systems improve service access with personalized help to the public sector.

AI implementations for service delivery operations make government resources reach their maximum efficiency. With AI data analysis organizations can detect service delivery deficiencies and expect population needs and arrange resources for maximum efficiency. AI predictive systems running in social welfare programs detect qualified recipients of assistance which generates reduced errors and enhanced service delivery speed. Public service delivery reaches higher efficiency because AI-derived decision systems enable data-based governance according to Janssen and van den Berg (2020).

AI boosts real-time governance responsiveness through its automated system that gives predictive functions and real-time monitoring capabilities. AI-integrated systems process extensive information collected from multiple foundations that allow the detection of irregularities alongside the forecasting of forthcoming problems alongside recommendations for urgent actions. AI systems that monitor public security analyze ongoing surveillance information to stop security risks making it possible to also leverage AI in disaster response through forecasting and warning detection. Real-time governance supported by AI according to Meijer and Bolívar (2018) gives authorities faster and more efficient means to tackle emergencies.

AI enhances e-governance because it enables the automation of administrative operations and boosts service delivery efficiency and delivers immediate processing. AI technology is expected to enhance its contribution to efficient governance which also includes transparency governance as well as citizen-focused implementation.

Data-Driven Policy Making

The interaction between citizens and public authorities transformed through AI-based virtual assistants because they deliver quick answers to questions together with minimized delays for services and elevated public service accessibility. AI-created systems with NLP technology analyze fast real-time public questions to execute automated administrative services while reducing human personnel involvement. The automated service executions done by chatbots enable Government staff to handle challenging and important matters. AIMed conversational agents demonstrated their capability to improve service times and user engagement while making government services more citizen-focused as Laranjo et al. (2018) reported.

The application of AI-driven data analytics effectively speeds up service provision because it directly supports policy development. High-volume datasets about socio-economic indicators and public opinions and population composition belong to state government institutions. AI calculates this data using statistical models to detect relationships which help public figures create decisions by evidence. AI analytics help identify upcoming challenges while predicting different aspects of change to let governance systems lead ahead of developments. According to Janssen and Kuk (2016) the use of data-based policy creation leads to better public sector decisions by minimizing uncertain factors while optimizing resource allocation.

Through its analysis of current data AI allows governmental institutions to craft reformable policies which help them deliver quick reactions to changing social requirements. AI analytics provides employment trend assessments which guide authorities to build job creation strategies during economic slumps. AI systems survey disease outbreaks to produce alert patterns which healthcare professionals use for developing precise public health measures. AI system-supported policymaking promotes visibility and answerability because data-driven evidence serves instead of individual preferences as Wirtz et al. (2019) explains.

AI public sentiment analysis systems help government authorities measure the opinions which citizens have toward their initiatives. Policymakers acquire insights into public matters through social media analytics which machine learning technology powers to make policy adjustments. Participatory governance emerges through such a mechanism which intentionally includes citizen input for decision-making processes. AI technology applied to public feedback systems enhances democratic processes while building government institution trust according to Chen and Aklikokou (2021).

Doctoral virtual assistants and chatbots aid public service delivery because they eliminate bureaucratic hurdles and AI models enable better policies through analysis of economic conditions combined with public requirements. Defaulting AI technology development will result in better governance through increased efficiency and better citizen participation and better service responsiveness.

AI IN PUBLIC SERVICE DELIVERY

Artificial Intelligence (AI) drives urban changes through smart city standards which make technology optimize infrastructure and enhance public services and improve citizen quality of life. The combination of AI technology with IoT devices enables cities to control traffic systems while optimizing the distribution of energy resources as well as waste treatment and security systems according to Batty (2018). City planners achieve sustainable urban development through data-driven predictive analytics that AI provides (Zhang, Zhang, & Du, 2021). The growing human population together with increasing trends of urbanization makes AI in smart cities essential for achieving both operational excellence and environment-friendly management alongside democratic government services.

Through AI technologies e-governance functions better by optimizing operation processes along with service achievement and it increases public transparency across government activities. AI-powered chatbots and virtual assistants provide easy citizen communication channels which reduce bureaucratic interference to enhance public service access (Janssen & van den Hoven, 2020). Machine learning algorithms improve policy development through their capacity to process large amounts of data about trends which helps predict coming requirements thereby creating more data-based governance systems (Meijer, 2019). Use of blockchain technology with artificial intelligence protects secure electronic transactions that achieve integrity while avoiding public sector corruption and improving administrative accountability. The growth of digital governance depends heavily on AI because it develops operational administrative systems that deliver accessibility and efficiency and prompt feedback capabilities.

The use of artificial intelligence adjusts public service operations to deliver quicker and simpler processes while maintaining heightened service responsiveness in healthcare, social welfare and taxation domains. AI-driven automation systems enhance the processing of social benefit applications by decreasing administrative workload while reducing both administrative mistakes (Eggers, Schatsky, & Viechnicki, 2017). Healthcare services benefit from AI predictive analytics which enhance both disease prevention and hospital resources management to deliver improved patient results (Esteva et al., 2019). Artificial intelligence platforms used for producing tax documentation and legal agreements boost processing accuracy and speed up operations thus curtailing payment delays along with cases of fraud (Margetts & Dunleavy, 2013). Public service delivery needs proper ethical and inclusive AI implementation from governments to achieve maximum benefits for their citizens.

Enhancing Efficiency and Accessibility

The transformation of public service delivery occurs through AI because it leads to enhanced operational efficiency together with better accessibility and broader service inclusivity. The integration of artificial intelligence technology into automated systems leads to efficient administrative processing through expanded abilities for social benefits applications together with tax document processing and legal documentation. AI systems cut down human interaction to deliver efficient services while eliminating delays and boosting transparent service distribution across the population.

AI provides substantial transformation in public service delivery through its impact on social welfare program administration. AI automation systems allow governments to handle unemployment benefit applications together with pension applications and healthcare applications with high accuracy and accelerated processing times. The application of machine learning algorithms over large datasets allows programs to evaluate eligibility requirements thus lowering cases of fraud and directing support to the appropriate beneficiaries. Public welfare program decision-making through AI implementation increases effectiveness along with fairness while also reducing errors and discriminatory biases according to Desouza and Bhagwatwar (2012).

Temperature-controlled lockers should be located in conspicuous places with real-time monitoring to prevent fraud. The technology should have the ability to thwart all forms of tampering attempts and upgrades should be periodically conducted to ensure robustness against newer devices and techniques. The use of AI-driven chatbots enables taxpayers to get responses to questions and follow step-by-step filing procedures and obtain tailored suggestions. Through financial record analysis AI detects inaccurate patterns in order to stop tax evasion while advancing regulatory compliance. AI analytics systems equipped with AI technologies use pattern recognition to detect tax-related fraud thus generating more revenue for public service operations according to Cockcroft and Russell (2018).

The process of legal documentation combined with judicial procedures receives automatic advancements through artificial intelligence. The processing of legal documents using AI systems operates through complete automation to handle permits licenses and contracts. NLP tools enable law document preparation which allows government agencies to reduce their administrative workload. The capability of AI predictive analytics to examine court cases and suggest judicial decisions brings extra support to the judicial system. The use of AI in legal services creates better access to justice through faster court decisions which also result in decreased expenses from judicial activities according to Susskind (2020).

People with disabilities benefit from AI-enablement of public service delivery through tools that support multilingual communication alongside disabled-person-friendly speech-to-text capabilities and digital accessibility functions. AI virtual assistants now provide their services through various language options which enable all speakers including non-native and marginalized people to access government services without limitation. Margetts and Dunleavy (2013) state that AI-powered digital government programs help achieve social inclusion through resolving inequality in public service accessibility.

The implementation of AI technologies helps public service institutions to optimize their administrative workflows and achieves both better efficiency alongside universal access to services. The upcoming AI technological growth will enable public administration institutions to improve public service access and remove bureaucratic processes for the development of governance systems that focus on citizens.

AI in Healthcare and Education

Medical services experience a transformation through artificial intelligence because it lets doctors make better diagnostic predictions along with generating individual treatment strategies and delivering healthcare remotely. The modernized healthcare technology works to create better medical outreach which includes early disease detection, precise treatments and service delivery to remote regions where healthcare access fails.

Large medical data sets undergo AI algorithm processing to create patterns which detect upcoming health dangers in predictive diagnostic models. Machine learning models analyze DNA information together with life patterns and medical treatment backgrounds to discover diseases such as cancer and diabetes and heart disorders during their early development. Topol (2019) explains how AI predictive analytics strengthen disease prevention methods by enabling prompt medical assistance that lowers healthcare expenses while improving diagnosis results.

Below lie benefits of AI which include patient-specific treatment recommendations produced through the examination of individual medical data. Healthcare staff benefit from AI decision support systems which enable them to identify suitable treatments after reviewing genetic information alongside treatment reaction histories combined with immediate health parameter scans. The application of AI-based precision medicine by Obermeyer and Emanuel (2016) leads to better treatment results together with decreased adverse effects and superior patient care standards.

The combination of telemedicine and artificial intelligence produces services that unite medical professionals with their patients particularly in sparsely populated locations. Biometric systems enable preliminary assessments and scheduling and offer virtual health assistance that provides follow-up healthcare services. AI technology operates wearable devices for patient remote monitoring which detects vital signs abnormalities and lets healthcare providers know about such problems. Keesara, Jonas and Schulman (2020) demonstrate how AI telemedicine services increase healthcare accessibility while decreasing hospital crowding and improving patient medical care continuity.

AI platforms apply customized student learning designs which create adjusted education programs that address different student requirements. There are two benefits which Adaptive learning systems bring to students: they evaluate their performance data to customize educational content that supports knowledge absorption. Students receive live assessments from AI tutors who aid in their fight against academic problems. According to Luckin et al. (2016) personal learning systems enhanced by artificial intelligence drive better student involvement while teaching them to learn independently and leads to stronger academic performance.

AI also streamlines administrative management in educational institutions. Applied to grading tasks and supporting enrollment and student performance evaluation activities these systems enhance both resource optimization and academic operational performance. AI-based chatbots support students who need help by responding to their questions and thus minimize the burdens on staff. The automated education system powered by AI technology enables instructors to dedicate more time toward teaching and mentoring because it improves operational effectiveness according to Holmes et al. (2019).

Through AI technology healthcare professionals conduct predictive diagnostics and medical professionals establish tailored treatments and telemedicine practices and educators deliver unique lessons to students. AI developments continue to enhance both the accessibility features and operational effectiveness and end results that benefit communities and individual beneficiaries.

CHALLENGES AND ETHICAL CONSIDERATIONS

Artificial Intelligence (AI) creates intelligent urban structures for smart cities through technological means that improve the quality of public services and infrastructure and civil existence standards. Smart cities utilize AI to operate the IoT along with big data analytics and automation systems which dominate traffic control management and distribute energy and control waste systems and security systems (Batty, 2018). Predictive analytics that operate through artificial intelligence help city planners base their choices on data to create sustainable urban developments (Zhang, Zhang, & Du, 2021). Smart cities achieve efficient operation and sustainable development and citizen-oriented government administration by using AI technologies while populations increase and urbanization increases.

The governance empowerment from AI involves the optimization of administrative systems and improved service quality and open government transparency measures. AI-based chatbots together with virtual assistants enable effective citizen conversations through which bureaucratic obstacles are minimized and essential services become more accessible to the public (Janssen & van den Hoven, 2020). Using machine learning algorithms helps policymakers understand vast datasets which allows them to discover patterns and forecast future requirements to create governance based on data (Meijer, 2019). Blockchain integration with AI solutions provides protected transactions that cannot be altered and this security practice helps reduce public administration corruption and boost accountability. AI play an essential role in digital governance development because it enables public institutions to become more efficient and nurturing for all their constituents while providing better service responses.

Through AI technology public service delivery experiences more efficient operations and improved accessibility joined with better response times when dealing with healthcare and social welfare situations and taxation services. Artificial intelligence enables the automation of social benefit application processing thus cutting down administrative workloads and error rates (Eggers, Schatsky, & Viechnicki, 2017). Robotics predictive analysis within healthcare creates early disease identification capabilities along with enhanced hospital resource distribution for better patient results (Esteva et al., 2019). AI technology in taxation and legal documentation works to automate vital processes which creates precise work while accelerating process speed and decreasing time spend waiting together with reducing inaccuracies and fraud (Margetts & Dunleavy, 2013). Public service delivery benefits require essential ethical along with inclusive implementation of AI by governments to ensure benefits reach all citizens.

The extensive advantages of AI in governance management accompany critical issues together with ethical complexities. Data privacy together with algorithmic biases and transparency and accountability issues need solution to build fair and responsible AI implementations (Mittelstadt et al., 2016). The extensive use of big data by AI systems generates two principal challenges because it increases data vulnerabilities and creates new opportunities for unapproved system exploitation (Brundage et al., 2018). AI models which show biases in their algorithms generate discriminatory results that consistently affect minority groups according to Buolamwini & Gebru (2018). The deployment of ethical AI systems needs standardized regulations together with systematic decision-making disclosure combined with bias prevention methods (Jobin, Ienca, & Vayena, 2019). Workforce training initiatives together with economic adaptation programs must be developed due to the job elimination capability of AI-based automation. To achieve maximum societal benefits with public trust AI deployment needs proper ethical and equitable governance implementation.

Addressing Bias and Privacy Concerns

When AI systems become part of governance operations they provide substantial improvements yet create three primary problems regarding data safety and algorithms that show bias and answerability issues. Solving these problems demands thorough legislation along with simple decision processes and continuous efforts to stop bias from occurring.

Data privacy problems represent the central issue which people face when using AI in governmental systems. AI systems analyze extensive personal data that public officials obtain from citizens for improving public service quality. Data mishandling produces breaches alongside unauthorized surveillance events that systematically destroy public trust. According to Zuboff (2019) unregulated AI systems enable the collection of extensive data thus threatening both freedom and democratic authority of the population. Public protection legislation including the GDPR must be strictly enforced by governments to safeguard both security and privacy during the delivery of AI services by AI systems.

The use of algorithms present substantial challenges to governing through artificial intelligence systems. The data processing methods in machine learning depend on historical records that sometimes include system-based biases to generate unfair results through their models. Social inequalities become stronger because of discriminatory biases that exist within AI applications which primarily affect law enforcement and hiring as well as social welfare distribution systems. O'Neil (2016) wrote that societal inequalities continue because biased algorithms exist which requires strong bias detection systems with correction capabilities. The execution of machine learning models with fairness elements together with skilled data sets permits the reduction of algorithmic prejudice while creating equal AI decision operations.

When AI rules governance there are significant challenges related to accountability since automated choices lack obvious human supervision capabilities. Official bodies need to develop systems which will enable the assignment of accountability when AI makes critical determinations particularly in instances of criminal justice and public benefits distribution. The implementation of explainable AI (XAI) according to Binns (2018) achieves transparency because it makes algorithmic choices accessible to public audiences and decision-makers. Open AI governance systems needs to include mandatory impact analyses along with ethical oversight tests in addition to ongoing performance checks for maintaining accountability practices.

Regulatory frameworks used for ethical AI deployment need to hold a dual ability to adjust and enforce their policies. Lawmakers need to work with researchers who study AI systems and civil society activists and legal specialists to create complete instructions which merge progressive developments with moral guidelines for AI applications. According to Floridi and Cowls (2019) fundamental ethical AI management principles need to incorporate beneficence and non-maleficence and justice to protect common interests.

The productive network capabilities of AI need to be supported by adequate efforts to handle questions about privacy protection and unbiased decisions and system transparency. Society will receive ethically and equitable service from AI through strong regulatory frameworks together with transparency promotion and bias mitigation strategy implementation.

Ensuring Digital Inclusivity

National governments need to establish digital inclusion priorities which aim to stop underserved populations from becoming excluded in an AI-based society. The essential part of digital progress is giving equal opportunity to technology and public services so everyone from all backgrounds can benefit regardless of their financial status. The solution to the digital exclusion requires both strategic policy development supported by infrastructure funding and artificial intelligence solutions that keep users accessible.

Digital exclusivity causes substantial impact on low-income communities together with rural areas and elderly demographics and persons with disabilities because these groups struggle to access basic public services including healthcare and education and employment resources. The research of van Dijk (2020) shows that digital inequalities make existing societal differences worse because they create perpetual poverty and social seclusion. The government needs to improve broadband installation while subsidizing digital equipment to execute digital literacy initiatives that teach social disadvantage communities how to use AI-driven platforms.

The deployment of AI systems for fair purposes requires eliminating biases which exist within algorithms that could produce discriminatory results. Multiple AI systems base their training on undersampled minority populations which produces discriminatory output decisions throughout industries such as recruiting, law enforcement and social program distributions. According to Buolamwini and Gebru (2018) facial recognition technology demonstrates racial and gender prejudices because training datasets remain biased which shows the need for representative and diversified data collections. AI fairness entails gathering data from all populations while offering clear views into automated processes along with procedures to monitor biases that emerge during AI operations.

The fundamental aspect of digital inclusivity includes full accessibility of services. Public services which incorporate AI technologies must have built-in accessibility features that support multiple languages and speech-to-text functions and user interfaces for individuals with disabilities. According to West (2019) inclusive design increases usability and maintains technology usability for diverse consumer groups. National governments need to establish mandatory accessibility guidelines during AI development which requires digital services to serve every population member effectively.

Partnerships between public and private organizations have a key position in advancing digital inclusivity. Shared government partnerships with technological companies and social organizations enable cost-effective development of AI technology solutions that everyone can access. According to Eubanks (2018) modern computer systems known as digital poorhouses create social inequalities through their resource distribution to the disadvantaged population. Government regulations should control AI implementation to prevent it from achieving exclusion instead of empowering people.

AI governance requires digital inclusivity as its main objective because marginalization would otherwise exist. The government should spend on infrastructure development and eliminate algorithmic discrimination and force accessibility protocols alongside business-government cooperation to develop an equal digital world which provides technological advantages to every resident.

CONCLUSION

AI implements transformative changes into three areas of governance including smart cities and e-governance and public service delivery. Advanced technologies in this system lead to operational improvements through data-based decision-making and increased transparency as well as citizen participation. The implementation of AI depends on both the resolution of ethical problems and fair AI usage practices to support sustainable governance that includes everyone. Governments should properly use AI technology to create public services which respond better to citizens while being more technologically advanced.

Smart city development heavily depends on Artificial Intelligence because it enhances the operation of infrastructure alongside resource management and urban planning systems. The integration of AI-powered systems enhances traffic control methods as well as energy and waste management systems which results in better environmental preservation and superior quality of living standards. Batty (2018) explains that artificial intelligence analytics systems provide predictive infrastructure maintenance which lowers expenses and avoids disruptions during services. AI-based security systems provide better safety to the public by processing live data streams to identify security risks as they develop (Zhang et al., 2021). The applications enhance urban governance through their role in providing efficient service delivery and risk mitigation.

AI enables significant improvement of both public service accessibility and administrative efficiency in the domain of e-governance. Virtual assistance supported by AI technology enables customers to interact more quickly with administrators which reduces bureaucratic delays and enhances their service speed. AI operates in public administration to handle taxes and social benefits submissions through automated systems which both cut down human involvement and elevate accuracy (Janssen & van den Hoven, 2020). Artificial Intelligence analytics processes generate economic insights from social trends which enhance decision making through the allocation of better resources. The application of AI-based governance systems allows instant data access according to Meijer (2019) which establishes trustworthy public systems and creates transparent environments.

Artificial intelligence delivers advantages to public service delivery by implementing automated system mechanisms which increase efficiency and improve accessibility to services. Artificial Intelligence controls healthcare through predictive medical tests and customized treatment plans and remote medical care which boost healthcare access (Topol, 2019). AI learning platforms in educational institutions create tailored educational programs and allocate academic resources effectively to produce superior educational achievements according to Luckin et al. (2016). Your paper demonstrates that AI enables faster legal proceedings combined with data-based operational choices through O'Neil (2016). Such applications show how AI can create an inclusive and efficient public sector through its applications.

For AI-driven government management to remain viable the essential ethical problems regarding privacy protection and algorithmic prejudice and responsibility must receive solution-based remedies. AI systems handle enormous amounts of personal data which generates privacy and protection of confidential information issues. Uncontrolled use of AI systems threatens to violate human freedoms along with democratic institutions according to Zuboff (2019). The General Data Protection Regulation (GDPR) with its strict data protection rules should become enforced by governments to secure privacy rights and stop unauthorized data use.

The problem of algorithmic bias emerges as an essential problem because AI platforms which use biased datasets produce discriminatory and unfair results. Statistics show that biased algorithms create social inequality instead of preventing it in various fields like law enforcement and social welfare distribution and hiring processes. Facial recognition systems develop racial and gender biases because they process training data that is not balanced according to Buolamwini and Gebru (2018). A solution to these problems should include fairness-aware machine learning together with diverse training datasets and transparent algorithm decision-making methods according to Floridi and Cowls (2019).

AI-decision making requires accountable governance systems to maintain responsible decision operations. High-stakes systems which use automated decisions in areas like criminal justice and public benefits allocation need proper accountability systems to stop discrimination and errors from happening. The system behind explainable AI (XAI) allows policymakers and the public to understand the decisions made by algorithms according to Binns (2018). The maintenance of public trust requires government institutions to perform periodic checks of AI systems together with visual examinations of their effects and ethical evaluations for maintaining responsibility.

The proper execution of AI systems must take place fairly for underserved communities to avoid their dismissal from the system. The implementation of AI-driven public services creates a digital exclusion barrier which primarily affects those belonging to lower-income brackets as well as residents from rural areas and elderly citizens and disables persons. Digital inequality intensifies economic inequalities between populations based on research conducted by van Dijk (2020). Government authorities should improve broadband structures and fund technology devices as well as train underserved populations to operate AI-driven platforms.

AI deployment for the public sector needs to resolve accessibility issues that exist within digital service platforms. The author West (2019) demonstrates how inclusive design processes both improve user interactions with technology and establish equal opportunities for device access. Guyanese governments need to set standards for AI development which will generate accessible public services for all citizens regardless of their differences.

AI-driven government operations benefit from public-private collaborations since these relationships enable innovation of new technologies coupled with equal access to technology. The development of affordable yet accessible AI solutions happens best through government and technology company and civil organization co-operation. According to Eubanks (2018) the implementation of digital poorhouses will occur when AI systems restrict available resources for vulnerable population groups. Public authorities need to establish control measures for AI to make sure its use benefits citizens instead of separating them from equal opportunities.

AI transforms governance by transforming smart cities and implementing e-governance systems together with public service delivery tools that generate efficient services along with transparent governance methods in addition to higher citizen participation in public matters. The successful use of AI depends on both ethical principles and equal ways of deploying the technology to achieve sustainable governance. Governments should establish regulatory standards which combine bias reduction techniques with data protection practices in order to use AI smartly. A government-driven approach will create public services that are smarter as well as more responsive to citizens' needs while benefiting the entire society.

REFERENCES

Ahmed, K., Mahmood, A., & Irfan, M. (2021). AI-driven environmental monitoring for smart cities: A systematic review. *Environmental Science & Policy*, *122*, 1–12.

Batty, M. (2018). Artificial intelligence and smart cities. *Environment and Planning. B, Urban Analytics and City Science*, *45*(1), 3–6.

Bertot, J. C., Estevez, E., & Janowski, T. (2016). Universal and contextualized public services: Digital public service innovation framework. *Government Information Quarterly*, *33*(2), 211–222.

Bertot, J. C., Jaeger, P. T., & Grimes, J. M. (2010). Using ICTs to create a culture of transparency: E-government and social media as openness and anti-corruption tools for societies. *Government Information Quarterly*, *27*(3), 264–271.

Binns, R. (2018). *Fairness in machine learning: Lessons from political philosophy. Proceedings of the 2018 Conference on Fairness, Accountability, and Transparency*, 149-159.

Brundage, M., Avin, S., Wang, J., Belfield, H., Krueger, G., Hadfield, G., . . . Anderljung, M. (2018). *The malicious use of artificial intelligence: Forecasting, prevention, and mitigation*. arXiv preprint arXiv:1802.07228.

Buolamwini, J., & Gebru, T. (2018). Gender shades: Intersectional accuracy disparities in commercial gender classification. *Proceedings of Machine Learning Research*, *81*, 1–15.

Chen, Y. C., & Aklikokou, A. K. (2021). Artificial intelligence and public engagement: Enhancing governance through sentiment analysis and predictive analytics. *Government Information Quarterly*, *38*(4), 101590.

Chen, Y. C., & Hsieh, T. C. (2014). Big data and public governance: The innovation and challenges of data-driven governance. *Government Information Quarterly*, *31*(1), 1–7.

Cockcroft, S., & Russell, M. (2018). *Big data opportunities for tax administration*. eJournal of Tax Research, 16(3), 184-201.

Desouza, K. C., & Bhagwatwar, A. (2012). Citizen apps to engage with local governments: An empirical investigation. *Government Information Quarterly*, *29*(1), 39–49.

Eggers, W. D., Schatsky, D., & Viechnicki, P. (2017). *AI-augmented government: Using artificial intelligence to improve public sector performance*. Deloitte Insights.

Esteva, A., Robicquet, A., Ramsundar, B., Kuleshov, V., DePristo, M., Chou, K., & Dean, J. (2019). A guide to deep learning in healthcare. *Nature Medicine*, *25*(1), 24–29. PMID: 30617335

Eubanks, V. (2018). *Automating inequality: How high-tech tools profile, police, and punish the poor*. St. Martin's Press.

Floridi, L., & Cowls, J. (2019). A unified framework of five principles for AI in society. *Harvard Data Science Review*, *1*(1).

Holmes, W., Bialik, M., & Fadel, C. (2019). *Artificial intelligence in education: Promises and implications for teaching and learning*. Center for Curriculum Redesign.

Janssen, M., & Kuk, G. (2016). The challenges and limits of big data algorithms in technocratic governance. *Government Information Quarterly*, *33*(3), 371–377.

Janssen, M., & van den Berg, R. (2020). Data-driven governance: Creating value through open government data. *Government Information Quarterly*, *37*(3), 101477.

Janssen, M., & van den Hoven, J. (2020). Big data and artificial intelligence for digital transformation in government: The challenges for ethics. *Information Polity*, *25*(3), 267–280.

Jobin, A., Ienca, M., & Vayena, E. (2019). The global landscape of AI ethics guidelines. *Nature Machine Intelligence*, *1*(9), 389–399.

Keesara, S., Jonas, A., & Schulman, K. (2020). COVID-19 and health care's digital revolution. *The New England Journal of Medicine*, *382*(23), e82. PMID: 32240581

Khan, M. A., Mittal, S., Roy, R., & Kumar, N. (2020). AI-based energy management for sustainable smart cities: A review. *IEEE Access : Practical Innovations, Open Solutions*, *8*, 206656–206674.

Laranjo, L., Dunn, A. G., Tong, H. L., Kocaballi, A. B., Chen, J., Bashir, R., Surian, D., Gallego, B., Magrabi, F., Lau, A. Y. S., & Coiera, E. (2018). Conversational agents in healthcare: A systematic review. *Journal of the American Medical Informatics Association : JAMIA*, *25*(9), 1248–1258. PMID: 30010941

Lee, J., Jin, C., & Bagheri, B. (2018). Cyber-physical systems for predictive maintenance using deep learning techniques. *Journal of Manufacturing Science and Engineering*, *140*(4), 041017.

Luckin, R., Holmes, W., Griffiths, M., & Forcier, L. B. (2016). *Intelligence unleashed: An argument for AI in education*. Pearson Education.

Margetts, H., & Dunleavy, P. (2013). *The second wave of digital-era governance: A quasi-paradigm for government on the Web*. Philosophical Transactions of the Royal Society A: Mathematical, Physical and Engineering Sciences, 371(1987), 20120382.

Meijer, A. (2019). Public administration and the data revolution: Transparency and data-driven decision-making in the public sector. *Government Information Quarterly*, *36*(4), 100383.

Meijer, A., & Bolívar, M. P. R. (2016). Governing the smart city: A review of the literature on smart urban governance. *International Review of Administrative Sciences*, *82*(2), 392–408.

Mittelstadt, B. D., Allo, P., Taddeo, M., Wachter, S., & Floridi, L. (2016). The ethics of algorithms: Mapping the debate. *Big Data & Society*, *3*(2), 1–21.

Mittelstadt, B. D., Allo, P., Taddeo, M., Wachter, S., & Floridi, L. (2016). The ethics of algorithms: Mapping the debate. *Big Data & Society*, *3*(2), 2053951716679679.

O'Neil, C. (2016). *Weapons of math destruction: How big data increases inequality and threatens democracy*. Crown Publishing Group.

Obermeyer, Z., & Emanuel, E. J. (2016). Predicting the future—Big data, machine learning, and clinical medicine. *The New England Journal of Medicine*, *375*(13), 1216–1219. PMID: 27682033

Pires, A., Martinho, G., & Chang, N. B. (2019). Solid waste management in smart cities: A review of waste management practices and AI-driven solutions. *Waste Management (New York, N.Y.)*, *91*, 1–14.

Susskind, R. (2020). *Online courts and the future of justice*. Oxford University Press.

Tang, J., Liu, F., Zou, M., & Yang, H. (2020). AI-based dynamic traffic management in smart cities: Trends and applications. *Transportation Research Part C, Emerging Technologies*, *115*, 102622.

Topol, E. (2019). *Deep medicine: How artificial intelligence can make healthcare human again*. Basic Books.

Van Dijk, J. A. (2020). *The digital divide*. John Wiley & Sons.

Wang, X., Zhang, Y., & Zha, Z. J. (2019). Intelligent surveillance systems: AI-powered video analytics for public safety. *IEEE Transactions on Multimedia*, *21*(9), 2293–2307.

West, S. M. (2019). Data capitalism: Redefining the logics of surveillance and privacy. *Business & Society*, *58*(1), 20–41.

Wirtz, B. W., Weyerer, J. C., & Geyer, C. (2019). Artificial intelligence and the public sector—Applications and challenges. *International Journal of Public Administration*, *42*(7), 596–615.

Zhang, K., Zhang, L., & Du, M. (2021). Artificial intelligence and smart governance: A systematic literature review. *Government Information Quarterly*, *38*(4), 101566.

Zheng, Z., Capra, L., Wolfson, O., & Yang, H. (2016). Urban computing: Concepts, methodologies, and applications. [TIST]. *ACM Transactions on Intelligent Systems and Technology*, *7*(3), 1–25.

Zuboff, S. (2019). *The age of surveillance capitalism: The fight for a human future at the new frontier of power*. PublicAffairs.

Chapter 6
Accurate Rainfall Prediction With Integrated BI LSTM in Deep Learning

Usharani Bhimavarapu
https://orcid.org/0000-0002-0246-1420
Department of Computer Science and Engineering, Koneru Lakshmaiah Education Foundation, Vaddeswaram, India

ABSTRACT

Accurate rainfall prediction is essential for agricultural planning and water resource management, particularly in regions like Andhra Pradesh, where the economy relies heavily on monsoon-dependent agriculture. Traditional statistical and empirical models, such as linear regression and ARIMA, have been commonly employed for rainfall forecasting in the region. However, these models often fail to account for the complex, non-linear relationships between variables that influence rainfall, resulting in inaccurate predictions, especially during extreme weather events. This study proposes a hybrid deep learning model combining Bi-LSTM (Bidirectional Long Short-Term Memory) and GRU (Gated Recurrent Unit) to improve rainfall prediction accuracy. The model leverages the strengths of both Bi-LSTM and GRU networks to capture both short- and long-term dependencies in historical rainfall data.

INTRODUCTION

Andhra Pradesh rainfall is very unpredictable since it is dependent on complex climatic conditions, geographical conditions, and seasonal conditions. Andhra Pradesh

DOI: 10.4018/979-8-3373-2387-9.ch006

has a tropical climate with heavy southwest monsoon rains (June to September) and dry weather in winter and summer. Depending on its agrarian economy, rainfall becomes a deciding factor for determining the crop production and food production in the region (Bhatia & Singh, 2024). Precise rainfall forecast is therefore extremely significant in helping the farmers to schedule activities and conserve water in the best manner. However, it is a complex task to predict rainfall in Andhra Pradesh as the state has varying topography, climatic heterogeneity over the areas, and temporal heterogeneity in the weather pattern (Rajesh et al., 2024).

Statistical and empirical models have been conventionally employed to forecast rainfall in Andhra Pradesh, and they have served as the backbone of weather prediction for decades (Ahmar et al., 2023). Historically, among the most widely used techniques are the application of historical rainfall data and linear regression models. These models are based on the premise that it is possible to forecast future rain patterns with the help of history, in which past weather occurrences are attributed to future occurrences. Statistical models like ARIMA (AutoRegressive Integrated Moving Average) have been employed for rainfall forecasting by analyzing time series data with the premise that future observations and trends will linearly relate to their past values (Amshi & Prasad, 2023; Rezaiy & Shabri, 2024; Mulla et al., 2024).

All such traditional models possess some limitations. Firstly, they are not able to effectively interpret the involved and non-linear rainfall processes. Rainfall consists of numerous parameters, such as atmospheric pressure, temperature, humidity, along with topography, modeling of which becomes difficult under the linearity assumption (Kahrari et al., 2024; Shan et al., 2023; Ji et al., 2024; Pawade & Charhate, 2024). Therefore, these models may provide erroneous predictions, especially during unfavorable weather conditions like cyclones, which hit with regular frequency in Andhra Pradesh during monsoon seasons. These models are also not in a position to adapt to evolving weather conditions and are not likely to be useful under real-time prediction of extreme events.

Traditional methods are also constrained by their inability to handle humongous, high-dimensional data. Today's weather forecasting is less concerned with coordinating data from multiple sources, such as satellite pictures, weather stations, and atmospheric models (Rivera et al., 2023). The older techniques do not have the capability to bring the large majority of data into a efficient coordinating manner, thus yielding less precise forecasts. Apart from that, traditional models don't support spatial and temporal interdependencies among rainfall data, and thus they might all fail to capture all the intricate relationships between various geography regions and time periods. That is particularly true in a region like Andhra Pradesh whose rain is highly variant among the various regions.

Seasonal patterns and long-term forecasting are issues with traditional models. There is a significant influence of seasonal monsoon patterns on Andhra Pradesh rainfall, and long-term forecasting is needed for agricultural planning (Thirumal & Latha, 2023; Mohanty et al.2020). The conventional models cannot model the cyclical patterns in rainfall or do not forecast in the long term. For example, most statistical models fail to precisely predict whether monsoon rains are going to be average, sub-average, or super-average since they also oversimplify such complex patterns.

Second, conventional models tend to rely on fixed assumptions about how the variables interact with one another, and therefore, they err when the weather patterns deviate from well-documented past standards. For instance, when the atmospheric conditions are altered due to climate change, normal models will not be able to re-calibrate their predictions accordingly. This lack of adaptability is another fundamental flaw since it does not allow the models to react to new conditions or altering rain patterns. All these limitations render classical models poorer at predicting weather pattern extremes, which have been exacerbated as a result of climatic condition alterations.

The conventional rain forecasting models have been extremely useful in the past but are constrained by several factors that restrict their potential use within the context of advanced, dynamic, and extremely evolving rainfall situations in Andhra Pradesh (Gopinadh Garre & Aswathy, 2024; Swanth & Sheela, 2024; Murthy, 2020). Linearity assumptions, low processing power in dealing with bulk amounts of data, and inability to learn new situations are the areas where more sophisticated models are required. To overcome such limitations and making rainfalls' predictions more predictable, integrating machine learning and deep learning models with the ability to identify abstract patterns, learn to adapt to new cases, and providing more accurate real-time predictions has become more prominent.

Deep learning models have revolutionized rainfall prediction by overcoming some of the built-in faults in traditional methods. Traditional models, such as statistical and empirical models, collapse with the non-linearity and intricacy of rainfall data. These models convert variable relationships to linear dependences or eliminate dynamic interactions between atmospheric conditions, geographical factors, and time-series patterns. On the other hand, deep learning models in particular recurrent neural networks (RNNs) and their variants like Bi-LSTM (Bidirectional Long Short-Term Memory) and GRU (Gated Recurrent Unit) can recognize fine-grained non-linear patterns by learning large and complex pattern databases (Wardani et al., 2024).

Deep learning models are one of the strongest areas of deep models in that they can process vast datasets, unlike other models. Most of the classical models of prediction like ARIMA and regression have permanent assumptions about data and are unable to process large amounts of information without assumptions (Suman, 2024; Seyedan et al., 2023).

Deep learning models, however, do not require pre-defined feature engineering and are able to learn important features from the data itself. This renders them highly efficient in processing large-scale rainfall data sets. For example, the Bi-LSTM+G-RU model is able to process large-scale time-series data and learn to automatically extract the most important features for rainfall prediction.

Classical models are also baffled to cope with advanced temporal and spatial dependency, which has great importance in accurate rainfall prediction. Rainfall behavior is guided by a number of determinants like geographical components, seasonally varying components, and interaction of atmospheric components. Classical models could be unable to cope with such advanced dependencies when the rainfall phenomenon involves long-range processes or interrupted changes. The Bi-LSTM+GRU model, possessing the ability to comprehend both long-range dependencies using Bi-LSTM and noisy data elimination using GRU's gate mechanism, is able to comprehend such spatial and temporal dependencies with ease and predict more precisely.

Further, the traditional models are also limited when it comes to integrating real-time data, especially when weather conditions are changing at a rapid rate. All except for the majority of traditional techniques are not dynamically calibrated according to recent meteorological information, thus inferior in the case of extreme weather. Models of deep learning like Bi-LSTM+GRU learn over time from most recent available information and revise their predictions by getting real-time inputs. This process of dynamic learning enables the model to learn rapidly from sudden weather variations, enabling accurate and timely forecasts of rainfall even in rapid-shifting weather conditions.

The second best aspect of the Bi-LSTM+GRU model is its ability to respond to seasonal effects and long-range forecasting. Majority of traditional models never consider precipitation cycles, such as monsoon cycles that annually function in the states of Andhra Pradesh. The Seasonal patterns are governed by Bi-LSTM network with respect to forward and backward pass of input, thereby remembering the history patterns of rainfall and predicting future climatic conditions. GRU and gate mechanism does not allow it to remember everything of season pattern knowledge and throw the rest of them away and hence making model efficient while forecasting rainfall for short- and long-time scales.

The hybrid Bi-LSTM+GRU model also works best when predicting extreme rainfall, which is often most important for decision-making in agriculture, water planning, and disaster readiness. Conventional models are inferior to predict extreme rain events such as heavy rain resulting from cyclones or prolonged dry spells during drought. The ability of the Bi-LSTM+GRU model to uncover underlying patterns in rain data, including extreme event prediction, is making it an invaluable tool for states like Andhra Pradesh, whose economy and public safety are directly impacted by the extremes. With learning from historical extreme events and using its gated and bidirectional memory, the model enhances the accuracy of forecasts, making more accurate future rain event predictions possible.

Bi-LSTM+GRU deep learning models possess the great benefit of conventional rainfall forecasting models. With the ability to efficiently surpass the shortcomings of conventional methods, i.e., inability to identify non-linear relationships, manage huge data, and learn from past data, Bi-LSTM+GRU models can provide more precise, dynamic, and complete rainfall forecasts. Their ability to generalize from past and future rain data, refine their forecasts by gated memory operations, and learn predicting on the basis of novel weather conditions renders them effective in enhancing the forecasting ability of Andhra Pradesh. It can be employed in enhancing agricultural decision-making, water resource management, and disaster relief in the case of catastrophe and end up resulting in more proactive planning grounded on good information under new climate conditions.

MATERIALS AND METHODOLOGY

The strategy begins with the fetching of the daily rainfall data from the WRIS database, for historical rainfall patterns in years 1980-2023. Preprocessing includes missing value treatment, normalization, and feature extraction as temporal features and lag values. The Bi-LSTM+GRU model introduced here faces the data with both short- and long-term relations extracted, with bidirectional patterns learned by Bi-LSTM and GRU fine-tuning the sequence data.

Materials

For the data collection of this composite weather forecast model for Andhra Pradesh, the process is to gather daily rainfall data from the Water Resources Information System (WRIS), a systematic and exhaustive database overseen by the Indian Government's Ministry of Jal Shakti. WRIS offers a rich set of hydrological and meteorological data, with access to required historical rainfall data across India. Rainfall information was pulled from WRIS for the purposes of this study to offer a good foundation for modelization and analysis, (Shah et al., 2021). The rains are daily records spread across over four decades, from 1980 up to 2023, offering the model good historical data on rainfall trends and patterns. All this historical information helps capture seasonality of the data, long-term drift, and exceptional events, which are all essential for proper model training. Given so much of this kind of historical data available for rainfall, the model achieves a tighter understanding of local climatic conditions and lays the stage for high-accuracy forecasts which are well suited for Andhra Pradesh.

Preprocessing

There is a need to preprocess the WRIS daily rainfall data in ensuring data quality and readiness for modeling.

Data cleaning is the first step where missing values are found and corrected. The gaps could be filled via interpolation or through substituting the missing values using season or monthly means, thereby having continuity of data. Outliers, usually a product of data entry or anomalous weather, are also picked up and corrected, usually by using statistical methods or domain knowledge to eliminate or normalize outlier values. The dataset is then cleaned to ready it for machine learning following this step. Temporal aggregation is performed, especially for exploratory purposes, but data at the daily level is retained for training the models. Additionally, rainfall values are standardized or normalized so that they are brought to the same level in terms of comparability, thus enhancing the performance and convergence of the neural networks during learning.

Feature Extraction

Feature extraction is a highly crucial step where the trend and seasonality features are induced which reflect trends such as seasonal rainfall peaks or long-run drifts.

Lagged indicators are also introduced, like precipitation in previous days, weeks, or months, to provide the model with some context to base its predictions upon. Moving averages and smoothing procedures then purify the dataset some more by weeding out the noise, extracting important trends. Temporal encoding follows, where periodic date characteristics like month or season are encoded using sine and cosine functions to elicit the seasonality in rainfall data. The data is then split into training, validation, and test sets for training without disrupting the sequence of time so that future data can be utilized as the test phase without disrupting model training. Data is restructured in order to match the input requirement of sequence models, where slid windows of lagged days act as input for each target day to be predicted.

The entire preprocessing task sets the dataset up to be uniform, clean, and prepared in order to trap historical weather patterns, thereby the model capacity of predicting rainfall daily for Andhra Pradesh with much accuracy.

Hybrid Model

Hybrid GRU model and Bi-LSTM model utilizes data sequentially to recognize temporal relationships between input time series data and output time series data in a highly well-organized thought process. The following is a step-by-step description of how the data passes through each block of the model from input to output:

Input Sequence

The input to the model is in the form of a time step sequence such that for every time step there exists a corresponding day of rain data.

The model uses a sliding window approach to predict rain on any day based on the data of past days as features.

For instance, to forecast rain on Day(t), the input sequence would be rainfall amounts for the last 7 days (rain on Day (t-1), Day (t-2), ., Day (t-7)).

This enables the model to observe past rain patterns and make wiser forecasts. This input series is first propagated to the Bi-LSTM layer, which takes the input bidirectionally. Through the forward pass, the initial LSTM network learns from the sequence from Day (t-7) up to Day(t), which comprises long dependencies and trends in the rainfall. Through the backward pass, the second LSTM travels over the sequence in reverse order, from Day (t) to Day (t-7).

The bidirectional pass enables both future and past contexts to be utilized by the model in order to augment each time step representation. Features from forward passes and backward passes are combined against each other, and this provides a high-feature representation with the presence of good dependencies in one direction or the other. Two-way processing of the data allows the Bi-LSTM layer such that it allows the model to learn not only the impact of the previous rain but also the manner in which conditions in the future can influence the prediction and, thus, enhances the performance of the model. This enhanced output is then transferred to subsequent layers, i.e., the GRU layer or dense layers, to further train and predict. Lastly, the two-way learning procedure makes the model capable of proper extraction of temporal patterns out of rain data such that it is able to better predict future rain based on better understanding past and contextual trends.

Bi-LSTM Layer

In the Bi-LSTM layer, the input sequence is passed through two LSTM networks operating in opposite directions: one in the forward direction from past to future and another in the backward direction from future to past. The forward LSTM reads the input sequence in its original sequence, placing the dependencies of previous time steps upon it and recognizing patterns and trends affecting data as it moves towards the future.

This forward pass helps the model realize how past rainfall data is affecting current and future values.

The backwards LSTM reads from the sequence from newer data, in reverse. Back-tracking with this preserves dependencies and dynamics potentially introduced by forward values in each individual time step, allowing the model to learn potential influences that future states have and use those for all prediction. This is facilitated for the Bi-LSTM layer due to two-way processing, enabling the layer to learn additional dependency and detail contained in the data while taking past as well as future context into account.

Once both the forward and backward LSTMs have processed the input sequence, their outputs are combined at each time step to create a rich feature representation. The combined output includes both directions' understanding, giving the model a richer context for each day with knowledge of what has happened already and what will probably come next. This less overt representation is the foundation for accurate forecasting through enabling the model to leverage history and context.

GRU Layer

The GRU layer receives the concatenated output of the Bi-LSTM layer and again extract essential sequential relationships and remove redundancy.

The gating mechanism of the GRU—i.e., the reset gate and update gate—allows it to selectively preserve or ignore information while computing each step of the sequence.

This allows the GRU layer to consider only the most important features from the Bi-LSTM output, essentially propagating the most important insights while keeping the computational complexity under control.

The reset gate in the GRU controls how much previous information is "forgotten" in generating the current output, and the update gate controls how much information from the current input should come into the output. These gates together allow the GRU to focus on important patterns and disregard noise or less important detail. By fine-grained enriching the sequence data in this way, the GRU layer provides a terminal context-rich representation of the rainfall data that contains important sequential information obtained from the bidirectional processing of the Bi-LSTM layer. This last representation, which best integrates both past and future contexts, is then ready to be used by the forecasting output layer, so that the model's predictions are based on a consistent well-processed realization of the temporal patterns in the data.

Fully Connected (Dense) Layer

The output of the GRU layer is passed into a dense (fully connected) layer, and that is the final step of taking processed sequence data from the model and spitting it out into target prediction form. The dense layer takes the input from the GRU and goes through the input and takes the processed and filtered sequence data and plugs that into the final output value—a predicted amount of rainfall for the target day.

Here, the neuron is connected to the learned features from the output of the GRU, therefore enabling the model to learn rainfall values in relation to the learned features. It is in learning the relations through updated weights during training utilizing the dense layer that the model's prediction accuracy is enhanced. By this last conversion, the dense layer properly transforms the temporal knowledge acquired throughout the network into a proper prediction of rainfall.

Output

The output of the model is an estimated quantity of rainfall for the target day or days as requested, depending on the chosen prediction horizon.

During training time, this predicted output is matched against the true rainfall values to calculate the error of the model, typically with a loss function such as Mean Squared Error (MSE).

Thereafter, an optimizing algorithm, such as the Adam optimizer, adjusts the model's weights in the Bi-LSTM and GRU layers to minimize such prediction errors over time.

Through this, the model learns over time to become more accurate, and its ability to discover and apply similar patterns in the rainfall data. This time processing chain—from the bidirectional learning of the Bi-LSTM layer for detecting implicit past and future dependencies through to the selective memory mechanism of the GRU layer—allows the model to be able to sufficiently detect short- and long-range dependencies in the rainfall data. With an integration of these mechanisms, hybrid Bi-LSTM and GRU model creates highly accurate and effective forecasting system transforming sequential input into precise predictions with the ability to discover temporal patterns in order to deliver quality rainfall forecasts.

Model Optimization

For guaranteeing the forecast model to be efficient in training and achieving maximum prediction accuracy, grid search (GS) and cross-validation (CV) are used for identifying the optimal set of hyperparameters.

Grid search performs a list of hyperparameters on its own, e.g., units per layer, batch size, and learning rate, in order to select the list which works best.

Cross-validation wraps up by measuring model performance across many subsets of the training set to see if the best hyperparameters are correctly generalizing and not being trained on one subset of the data.

Concurrently, the procedure prevents overfitting and yields an efficient model configuration. Once hyperparameters have been optimized, the Adam optimization algorithm still adjusts internal weights and bias of the model during training. Adam, adaptive learning rates and sparse gradient effective, incrementally updates weights from gradients of computed loss function. Continuous updating minimizes prediction errors and increases model convergence.

Optimization of the weights and biases with Adam makes the model more cost-efficient to identify the underlying patterns in the data and thereby offer better accuracy for rainfall prediction. This end-to-end optimization process with grid search, cross-validation, and Adam optimizer optimizes the model as highly efficient as well as perfectly tuned for accurate prediction.

Performance Measures

To evaluate the effectiveness of different forecast models in quantitative analysis, several error metrics are commonly used, including Mean Square Error (MSE), Root Mean Square Error (RMSE), and Mean Absolute Error (MAE). Each of these metrics provides unique insights into the model's predictive performance by measuring the discrepancy between the predicted and actual values.

Mean Square Error (MSE)

This metric calculates the average of the squared differences between predicted and actual values. It is represented as:

$$\text{MSE} = \frac{1}{n}\sum_{i=1}^{n}(y_i - \hat{y}_i)^2$$

where y_i is the actual value, $\hat{y}_i$ is the predicted value, and n is the total number of predictions. MSE gives a higher penalty to larger errors, making it sensitive to outliers and particularly useful for identifying large deviations in predictions.

Root Mean Square Error (RMSE)

RMSE is the square root of MSE, providing a measure in the same units as the target variable. The formula is:

$$\text{RMSE} = \sqrt{\frac{1}{n}\sum_{i=1}^{n}(y_i - \hat{y}_i)^2}$$

RMSE is often used to gauge the average magnitude of prediction errors, as it combines both the frequency and severity of errors, helping to understand the overall accuracy of the model in real-world terms.

Mean Absolute Error (MAE)

MAE calculates the average of the absolute differences between predicted and actual values. It is given by:

$$\text{MAE} = \frac{1}{n}\sum_{i=1}^{n}|y_i - \hat{y}_i|$$

Unlike MSE and RMSE, MAE does not square the error, making it less sensitive to outliers. It provides a straightforward measure of the average error magnitude and is often easier to interpret.

Using these metrics together provides a comprehensive evaluation of the forecast model's accuracy, reliability, and sensitivity to larger deviations, enabling a more thorough comparison of different models' performance.

Experimental Results

The performance is confirmed using measures like MSE, RMSE, MAE, and R^2 to compare with traditional models like ARIMA and machine learning models. The performances are compared based on prediction accuracy with a suggestion of deep learning dominance in rain forecasting.

Table 1 represented the performance of the rain fall forecast. The three tables indicate the performance of various forecasting models employed to predict daily rainfall in Andhra Pradesh, in terms of Mean Squared Error (MSE), Root Mean Squared Error (RMSE), Mean Absolute Error (MAE), and R^2, which indicate the reliability and accuracy of each model. The highest performing model is Bi-LSTM + GRU in Table 1(a) with train results, having lowest MSE (0.012), RMSE (0.109), and MAE (0.085) which signifies that it performs best when trained. It also has an R^2 value of 0.92 which signifies that it accounts for 92% of variability in the train data. LSTM, GRU, and CNN + LSTM models also show competitive performance, but with slightly higher MSE and RMSE values and lower R^2 scores. ARIMA, Random Forest, Support Vector, and Decision Tree classical models show very poor performance, as evidenced by higher error metrics and lower R^2 values.

In Table 1(b) with results validated, Bi-LSTM + GRU is once more leading the rest with MSE of 0.015, RMSE of 0.122, and MAE of 0.091. These are slightly larger than during training but the model once again performs well with excellent generalization and an R^2 of 0.90. Both GRU and LSTM models perform similarly but with more distinct variations from the Bi-LSTM + GRU model. Conventional models once more suffer from performance decline, particularly with their higher MSE and RMSE values, reflecting difficulty to generalize along with the deep learning models.

Finally, in Table 1(c), the testing performance, Bi-LSTM + GRU is still the best with an MSE of 0.017, RMSE of 0.130, and MAE of 0.095, and R^2 score of 0.89. While the performance is slightly decreased from training and validation phase, the model is still very effective in handling unseen data. The next are the other deep learning models such as LSTM, GRU, and CNN + LSTM but with increasingly higher error measurement. More traditional models such as ARIMA, Random Forest, SVR, and Decision Tree are still recording mounting errors and R^2 values showing their inadequacies in predicting daily rainfall in relation to superior contemporary deep learning models.

Overall, the Bi-LSTM + GRU model gives better performance than all the other models for training, validation, and testing phases. The model can place itself as a strong model to predict rainfall on a daily basis from long-range dependencies and complex patterns in the data. Compared to the traditional models like ARIMA, Random Forest, Support Vector, and Decision Tree, they do not deliver when handling the complexity of predicting rainfall on a day-by-day basis, as evident from their high value of error and low R^2 values. The Bi-LSTM + GRU models and deep learning models are much more accurate and consistent in rainfall prediction, an indicator of their stronger capacity to extract the complex, nonlinear time-varying relations present in the data.

Table 1-3 represents model performance metrics for daily rainfall forecasting among other measurements.

Table 1. Training Results

Model	MSE	RMSE	MAE	R^2
Bi-LSTM + GRU	0.012	0.109	0.085	0.92
LSTM	0.018	0.134	0.101	0.89
GRU	0.022	0.148	0.113	0.87
CNN + LSTM	0.024	0.155	0.115	0.86
Transformer	0.026	0.161	0.118	0.85
CNN	0.030	0.173	0.125	0.83
ARIMA	0.034	0.184	0.130	0.81
Random Forest	0.036	0.190	0.133	0.80
Support Vector	0.040	0.200	0.140	0.78
Decision Tree	0.045	0.212	0.148	0.76

Table 2. Validation Results

Model	MSE	RMSE	MAE	R^2
Bi-LSTM + GRU	0.015	0.122	0.091	0.90
LSTM	0.020	0.141	0.104	0.88
GRU	0.024	0.155	0.115	0.86
CNN + LSTM	0.026	0.161	0.120	0.85
Transformer	0.029	0.170	0.123	0.83
CNN	0.032	0.179	0.128	0.82
ARIMA	0.035	0.187	0.132	0.80
Random Forest	0.038	0.195	0.135	0.79
SVR	0.042	0.205	0.142	0.77
Decision Tree	0.047	0.216	0.149	0.75

Table 3. Testing Results

Model	MSE	RMSE	MAE	R^2
Bi-LSTM + GRU	0.017	0.130	0.095	0.89
LSTM	0.022	0.148	0.108	0.87
GRU	0.026	0.161	0.118	0.85
CNN + LSTM	0.029	0.170	0.124	0.84
Transformer	0.032	0.179	0.129	0.82
CNN	0.036	0.190	0.135	0.80
ARIMA	0.038	0.195	0.138	0.78
Random Forest	0.041	0.202	0.143	0.77
SVR	0.044	0.210	0.146	0.76
Decision Tree	0.048	0.219	0.152	0.74

Figure 1 depicts the predicted and actual rainfall in Andhra Pradesh. The model prediction performance is also very heterogeneous with Bi-LSTM + GRU performing the best as it has the capability to capture long-range and short-range dependencies efficiently.

The model also produces predictions nearest to the actual rainfall values and demonstrate the performance of the model in processing difficult sequential data. LSTM also performs reasonably well in identifying sequential patterns but with relatively higher discrepancies from Bi-LSTM + GRU outputs, with a moderate error rate in rainfall prediction.

The GRU model, while efficient, shows slightly greater errors compared to LSTM, showing greater deviations in the prediction. The CNN + LSTM model is less time-series oriented and shows greater error rates. While convolutional layers are stronger in feature extraction, the model is not properly predicting rainfall and thus shows greater deviations from actual values. Likewise, the Transformer model, while good at capturing dependency through self-attention methods, performs badly with this particular issue of prediction, committing more mistakes in its prediction with its complexity.

The CNN model, better than the image processing task, is cautious while performing a correct prediction of time-series data such as rain and provides more uncertain predictions. The conventional time-series model ARIMA also forecasts intricate, non-stationary data such as rainfall and is subjected to huge errors in relation to the real values of rainfall. The conventional methods such as Random Forest and Support Vector Regressor (SVR) are with relatively higher errors, which show lower reliability in rainfall forecast.

Finally, the Decision Tree model does the worst when it comes to prediction, likely because of overfitting and sensitivity to noisy data. It results in extreme variation of predicted and actual values. Although deep models such as Bi-LSTM + GRU and LSTM have higher and more effective predictions, simple models such as ARIMA, Random Forest, and Decision Tree are less in this case, with increased rates of prediction errors.

Figure 1. Actual and predicted rainfall comparison

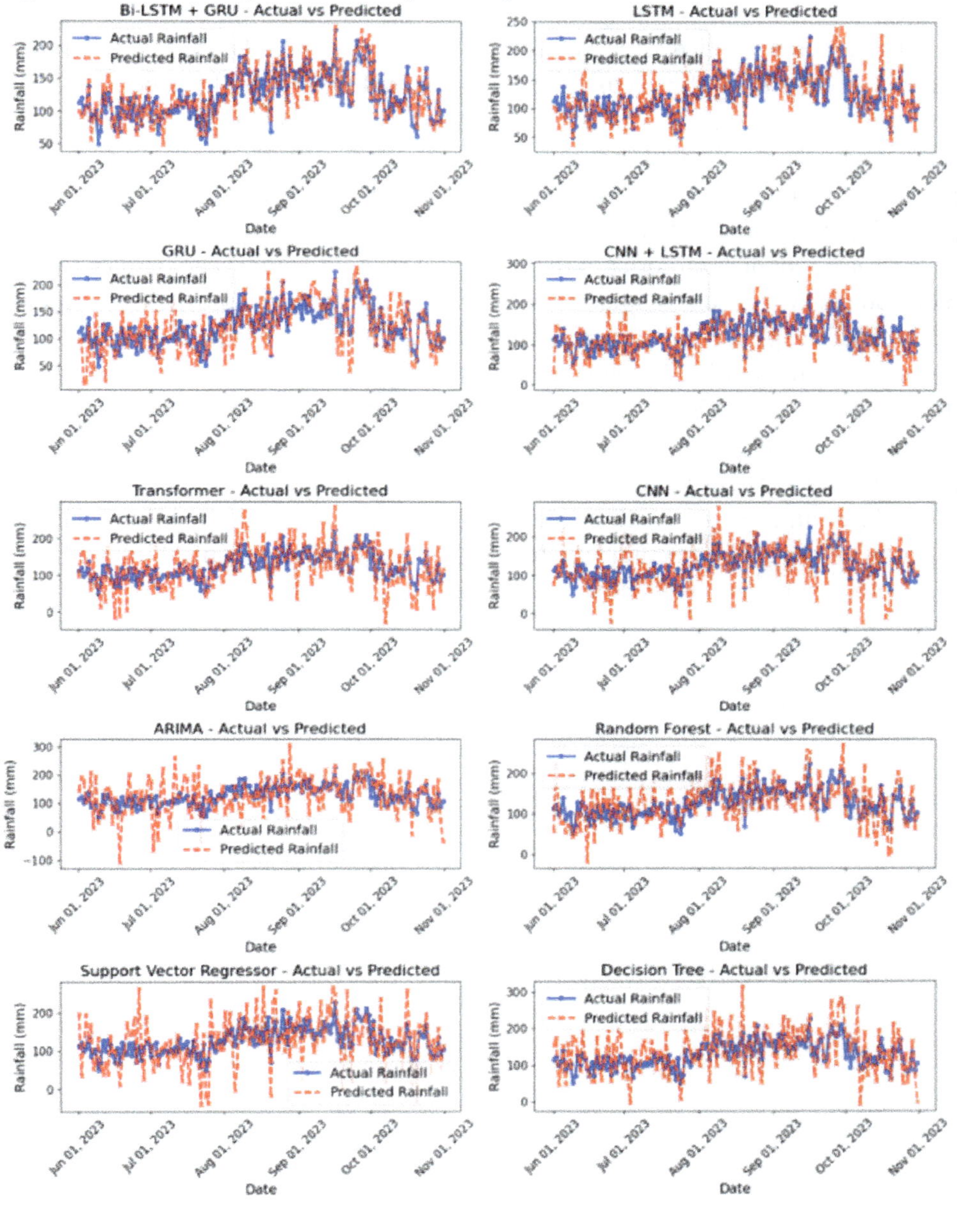

CONCLUSION

The research confirms the validity of hybrid Bi-LSTM+GRU deep learning models in enhancing the accuracy of Andhra Pradesh's rainfall prediction. Compared to conventional models that lack the capability to identify weak non-linear interrelationship and trends of rainfall records, the suggested model is efficient in effectively intertwining temporal and spatial features that enhance its ability in predicting outcomes. With bidirectional processing of rain data and GRU's capacity to eliminate redundant information, the Bi-LSTM+GRU model can predict rainfall more precisely, especially under dynamic seasonal and geographical conditions. The model's capacity to learn from new data and manage big data makes it ideal for real-time forecasting in dynamic climates. The findings of this research unveil the capability of deep learning models to surpass the shortcomings of conventional forecasting techniques and provide a beneficial tool for enhanced water resource planning and supporting agricultural decision-making in regions such as Andhra Pradesh. Future research will be directed towards further refining the model by including more environmental variables and improving its generalizability for more widespread applications in climate prediction.

REFERENCES

Ahmar, A. S., Singh, P. K., Ruliana, R., Pandey, A. K., & Gupta, S. (2023). Comparison of ARIMA, SutteARIMA, and holt-winters, and NNAR models to predict food grain in India. *Forecasting*, *5*(1), 138–152.

Amshi, A. H., & Prasad, R. (2023). Time series analysis and forecasting of cholera disease using discrete wavelet transform and seasonal autoregressive integrated moving average model. *Scientific African*, *20*, e01652.

Bhatia, S., & Singh, S. P. (2024). Assessing Groundwater Use Efficiency and Productivity across Punjab Agriculture: District and Farm Size Perspectives. *Agriculture*, *14*(8), 1299.

Gopinadh Garre, S. S., & Aswathy, V. K. (2024). Examining Rainfall Trends in Guntur District, Andhra Pradesh, India, Amidst the Climate Change Challenge: A Comprehensive Analysis of Global Warming Impacts. In *Climate Change and Human Adaptation in India: Sustainability and Public Policy* (pp. 79–100). Springer Nature Switzerland.

Ji, R., Wang, C., Cui, A., Jia, M., Liao, S., Wang, W., & Chen, N. (2024). Assessing terrestrial water storage dynamics and multiple factors driving forces in China from 2005 to 2020. *Journal of Environmental Management*, *370*, 122464. PMID: 39265495

Kahrari, P., Khaledi, S., Keikhosravi, G., & Alavi, S. J. (2024). Application of machine learning and deep learning techniques in modeling the associations between air pollution and meteorological parameters in urban areas of tehran metropolis. *Environmental Monitoring and Assessment*, *196*(10), 994. PMID: 39352511

Mohanty, U. C., Sinha, P., Rao, M. N., Swain, D. K., & Singh, K. K. (2020)Climate Risk Management in Agriculture.

Mulla, S., Pande, C. B., & Singh, S. K. (2024). Times Series Forecasting of Monthly Rainfall using Seasonal Auto Regressive Integrated Moving Average with EXogenous Variables (SARIMAX) Model. *Water Resources Management*, *38*(6), 1825–1846.

Murthy, R. V. R. (2020). *Mapping Spatio-Temporal Cropland Changes Due To Water Stress In Krishna River Basin Using Temporal Satellite Data* (Doctoral dissertation, College of Engineering (A), Andhra University, Visakhapatnam).

Pawade, A., & Charhate, S. (2024). Assessing environmental influences on radon levels: Analysis of independent variables. *Mathematical Models in Engineering*, *10*(3), 168–192.

Rajesh, R., Mathews, G. V., Rao, N. P., & Begum, S. K. (2024). Groundwater-level prediction in Visakhapatnam district, Andhra Pradesh, India, using Bayesian Neural Networks. *Acta Geophysica*, *72*(4), 2759–2772.

Rezaiy, R., & Shabri, A. (2024). An innovative hybrid W-EEMD-ARIMA model for drought forecasting using the standardized precipitation index. *Natural Hazards*, ●●●, 1–30.

Rivera, A., Ponce, P., Mata, O., Molina, A., & Meier, A. (2023). Local weather station design and development for cost-effective environmental monitoring and real-time data sharing. *Sensors (Basel)*, *23*(22), 9060. PMID: 38005448

Seyedan, M., Mafakheri, F., & Wang, C. (2023). Order-up-to-level inventory optimization model using time-series demand forecasting with ensemble deep learning. *Supply Chain Analytics*, *3*, 100024.

Shah, N. V., & Patel, Y. S., & DBhangaonkar, P. (2021). Assessing impact of climate change on rainfall patterns of Vadodara District, Gujarat, India. [). IOP Publishing.]. *Journal of Physics: Conference Series*, *1714*(1), 012046.

Shan, S., Wang, Y., Xie, X., Fan, T., Xiao, Y., Zhang, K., & Wei, H. (2023). Analysis of regional climate variables by using neural Granger causality. *Neural Computing & Applications*, *35*(22), 16381–16402.

Suman, D. (2024). Deep Learning Methods for Demand Time Series Forecasting.

Swanth, B., & Sheela, J. (2024, January). Agricultural Yield Forecasting with the Fusion of Transfer Learning and LSTM Approach. In *2024 2nd International Conference on Intelligent Data Communication Technologies and Internet of Things (IDCIoT)* (pp. 1268-1277). IEEE.

Thirumal, S., & Latha, R. (2023). Machine Learning Based Predictive Assessments of Impacts of Influential Climatic Conditions for the Sustainable Productivity of Paddy Crops. *SSRG International Journal of Electronics and Communication Engineering*, *10*(5), 117–128.

Wardani, A. K., Kristalina, P., Hadi, M. Z. S., & Pratiarso, A. (2024, August). Bidirectional Long Short-Term Memory Method for Weather Prediction in Terms of Evacuation of River Drifting Victims. In *2024 International Electronics Symposium (IES)* (pp. 663-668). IEEE.

Chapter 7
Air Pollution Prediction Using the Deep Learning Stacked Approach

Usharani Bhimavarapu
https://orcid.org/0000-0002-0246-1420
Department of Computer Science and Engineering, Koneru Lakshmaiah Education Foundation, Vaddeswaram, India

ABSTRACT

Air pollution prediction plays a critical role in managing public health and environmental policies, especially in regions like India, where air quality is rapidly deteriorating due to urbanization, industrialization, and other anthropogenic activities. This study aims to predict air pollution levels, specifically PM2.5 concentrations, using a deep learning approach—stacked Bidirectional Gated Recurrent Units (BiGRU). The proposed model leverages the advantages of BiGRU to capture both temporal dependencies and complex, non-linear relationships in air pollution data. The study compares the performance of the stacked BiGRU model with traditional statistical and machine learning models, such as Linear Regression, ARIMA, and Support Vector Machines (SVM).

INTRODUCTION

Air pollution is the presence of toxic substances in the air, including particulate matter (PM), gases like nitrogen dioxide (NO_2), sulfur dioxide (SO_2), carbon monoxide (CO), and volatile organic compounds (VOCs), not only harmful to the environment but also to human health. They are typically released by industry, motorized vehicles, agriculture, and natural occurrences like forest fires or dust storms. Air

DOI: 10.4018/979-8-3373-2387-9.ch007

quality in a location is typically measured in terms of the concentration of suspended particles, especially PM2.5 and PM10, suspended particles with diameters of 2.5 and 10 micrometers, respectively. Suspended particles can penetrate the blood and lungs deep and lead to serious health issues.

Air pollution has become a growing issue in India during the past few years with specific focus on urban cities like Delhi, Mumbai, and Kolkata. The country has some of the globe's worst air with PM2.5 readings oftentimes well into unhealthy levels. Urbanization and industrialization combined with an increasing number of automobiles have caused heavily poor air. Crop burning and weather conditions elsewhere in the country during crop seasons and even natural seasonal conditions contribute to the situation, especially during winters when the pollution is the worst.

India's air pollution has a gigantic reach and severity. Health suffers most from the constant exposure to filthy air making the gambit of respiratory disease, cardiovascular disease, and cancer worse. The most vulnerable are particularly most exposed, such as children, the aged, and those with pre-existing condition. Reports by World Health Organization (WHO) indicate that air pollution alone results in tens of millions of premature deaths annually in India. Furthermore, air pollution is also economically costly to productivity as it contributes to increased healthcare costs, reduced worker productivity, and loss of working days due to illness. The economic burden of air pollution is significant and puts economic strain on the individual and the health system.

Apart from health, air pollution destroys the environment. Air pollution increases the level of greenhouse gases, mainly carbon dioxide (CO_2) and methane, that contribute to global warming. Pollution also kills natural ecosystems and negatively affects soil and plants. Air pollutants like sulfur dioxide contribute to acid rain, which deteriorates water bodies and destroys aquatic organisms in some areas. The agriculture industry in India is also compromised by pollution because polluted air can delay plant growth, reduce farm production, and affect food quality. Curbing air pollution in India is not only being tried but done, from tightening automobile exhaust emission controls to promoting the use of renewable energy and enhanced waste management. The problem, though, is one that is difficult to rectify with the rate of development in India and the complexity of the problem.

Air pollution forecasting is significant for many reasons. It allows governments to forecast air quality levels, which provides individuals and governments with sufficient notice to reduce the impact of poor air quality on health. Anticipatory forecasting can initiate the release of health advisories, preventing sensitive groups such as children, the elderly, and individuals with pre-existing illness from going outside for recreation. Furthermore, the prediction of air pollution concentration helps urban planning to enable governments to control industrial emissions, transportation policy, and waste management. Accurate predictions help in estimating the long-term impacts of pollution on the environment, public health, and economy, and guide the mitigation efforts to reduce exposure. Past air pollution prediction models utilize statistical modeling, machine learning techniques, and deterministic models. Several of the traditionally used methods that are widely used include Linear Regression, Multiple Regression, Time Series Prediction (e.g., ARIMA models), and Support Vector Machines (SVMs). These models work by reading past data and identifying trends and employing them to predict future air quality levels. Linear regression models, for instance, operate on establishing a linear relationship between independent variables (e.g., weather or traffic) and dependent variables (air quality indices). Similarly, ARIMA models have made use of time series to predict future concentrations of pollutants.

These traditional models do possess some limitations, however. First, they rely on linear relations among input variables, and that is not always true with complex environmental data where the air can be affected by non-linear and interconnected variables. Second, such models are vulnerable to overfitting, especially when they try to simulate complex interactions using very simple forms. Third, traditional models are not very efficient in handling large and high-dimensional data that are prevalent in air pollution data and do not handle temporal and spatial interdependencies with ease. The models are also not easy to handle dynamic environmental fluctuations, such as quick spikes in vehicle emissions or unexpected weather patterns, that tend to affect air quality very much.

Deep learning offers a solution to the limitation of conventional models through a stronger, more flexible, and scalable approach in air pollution forecasting. Deep learning models or Artificial Neural Networks (ANNs) can learn intricate patterns from data without needing explicit feature engineering like conventional models. They perform best in capturing intricate interactions between different input features, including weather, traffic flow, and pollutant concentrations, which classical models will lose. In addition, deep learning models are highly efficient in dealing with large data of high dimensions and generalize better than classical models to reduce the problem of overfitting.

Deep learning has the ability to learn non-linear interactions between the input features, which in air pollution prediction comes handy since most parameters, for example, traffic, wind direction, and temperature, are nonlinearly combined to represent air quality. Deep learning models better capture these interactions than traditional models. Deep learning models are also driven by data and require fewer human efforts for feature engineering as well as feature selection. This makes them efficiently handle complex data sets and changing environmental conditions.

The Stacked Bidirectional Gated Recurrent Units (BiGRU) model is a robust deep learning method that clearly improves the prediction accuracy of air pollution over other deep learning methods. The BiGRU model is an enhanced version of the

Gated Recurrent Unit (GRU) model, which is a recurrent neural network (RNN) that is highly effective in dealing with sequential data. BiGRU, particularly, can process data both in forward and reverse directions and thus learn the complete temporal context of data more easily. This is particularly helpful in the case of forecasting air pollution because pollutant concentrations are set by numerous variables that change over time, e.g., traffic volume and weather.

Stacking refers to the practice of stacking several GRU layers in a bid to have the model learn complex patterns better. In the case of a stacked BiGRU architecture, the GRU layers are overlaid one on top of another in a manner that allows the network to learn successively and increasingly complex features from one layer to the next. This enables the model to learn short and long dependencies in air pollution data in an adequate manner, which is critical for accurate forecasting. Stacked layers enable deeper and more expressive models to have the capacity to learn strongly non-linear relationships and intricate patterns of data.

The study provides an overview of sources, impacts, and solutions to air pollutants but in the absence of empirical data or case study analysis, the applicability of such an overview to real-world context is limited (Odubo & Kosoe, 2024). The suggested solutions are also general and do not take into account socioeconomic or environmental conditions of different places (Odubo & Kosoe, 2024).

The research is said to find a correlation with particulate matter and COVID-19 impact in Milan but is geographically specific and may not be extended to regions of another climatic or population profile. Second, utilization of observation data includes potential confounding variables, which were not entirely adjusted for (Zoran et al., 2020).

Although the research provides full morphological and biochemical characteristics of particulate matter, it is incomplete because it only considers urban and not rural and industrial ones. Additionally, the study does not measure the health implication of these characteristics, hence creating a gap for understanding how they influence human health directly (Ahmad et al., 2023).

The study is able to link air quality to trends in the growth of eight Indian cities but is constrained by cross-sectional design that doesn't allow for causality to be determined. Additionally, the analysis isn't able to account properly for policy interventions and technological advancements that could have influenced the trends in the urban air quality (Sharma & Ghuge, 2024).

This longitudinal assessment provides critical data on inter-seasonal and urban air pollutant variability; however, its drawback lies in the lack of predictive modeling or future scenario analysis. Second, it is heavily reliant on past data without integrating real-time monitoring systems, thus becoming less user-friendly for anticipatory policy actions (Sharma et al., 2024).

While the review appropriately integrates the interrelationship between air quality and urbanization, the review does not integrate empirical data to validate the proposed models of sustainable urbanization. The study also does not clarify potential contradictions between green infrastructure implementation and rapid urbanization for developing countries (Zhang et al., 2022).

The article offers methodological critical issues in low air pollution level studies but focuses mostly on Western environments and does not account for baseline high-pollution communities. It also gives priority to conceptual overviews rather than empirical solutions and hence is of limited near-term policy-relevance (Papadogeorgou et al., 2019).

The study estimates India's reduction in premature mortality, but the study does not pay much attention to internal regional differences in the country. Furthermore, the analysis assumes the continued scale-up of WHO-recommended interventions, which may not always hold true in all states and economic levels (Kulothungan et al., 2024).

Although multivariate adaptive regression splines usage offers advanced modeling, secondary data use for research limits it from passing through global micro-level forces, such as neighborhood labor policy or underground labor markets. The model does not account for whether it has lag effects for air pollution exposure and productivity (Muzayyanah et al., 2023).

This chapter provides a very sound theoretical case for carbon dioxide and global climate change but lacks empirical case studies showing actual practice of decarbonization initiatives. Conceptual methods as a focus narrow the capacity to measure the concrete practicability and cost aspects of suggested measures in practice (Ramirez-Corredores et al., 2023).

The study completely calculates national contributions towards global warming but is constrained by the uncertainties in past emission inventories and harmonization of data between countries. Also, the study does not consider the contribution of emerging economies for future projections and only handles historical trends (Jones et al., 2023).

Though the paper has a general impression of Indian city emission sources, its data are relatively outdated and therefore guaranteed to downplay the contribution of emerging industrial and automotive expansion. Moreover, the study does not examine the efficacy of contemporary abatement measures, and hence the study is less relevant to contemporary policymaking objectives (Guttikunda et al., 2014).

The study shows the application of CNN-LSTM and CONV-LSTM models for PM2.5 prediction but with the use of historic data to a large extent, ignoring real-time adaptability as well as the limitations of sensor networks. The study further fails to give comparative studies with simple models to investigate the cost-effectiveness of large-scale implementation (Putri et al., 2024).

The study best employs an ANN-based regression model when predicting NOx emissions for underground mining machinery but is plagued predominantly by being domain-specific in reference to a dataset that is not generalizable across industries. In addition, the study does not explore hybrid or ensemble methods with which enhanced predictability can be achieved under varying operating conditions (Banasiewicz et al., 2023).

While the study shows improved air quality forecasting accuracy by combining machine learning with CAMS output, the weakness of reliance on Copernicus data itself is that it might not reflect local microclimates. Heterogeneous geography and scalability of the model to the size of the world are also not appropriately tested (Riccio & Chianese, 2023).

The suggested hybrid ARIMA-ML approach is new but computationally limited and demanding large historical data for training. The research does not tackle general time series forecasting as compared to domain-specific concerns such as environmental volatility (Júnior et al., 2019).

Although comparative modeling of ARIMA, SARIMA, and SVR is beneficial, the study includes only one case study, inhibiting generalizability to a different market for energy or environmental factor. Incorporation of deep learning techniques, which have been demonstrated to be superior to time series forecasting, even more restricts the scope (Szostek et al., 2024).

Empirical confirmation of univariate models for forecasting generates strong results; the research, however, does not permit for the possibility that the multivariate models with greater capacity to accommodate intricate interrelations among environmental factors may be superior. The modelled ones are also missing real-time learning adjustments to conditions critical under dynamic requirements (Effrosynidis et al., 2023).

The SVM-based simulation equation model of AI also presents a new perspective to the contribution made by IoT and economic factors in air pollution but is in its limitation in application in real-world situations based on simulated data. Further, the study does not explore the potential contributions of various quality data from IoT sensors, with potentially considerable effects on the performance of the model (Dang et al., 2024).

The BiGRU-AM technique enhances high-resolution air quality monitoring but is hindered by the need for vast computational resources, which in some cases is a resource limitation. Additionally, the study fails to include interpretation assessment, and as such, policymakers cannot depend and make decisions based on the model output (Williams et al., 2023).

Comparative analysis pre- and post-COVID of air quality is useful but limited by inability to carry out causal analysis in order to establish the link between policy interventions and changes in air quality being observed (Dhar, 2023). Additionally, the study is based on aggregated data, which can mask differentiated air pollution patterns at a local scale (Dhar, 2023).

Response paper is in scope as far as z-score standardized RSEI use problems are concerned but not in the sense that it does not offer options for time-series ecological change detection. In addition, the argument is not yet empirically supported because no empirical testing of the presented arguments exists (Zheng et al., 2023).

The proposed reinforcement-based optimization with BiGRU is very predictive in performance, but the study doesn't take into consideration computational cost or performance on a variety of varying real-time situations. Additionally, the need for extensive hyperparameter tuning might render the method less practical for deployment at scale (Gurumoorthy et al., 2023).

The RBOSR method can improve air pollution prediction, but its resource demand and dependency on Bayesian optimization add to the need for resources, limiting usability in low-resource environments. Secondly, the study fails to include a comparison with new emerging lean deep learning libraries that could be having competitive accuracy but with less computationally intensive demands (Djarum et al., 2023).

BiGRU-based AQI forecast model shows improved performance in medium-term prediction, but the study is region-specific in terms of selected regions of Bangladesh and not generalizable to different climatological and urban areas. Secondly, the absence of uncertainty quantification in the predictions discourages sound outcomes for decision-making (Mandal & Sen, 2024).

Stacked BiGRU model, being different from other deep models, has several strengths. All the typical feedforward neural networks (FNN), Long Short-Term Memory (LSTM) networks, and the rest of the RNN-based models do not handle learning long-term dependencies from sequence data well due to issues such as vanishing gradients. BiGRU beats this with the simpler gating mechanism that allows it to learn long-term dependencies without computing at high expense. Also, BiGRU outperforms Convolutional Neural Networks (CNNs) if one is dealing with sequential data like air pollution because CNNs are excellent at identifying spatial features but struggle with handling time-series data that involve time dependencies. The stacked BiGRU model best performs air pollution forecasting because it can handle temporal and spatial dependencies very well.

Air quality levels are likely to exhibit temporal correlations, whose values of concentration at any point in time are a function of past measurements along with ambient conditions like weather. Stacked BiGRU can utilize these temporal relationships as it processes the data bidirectionally sequentially and thus provides overall context to the model while predicting. Second, the layering enables the model to learn abstract features, and this greatly enhances the precision of the model. To add, air pollution is both dynamic and multi-variable, where different variables interact intricately with one another.

BiGRU's two-way capability, in both upstream and downstream, enables the model to consider both future and past data points, thereby making it more suitable to learn how the concentrations of pollutants are influenced by environmental factors, i.e., wind speed, humidity, and temperature, over time. This makes the stacked BiGRU model extremely effective in making precise predictions as it can learn from changes in the input data and identify short-term variations and long-term trends. The second major strength of the stacked BiGRU is its ability to make real-time predictions.

In air pollution forecasting, it is necessary to be able to make forecasts in a timely fashion so that they will be available to inform public health interventions and policy decisions. The BiGRU stacked model, its inference speed, and training speed can afford to process real-time data, provide continual monitoring and forecasting of air quality levels. This is especially significant where there is mixed pollution in urban places, as early warning will minimize health effect and prevent further worsening of air quality.

MATERIALS AND METHODOLOGY

Methodology is the application of a stacked Bidirectional Gated Recurrent Unit (BiGRU) model for PM2.5 concentration prediction in India. The model performs air pollution data processing, including wind speed, temperature, and traffic variables, to capture temporal dependencies and non-linearities. Data preprocessing such as normalization and feature selection is performed to improve model accuracy.

Material

Indian air pollution data, sourced from the Central Pollution Control Board (CPCB), cover the period 2015 to 2023 and include a wide range of meteorological as well as air quality variables. The eight most important features in the dataset are wind speed, rain, wind direction, snow, dew point, concentration of PM2.5, air pressure, and temperature. All these attributes provide useful information about weather as well as pollutant concentration over some interval. The inclusion of PM2.5 concentration is particularly vital since it is a real-time measure of particulate matter concentrations that affect public health. Meteorological variables like wind direction and speed offer information regarding atmospheric dispersion conditions that dictate the degree to which the pollutants become dispersed and deposited within a given area. Parameters like temperature, rain, and dew point all indirectly determine air quality because they will interact with air pollutants. Snow and air pressure are part of the description of the seasonality and air stability dynamic, which is relevant to studying air pollution. Together, these diverse characteristics constitute a data set which can be employed to qualitatively examine air quality patterns, seasonal patterns, and impacts of meteorological factors on pollution concentration in India over nearly a decade of time.

Pre Processing

Pre-processing of air pollution data involves a series of steps to pre-clean data, maintain consistency, and make it ready for analysis. Missing values treatment is the initial step, where in the air pollution data missing values are common due to malfunctioning measurement or errors in recording. Missing values in attribute fields like the concentration of PM2.5, wind speed, or rain can be managed with imputation methods, e.g., mean or median replacement, or by utilizing interpolation techniques of the surrounding timestamps. For treatment and outliers, we consider each feature to identify abnormal spikes or dips, especially for meteorological variables such as temperature and wind speed, which may influence pollutant concentration and dispersion. Outliers are trimmed or replaced according to standard statistical procedures or domain expertise.

Normalization and standardization of the data are then done in order to put the features, especially those with variable scales and units (e.g., wind speed in km/h, PM2.5 concentration in $\mu g/m^3$), onto a standard scale. One can undertake Z-score standardization as per model requirements. Categorical variables like wind direction may need encoding in order to convert these categories to numerical values. One-hot encoding or ordinal encoding would be applied depending on the categorical feature type and type of analysis to be performed.

Finally, time-series decomposition and feature engineering enrich the dataset by capturing temporal patterns such as seasonality and yearly trends. Other features such as monthly averages or deviation from daily mean could provide further information about air quality trends. Such preprocessing actions lead to a systematic and consistent dataset, paving the way for accurate modeling and meaningful air quality analysis.

Correlation

To identify the most important contributors for precise air pollution forecasting, we compute the correlation coefficients (CCs) of every feature in the dataset, i.e., wind speed, rain, wind direction, snowfall, dew point, level of PM2.5, air pressure, and temperature. To compute the correlation matrix between variables, we obtain magnitudes and directions of correlation between each pair of variables ranging from

-1 (perfect negative correlation) to +1 (perfect positive correlation). To determine precisely which meteorological factors have the largest effects on pollution levels, looking at the correlation of PM2.5 concentration with all of these meteorological factors can uncover the most significant ones. For example, strong negative correlation between PM2.5 and wind speed might suggest that stronger winds allow for particle dispersal and therefore lower concentrations of pollutants. In addition, correlations between the other variables to themselves need to be checked to prevent multicollinearity, whereby two or more characteristics are extremely correlated with themselves, distorting model outputs.

For example, dew point and temperature can be extremely correlated, and both will not be adding anything towards the forecast value if they are added to the forecast model. Heatmap can be an excellent option to display the correlation matrix and get a direct first-hand impression about such correlations and highly correlated pairs along with uncorrelated variables. Lastly, establishing a threshold of say 0.5 enables the use of only features with significant correlations to PM2.5 to be used as input into the model in order to keep it centered on the most predictive variables without being overly complicated.

Feature Optimization

In feature optimization for air pollutant prediction, Bayesian Optimization with Lasso Regression provides an efficient method by progressively discarding the most significant variables.

Bayesian Optimization is a stochastic approach that optimizes the feature space effectively by balancing exploration (conducting experiments on new features) and exploitation (optimizing previously found important features). Bayes Optimization starts with selecting some features and estimating the target function—such as minimizing prediction error in this case—by perturbing sets of features based on prior evaluation. Bayes Optimization creates a posterior distribution over possible solutions, which guides the search towards the highest-performing features. Lasso Regression substitutes this operation with regularization, introducing a penalty that causes smaller influence feature coefficients to converge towards zero and thus remove them from the model.

Lasso regularization is particularly powerful when dealing with air pollution data, where environmental variables may be collinear (for example, temperature and dew point), eliminating redundancy by choosing the most relevant predictors automatically. Through this hybrid approach, Bayesian Optimization chooses the optimal feature sets, and Lasso Regression adjusts the choice to include only variables that are most contributory to pollution indicators, delivering an additional optimized and interpretable model.

AIR POLLUTION PREDICTION

Stacked Bidirectional GRU model is employed by the Air Quality Prediction model, tapping into the strength of Recurrent Neural Networks (RNNs), specifically the Gated Recurrent Unit (GRU), and builds on this with a stacked, bidirectional method to detect subtle, sequential patterns in time-series air quality data. The following is a step-by-step explanation of how this model forecasts the degree of air quality with particular emphasis on the bidirectional and stacked GRU layers:

Data Preparation and Sequence Input Creation

In forecasting air quality, time series data—such as past air pollutants (for example, PM2.5), meteorology (for example, temperature, humidity, wind speed), and day or season trends—are collected and preprocessed. This is thereafter transformed into sequences wherein an input sequence of time steps appears in the window format of a sequence of previous time steps (for example, the last 24 hours or days) that is input to the model so that it may learn temporal patterns.

GRU and its Use in Sequential Data Processing

GRU is an extension of RNNs that attempts to address issues like vanishing gradients, which detract from the ability of normal RNNs to learn long-term dependencies. GRU consists of two main gates—a reset gate and an update gate—used to decide how much past information to retain or discard. Through this gating mechanism, the model can learn important past dependencies in an adaptive way even when temporal variability is complex in air pollution data.

Bidirectional GRU (BIGRU) Layer for Pattern Identification

Both the forward GRU layer and the backward GRU layer in a biGRU move through the input sequence in two opposing directions:

Forward Layer

Reads from start to end within the sequence and learns about dependencies later on within the sequence.

Backward Layer

It runs from the end of the sequence to the start, picking out relationships that can occur towards the end of the sequence.

By overlapping the forward and backward layers, a biGRU is able to observe both prior and future context, something that is valuable in air quality forecasting because the effects of some pollutants are linked with both prior and following environmental changes. Through such consideration from two sides, the model has better insight into temporal dynamics between air quality variables and is therefore more precise.

Stacked BIGRU Layers for Capturing Higher-Level Features

Multiple biGRU layers are layered over each other vertically in the stacked model. The output of one previous biGRU layer is provided as the input to the next layer, and hence the model can detect hierarchical or higher-order temporal patterns. The initial layer detects broad temporal relationships in data, and following layers detect more complex patterns, such as cyclical air quality patterns or seasonality, that are important for correct long-term forecasts.

Dense Output Layer for Final Prediction

The stacked biGRU output is fed to a fully connected (dense) layer which projects the learned features onto the target variable, i.e., the level of PM2.5 at a subsequent time step. The dense layer adds up the sequential information from GRU layers and does the final prediction.

Training with Loss Minimization

At training, the model is taught to reduce a loss function (in this case, Mean Squared Error for regression), i.e., the difference between output and input air quality levels. The model updates its weights using backpropagation as it attempts to reduce this error step-wise. Through such learning, the stacked biGRU learns to find useful patterns in historical data to use in successfully predicting future air quality levels.

After having been trained, the stacked biGRU model employs the recent environmental and air quality input data sequence to predict future time step air quality levels. As past and future dependency has been utilized and the model has been trained from multiple stacked layers, the model can efficiently identify intricate patterns and therefore can provide accurate and reliable estimations of the levels of air pollution under varying environmental conditions.

The ability of the stacked biGRU model to learn bidirectional dependencies and hierarchical temporal relationships enhances its forecasting accuracy in air quality prediction.

EXPERIMENTAL RESULTS

Table 1 illustrates comparative performance between various models used in PM2.5 air pollution forecasting, where the highest performing in predictive accuracy is the proposed Stacked biGRU. Stacked biGRU recorded the highest Mean Absolute Error (MAE) of 5.2 and Root Mean Squared Error (RMSE) of 12.1, MSE of 50.2, indicating a best fit with zero error. Its Symmetric Mean Absolute Percentage Error (SMAPE) was 7.8%, indicating its high degree of accuracy. For all the traditional models, ARIMA produced significantly larger errors, i.e., 10.5 MAE, 18.2 RMSE, and 12.4% SMAPE, indicating ineffectiveness in capturing complex air pollution dynamics. Random Forest also indicated larger errors, i.e., MAE of 12.3, RMSE of 19.4, and SMAPE of 14.2%, indicating lower suitability in this prediction exercise.

Deep learning models such as LSTM and GRU performed better than standard models with LSTM achieving MAE of 6.7 and RMSE of 14.8, and GRU achieving an MAE of 7.5 and RMSE of 13.7. Both these models were surpassed by the Stacked biGRU. Support Vector Regression (SVR) and XGBoost acted fairly well, with SVR yielding an MAE of 9.1 and SMAPE of 11.5%, whereas XGBoost yielded an MAE of 8.3 and SMAPE of 9.8%. Prophet model, even though trained to be used for time series tasks, had greater errors of MAE equal to 9.0 and RMSE equal to 16.5. The result validates the strong predictive capability of the proposed Stacked biGRU model over the traditional and alternative deep learning models in predicting PM2.5 concentration based on Indian air quality information.

Table 1. Performance comparison for PM2.5 air pollution prediction

Model	MAE	RMSE	MSE	SMAPE
Proposed Stacked biGRU	5.2	12.1	50.2	7.8%
ARIMA	10.5	18.2	120.6	12.4%
Random Forest	12.3	19.4	160.5	14.2%
LSTM	6.7	14.8	85.3	9.1%
GRU	7.5	13.7	74.9	10.3%
SVR	9.1	15.5	99.7	11.5%
XGBoost	8.3	14.2	85.7	9.8%
Prophet	9.0	16.5	102.4	11.2%

Table 2 offers a comparison of model performance on air pollution data before and after preprocessing, illustrating the impact data preprocessing has had on predictive accuracy. The model achieved a Mean Absolute Error (MAE) of 12.6 and a Root Mean Squared Error (RMSE) of 20.5 in the Non-preprocessed data, with a fairly low R^2 measure of 0.72. These values indicate that if preprocessing were not done, the model fails to capture patterns in the data very well, with increased prediction errors. With Preprocessed data, the performance of the model improved immensely. The MAE reduced to 5.2, and the RMSE reduced to 12.1, showing an enormous decrease in prediction errors. The R^2 value also improved immensely to 0.91, showing a much improved fit between the model and observed data. In addition, the Mean Absolute Percentage Error (MAPE) decreased from 22.4% to 9.3%, and Symmetric Mean Absolute Percentage Error (SMAPE) decreased from 15.8% to 7.8%, indicating a higher level of precision and reliability in model prediction after preprocessing.

Table 2. Performance analysis of the proposed preprocessed technique with non-preprocessed data and preprocessed data

Model	MAE	SMAPE	RMSE	MSE	MAPE	R^2
Non-preprocessed data	12.6	15.8%	20.5	420.5	22.4%	0.72
Preprocessed data	5.2	7.8%	12.1	50.2	9.3%	0.91

Table 3 displays the comparison of performance of multiple machine learning models for agricultural vulnerability analysis on the basis of different evaluation criteria. The Proposed Stacked biGRU model performed better than the rest of them, with the lowest Mean Absolute Error (MAE) value being 4.9, Symmetric Mean Absolute Percentage Error (SMAPE) value being 7.5%, Root Mean Square Error (RMSE) value being 11.8, Mean Square Error (MSE) value being 46.1, and Mean Absolute Percentage Error (MAPE) value being 8.9%, and the highest R^2 score being 0.93, indicating high precision and reliability. The LSTM model also performed with an MAE of 6.3, SMAPE of 8.9%, RMSE of 14.3, MSE of 81.5, and MAPE of 10.0% with an R^2 of 0.89. The CNN-LSTM also produced similar performance with an MAE of 6.0, SMAPE of 8.3%, RMSE of 12.9, and an R^2 of 0.90, but slightly higher than that of the BiLSTM model, which produced similar values with an R^2 of 0.88.

MAE for GRU model was 7.1, SMAPE was 10.0%, RMSE was 13.5, MSE was 72.9, and MAPE was 10.7%, with R^2 being 0.87. The RNN model with higher errors (MAE of 7.8, SMAPE of 11.9%, RMSE of 15.8) and a relatively low R^2 of 0.82 was not as precise. Finally, the Deep Neural Network (DNN) performed poorest with the largest MAE of 9.0, SMAPE of 14.1%, RMSE of 18.2, MSE of 119.2, and MAPE of 12.3%, and lowest R^2 of 0.77.

Table 3. Performance comparison for air pollution prediction

Model	MAE	SMAPE	RMSE	MSE	MAPE	R^2
Proposed Stacked biGRU	4.9	7.5%	11.8	46.1	8.9%	0.93
LSTM	6.3	8.9%	14.3	81.5	10.0%	0.89
GRU	7.1	10.0%	13.5	72.9	10.7%	0.87
CNN-LSTM	6.0	8.3%	12.9	66.4	9.5%	0.90
BiLSTM	6.2	8.1%	13.2	71.0	9.9%	0.88
RNN	7.8	11.9%	15.8	86.6	11.6%	0.82
Deep Neural Network (DNN)	9.0	14.1%	18.2	119.2	12.3%	0.77

Table 4 summarizes an extensive comparison of different optimization algorithms, Gradient Descent (GD) posted lower accuracy with increased MAE of 7.4 and R^2 of 0.83, representing worse fit and greater prediction errors. RMSProp posted well-balanced results with MAE of 6.2 and R^2 of 0.88, indicating stable but mediocre accuracy compared to Adam. The remaining models, like Adagrad and SGD, also had moderate to severe errors; Adagrad had an MAE of 7.0 and R^2 of 0.85 while SGD had the biggest errors with an MAE of 7.8 and an R^2 of 0.81, which was worse model performance. Adadelta had decent accuracy with an MAE of 6.6 and R^2 of 0.87, a good but not ideal fit. Last but not least, Nesterov Accelerated Gradient (NAG) was also good with an MAE of 6.0, SMAPE of 8.3%, and R^2 of 0.89 due to its application of momentum to assist in boosting precision. Generally, Adam was the best performing optimization algorithm with the least prediction error and greatest prediction accuracy according to the measures, which supports the fact that it is best suited for air quality forecasting in this study.

Table 4. Optimizer performance

Optimizer	MAE	SMAPE	RMSE	MSE	MAPE	R^2
Adam	5.2	7.8%	12.1	50.2	9.3%	0.91
Gradient Descent (GD)	7.4	10.2%	15.6	93.0	11.1%	0.83
RMSProp	6.2	8.6%	13.4	69.4	10.5%	0.88
Adagrad	7.0	9.8%	14.9	88.6	10.9%	0.85
SGD (Stochastic Gradient Descent)	7.8	11.5%	16.2	97.6	12.4%	0.81
Adadelta	6.6	9.1%	13.8	75.7	10.3%	0.87
Nesterov Accelerated Gradient (NAG)	6.0	8.3%	13.0	70.4	9.9%	0.89

CONCLUSION

Here in this paper, we presented a deep learning method based on the stacked BiGRU model to forecast PM2.5 concentration in India. The stacked BiGRU model was more accurate than the conventional models such as Linear Regression, ARIMA, and SVM. By accurately representing temporal dependencies alongside intricate interactions between the different factors affecting air pollution, BiGRU produced more precise predictions with higher MAE, RMSE, and R^2 scores. The bidirectional and stacked model allowed it to identify short-term variations and long-term patterns with high accuracy, which is critical in achieving precise air quality prediction. Considering the limitations of real-time monitoring of air quality in dynamic cities, the BiGRU stacked model is a useful tool in being able to supply accurate and timely predictions. The findings indicate that incorporating deep learning methods such as stacked BiGRU into air quality monitoring frameworks can make air quality management more efficient, lower health threats, and contribute to the development of effective environmental policies in India and other countries facing similar issues.

REFERENCES

Ahmad, S., Zeb, B., Ditta, A., Alam, K., Shahid, U., Shah, A. U., & Alqurashi, M. (2023). Morphological, mineralogical, and biochemical characteristics of particulate matter in three size fractions (PM10, PM2. 5, and PM1) in the urban environment. *ACS Omega*, *8*(35), 31661–31674. PMID: 37692244

Banasiewicz, A., Moosavi, F., Kotyla, M., Śliwiński, P., Krot, P., Wodecki, J., & Zimroz, R. (2023). Forecasting of NOx emissions of diesel LHD vehicles in underground mines—An ANN-based regression approach. *Applied Sciences (Basel, Switzerland)*, *13*(17), 9965.

Dang, W., Kim, S., Park, S., & Xu, W. (2024). The impact of economic and IoT technologies on air pollution: An AI-based simulation equation model using support vector machines. *Soft Computing*, *28*(4), 3591–3611.

Dhar, S. B. (2023). A comparative study of air quality between pre and post COVID-19 periods in India. *Environment, Development and Sustainability*, •••, 1–25.

Djarum, D. H., Ahmad, Z., & Zhang, J. (2023). Reduced Bayesian Optimized Stacked Regressor (RBOSR): A highly efficient stacked approach for improved air pollution prediction. *Applied Soft Computing*, *144*, 110466.

Effrosynidis, D., Spiliotis, E., Sylaios, G., & Arampatzis, A. (2023). Time series and regression methods for univariate environmental forecasting: An empirical evaluation. *The Science of the Total Environment*, *875*, 162580. PMID: 36906023

Gurumoorthy, S., Kokku, A. K., Falkowski-Gilski, P., & Divakarachari, P. B. (2023). Effective air quality prediction using reinforced swarm optimization and bi-directional gated recurrent unit. *Sustainability*, *15*(14), 11454.

Guttikunda, S. K., Goel, R., & Pant, P. (2014). Nature of air pollution, emission sources, and management in the Indian cities. *Atmospheric Environment*, *95*, 501–510.

Jones, M. W., Peters, G. P., Gasser, T., Andrew, R. M., Schwingshackl, C., Gütschow, J., & Le Quéré, C. (2023). National contributions to climate change due to historical emissions of carbon dioxide, methane, and nitrous oxide since 1850. *Scientific Data*, *10*(1), 155. PMID: 36991071

Júnior, D. S. D. O. S., de Oliveira, J. F., & de Mattos Neto, P. S. (2019). An intelligent hybridization of ARIMA with machine learning models for time series forecasting. *Knowledge-Based Systems*, *175*, 72–86.

Kulothungan, V., Ramamoorthy, T., Mohan, R., & Mathur, P. (2024). Assessing progress of India in reduction of premature mortality due to four noncommunicable diseases towards achieving the WHO 25× 25 goal and the sustainable development goals. *Sustainable Development*, *32*(3), 2020–2030.

Mandal, A. K., & Sen, R. (2024). Medium-Term AQI Prediction in Selected Areas of Bangladesh Based on Bidirectional GRU Network Model. *SN Computer Science*, *5*(5), 627.

Muzayyanah, S., Hong, C. Y., Adha, R., & Yang, S. F. (2023). The non-linear relationship between air pollution, labor insurance and productivity: Multivariate adaptive regression splines approach. *Sustainability*, *15*(12), 9404.

Odubo, T. C., & Kosoe, E. A. (2024). Sources of Air Pollutants: Impacts and Solutions.

Papadogeorgou, G., Kioumourtzoglou, M. A., Braun, D., & Zanobetti, A. (2019). Low levels of air pollution and health: Effect estimates, methodological challenges, and future directions. *Current Environmental Health Reports*, *6*, 105–115. PMID: 31090042

Putri, T. H., Caraka, R. E., Toharudin, T., Kim, Y., Chen, R. C., Gio, P. U., ... & Pardamean, B. (2024). Fine-Tuning of Predictive Models CNN-LSTM and CONV-LSTM for Nowcasting PM 2.5 Level. *IEEE Access*.

Ramirez-Corredores, M. M., Goldwasser, M. R., & Falabella de Sousa Aguiar, E. (2023). Carbon dioxide and climate change. In *Decarbonization as a Route Towards Sustainable Circularity* (pp. 1–14). Springer International Publishing.

Riccio, A., & Chianese, E. (2023). Accurate, reliable and high resolution air quality predictions by improving the Copernicus Atmosphere Monitoring Service using machine learning techniques. *EGUsphere*, *2023*, 1–27.

Sharma, G. K., & Ghuge, V. V. (2024). How urban growth dynamics impact the air quality? A case of eight Indian metropolitan cities. *The Science of the Total Environment*, *930*, 172399. PMID: 38631640

Sharma, M., Singh, K., Gautam, A. S., & Gautam, S. (2024). Longitudinal Study of Air Pollutants in Indian Metropolises: Seasonal Patterns and Urban Variability. *Aerosol Science and Engineering*, 1-16.

Szostek, K., Mazur, D., Drałus, G., & Kusznier, J. (2024). Analysis of the Effectiveness of ARIMA, SARIMA, and SVR Models in Time Series Forecasting: A Case Study of Wind Farm Energy Production. *Energies (19961073)*, *17*(19).

Williams, D. P., Srinivas, G., Bajpai, A., Ghamande, M. V., Dhyani, B., & Pal, S. (2023, November). Fine Grained Air Quality Monitoring Based on BiGRU and AM Model for Enhanced Public Health. In *2023 7th International Conference on Electronics, Communication and Aerospace Technology (ICECA)* (pp. 235-240). IEEE.

Zhang, X., Han, L., Wei, H., Tan, X., Zhou, W., Li, W., & Qian, Y. (2022). Linking urbanization and air quality together: A review and a perspective on the future sustainable urban development. *Journal of Cleaner Production*, *346*, 130988.

Zheng, Z., Wu, Z., & Marinello, F. (2023). Response to the letter to the editor "is the z-score standardized RSEI suitable for time-series ecological change detection? Comment on Zheng et al.(2022)". *The Science of the Total Environment*, *855*, 1–4. PMID: 36150590

Zoran, M. A., Savastru, R. S., Savastru, D. M., & Tautan, M. N. (2020). Assessing the relationship between surface levels of PM2. 5 and PM10 particulate matter impact on COVID-19 in Milan, Italy. *The Science of the Total Environment*, *738*, 139825. PMID: 32512362

Chapter 8
Harnessing Artificial Intelligence for Sustainable Innovation and Policy: The Eco-Intelligence

Ananya Pandey
https://orcid.org/0000-0002-2419-6314
Christ University, Bangalore, India

ABSTRACT

Artificial Intelligence (AI) is revolutionizing sustainable innovation and policymaking by optimizing resource management, enhancing environmental monitoring, and fostering circular economies. This chapter explores Eco-Intelligence—the integration of AI-driven analytics, predictive modeling, and automation in addressing environmental challenges. By leveraging machine learning, and digital twins, AI enables real-time decision-making for climate adaptation, carbon footprint reduction, and green supply chains. Also, AI-driven regulatory frameworks enhance compliance with sustainability standards, bridging the gap between technological advancement and environmental governance. However, ethical concerns, algorithmic biases, and data privacy issues pose challenges to AI's effective deployment in sustainability policy. This chapter critically examines the intersection of AI, environmental stewardship, and regulatory landscapes, proposing a balanced approach to harness AI's potential for long-term ecological and economic resilience.

DOI: 10.4018/979-8-3373-2387-9.ch008

INTRODUCTION

Eco-intelligence represents a paradigm shift in how artificial intelligence (AI) is leveraged to drive sustainable innovation, addressing the pressing environmental challenges of the 21st century while ensuring economic and social benefits (Vinuesa et al., 2020). In an era where climate change, resource depletion, and environmental degradation pose existential threats, AI emerges as a transformative tool that can enable data-driven decision-making, optimize resource efficiency, and foster the development of green technologies (Nishant et al., 2020). At its core, eco-intelligence integrates AI with sustainability principles to create intelligent systems capable of mitigating ecological risks, enhancing environmental governance, and promoting responsible consumption and production. This synergy extends beyond mere technological advancements; it necessitates a holistic approach that involves policy frameworks, ethical considerations, and multi-stakeholder collaboration. The intersection of AI, sustainability, and policy is, therefore, a crucial nexus that determines how effectively AI can be harnessed for environmental and societal well-being (Bibri et al., 2024). Governments, businesses, and researchers must navigate this complex landscape, ensuring that AI applications align with sustainable development goals (SDGs) and adhere to ethical and regulatory standards.

AI-driven sustainable innovation manifests in diverse sectors, from renewable energy optimization to precision agriculture, waste management, and climate modeling. In renewable energy, AI enhances the efficiency of solar and wind power by predicting energy generation patterns, optimizing grid distribution, and reducing reliance on fossil fuels (Rehman et al., 2024). AI-powered smart grids can balance energy demand and supply in real-time, minimizing wastage and improving resilience against disruptions. Similarly, in agriculture, AI-driven precision farming techniques—such as machine learning algorithms for crop monitoring, automated irrigation systems, and predictive analytics for pest control—reduce resource consumption while maximizing yield (Issa et al., 2024). AI's role in waste management includes intelligent sorting systems that improve recycling efficiency, predictive maintenance for waste treatment plants, and blockchain-based traceability for circular economy models. Furthermore, AI-driven climate models provide accurate predictions for extreme weather events, enabling policymakers and disaster response teams to implement proactive mitigation strategies. These applications underscore AI's potential in revolutionizing sustainability efforts, but their success hinges on supportive policy mechanisms that ensure responsible deployment (Koshariya et al., 2023).

Policy plays a pivotal role in guiding AI applications towards sustainable outcomes by setting regulatory frameworks, incentivizing green innovation, and addressing ethical concerns. Governments and international organizations have introduced various policies to integrate AI into sustainability strategies, including the European Green Deal, the United Nations AI for Good initiatives, and national AI strategies that emphasize environmental stewardship (Truby, 2020). However, the dynamic and complex nature of AI poses regulatory challenges, including issues of accountability, transparency, and fairness. For instance, AI-driven environmental monitoring systems may rely on vast amounts of data, raising concerns about privacy, surveillance, and data ownership. Additionally, AI algorithms can inherit biases, leading to unintended environmental injustices where marginalized communities face disproportionate environmental harm (Mennella et al., 2024). To counteract these risks, policymakers must establish ethical AI guidelines that prioritize transparency, inclusivity, and sustainability metrics. Moreover, AI's own carbon footprint—stemming from energy-intensive computations—must be addressed through the development of green AI models that optimize computational efficiency and utilize renewable energy sources for data centers (Cowls et al., 2023).

The intersection of AI, sustainability, and policy necessitates a multidisciplinary approach where technology, governance, and social responsibility converge to create systemic change. AI alone cannot drive sustainability; it must be embedded within comprehensive policy frameworks that foster responsible innovation, equitable access, and long-term environmental stewardship (Kar et al., 2022). Governments must collaborate with industry leaders, research institutions, and civil society organizations to create policies that balance innovation with ethical and ecological considerations. Public-private partnerships can accelerate the adoption of AI-driven sustainability solutions by providing funding, knowledge exchange, and infrastructure support (Vis, 2020). Furthermore, international cooperation is crucial in establishing standardized regulations that prevent the misuse of AI and promote sustainable practices across borders. The ethical dimension of AI in sustainability also requires ongoing dialogue on AI governance, ensuring that AI solutions do not exacerbate existing inequalities but rather contribute to a just transition towards a low-carbon and resilient future.

As AI continues to evolve, its role in sustainability will expand, creating both opportunities and challenges that demand proactive policy responses. AI-driven sustainability strategies must align with global environmental targets, such as the Paris Agreement and the UN SDGs, ensuring that AI applications contribute to carbon neutrality, biodiversity conservation, and responsible consumption (Lampropoulas et al., 2024). The future of eco-intelligence lies in integrating AI-driven solutions with circular economy models, regenerative practices, and community-led environmental initiatives. To achieve this, regulatory bodies must implement forward-looking policies that incentivize green AI development while mitigating potential risks (Patahn et al., 2023). Ethical AI governance frameworks should emphasize environmental impact assessments, algorithmic transparency, and inclusive decision-making processes.

The emergence of AI for sustainability signals a transformative era where technology and policy must coalesce to address planetary challenges, ultimately shaping a future where AI-driven intelligence serves as a catalyst for ecological resilience, economic sustainability, and social well-being (Daly et al., 2022).

In essence, this chapter will serve as a comprehensive roadmap for understanding how AI can be harnessed to foster sustainable innovation, outlining the synergies between AI, environmental policies, and governance structures. It will critically assess both the potential and limitations of AI-driven sustainability, advocating for a balanced, ethically sound, and policy-aligned approach to Eco-Intelligence. By delving into the technical, regulatory, and strategic dimensions of AI for sustainability, this chapter aims to contribute to a more informed, responsible, and forward-thinking discourse on the role of AI in achieving a greener, more sustainable, and technologically advanced future.

AI AND SUSTAINABLE INNOVATION: A TRANSFORMATIVE PARADIGM

AI is revolutionizing the landscape of sustainability by offering data-driven, intelligent, and automated solutions to some of the world's most pressing environmental challenges. As the global climate crisis intensifies, governments, industries, and researchers are increasingly leveraging AI to optimize resource management, reduce carbon footprints, and promote circular economies (Gunther & Rose, 2020). AI-driven technologies enhance decision-making processes, automate sustainable practices, and improve efficiency across sectors, ensuring that economic growth aligns with environmental responsibility. AI-powered systems enable real-time monitoring, forecasting, and optimization, which are critical for tackling issues such as climate change, energy consumption, and waste management (Chen et al., 2024). Through machine learning (ML), deep learning, and advanced analytics, AI facilitates predictive and prescriptive decision-making, driving significant progress in the development of eco-friendly solutions (Schmitt, 2023).

One of the most promising areas where AI is making a substantial impact is climate technology (climate tech). AI algorithms are being deployed to analyze vast datasets from satellite imagery, weather patterns, and environmental sensors, providing precise climate forecasts and risk assessments. This predictive capability enhances disaster preparedness, enabling governments and organizations to mitigate the effects of climate change (Olawade et al., 2024). For example, AI-driven climate models developed by organizations like NASA and Google's DeepMind have significantly improved the accuracy of climate predictions, offering insights into extreme weather events, rising sea levels, and deforestation patterns. Furthermore,

AI is instrumental in tracking greenhouse gas emissions, optimizing carbon capture technologies, and supporting sustainable agriculture by predicting soil health, monitoring crop growth, and reducing water wastage. AI-powered irrigation systems analyze weather data and soil moisture levels to ensure optimal water usage, thereby minimizing environmental impact and enhancing agricultural sustainability (Popescu et al., 2024).

The circular economy, which emphasizes reducing waste and maximizing resource efficiency, is another domain where AI is transforming sustainability efforts. Traditional linear economic models—based on the "take, make, dispose" approach—have led to significant environmental degradation and resource depletion. AI-driven solutions help transition toward circular business models by enabling smart recycling, waste management, and sustainable supply chain logistics (Zhang, 2024). For example, AI-based computer vision and robotics are being used to automate waste sorting, increasing recycling efficiency and reducing landfill waste. Companies such as AMP Robotics have developed AI-powered sorting systems that identify and separate recyclable materials with high precision, significantly improving the recycling process. Additionally, AI facilitates product life cycle analysis, allowing manufacturers to design products that are more durable, repairable, and recyclable. By leveraging AI-driven insights, companies can adopt sustainable materials, optimize production processes, and reduce excess inventory, ultimately minimizing environmental footprints (Lodhi et al., 2024).

AI is also playing a pivotal role in green energy innovation by enhancing the efficiency, reliability, and scalability of renewable energy sources such as solar, wind, and hydroelectric power. The intermittency of renewable energy sources has historically posed a challenge to their widespread adoption; however, AI is mitigating this issue through intelligent forecasting and grid optimization (Ashfaq et al., 2022). AI-driven predictive analytics can accurately forecast solar radiation levels and wind patterns, enabling energy providers to optimize power generation and distribution. For instance, Google's DeepMind has successfully used AI to predict wind energy output 36 hours in advance, improving grid integration and reducing reliance on fossil fuels. AI-powered smart grids further enhance energy distribution by dynamically adjusting power flows based on real-time demand, reducing wastage, and increasing overall efficiency (Arya, 2024). Moreover, AI is being leveraged to optimize battery storage systems, ensuring that excess renewable energy is stored efficiently and deployed when needed. This advancement is crucial in accelerating the transition to a fully renewable energy infrastructure (Kajela & Manshahia, 2017).

Beyond climate tech, circular economy, and green energy, AI is also transforming sustainable urban planning and eco-conscious design through digital twins and predictive analytics. Digital twins—virtual models of physical systems—are being utilized to simulate and optimize energy usage, transportation networks, and building efficiency (Alnaser et al., 2024). AI-driven digital twin technology allows city planners to analyze the environmental impact of urban expansion, optimize traffic flow, and design sustainable infrastructure. For example, AI-powered smart traffic management systems can reduce congestion, lower emissions, and enhance public transportation efficiency. AI also plays a crucial role in sustainable architecture by enabling eco-friendly building design (Mitra et al., 2023). Machine learning algorithms can optimize building materials, assess energy efficiency, and suggest green construction techniques that minimize carbon footprints. Furthermore, AI-driven climate control systems in smart buildings automatically adjust heating, ventilation, and air conditioning (HVAC) settings based on occupancy patterns and weather conditions, significantly reducing energy consumption (Strubell et al., 2020). Predictive analytics, another powerful AI capability, is driving proactive decision-making in sustainability efforts. By analyzing historical and real-time data, AI-powered predictive models can identify trends, anticipate environmental risks, and recommend preventive measures. In the agricultural sector, AI-driven predictive analytics help farmers optimize crop yields, reduce pesticide usage, and implement precision farming techniques that enhance soil health (Okeleke et al., 2024). Similarly, AI-powered environmental monitoring systems track air and water quality, detect pollution sources, and provide early warnings for contamination, enabling authorities to take swift action to protect ecosystems and public health (Olawade et al., 2024).

Despite the transformative potential of AI in sustainable innovation, several challenges must be addressed to maximize its impact. The energy consumption of AI itself is a growing concern, as large-scale machine learning models require substantial computational power, leading to increased carbon footprints (Perc et al., 2019). However, advancements in energy-efficient AI models and green computing are actively addressing this issue. Additionally, ethical considerations related to AI-driven sustainability must be carefully managed, ensuring transparency, fairness, and accountability in AI decision-making processes (Raman et al., 2024). Therefore, AI is playing a pivotal role in driving sustainable innovation by offering intelligent, data-driven solutions for climate technology, circular economy, and green energy. By leveraging AI-driven digital twins, predictive analytics, and eco-conscious design principles, industries and governments can optimize resource utilization, mitigate environmental risks, and transition toward a more sustainable future (Gundeti et al., 2024). While challenges such as AI's energy consumption and ethical concerns remain, the potential of AI to accelerate sustainability efforts is undeniable. Through continued research, policy support, and interdisciplinary collaboration, AI-powered sustainability initiatives can help achieve global climate goals and create a more resilient and eco-friendlier world.

POLICY FRAMEWORK FOR AI AND SUSTAINABILITY

The integration of AI into sustainability efforts has gained significant traction, with global policy frameworks emerging to guide its ethical and effective implementation. Various international and regional initiatives, such as the UN SDGs, the European Green Deal, and AI ethics guidelines, provide a structured approach to leveraging AI for environmental and social sustainability (Cumming et al., 2024). These frameworks are designed to ensure that AI contributes to climate action, resource efficiency, and environmental protection while adhering to principles of transparency, accountability, and fairness. The UN SDGs, particularly Goals 7 (Affordable and Clean Energy), 9 (Industry, Innovation, and Infrastructure), 12 (Responsible Consumption and Production), and 13 (Climate Action), emphasize the role of emerging technologies like AI in addressing sustainability challenges. AI-driven solutions, such as predictive analytics for climate change mitigation, intelligent resource allocation in agriculture, and digital twins for industrial sustainability, align with these objectives (Greif et al., 2024). Furthermore, AI can enhance the measurement and tracking of SDG progress through automated data collection and real-time environmental monitoring, allowing policymakers to make informed decisions and improve sustainability strategies.

At the regional level, the European Green Deal, launched by the European Commission, aims to make Europe climate-neutral by 2050 through policy mechanisms that integrate AI and digital transformation into sustainability objectives. AI technologies play a crucial role in the implementation of this policy by optimizing energy consumption, reducing emissions, and enabling the circular economy (Almeida et al., 2023). The EU Artificial Intelligence Act, currently under development, seeks to regulate AI systems based on their risk levels, ensuring that high-risk AI applications, including those related to sustainability and environmental monitoring, adhere to strict safety and ethical standards. This legal framework aims to mitigate AI-induced risks, such as biased environmental impact assessments or unsustainable data-processing practices, while promoting the responsible use of AI in achieving the European Green Deal's climate and environmental goals. Additionally, the EU Taxonomy for Sustainable Activities provides a classification system for sustainable investments, influencing AI-driven green finance initiatives and corporate sustainability reporting.

Despite the potential of AI in advancing sustainability policies, several regulatory challenges and ethical considerations must be addressed to ensure the responsible deployment of AI technologies. One of the key challenges is the lack of standardized AI governance frameworks across different jurisdictions, leading to inconsistencies in how AI is regulated for sustainability applications. While some regions, such as the EU, are adopting stringent AI regulations, others have yet to develop comprehensive legal guidelines, creating a fragmented global regulatory landscape. Another concern is the transparency and explainability of AI algorithms used in sustainability-related decision-making. Many AI models, including deep learning systems for climate prediction or biodiversity conservation, operate as "black boxes," making it difficult for policymakers and stakeholders to interpret how decisions are made. This lack of interpretability raises ethical concerns, particularly when AI-driven environmental policies affect vulnerable communities or result in unintended socio-economic consequences. Moreover, AI systems that optimize industrial processes for sustainability may also contribute to job displacement, necessitating policies that balance automation-driven efficiency with workforce transition strategies.

Another pressing issue is the environmental impact of AI itself, as high-performance AI models often require substantial computing power, leading to increased energy consumption and carbon emissions. The irony of using energy-intensive AI systems to combat climate change highlights the need for Green AI initiatives—strategies aimed at developing energy-efficient AI algorithms and promoting sustainable computing practices. Regulatory bodies are increasingly advocating for the adoption of low-carbon AI infrastructure, encouraging technology companies to implement sustainable AI training methods, such as federated learning and energy-efficient neural networks. Additionally, data privacy concerns must be addressed, particularly in AI applications that rely on vast amounts of environmental and social data. AI-driven sustainability initiatives, such as smart grids, precision agriculture, and carbon footprint tracking, require extensive data collection, raising concerns about data security, consent, and ownership. Regulatory frameworks must ensure that AI systems comply with international data protection laws, such as the General Data Protection Regulation (GDPR), while maintaining data integrity for sustainability-driven decision-making.

The role of AI in Environmental, Social, and Governance (ESG) compliance has become increasingly critical as companies and investors seek to align their operations with sustainability goals. AI-driven ESG assessment tools enable businesses to analyze their environmental impact, monitor supply chain sustainability, and ensure ethical corporate governance. By leveraging natural language processing (NLP) and machine learning, AI can analyze vast datasets, including sustainability reports, regulatory filings, and climate risk disclosures, to assess a company's ESG performance. This automated ESG evaluation process enhances transparency and reduces the risk of greenwashing, where organizations falsely claim to be environmentally responsible. Furthermore, AI-powered climate risk modeling allows investors to evaluate the financial implications of climate change on asset portfolios, promoting sustainable investment strategies. Regulatory bodies, such as the Securities and Exchange Commission (SEC) in the United States and the EU Sustainable Finance

Disclosure Regulation (SFDR), are increasingly mandating ESG disclosures, pushing companies to integrate AI-driven analytics for compliance reporting.

Beyond corporate compliance, AI contributes to policy-driven sustainability reporting by enhancing environmental data accuracy and streamlining regulatory compliance processes. Governments and international organizations use AI to track emissions, detect regulatory violations, and enforce environmental laws. For example, satellite-based AI systems can monitor deforestation, illegal mining, and ocean pollution in real time, enabling authorities to take immediate action against environmental violations. Additionally, AI-driven blockchain technology is being explored to improve ESG data transparency by securely recording corporate sustainability commitments and ensuring that environmental claims are verifiable. The convergence of AI, blockchain, and IoT (Internet of Things) has the potential to revolutionize ESG compliance by creating automated, tamper-proof sustainability tracking systems. However, the ethical implications of AI-driven surveillance for environmental regulation must be carefully managed to prevent privacy infringements and ensure that sustainability monitoring is conducted in a fair and unbiased manner.

To maximize the positive impact of AI on sustainability policy frameworks, multi-stakeholder collaboration is essential. Governments, regulatory bodies, industry leaders, academia, and civil society must work together to establish global AI governance mechanisms that promote sustainability while addressing ethical and regulatory challenges (Francisco & Linnér, 2023). The development of AI ethics guidelines for sustainability, similar to the EU's AI Ethics Guidelines for Trustworthy AI, could provide a foundation for responsible AI deployment in environmental and social governance contexts. Furthermore, capacity-building initiatives are needed to equip policymakers, businesses, and communities with the knowledge and skills required to integrate AI into sustainability strategies effectively. By fostering an ecosystem of responsible AI innovation, regulatory frameworks can ensure that AI serves as a force for climate resilience, resource conservation, and inclusive economic development (Danish & Senjyu, 2023).

AI FOR GREEN GOVERNANCE AND DECISION MAKING

AI has emerged as a transformative force in green governance, revolutionizing how policymakers, governments, and institutions address environmental challenges. One of the most promising applications of AI in sustainability governance is AI-powered policy simulations and impact assessments, which enable data-driven decision-making. Traditional policy-making often relies on historical data and theoretical models, which may not accurately predict future environmental challenges (Ren et al., 2022). AI, with its machine learning and predictive analytics capabilities, can model complex environmental scenarios, assess the impact of policy interventions, and suggest optimal strategies for sustainability. For example, AI-driven simulations can analyze the effects of carbon pricing, emissions regulations, or renewable energy subsidies by factoring in real-time environmental and economic data (Olawade et al., 2024). These models enable policymakers to anticipate unintended consequences, optimize resource allocation, and refine regulations before implementation. Additionally, AI-powered Natural Language Processing (NLP) can analyze legislative texts, international agreements, and scientific literature to provide policymakers with comprehensive insights into best practices and emerging regulatory trends. AI also enhances the ability to track compliance with international agreements, such as the Paris Agreement, by assessing whether nations are meeting their climate commitments based on real-world data (Rashid & Kausik, 2024).

Another critical application of AI in green governance is AI for smart cities, carbon footprint monitoring, and biodiversity conservation. Smart cities leverage AI to improve energy efficiency, optimize urban planning, and reduce environmental footprints. AI-driven systems can analyze energy consumption patterns, detect inefficiencies in electricity grids, and optimize energy distribution, thereby reducing carbon emissions (Greif et al., 2024). For example, AI-powered traffic management systems use real-time data to optimize traffic flow, reducing congestion and emissions. Similarly, AI-driven waste management systems use predictive analytics to optimize waste collection routes, minimize landfill usage, and enhance recycling efficiency. AI is also pivotal in carbon footprint monitoring, as it enables real-time tracking of greenhouse gas (GHG) emissions across industries, transportation systems, and urban infrastructure. AI algorithms can process satellite imagery, sensor data, and industrial emissions reports to assess carbon footprints at a granular level, allowing policymakers to design more targeted carbon reduction strategies (Fang et al., 2023). Furthermore, AI is instrumental in biodiversity conservation, as it helps monitor endangered species, detect illegal deforestation, and combat wildlife trafficking. Machine learning models trained on drone imagery and satellite data can identify deforestation patterns, track changes in ecosystems, and predict areas at high risk of biodiversity loss (Raihan, 2023). AI-powered bioacoustic monitoring systems analyze soundscapes in forests and oceans to detect the presence of endangered species and assess ecosystem health. These technologies enable conservationists and policymakers to take proactive measures in preserving biodiversity and mitigating environmental damage (Ramadan et al., 2024).

A crucial yet often overlooked aspect of AI in green governance is strengthening institutional capacity with AI-driven governance models. AI can enhance institutional efficiency by automating administrative processes, improving regulatory compliance monitoring, and facilitating evidence-based policy formulation. Governments and international organizations are increasingly adopting AI-driven dashboards and decision-support systems to assess sustainability metrics, identify policy gaps, and coordinate multi-stakeholder initiatives (Wilson & van der Veldon, 2022). AI-powered governance models enhance transparency and accountability by automating data collection, processing, and reporting, reducing human errors and biases in sustainability assessments. Furthermore, AI enables decentralized governance by facilitating participatory decision-making, where citizens can engage in environmental policy discussions through AI-powered platforms. Blockchain-integrated AI solutions provide immutable records of environmental commitments, ensuring transparency and preventing greenwashing by corporations and governments (Vinueasa et al., 2020). Additionally, AI enhances disaster risk management by analyzing climate models, forecasting extreme weather events, and informing disaster preparedness strategies. AI-driven early warning systems help governments respond proactively to natural disasters such as hurricanes, floods, and wildfires, minimizing environmental and human losses. The integration of AI into governance structures is not without challenges, as ethical considerations such as algorithmic biases, data privacy, and the energy consumption of AI models must be addressed to ensure responsible implementation (Ghaffarian et al., 2023). However, when deployed effectively, AI has the potential to revolutionize environmental governance by providing actionable insights, improving policy coherence, and fostering a sustainable future. By harnessing AI for green governance, policymakers can create more resilient, adaptive, and environmentally conscious regulatory frameworks, ensuring that sustainability goals are achieved efficiently and equitably (Albahri et al., 2024).

CHALLENGES AND RISKS IN AI-DRIVEN SUSTAINABILITY

AI has immense potential to drive sustainable innovation, but its deployment comes with several challenges and risks, particularly in areas such as bias, transparency, accountability, energy consumption, and cybersecurity (Rayhan, 2023). One of the most pressing concerns is the issue of bias in AI models, which can lead to discriminatory outcomes and undermine the effectiveness of sustainability initiatives. AI systems rely on vast datasets, and if these datasets contain historical biases, the models can perpetuate and even amplify existing inequalities. For example, AI-driven environmental policies or resource allocation models may unintentionally favor certain regions or communities while marginalizing others (Murikah et al., 2024). This is especially problematic in climate adaptation strategies, where AI recommendations could be skewed due to biased training data, potentially exacerbating environmental injustices. Addressing bias requires robust data governance, inclusive dataset curation, and fairness-aware algorithms that ensure equitable outcomes for all stakeholders (Sanchez et al., 2024).

Transparency and accountability are also major challenges in AI-driven sustainability efforts. Many AI models, particularly deep learning systems, function as "black boxes," making it difficult to interpret their decision-making processes. This lack of transparency can hinder public trust and make it challenging for policymakers to rely on AI-driven insights for sustainability planning (Wischmeyer, 2019). For instance, if an AI system recommends deforestation in a certain area to optimize land use but fails to explain the rationale behind this decision, it may face resistance from environmental groups and policymakers. Accountability becomes even more complex when AI systems make critical decisions about environmental management, carbon credits, or conservation strategies. Without clear mechanisms to trace responsibility, it becomes difficult to hold entities accountable for unintended negative consequences. Therefore, there is a pressing need for explainable AI (XAI) techniques, regulatory frameworks, and third-party audits to ensure that AI-driven sustainability solutions remain transparent and accountable (Dwivedi et al., 2022).

Another significant concern is the paradox of AI's own energy consumption versus its role in promoting sustainability. Training and running AI models require vast computational power, leading to substantial energy use and carbon emissions (Nelson et al., 2023). For instance, training a single deep learning model can emit as much carbon dioxide as five cars over their entire lifetimes. While AI is being utilized to optimize energy grids, enhance renewable energy adoption, and reduce waste, its own energy footprint raises ethical concerns about sustainability. Data centers housing AI models consume massive amounts of electricity, often relying on non-renewable energy sources. This raises the question of whether AI is genuinely contributing to sustainability or merely shifting environmental burdens (Olawade et al., 2024). To mitigate this impact, there is an increasing focus on "green AI," which emphasizes energy-efficient algorithms, carbon-conscious data centers, and optimized hardware. Additionally, integrating AI with renewable energy sources and adopting federated learning techniques can help minimize its carbon footprint while maximizing its sustainability contributions (Biggi et al., 2025).

Cybersecurity and data privacy in eco-intelligent solutions represent another critical challenge. As AI-powered sustainability initiatives rely on vast amounts of environmental, corporate, and personal data, they become attractive targets for cyberattacks. A breach in an AI-driven smart grid system, for example, could lead to widespread energy disruptions, financial losses, and compromised sustainability goals (Kaur et al., 2023). Similarly, AI-based climate monitoring systems that collect data from satellites, IoT sensors, and weather stations could be vulnerable to hacking, leading to misinformation and manipulation of environmental data. Data privacy concerns also arise when AI models collect and process personal information related to energy consumption, carbon footprints, or sustainable behaviors. Without strict data protection regulations, individuals and organizations risk their data being misused or exploited (Popescu et al., 2024). Ensuring cybersecurity in AI-driven sustainability efforts requires robust encryption protocols, decentralized data storage, and compliance with privacy laws such as GDPR. Moreover, fostering collaboration between AI developers, policymakers, and cybersecurity experts is essential to building resilient and secure eco-intelligent systems (Ansari et al., 2022).

FUTURE DIRECTIONS AND RECOMMENDATIONS

The future of sustainable innovation hinges on a symbiotic relationship between AI and policy, where regulatory frameworks guide responsible AI deployment while AI enhances the efficiency and effectiveness of sustainability initiatives. This AI-policy symbiosis is crucial to ensuring that technological advancements align with environmental and ethical standards, fostering a balance between economic growth and ecological preservation (Rame et al., 2024). Governments must establish adaptive policies that promote transparency, fairness, and accountability in AI applications for sustainability, while industries should integrate AI-driven sustainability strategies into their operational models. Academia plays a pivotal role in advancing research on AI-driven environmental solutions, offering empirical insights that inform evidence-based policymaking and industry practices (Vinuesa et al., 2020).

Advancements in AI ethics, green AI, and regenerative technologies further underscore the potential for AI to drive sustainable transformation. Ethical AI frameworks should be embedded in regulatory policies to mitigate bias, ensure inclusivity, and prevent unintended consequences that may exacerbate environmental or social inequalities (Bayan, 2024). Green AI, which focuses on reducing the carbon footprint of AI models through energy-efficient computing and sustainable data processing, is imperative for minimizing the paradox of AI's environmental impact. Additionally, regenerative technologies—AI-driven solutions that go beyond sustainability to actively restore and replenish ecosystems—must be prioritized. Innovations such as AI-powered carbon capture, biodiversity monitoring, and precision reforestation exemplify how AI can contribute to reversing environmental damage rather than merely reducing harm (Konietzko et al., 2023).

Achieving these advancements necessitates multi-stakeholder collaboration, where governments, industries, and academia work together to drive AI-powered sustainability initiatives. Policymakers must engage with AI experts and sustainability researchers to develop robust regulations that facilitate responsible AI innovation (Greif et al., 2024). Industries should invest in AI-driven green solutions while ensuring compliance with evolving regulatory frameworks. Academia should foster interdisciplinary research that bridges AI, environmental science, and policy development. By fostering this collaborative ecosystem, AI can become a transformative force for sustainability, driving innovative solutions that address global environmental challenges while ensuring economic and social equity (Adanma & Ogunbiyi, 2024).

CONCLUSION

AI has emerged as a transformative force in driving sustainability and shaping policy frameworks for a greener future. Its applications in optimizing energy efficiency, reducing carbon footprints, enabling circular economies, and enhancing environmental monitoring have demonstrated significant potential in addressing global sustainability challenges. AI-powered predictive analytics, machine learning models, and digital twins have revolutionized decision-making processes, providing policymakers and industries with data-driven insights to design and implement effective sustainability strategies (Johnson & Olanite Enoch, 2021). However, while AI presents immense opportunities, it also raises concerns about ethical deployment, data privacy, algorithmic biases, and energy consumption. Therefore, harnessing AI for sustainability requires a balanced approach that integrates technological advancements with robust regulatory frameworks to ensure equitable and responsible implementation.

The roadmap for AI-powered sustainable innovation lies in fostering interdisciplinary collaboration between governments, industries, academia, and civil society. Policymakers must establish clear regulations that promote transparency, accountability, and inclusivity in AI development while mitigating potential risks (Goralski & Tan, 2020). Investment in green AI i.e., AI models optimized for energy efficiency—alongside the promotion of ethical AI design principles can enhance its positive environmental impact. Moreover, AI-driven sustainability initiatives should align with global sustainability frameworks such as the UN SDGs and the Paris Agreement to maximize their contributions to climate action.

A call to action for responsible AI deployment demands a multi-stakeholder approach where technology is designed and used for the collective good. Governments must enforce policies that encourage sustainable AI applications, while businesses should integrate AI-driven environmental strategies into their operations. Academia and research institutions must continue innovating AI models that prioritize sustainability and ethical considerations. Public awareness and engagement are equally crucial in fostering responsible AI adoption. By embedding sustainability at the core of AI development and policy design, societies can ensure that AI serves as a catalyst for environmental protection, economic resilience, and social equity in the transition toward a more sustainable future.

REFERENCES

Adanma, U. M., & Ogunbiyi, E. O. (2024). Artificial intelligence in environmental conservation: Evaluating cyber risks and opportunities for sustainable practices. *Computer Science & IT Research Journal*, *5*(5), 1178–1209.

Albahri, A. S., Khaleel, Y. L., Habeeb, M. A., Ismael, R. D., Hameed, Q. A., Deveci, M., & Alzubaidi, L. (2024). A systematic review of trustworthy artificial intelligence applications in natural disasters. *Computers & Electrical Engineering*, *118*, 109409.

Almeida, D. V., Kolinjivadi, V., Ferrando, T., Roy, B., Herrera, H., Gonçalves, M. V., & Van Hecken, G. (2023). The "greening" of empire: The European Green Deal as the EU first agenda. *Political Geography*, *105*, 102925.

Alnaser, A. A., Maxi, M., & Elmousalami, H. (2024). AI-Powered Digital Twins and Internet of Things for Smart Cities and Sustainable Building Environment. *Applied Sciences (Basel, Switzerland)*, *14*(24), 12056.

Ansari, M. F., Dash, B., Sharma, P., & Yathiraju, N. (2022). The impact and limitations of artificial intelligence in cybersecurity: A literature review. *International Journal of Advanced Research in Computer and Communication Engineering*.

Arya, S. (2024). Harnessing Big Data and Machine Learning for Climate Change Predictions and Mitigation. In *Maintaining a Sustainable World in the Nexus of Environmental Science and AI* (pp. 383–408). IGI Global.

Ashfaq, A., Kamran, M., Rehman, F., Sarfaraz, N., Ilyas, H. U., & Riaz, H. H. (2022, March). Role of artificial intelligence in renewable energy and its scope in future. In *2022 5th International Conference on Energy Conservation and Efficiency (ICECE)* (pp. 1-6). IEEE.

Bayan, F. M. H. (2024). The Ethics of AI: Navigating the Moral dilemmas of Artificial Intelligence. *Arab Journal for Scientific Publishing (AJSP). ISSN*, *2663*, 5798.

Bibri, S. E., Huang, J., Jagatheesaperumal, S. K., & Krogstie, J. (2024). The synergistic interplay of artificial intelligence and digital twin in environmentally planning sustainable smart cities: A comprehensive systematic review. *Environmental Science and Ecotechnology*, •••, 100433. PMID: 38831974

Biggi, G., Iori, M., Mazzei, J., & Mina, A. (2025). Green Intelligence: The AI content of green technologies. *Eurasian Business Review*, 1-38.

Chen, W., Men, Y., Fuster, N., Osorio, C., & Juan, A. A. (2024). Artificial intelligence in logistics optimization with sustainable criteria: A review. *Sustainability, 16*(21), 9145.

Cowls, J., Tsamados, A., Taddeo, M., & Floridi, L. (2023). The AI gambit: Leveraging artificial intelligence to combat climate change—opportunities, challenges, and recommendations. *AI & Society*, •••, 1–25. PMID: 34690449

Cumming, D., Saurabh, K., Rani, N., & Upadhyay, P. (2024). Towards AI ethics-led sustainability frameworks and toolkits: Review and research agenda. *Journal of Sustainable Finance and Accounting*, *1*, 100003.

Daly, A., Hagendorff, T., Hui, L., Mann, M., Marda, V., Wagner, B., & Wei Wang, W. (2022). AI, Governance and Ethics: Global Perspectives.

Danish, M. S. S., & Senjyu, T. (2023). Shaping the future of sustainable energy through AI-enabled circular economy policies. *Circular Economy*, *2*(2), 100040.

Dwivedi, Y. K., Hughes, L., Kar, A. K., Baabdullah, A. M., Grover, P., Abbas, R., & Wade, M. (2022). Climate change and COP26: Are digital technologies and information management part of the problem or the solution? An editorial reflection and call to action. *International Journal of Information Management*, *63*, 102456.

Fang, B., Yu, J., Chen, Z., Osman, A. I., Farghali, M., Ihara, I., & Yap, P. S. (2023). Artificial intelligence for waste management in smart cities: A review. *Environmental Chemistry Letters*, *21*(4), 1959–1989. PMID: 37362015

Francisco, M., & Linnér, B. O. (2023). AI and the governance of sustainable development. An idea analysis of the European Union, the United Nations, and the World Economic Forum. *Environmental Science & Policy*, *150*, 103590.

Ghaffarian, S., Taghikhah, F. R., & Maier, H. R. (2023). Explainable artificial intelligence in disaster risk management: Achievements and prospective futures. *International Journal of Disaster Risk Reduction*, *98*, 104123.

Goralski, M. A., & Tan, T. K. (2020). Artificial intelligence and sustainable development. *International Journal of Management Education*, *18*(1), 100330.

Greif, L., Kimmig, A., El Bobbou, S., Jurisch, P., & Ovtcharova, J. (2024). Strategic view on the current role of AI in advancing environmental sustainability: A SWOT analysis. *Discover Artificial Intelligence*, *4*(1), 45.

Gundeti, R., Vuppala, K., & Kasireddy, V. (2024). The future of AI and environmental sustainability: Challenges and opportunities. *Exploring Ethical Dimensions of Environmental Sustainability and Use of AI*, 346-371.

Gunther, H., & Rose, J. (2020). Governing AI: The importance of environmentally sustainable and equitable innovation. *Envtl. L. Rep.*, *50*, 10888.

Issa, A. A., Majed, S., Ameer, S. A., & Al-Jawahry, H. M. (2024). Farming in the digital age: Smart agriculture with ai and iot. In *E3S Web of conferences* (Vol. 477, p. 00081). EDP Sciences.

Johnson, J., & Olanite Enoch, E. O. (2021). Building Resilient Cloud Ecosystems: The Role of Technological Advances in Data Center Infrastructure.

Kajela, D., & Manshahia, M. S. (2017). Optimization of renewable energy systems: A review. *International Journal of Scientific Research in Science and Technology*, *3*(8), 769–795.

Kar, A. K., Choudhary, S. K., & Singh, V. K. (2022). How can artificial intelligence impact sustainability: A systematic literature review. *Journal of Cleaner Production*, *376*, 134120.

Kaur, R., Gabrijelčič, D., & Klobučar, T. (2023). Artificial intelligence for cybersecurity: Literature review and future research directions. *Information Fusion*, *97*, 101804.

Konietzko, J., Das, A., & Bocken, N. (2023). Towards regenerative business models: A necessary shift? *Sustainable Production and Consumption*, *38*, 372–388.

Koshariya, A. K., Kalaiyarasi, D., Jovith, A. A., Sivakami, T., Hasan, D. S., & Boopathi, S. (2023). Ai-enabled iot and wsn-integrated smart agriculture system. In *Artificial Intelligence Tools and Technologies for Smart Farming and Agriculture Practices* (pp. 200–218). IGI global.

Lodhi, S. K., Gill, A. Y., & Hussain, H. K. (2024). Green innovations: Artificial intelligence and sustainable materials in production. *BULLET: Jurnal Multidisiplin Ilmu*, *3*(4), 492–507.

Mennella, C., Maniscalco, U., De Pietro, G., & Esposito, M. (2024). Ethical and regulatory challenges of AI technologies in healthcare: A narrative review. *Heliyon*, *10*(4). PMID: 38384518

Mitra, S., Kumar, H., Gupta, M. P., & Bhattacharya, J. (2023). Entrepreneurship in smart cities: Elements of the start-up ecosystem. *Journal of Science and Technology Policy Management*, *14*(3), 592–611.

Murikah, W., Nthenge, J. K., & Musyoka, F. M. (2024). Bias and ethics of AI systems applied in auditing-A systematic review. *Scientific African*, •••, 02281.

Nelson, J. P., Biddle, J. B., & Shapira, P. (2023). Applications and societal implications of artificial intelligence in manufacturing: A systematic review. *arXiv preprint arXiv:2308.02025.*

Nishant, R., Kennedy, M., & Corbett, J. (2020). Artificial intelligence for sustainability: Challenges, opportunities, and a research agenda. *International Journal of Information Management*, *53*, 102104.

Okeleke, P. A., Ajiga, D., Folorunsho, S. O., & Ezeigweneme, C. (2024). Predictive analytics for market trends using AI: A study in consumer behavior. *International Journal of Engineering Research Updates*, *7*(1), 36–49.

Olawade, D. B., Wada, O. Z., David-Olawade, A. C., Fapohunda, O., Ige, A. O., & Ling, J. (2024). Artificial intelligence potential for net zero sustainability: Current evidence and prospects. *Next sustainability, 4*, 100041.

Perc, M., Ozer, M., & Hojnik, J. (2019). Social and juristic challenges of artificial intelligence. *Palgrave Communications*, *5*(1).

Popescu, S. M., Mansoor, S., Wani, O. A., Kumar, S. S., Sharma, V., Sharma, A., & Chung, Y. S. (2024). Artificial intelligence and IoT driven technologies for environmental pollution monitoring and management. *Frontiers in Environmental Science*, *12*, 1336088.

Raihan, A. (2023). Original Research Article Artificial intelligence and machine learning applications in forest management and biodiversity conservation.

Ramadan, M. N., Ali, M. A., Khoo, S. Y., & Alkhedher, M. (2024). AI-powered IoT and UAV systems for real-time detection and prevention of illegal logging. *Results in Engineering*, *24*, 103277.

Raman, R., Pattnaik, D., Lathabai, H. H., Kumar, C., Govindan, K., & Nedungadi, P. (2024). Green and sustainable AI research: An integrated thematic and topic modeling analysis. *Journal of Big Data*, *11*(1), 1–28.

Rame, R., Purwanto, P., & Sudarno, S. (2024). Industry 5.0 and sustainability: An overview of emerging trends and challenges for a green future. *Innovation and Green Development*, *3*(4), 100173.

Rashid, A. B., & Kausik, A. K. (2024). AI revolutionizing industries worldwide: A comprehensive overview of its diverse applications. *Hybrid Advances*, 100277.

Rayhan, A. (2023). The role of AI in sustainable development: Opportunities and challenges.

Rehman, A. U., Alamoudi, Y., Khalid, H. M., Morchid, A., Muyeen, S. M., & Abdelaziz, A. Y. (2024). Smart agriculture technology: An integrated framework of renewable energy resources, IoT-based energy management, and precision robotics. *Cleaner Energy Systems*, *9*, 100132.

Ren, Y., Xie, R., Yu, F. R., Huang, T., & Liu, Y. (2022). Green intelligence networking for connected and autonomous vehicles in smart cities. *IEEE Transactions on Green Communications and Networking*, *6*(3), 1591–1603.

Sanchez, T. W., Brenman, M., & Ye, X. (2024). The ethical concerns of artificial intelligence in urban planning. *Journal of the American Planning Association*, •••, 1–14.

Schmitt, M. (2023). Automated machine learning: AI-driven decision making in business analytics. *Intelligent Systems with Applications*, *18*, 200188.

Strubell, E., Ganesh, A., & McCallum, A. (2020, April). Energy and policy considerations for modern deep learning research. *Proceedings of the AAAI Conference on Artificial Intelligence*, *34*(09), 13693–13696.

Truby, J. (2020). Governing artificial intelligence to benefit the UN sustainable development goals. *Sustainable Development*, *28*(4), 946–959.

Vinuesa, R., Azizpour, H., Leite, I., Balaam, M., Dignum, V., Domisch, S., & Fuso Nerini, F. (2020). The role of artificial intelligence in achieving the Sustainable Development Goals. *Nature Communications*, *11*(1), 233. PMID: 31932590

Vis, Y. A. (2020). *Characteristics of a successful public-private-partnership on Artificial Intelligence* (Bachelor's thesis).

Wilson, C., & Van Der Velden, M. (2022). Sustainable AI: An integrated model to guide public sector decision-making. *Technology in Society*, *68*, 101926.

Wischmeyer, T. (2019). Artificial intelligence and transparency: opening the black box. In *Regulating artificial intelligence* (pp. 75–101). Springer International Publishing.

Zhang, Y. (2024). Circular economy innovations: Balancing fossil fuel impact on green economic development. *Heliyon*, *10*(18). PMID: 39328564

Chapter 9
Hate Speech:
Scope of AI for Its Legal Solution Through Real-Time Detection

Shrabana Chattopadhyay
https://orcid.org/0000-0001-7648-6535
Department of Law, University of Engineering and Management, Kolkata, India

Snehatit Sett
https://orcid.org/0009-0006-5093-409X
Symbiosis Law School, Noida, Symbiosis International University, Pune, India

Srijani Dasgupta
Strategic Marketing Solutions and Research Centre, Kolkata, India

ABSTRACT

Hate speech remains a pervasive issue in contemporary society, exacerbated by the rapid expansion of digital communication platforms. This article explores the use of Artificial Intelligence (AI) in combating hate speech, focusing on its detection, classification, and moderation capabilities. It explores how AI can be integrated into legal structures, ethical considerations, and the interplay between AI-driven hate speech detection and freedom of expression. The study provides a comprehensive overview of AI's role in mitigating hate speech, offering recommendations for policymakers and technology developers.

INTRODUCTION

In India, any speech that incites hatred, prejudice, or violence against any individual or group by discrimination based on religion, caste, status, gender/sexuality,

DOI: 10.4018/979-8-3373-2387-9.ch009

and race is termed hate speech, (Nayak, 2025; Narendrakumar & Fnu, 2023). In a multicultural country like India, where such speech can easily provoke an inter-communal riot leading to public disorder, it emerges to be an crucial social evil as well as a legal issue. The Indian legal system indeed tackles hate speech through statutory laws, court rulings, and constitutional requirements to combat hate speech, (Venkataramanan, 2022). While Article 19(1)(a) grants the right to free speech and expression, it also permits reasonable restrictions based on considerations such as sovereignty, morality, decency, and public order.

The "Bharatiya Nyaya Sanhita, 2023" (erstwhile the Indian Penal Code, 1860) comprises statutory provisions against hate speech such as Section 196 (previously Section 153A of IPC), directed against promoting any hatred amongst different groups; Section 299 (previously Section 295A of IPC), directed against anything provocative to religious sentiments; and Section 353 (erstwhile Section 505 of IPC), which deals with statements causing public mischief. Also relevant is Section 69A of the "Information Technology Act", which empowers the government to restrict access to any content threatening national security and public order and can be applicable in cases of online hate speech. The courts have also defined and established the scope of these existing legal standards.

"Shreya Singhal v. Union of India, 2015" (Gnanith, 2015) marks one of the landmark judgments in India that have dealt with online freedom of expression and the legitimacy of Section 66A of the "Information Technology Act", struck down for being too overbroad and ambiguous, (Chakrapani, 2025).

In India, hate speech consists usually of offensive comments directed against persons or groups on grounds of race, sex, caste, religion, or ethnicity. Some of the forms of hate speech that are commonly found are:

1. Religious prejudice: Hate speech quite often targets religious communities, anti-Muslim feelings, especially in a multireligious atmosphere like India, being most pervasive.
2. Caste-Based Discrimination: Although there are laws that prohibit caste discrimination, it is still common for people to speak disparagingly of someone in terms of caste, (Smrutirekha & Madheswaran, 2016). It includes derogatory words and statements that support preconceived ideas and stereotypes about that particular caste, (Das & Das, 2021)
3. Ethnic slurs: The ethnic diversity of India ensures that there are times when people belonging from different ethnicity nation face ethnic slurs that aggravate polarization and reinforce prejudicial stereotypes.
4. Gender-Based Hate Speech: Misogynistic hate speech, such as disparaging comments and menaces of gender-based violence, is frequently directed towards women.

5. Race-Based Inflammatory Language: Racial slurs and discriminatory language can be directed at certain communities, especially those of African heritage and those from the Northeastern states of India, (Hunt, 2016).

It is important to recognise that hate speech can happen both online and offline, but the popularity of social media has led to a quicker diffusion and possibly a bigger effect on public order and communal cohesion. Both legislative actions and proactive social initiatives are necessary in India's fight against hate speech. Whether we come across hate speech online or in person, it is our duty as citizens to confront and challenge it. Significant research gaps still exist, impeding effective intervention despite India's efforts to prevent hate speech. There is a huge absence of qualitative data which is a core problem that requires methodical collection of hate speech incidents across communities, regions, and platforms in India and evaluating the same for better understanding. Such data would allow for an in-depth understanding of the frequency, nature, and implications of online hate speech, (hate-alert, 2019). Further, the current legal framework is not only lacking in the context of keeping up with the changing nature of hate speech but also in the context of online hate speech in India. The only way to overcome such a challenge is by enhancing the role of platforms in data collection and analysis, which requires only a holistic approach, (Gupta & Gupta, 2020; Lepoutre, 2017). There is an urgent need for additional qualitative research to determine the extent to which sociopolitical dynamics, including campaign politics and ideological propaganda, shape hate speech and interpersonal relationships, (Zapata & Deroy, 2023). There is also a need for additional research to understand how social networking sites and media channels enable the spreading and escalation of hate speech, particularly in the context of accountability and responsibility of platform providers, (Omar & Hashem, 2022).

Understanding the impacts of these factors is crucial for developing effective mechanisms of interventions, (Müller & Schwarz, 2020). Filling in these research gaps could improve efforts to combat hate speech in India, improve policy and legal reforms, and provide a better knowledge of hate speech trends, (Vergani, 2024). In the Republic of India, hate speech is a major issue. Indian law, however, does not employ the term "hate speech." Different Indian regulations cover different types of what could be considered hate speech in different ways.

This paper lists some first concerns we discovered when thoroughly researching India's anti-hate speech legislation, (Hyman, 2021). It highlights some of the main issues that come up when hate speech occurs both online and offline, particularly when it is expressed as a possible encouragement to violence.

In order to outline the present legal framework utilised to deal with hate speech, we first discuss hate speech as inciting violence in India. This paper addresses the conflict between hate speech laws and freedom of expression as the legal framework has resulted in the suppression of free speech, (SELMA Partners, 2019). It also looks at the effects of hate speech laws and tactics other than criminalisation that are employed in India to combat hate speech online. We concentrate on state-led strategies rather than the attempts of non-state actors to address the issue of hate speech.

A lack of thorough studies on the actual application of hate speech laws in various Indian regions and a dearth of empirical information about the legal procedures from report to prosecution are two examples of research gaps. Furthermore, given the quickly changing digital context, more academic research is required to critically assess the balance that courts strike between allowing free speech and criminalising hate speech, (Paterson, Brown, & Walters, 2018).

Numerous reports around the world have dubbed 2018 the "year of online hate" (Simpson, 2012). In its "Transparency Report", social media behemoth Facebook revealed shocking figures regarding their hateful content, a staggering number of 3 million hateful posts was removed from its platform, (Free Word Centre, 2018). YouTube, which permits the free sharing of videos on its website, deleted over 25,000 videos in just one month, (National Law University Delhi, 2024). These figures merely represent the beginning of the problem and show how things are slowly getting out of hand. As we have seen recently in India, hate speech in its worst form has resulted in terrible hate crimes, including violent battles between religious communities and communal riots (Bajoria, 2016), all of which were caused by provocative speech spread by groups that seek to divide people, (Olsen et al., n.d). There were numerous accounts of horrific murders in which "hatred" for a different group or community manifested itself in a particularly twisted way through mob lynching, (Fowler & Harwell, 2018). Words were used in their most perilous form in these circumstances, "...as weapons to ambush, terrorise, wound, humiliate and degrade" (Facebook, n.d.) people and communities.

DEFINITION AND OUTLINE OF HATE SPEECH:

In modern times, hate speech has expanded beyond simply being offensive; it now includes communication that is demeaning, discriminatory, insulting, provocative, or even so hostile that it incites the use of violence or provokes violent retaliatory reactions. As a result, the peace and order of society as a whole are disturbed. More significantly, hate speech turns into a particularly horrible kind of hate crime that directly harms the victims' physical and mental health. It has intangible effects on its victims that stifle their freedom of speech and expression and prevent them from taking part in public conversation and the democratic process.

"United Nations Organisation" has defined the term hate speech as "any kind of communication in speech, writing or behaviour, that attacks or uses pejorative or discriminatory language with reference to a person or a group on the basis of who they are, in other words, based on their religion, ethnicity, nationality, race, colour, descent, gender or other identity factor" (FP Staff, 2013).

Supreme Court Directs States to Proactively Register FIRs Against Hate Speech

In a historic decision, the Supreme Court of India required all states to automatically register First Information Reports (FIRs) in hate speech cases without awaiting a formal complaint. The court stated that all persons guilty of hate speech regardless of their religion deserve punishment under this ruling and stressed the need to maintain the secular character of the state. The "Bharatiya Nyaya Sanhita, 2023" (BNS) was discussed and certain laws mentioned, such as Sections 196, 197, 299, and 353, to emphasize their utility in prosecuting offenders of hate speech.

The Supreme Court urged states to timely intervene in all instances of hate speech, whether any formal complaint has been lodged, thereby emphasizing the urgent need to protect India's secular character. In other words, the court explicitly stated that hate speech must fall under the purview of the penal provisions under the IPC mentioned above. Additionally, the court mandated that all state director generals of police make sure their subordinates are aware of this command, stressing that any resistance on the part of law enforcement to follow this order would be considered contempt of court.

Although the court's order was widely praised for its dedication to preventing hate speech, those around them were worried about possible violations of free speech rights. Advocates emphasised the significance of maintaining free speech while successfully combating hate speech. The necessity for a balanced approach based on current jurisprudence on hate speech and the implementation of the rule of law was emphasised as they warned against the introduction of harsh regulations that could unintentionally further restrict free expression.

Facebook, which has 2 billion users worldwide and hosts a third of the world's population, defines hate speech as a direct attack on individuals based on "protected characteristics" such as race, ethnicity, national origin, religious belief, sexual preferences, socioeconomic status, sex, gender, gender identity, or a serious illness or disability. However, there is no universally accepted definition of hate speech. It also defines "attacks" as requests for segregation or exclusion, declarations of inferiority, or violent or dehumanising speech, (The Indian Express, 2018). Apparently, some of these safeguards are also extended to refugees and immigrants of all types. Facebook owns Instagram and WhatsApp; thus its community rules are applicable to all of its products. Additionally, users are prohibited from promoting violence against or directly attacking or threatening other people on the basis of race, ethnicity, national origin, sexual preference, personality type, spiritual belief, age, disability, or serious disease, according to Twitter's "hateful content policy." Additionally, it asserts that it prevents users from expressing hatred for specific people or groups in display photos and online bios (Saldanha, 2017), as well as from posting hostile symbols or images. However, the generic and wide boundaries of social media platforms' norms for acceptable behaviour are rapidly failing to address the prevalence, dissemination, and impact of hate speech, forcing them to become more dynamic. They must adjust to linguistic, religious, or cultural sensitivity and be on guard against political propaganda abuse, especially in India. Facebook says it has learnt additional languages to use its AI technologies for identifying hate speech. According to the platform, throughout the two quarters between 2018 and 2019, technology improved its ability to identify and address hate speech before users report it by roughly 14%, (Webb, 2011).

In order to detect violent, abusive, or hateful content, the majority of platforms have started to give priority to the development of machine learning algorithms. In June 2019, YouTube, Google's video division, announced that it would take down films including white nationalist content. YouTube allows users to publish videos on its platform for public viewing. Moreover, it asserts that it has modified its algorithms to "halve the views of videos deemed borderline content," (Yadav, n.d.). In several instances, it was stated that YouTube, which gives users a portion of the advertising revenue generated by each click on their video, had simply removed the offending user's access to the revenue share while leaving content unaltered, (Guterres, 2019).

The concept of a "neutral platform," or one that can or is genuinely dedicated to a clean space online, is actually a lie, according to communications expert and scholar Tarleton Gillespie. Conflict attracts comments, criticism, and even abuse, which increases the quantity of hits and interactions. For traffic, the more controversial, the better. He claims that Twitter has largely gone unchecked in fostering a culture of harassment, especially against women. Due to the widespread use of explicit threats of rape and violence, as well as the doxing or release of users' personal information, Twitter was finally compelled to defend freedom of expression as the foundation for stricter safeguards against hate and abuse, "allowing users to remain and opinions to flourish," (Facebook, n.d.).

CEO, Jack Dorsey, was called before India's Parliamentary committee on information technology in February 2019 to address accusations of "liberal bias" (Twitter, n.d.). The ruling BJP-led committee's summons was based on a complaint by party members, many of whom had been charged with escalating the platform's toxicity since the Hindu right party's victory in the 2014 Indian general elections, which saw them rise to power without challenge, (Richard, 2018). With the enormous amount of support Prime Minister Narendra Modi and his party have on social media, the summons was viewed as nothing less than comical. Just four months prior to the summons of the Indian parliament committee, the summons was viewed as a blatant copy of President Trump's strategy, (The YouTube Team, 2019).

The Election Commission of India allegedly held a closed-door meeting in March 2016 to investigate political "hate speech" and "provocative advertisements" (Civic Space, 2018). Na-sim Zaidi, the Chief Election Commissioner, is accused of saying at this meeting:

> *...this [hate speech] is one of the issue[s] that we had flagged for the ongoing assembly polls in five states. All political parties have supported and have suggested and have committed that they will ensure that the upcoming elections are conducted with highest standards and decency and with decorum. The Commission is assured by all these political parties. We have also urged and appealed to them, (Civic Space, 2018).*

The term "hate speech," which has many different meanings, has no clear definition. The Cambridge Dictionary defines it as public statements that incite hatred or support violence against a person or group on the basis of characteristics such as ethnicity, gender, sexual orientation, or faith, (Gillespie, n.d.). This is expanded by the Encyclopaedia of the American Constitution (Mirchandani, 2019) to include communications that show hostility or denigration because of traits like sexual orientation, religion, race, or colour.

Because the terms "hate" and "disparagement" have no internationally accepted definition, there are differing legal interpretations of them around the world. There are continuous discussions about the relationship between hate speech laws and freedom of expression because different nations have different legal definitions, (Narayanan, 2019). Some countries select protected groups based on particular characteristics and define hate speech as acts that incite violence or prejudice against a group. Notably, many things that come under this category have constitutional protection in the United States, but the phrase "hate speech" is not recognised in the legal systems of certain other nations, (Mirchandani, n.d.).

Online Hate Speech

Governments trying to control online hate speech face difficulties because of the worldwide nature of the internet. The challenge is that since the internet crosses national boundaries, it is impossible to adopt and enforce extensive government rules consistently. Issues with jurisdiction and divergent viewpoints from other nations present challenges for governments, (Press Trust of India, 2016). A French court held Yahoo! Inc. liable for open Nazi memorabilia auctions in "Yahoo! Inc. v. La Ligue Contre Le Racisme et l'Antisemitisme", which serves as an example. Because Yahoo! refused to comply, a U.S. court decided that the French verdict was not enforceable in the United States. These disputes make the process of creating national regulations more difficult. Although there are international initiatives and legislation to combat hate speech online, the way these treaties are used and interpreted varies from nation to nation, which further complicates the regulatory (Cambridge Dictionary, 2019) environment.

Through their stated terms of service, which specify what content is allowed on their platforms and frequently forbid hate speech, many technological firms voluntarily regulate online hate speech. Facebook, Google, Microsoft, and Twitter made a major commitment to a European Union code of behaviour on May 31, 2016. The "majority of valid notifications for removal of illegal hate speech" posted on their platforms have to be reviewed within 24 hours, according to this agreement, (Brown-Sica & Beall, 1999). These businesses use a variety of methods to control hate speech, such as employee-performed manual content reviews, AI flagging, and user reporting, (Herz & Molnár, 2012). In order to reduce the amount of offensive content that appears in search results, major search engines like Google Search modify their algorithms, (Kinney, 2008). Despite these endeavours, online hate speech remains a persistent issue, (Banks, 2010).

HISTORICAL TRACES OF HATE SPEECH

American civil rights organisations vigorously pushed for restrictions on hate speech against racism and spiritual organisations in the 1940s and 1950s in response to the atrocities of World War II, (Gagliardone et al., 2015). These groups used the idea of group libel as a framework in their search for legal ways to combat the violence that is a part of hate speech. In his study of the history of criminal libel, scholar Jeremy Waldron (2012), highlights that these rules attempted to preserve a shared understanding of each person's standing, dignity, and reputation within the social structure in addition to preventing acts of violence.

In 1952, the United States Supreme Court upheld group libel statutes in the Beauharnais v. Illinois case, marking a key legal milestone for this viewpoint, (Hatano, 2023). However, the use of collective libel became less popular in the 1960s as the civil rights movements of that time grew more supportive of individual rights. Notably, those who support individual rights are not the only ones who criticise collective defamation laws. Critical race theorist Richard Delgado is in favour of limiting hate speech legally, but he contends that defamation is an insufficiently broad definition to effectively combat hate speech. Delgado highlights the difficulties in obtaining reparation within the current legal system (Schulze, 2019) and suggests a legal approach that would create a particular area of tort law to handle racist remarks, (ADL, 2021). The earliest known incidence of hate speech on the internet dates back to its early years, when neo-Nazi George Dietz developed a bulletin board system in 1983, (Walker, 1994).

FACTORS RESPONSIBLE FOR RISE OF HATE SPEECH

A complex web of interrelated causes contributes to the spread of hate speech globally, each of which has a unique but related impact. The rise in hate speech around the world is caused by a complex web of interrelated elements. Deep societal divisions are shown by social fragmentation and polarisation, which are best illustrated by incidents such as the Charlottesville demonstration in 2017. As evidenced by the Rohingya situation in Myanmar, political instability and authoritarianism show how politicians can use hate speech as a weapon, fuelling persecution and humanitarian catastrophes. As demonstrated in Greece during the Eurozone crisis, economic inequality can result in scapegoating and a rise in hate speech directed against vulnerable populations, such as immigrants.

Technological developments are a major factor in the spread of hate speech, especially on social media. The murders at the Christchurch Mosque in New Zealand serve as a reminder of how extremist ideas and acts of violence may be disseminated via internet platforms. Grievances from the past, like those in the Balkans in the 1990s, demonstrate how hate speech may take advantage of group trauma and spark mass violence.

Cultural conflicts are exacerbated by globalisation, as evidenced by the emergence of far-right movements in Europe, and lax enforcement and legal protections, as seen in Russia, can permit hate speech to proliferate without consequence. Groups like ISIS take advantage of internet echo chambers and filter bubbles, which fuel radicalisation and the spread of hateful ideology around the world. Hate speech is further fuelled by cultural and religious extremism, as demonstrated by the growth of Hindu nationalism in India.

Lastly, as evidenced by the Rohingya issue, a major aspect is their dearth of education and media literacy. Comprehensive efforts to address these interrelated factors, promote inclusivity, combat misinformation, and support global education and media literacy campaigns are necessary to combat the rise of hate speech on a worldwide scale. These instances demonstrate the complexity of hate speech and the ways in which various elements come together to foster an atmosphere that encourages its spread. These elements frequently reinforce one another, creating an environment that is conducive to the spread of hate speech across the globe. In order to effectively address these underlying issues, comprehensive approaches are needed that protect democratic principles while also fostering social cohesiveness and thwarting discrimination, (Waldron, 2012).

INSTANCES OF HATE SPEECH

Rohingya Crisis (2017-2018- Myanmar)

The violence against Myanmar's Rohingya Muslim minority was exacerbated in large part by hate speech on social media. The political and military leaders' discriminatory rhetoric stoked a humanitarian crisis that resulted in massive displacement, aggression, and accusations of ethnic cleansing. Crimes towards the Rohingya population increased as a result of the false narratives spreading on many platforms, (Waldron, 2012).

Christchurch Mosque Shootings (2019 - New Zealand):

A horrific attack on two mosques in Christchurch, New Zealand, in March 2019 by a white supremacist claimed 51 lives and injured numerous more. The assailant used online tools to disseminate hate speech and extremist ideology by live-streaming the shootings on social media. This tragedy highlighted the prevalence of hate speech around the world and the part that digital platforms play in spreading such violence, (Waldron, 2012).

Charlottesville Rally (2017 -USA)

The 2017 Charlottesville, Virginia, "Unite the Right" demonstration served as a centre of gravity for far-right, neo-Nazi, and white nationalist organisations. This incident intensified into violent altercations with opposing demonstrators, highlighting the real-world repercussions of hate speech. The episode demonstrated the practical effects of provocative discourse and brought attention to the rise of hate groups in the US, (Waldron, 2012).

Halle Synagogue Shooting (2019)

On Yom Kippur, an individual from the far right extremist tried to carry out a mass shooting at a synagogue in Halle, Germany. The livestreamed incident demonstrated how online platforms may be used to disseminate extremist views, (Waldron, 2012).

Pulwama Attack (2019)

India-Pakistan tensions increased after a suicide bombing in Pulwama, Kashmir. The violence was made worse by hate speech and nationalist rhetoric on social media platforms, demonstrating the connection between online debate and actual occurrences, (Waldron, 2012).

YouTube Shooting (2018)

The YouTube headquarters in San Bruno, California, was the target of a shooter. The episode sparked worries about the possible influence of online hate speech on people's behaviour, even if it was mostly connected to complaints about the site, (Waldron, 2012).

Xenophobic Attacks in South Africa (2019)

Foreign nationals were the subject of xenophobic attacks in South Africa. Hate speech that was stoked by anti-immigrant emotions and economic discontent resulted in violent attacks, looting, and community displacement, (Waldron, 2012).

Online Misogyny and Harassment (Global)

Online harassment and hate speech are problems for women everywhere. Discussions concerning the relationship between gender-based violence and digital spaces have been sparked by the usage of misogynistic rhetoric and threats on social media platforms, (Waldron, 2012).

Communal Violence (India)

In India, hate speech has occasionally resulted in intercommunal violence. Religious and ethnic tensions have been exacerbated by the use of social media platforms to spread divisive messages, (Waldron, 2012).

Paris Attacks (2015)

ISIS-affiliated radicals carried out coordinated terrorist strikes in Paris, France, which claimed many lives. Online hate speech and propaganda had played a role in radicalising the assailants, (Waldron, 2012).

El Paso Walmart Shooting (2019)

A mass shooting that targeted the Hispanic population in particular occurred when a white supremacist targeted a Walmart in El Paso, Texas. Anti-immigrant attitudes frequently heard in internet hate speech were reflected in the attacker's manifesto, (Waldron, 2012).

Synagogue Shooting in Poway (2019)

A gunman discharged a firearm at the Chabad of Poway synagogue in California, USA, amidst a Passover celebration. Influenced by anti-Semitic beliefs, the attacker published a hateful screed online prior to the assault, (Waldron, 2012).

Black Lives Matter Movement (2020-2021):

The Black Lives Matter movement encountered a lot of hate speech and false information online, but there was not a single incident. The campaign brought attention to how hate speech affects underprivileged groups and how internet platforms are necessary to address these problems, (Waldron, 2012).

Austria's Ibiza Scandal (2019)

A covertly recorded film of the vice chancellor of Austria participating in corrupt activities was the subject of a political crisis. The event sparked worries about how hate speech and social media might shape political narratives, (Waldron, 2012).

2022 FBI Hate Crimes Statistics Report

The Federal Bureau of Investigation (Stefancic & Delgado, n.d.) (FBI) released its extensive 2022 Hate Crimes Statistics report in October 2023, providing insight into the alarming prevalence of bias-motivated crimes that law enforcement agencies around the country have documented. The main conclusions of the research highlight a concerning rise in hate crimes, which reached 11,634 in 2022—a startling 794 increase from 10,840 the year before. Crimes based on race, ethnicity, or ancestry were the most common among the widespread patterns, accounting for 6,557 recorded occurrences. The finding that there were 3,421 anti-Black or African American events, more than three times as many as other racial or ethnic groups, was especially upsetting.

With 2,042 crimes based on religion, it was alarming to see that anti-Jewish prejudice was responsible for more than half of these events (1,122). In contrast to 2021, events involving anti-Muslim and anti-Sikh attitudes stayed mostly unchanged. A concerning increase in hate crimes against the LGBTQI+ community was one of the report's most notable findings.

The number of occurrences against homosexual males was 1,075, and the number of incidents against lesbians was 622. These figures are the highest in the last five years and reflect a rise of almost 10% since 2021. Notably, the number of reported anti-transgender events increased by over 40% to 338 in 2022. These figures highlight the urgent need for ongoing initiatives to prevent hate crimes, raise awareness, and put policies in place to protect the security and welfare of groups at risk of acts motivated by hatred.

Increased engagement by law enforcement agencies is seen in the Hate Crime Statistics, 2022 report Levin, 2002), as 14,631 agencies—representing 91.7% of the population—submitted incident reports. The records describe 13,337 related offences motivated by racism and 11,634 criminal occurrences. Over 11,000 single-bias hate crimes with 13,278 victims and 346 multiple-bias hate crimes with 433 victims were reported. Race/ethnicity/ancestry, religion, and sexual orientation were the top three areas of bias; among these, particular biases like anti-Black or African American, anti-Jewish, and anti-gay (male) were highly ranked.

Community Standards Enforcement Report by Meta

The Community Standards Enforcement Report by Meta on Facebook and Instagram provides a quarterly assessment of the prevalence of violating content by measuring the percentage of total views that included such content. This metric is given by the number of estimated views on violating content divided by the total estimated views on both platforms. With the consistent publication of this report, Meta is seeking to ensure tracking its progress in enforcing its community standards while also creating a safer and more humane online ecosystem, (Waldron, 2012).

Figure 1. Hate speech trend on Facebook

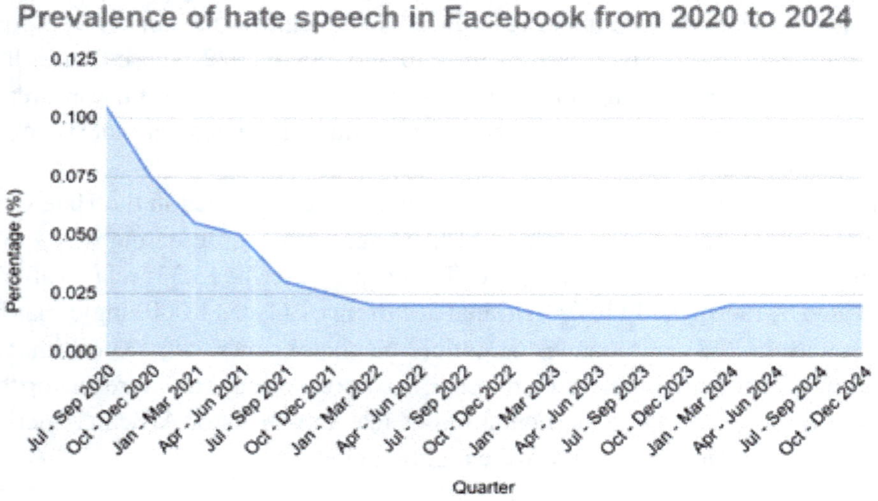

Figure 2. Hate speech trend on Instagram

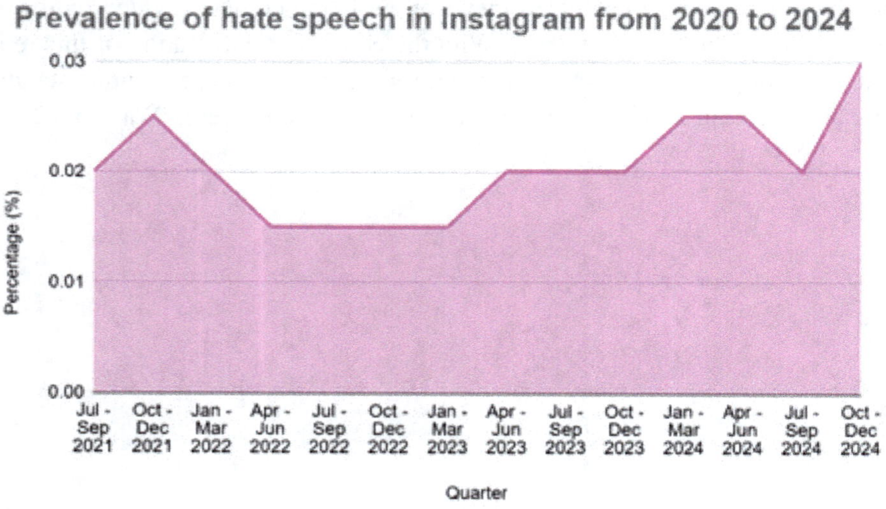

The data reveals a gradual decline in the prevalence of violating content over time, indicating improved content moderation and enforcement efforts. In earlier years, the percentage of views on violating content was notably higher, but it has since decreased, stabilizing at lower levels in recent quarters. Also to be noted that Instagram produces more Hate Speech content on average than Facebook. Despite this overall controlled trend, occasional fluctuations suggest that certain challenges, such as evolving forms of harmful content and detection limitations, persist.

LEGAL FRAMEWORK

Many criminal complaints regarding hate speech are filed under the "Bharatiya Nyaya Sanhita" (BNS), which regulates the majority of hate speech. However, some types of hate speech are also illegal under other laws, such as the Scheduled Tribes (Prevention of Atrocities Act) of 1989 and the "Scheduled Castes Act". Laws such as the "Cinematograph Act of 1952" and the "Cable TV Networks (Regulation) Act of 1995" (Cable TV Act) regulate speech according to certain mediums. Procedural laws, such as the Criminal Procedure Code, are utilised in addition to substantive laws to pre-censor specific speech categories. The "Customs Act of 1962" and other laws may also be invoked to stop publications from being circulated.

One important indicator of a nation's dedication to upholding social harmony and defending the rights of its inhabitants is how well its judicial system handles hate speech. The literature on India's hate speech-related legal system reveals a number of issues about its sufficiency, implementation, and difficulties, (Stefancic & Delgado, n.d.).

Sections 196 and 299 of the "Bharatiya Nyaya Sanhita, 2023" are two of the laws that India has in place to prevent hate speech. These laws make it illegal to do anything that incites animosity between groups or that is meant to offend religious sentiments. Furthermore, electronic hate speech is covered by other laws, such as the "Information Technology Act". Scholars and activists have expressed doubts over the efficacy and application of these statutes. The ambiguity of legal terminology is frequently highlighted in literature as a potential source of abuse and a barrier to enforcing laws against the actual propagation of hatred, (Levin, 2002).

The "Bharatiya Nyaya Sanhita, 2023"; the "Representation of the People Act"; and more modern laws pertaining to electronic communication are the main sources of important laws in India that handle hate speech:

Section 196 of BNS

Section 196 penalizes "Promoting enmity between different groups on grounds of religion, race, place of birth, residence, language, etc., and doing acts prejudicial to maintenance of harmony." Acts of hate speech that could cause discord or emotions of animosity, hatred, or malice between various castes and communities or groups based on religion, race, language, or geography are included in this, (Negi, 2024).

Section 299 of BNS

This section is for penalising "Deliberate and malicious acts, intended to outrage religious feelings of any class by insulting its religion or religious beliefs". It tackles hate speech that disparages or attempts to disparage any religion or religious beliefs.

Section 353 of BNS

This section penalises "Statements conducive to public mischief" encompassing statements that incite or are likely to incite, based on caste, language, race, community, religion, residence, or place of birth, sentiments of animosity, hatred, or hostility among various racial, caste, regional, linguistic, religious, or community groups, (U.S. Department of Justice, 2023).

The "Representation of the People Act, 1951"

According to this act, Section 123(3A) categorises as an act of corruption any promotion or attempt to incite resentment or antagonism among various classes of Indian citizens based on caste, race, community, religion, or language conducted through public meetings, actions, or published articles during election periods, (Union of India, 1951).

"Information Technology Act, 2000 (IT Act)"

This act, last amended in 2008, does not provide us with a specific definition of hate speech, however it does provide us with the legal for electronic governance by validating electronic records and digital signatures. It also provides us with the definition of cybercrimes along with prescribed punishment for such crimes. Several changes we incorporated in the IT Act to include provisions against identity theft, cyber terrorism, and child pornography. Section 66A introduced in this act regarded the sending of offensive messages through communication services as an act of crime. This section, however, was struck down by the Supreme Court of India in 2015 as unconstitutional and a violation of freedom of speech in the landmark "Shreya Singhal v Union of India" case, (Gnanith, 2015).

The "Information Technology Act, 2000" contains no provisions that directly address hate speech, hence cannot be considered a hate speech law. However, the mandate of this act help regulates online communication and provide mechanisms to deal with cybercrime, which may include hate speech disseminated via electronic means. Since Section 66A was rescinded, the remaining provisions of the Act, along with the various other sections of the IPC, are aggregated to battle online hate speech. For example, Section 69A of the IT Act empowers the government to block public access to content that in any way harm our sovereignty, integrity, or security of the state and to help maintain public order. This regulation is inclusive of online hate speech, (Meta, n.d.).

There exist special statutes which criminalize discriminatory or defamatory speech directed at certain marginalized or protected communities like the Scheduled Castes and the Scheduled Tribes. "Prevention of Atrocities Act 1989" deals with the abusive speech directed at certain caste groups in India, which have historically been victims of discrimination and violence. Chapter 2, Section 3(1)(x) of the Act describes the specific type of such acts as intentional "insults ... with intent to humiliate a member of a Scheduled Caste or a Scheduled Tribe in any place within public view" (Gupta & Gupta, 2020).

In addition to statutes like the IPC and the "Prevention of Atrocities Act", both of which criminalize speech, procedural law contained in the "Code of Criminal Procedure" (CrPC) is very effective. The mechanisms employed by CrPC can be considered as pre-censorship or prior restraint methods, (Lehning, 2021. For instance, Section 95 of the CrPC allows for the proscription of the circulation of written material which includes but is not limited to books, newspapers, etc., containing hate speech as defined under specific sections of the IPC. The Nagaland government invoked this statute to ban Dan Brown's book *The Da Vinci Code* three years after its release, (Rinchen, 2018). Similarly, the same law was invoked by the Central Government to place a ban on The True Furqan in 2005, alleging that it cast aspersions on Islam, (Kanalstein, n.d.). There exist other regulations that control speech based on the medium. The Central Government has issued guidelines under Section 5B(2) of the "Cinematograph Act of 1952", including a guideline on "visuals or words contemptuous of racial, religious or other groups". The Central Board of Film Censorship was recognized as a statutory body that can partially censor films falling short under these guidelines, (Citizens for Justice and Peace, 2022). Separately, the "Cable TV Act" has a program code under the Cable Television Networks Rules of 1994 which prohibits airing of content that "attacks religions or communities or visuals or words contemptuous of religious groups or which promote communal attitudes" (Das, 2024) and "is likely to encourage or incite violence or contains anything against maintenance of law and order or which promote-anti-national attitudes," (Das, 2024). The above-mentioned acts further contribute to the patchwork of laws governing hate speech in India, including Indian election laws, which prohibit "promoting enmity or hatred" during elections, (The Scheduled Castes and the Schedules Tribes (Prevention of Atrocities) Act, 1989).

Election-related corruption and the incitement of class animosity are targeted by election legislation, (The Scheduled Castes and the Schedules Tribes (Prevention of Atrocities) Act, 1989). Any candidate found violating these laws may, therefore, be disqualified for contesting elections.

In general, Indian legislation strives to protect hate speech through reasonable restrictions to preserve Article 19(1)(a) which encompasses freedom of speech and expression as guaranteed in the Indian Constitution. This right does not constitute an absolute privilege. Article 19 provides for reasonable restrictions on freedom of expression in the interests of Sovereignty, integrity, or security of the state; public order; friendly relations with foreign states; decency; morality; contempt of court; defamation; or incitement to an offense.

Sections 196 and 299 of the BNS indicate this balance (erstwhile Indian Penal Code, 1860). They define and limit forms of speech that might threaten public order or communal harmony but is also true to the democratic principle of free expression. However, the enforcement of such laws can become highly contentious and remains an area of tremendous concern to oversee in a fair, equal, and democratic manner, more so in this digital age where the reach and influence of speech are amplified. While appropriately requiring the prosecution of hate speech under these laws, there is also a need for a careful application of the laws so that regulation does not infringe upon the democratic rights of free speech, (Union of India, 1973).

International Legal Frameworks

"International Covenant on Civil and Political Rights" (ICCPR)

Under Article 20 (ICCPR), any incitement to national, racial, or religious hatred which constitutes incitement to discrimination, hostility, or violence is strictly prohibited, all of these can be constituted as hate speech. Accordingly, states parties are obligated to adopt measures that will criminalize such speech.

"International Convention on the Elimination of all Forms of Racial Discrimination" (ICERD)

ICERD calls for member states to criminalize hate speech and incitement to racial hatred in Article 4. It reinforces the need for prohibiting organizations that promote and incite racial discrimination.

"European Convention on Human Rights" (ECHR)

Article 10 of the ECHR guarantees freedom of speech while still allowing restrictions to prevent hate speech. This was ruled by the European Court of Human Rights, which accepted that the states may limit the speech inciting hatred, discrimination, or violence, (Waldron, 2012).

CHALLENGES IN CONTROLLING HATE SPEECH

Contemporary Legal Challenges

Implementing online hate speech laws in various online domains can be challenging and prop up a plethora of issues due to the internet being globally accessible. Jurisdictional complexities complicate the enforcement of such laws because something can be illegal in one country but totally legal in another. Moreover, this information can be stored on servers situated in a region with different legal standards regarding hate speech. This raises an all-important question of which laws would apply and how different jurisdictions could then apply their legal authority internationally.

Additionally another web of complexities arise due to the anonymity or pseudonymity afforded by online platforms which can substantially add to the difficulty of tracking down the individuals behind hate speech, thus hindering legal repercussions. The authorities and moderators of the site themselves find it a Herculean task to monitor hate speech in the myriad of uploads each day.

The burden is increased by the disparities in legal standards across the globe, which result in a patchwork of regulations that can be difficult to understand and consistently enforce. At the same time, constantly developing technology make matters more complicated. While decentralised platforms and encryption might protect individual privacy, they can also make it more difficult to monitor and control hate speech. Due to the quick and ongoing development of online speech, communication methods may evolve more quickly than legislation, possibly making current rules outdated. Furthermore, because many current regulations were written before social media became widely used, they are unclear when applied to the internet environment, which makes enforcement challenging and leaves gaps, (Meta, n.d.).

Effectiveness and Challenges Addressing Hate Speech Globally

In harmonizing legal responses, it is possible to strengthen the battle against the rampant spread of discriminatory hate perpetuated throughout all medium of electronic communications. Effective hate speech laws should be developed through an understanding of cultural sensibilities, considering various perspectives on what is considered offensive speech. One must achieve a balance that honours cultural variances, while protecting universal human rights. Adding to this notion is the acceptance that legal mechanisms may not fully address the root cause of the behaviour of hate speech, thus compelling us to adopt preventive tools such as education, awareness, and community participation an essential part of the promotion of tolerance and inclusion in society, (Waldron, 2012).

INITIATIVE TO COMBAT

Education Program

- Academic Course Integration: Training modules on tolerance, diversity, and responsible digital citizenship introduced in the school curriculum can help foster inclusive attitudes.
- Media Literacy Programs: Critical media literacy skills must be taught through educational initiatives enable people to differentiate reliable information from hateful content.

Community Engagement Strategies

- Platforms for Dialogue: Inclusive platforms must be created for open and constructive dialogue among all stakeholders including communities with different race, religion, ethnicity and gender to discuss issues and prejudice faced by them and find an implementable solution,
- Cultural Exchange Programs: These programs allow people hailing from different backgrounds to experience cultures not their own, and through experience, overcome cultural stereotypes and prejudice.
- Interfaith Initiatives: These programs open up dialogs between people from different religions thereby promoting religious peace and overcoming religious bigotry.

Online Awareness Campaigns

- Digital Literacy Workshops: Workshops create an understanding on how to use the online space without being a facilitator of hate speech.
- Social Media Awareness: Campaigns educate one on the impact of hate speech in online places and, thus, promote responsible engagement.

Legal Support and Advocacy

- Programs for Legal Awareness: Informing communities on the legal repercussions of hate speech raises awareness and discourages people from acting in a discriminatory manner.
- Supporting campaigns for stricter laws against hate speech guarantees that legal frameworks are resilient and adaptable to changing circumstances.

Media Responsibility Initiatives

- Media Regulations: By creating and advancing standards for ethical reporting, hate speech is less likely to proliferate through the media by discouraging sensationalism and slanted storylines.
- Journalists who receive media literacy training are better equipped to report impartially and refrain from unintentionally endorsing hate speech.

Youth Engagement Programs

- Workshops for Youth Empowerment: Giving young people the skills they need to combat hate speech through leadership initiatives and workshops creates a generation dedicated to inclusivity.
- Campaigns to Combat Bullying: By raising awareness of bullying in schools, hate speech is less likely to flourish there.

Government and NGO Collaborations

- Task Forces Against Hate Speech: Coordinated efforts to monitor and combat hate speech are made possible by governments and non-governmental organisations working together to form task forces.
- Funding for Initiatives: Providing funds and resources for educational initiatives, awareness campaigns, and community-based projects demonstrates a dedication to preventing hate speech. Together, these programs support a comprehensive strategy that tackles the underlying causes of hate speech and cultivates societies that value diversity, tolerance, and understanding, (Waldron, 2012).

Alternative Dispute Resolution of Hate Speech Cases

A paradigm changes in the way the judicial system delivers justice is suggested by alternative dispute resolution. It moves the emphasis from formal court-centric legal proceedings to the parties' agreement to resolve their differences through negotiation, mediation, arbitration, and/or conciliation. It is impossible to overstate the significance of this method for resolving conflicts because it operates in a time-bound manner with the goal of reaching a settlement between the parties rather than taking the case to a court of law, which is already overloaded with cases that have been pending for years and is constrained by formalities.

In certain jurisdictions around the world, a variety of alternative dispute resolution techniques have been successfully used in the context of criminal matters, including "victim-offender mediation, victim-offender panels, victim assistance programs, community crime prevention programs, community service, plea bargaining," (Suroor, 2012).

Adopting alternative methods of criminal issue settlement has significant benefits for the administration of criminal justice. First of all, it satisfies the goal of restorative justice for victims of crime by giving them an opportunity to reconcile with their perpetrators and starting the healing and atonement processes for both parties, (Suroor, 2012). Second, the alternative dispute procedure can be adjusted to meet the objectives while still operating in accordance with the legal framework and terms. Thirdly, from a financial perspective, it is a feasible approach for the parties because the expenses incurred by them are substantially less than those associated with the formal trial procedure. Fourthly, the parties might reach a settlement through the flexible method without having to endure the drawn-out judicial proceedings. However, there is a clear disclaimer when it comes to using alternative methods of resolution in criminal cases: not all offences can be resolved in the same way by this method. Its effectiveness has yet to be evaluated in the class of offences that are classified as grave, serious, or heinous. Although the use of other methods to resolve criminal cases has been fraught with anxiety and implemented with differing degrees of success in India, the trend worldwide is towards alternative methods of resolution, with the courts serving as the final choice.

When it comes to using mediation as an alternative to criminal procedures in hate speech cases, the story of Australia offers an intriguing case study. In addition to the existing criminal legal framework that forbids hate speech, it has done so by establishing a civil process. Australia has both federal laws made by Parliament and state laws within the federal system.

Similar to Australia, India stands to benefit greatly from the implementation of alternative dispute resolution procedures for hate speech crimes. However, it is important to remember that this type of strategy must be appropriately adjusted in order to function inside India's current system.

Counter-Speech

Counter-speech is a strict and decisive response to hate speech that is only intended to repair the harm that the hate speech initially caused. On social media, it is referred to as "crowd-sourced responses to extremist or hateful content" and is employed to "tone down the rhetoric" when users submit dissent or agreement in response to hate speech, (Union of India, 1951).

Depending on the platform used to spread hate speech, this responsive speech can take many different forms. For example, it can be a straightforward response to a hateful message that was created from a fabricated claim or fake news, a clarification of any questionable claims made, or even the se of humour, sarcasm, cartoons, memes, and caricatures to neutralize and defuse the tension that a hate message aim to provoke. Perhaps more crucial to emphasise, though, is the reality that anyone—even the victim herself—can advocate counter speech. The important thing is that such speech "fills a purifying role, facilitating a discontented message recipient to express his/her thoughts rather than indulge in harmful content" (WIPO, 2009) and has the "potential to contribute to the vitality of society," even though this makes it a more adaptable and straightforward response, (Union of India, 1951).

The #notinmyname or "Not In My Name" movement was recently introduced on social media in India in reaction to multiple instances of mob lynching, violence, and persecution of victims from different regions of the nation based on their religious, racial, or ethnic identities. The initial goals of this campaign were to rally public support and combat the hate speech that was being spread and led to those violent acts. The campaign gained popularity after a number of well-known public figures joined, and demonstrations condemning the violence were held in Indian cities. All things considered, it was regarded as a successful counterinitiative, and it still receives support from a variety of sources.

FINDINGS AND ANALYSIS

In order to assess people's expertise and interest in the intersection of AI and Hate speech detection in legal context, researchers have designed a questionnaire of 10 straightforward questions. Those questions were included in a Google form that was disseminated to respondents of various ages and genders. The survey results are succinctly summarised below. Respondents were initially asked to indicate their age range (Figure 3) before answering the subsequent questions.

Figure 3. Result summary of question 1

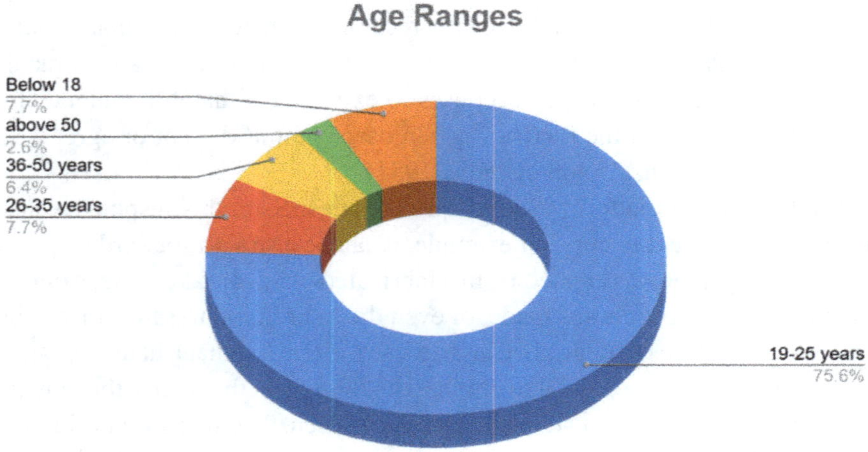

The subsequent section was to know people's perspective on Hate speech. The first question under this section was "How would define Hate speech?" with four possible options:

1. Any offensive statement
2. Speech targeting specific groups based on race, religion, gender, etc.
3. General negativity in communication
4. Other possible definitions.

Figure 4. Result summary of question 2

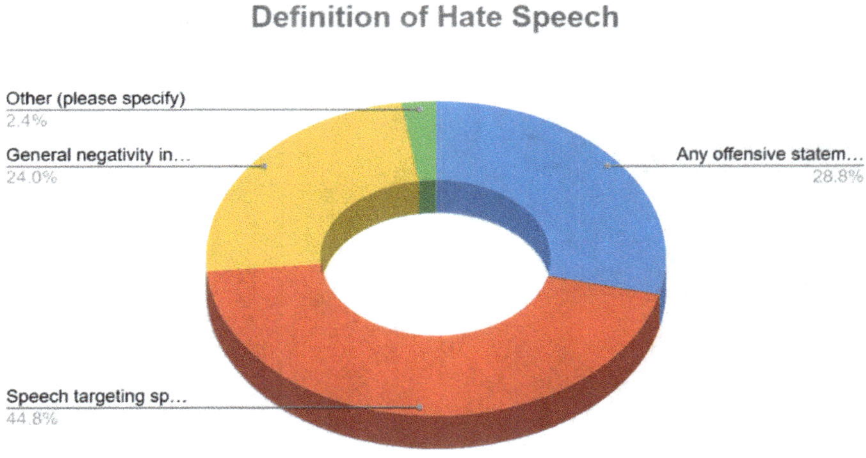

From Figure 4, we can derive that about 45% of the responders consider Hate speech to be speech targeting specific groups based on race, religion, gender etc. Another 24% just think of it as General negativity in communication and for another 29%, any offensive statement is Hate speech.

The second question was "On which platforms have you encountered hate speech the most?" with the following options:

1. Social Media (e.g., Facebook, Twitter)
2. Online Forums (e.g., Reddit)
3. Messaging Apps (e.g., WhatsApp)
4. Other *(please specify)*

Figure 5. Result summary of question 3

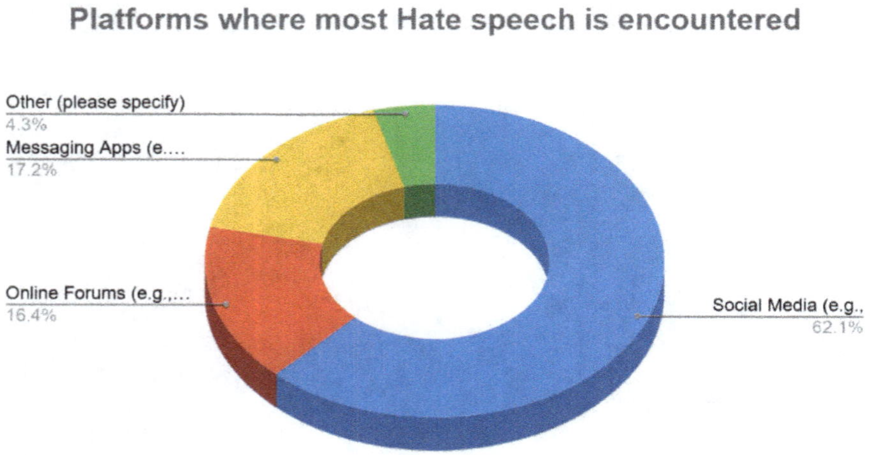

The pie chart in Figure 5 shows us that most Hate speech is perpetuated through Social Media Platforms like Faceboo, Instagram, etc.

The third question was "How frequently do you encounter hate speech online?", with the following options:

Figure 6. Result summary of question 4

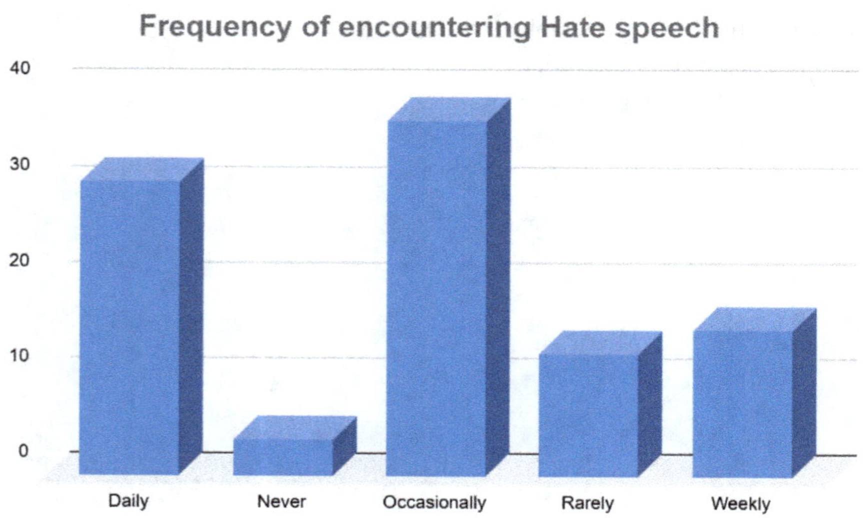

Figure 7. Comparative analysis of gender and frequency of hate speech encountered

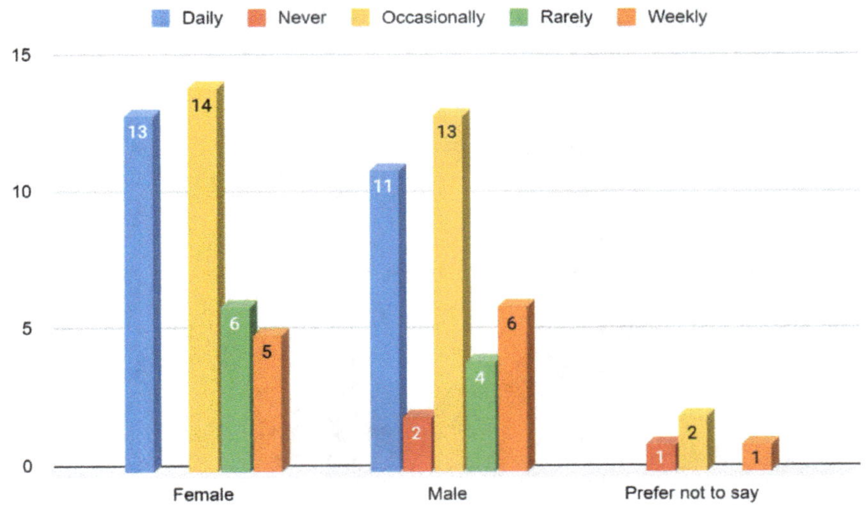

It is observed from Figure 6 that about 30.8% of the responders face online Hate speech on daily basis while 37.2% encounter Hate speech occasionally. It should be noted that only 3.8% of responders have never received online Hate speech, which reflects the persistent problem of Hate speech that has exponentially increased in the last decade. Drawing conclusions from Figure 7, that responders identifying as female almost always face online Hate Speech, thus suggesting a component of gender based prejudice in Hate speech.

The last question in this section was "In your opinion, how harmful is hate speech to societal harmony?". In answer to this question, most of the responders (62.8%) are of the opinion that in terms of societal harmony Hate speech is very harmful.

Figure 8. Result summary of question 5

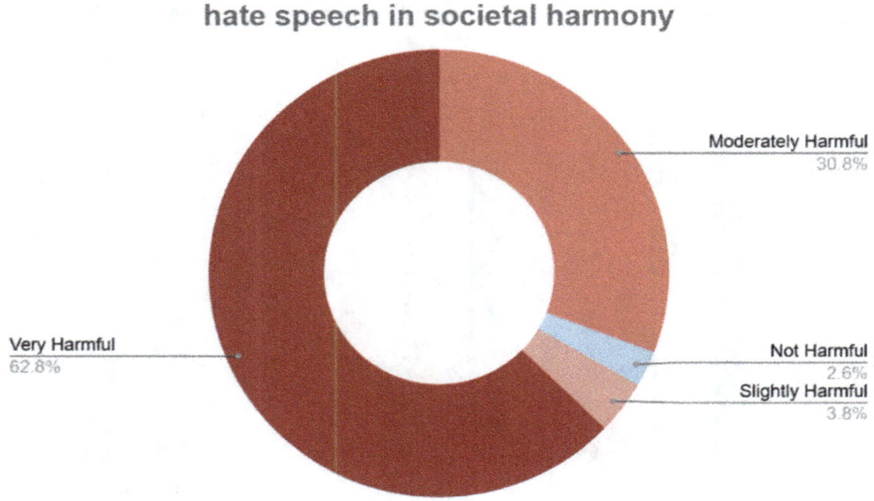

The next section of questions is constructed to give us perspective how AI and Hate speech detection corelate.

The section starts with the question "Are you aware of AI technologies being used to detect hate speech online?" where only 64.1% of responders are aware of Hate speech detection technology while the rest (35.9%) are unaware. This pie chart is interesting as it reflects on the digital literacy of our population.

Figure 9. Result summary of question 6

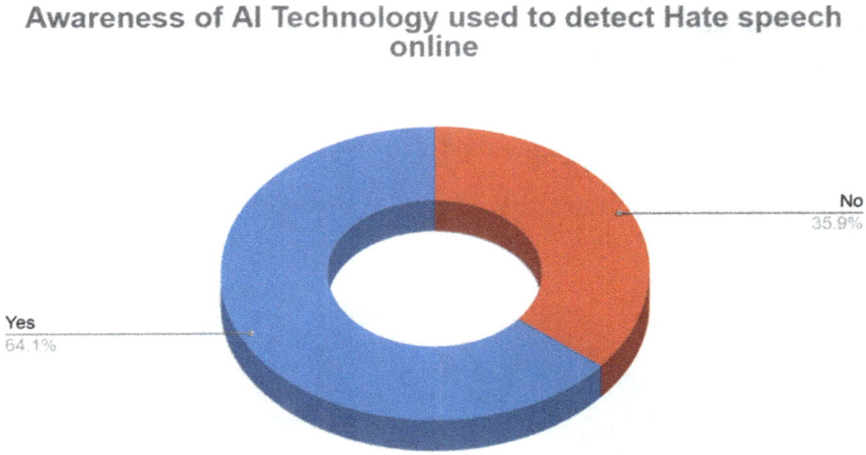

The next question was "Do you believe AI can effectively detect hate speech in real time?". Most of the responders (55.1%) are not sure if this technology is applicable or not.

Figure 10. Result summary of question 7

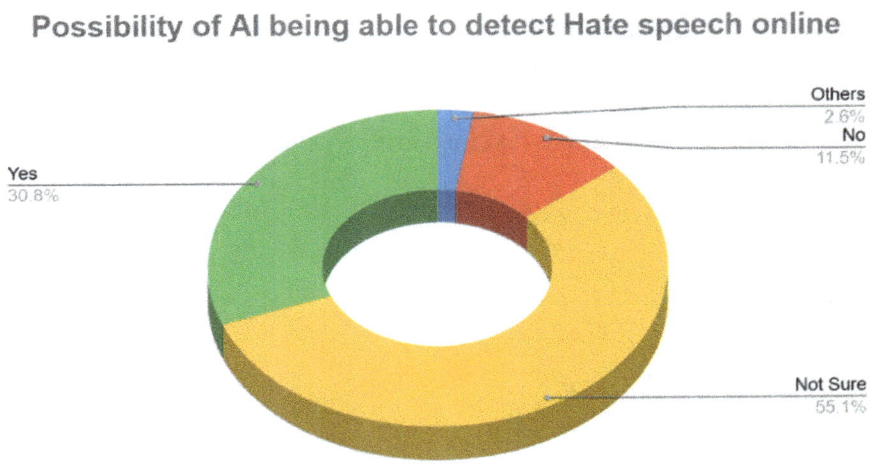

The next question was "What challenges do you foresee in using AI to detect hate speech?" The purpose of this question was to ascertain the various algorithmic challenges of Hate speech Detection. Figure 11 aptly demonstrates the percentage distribution of possible challenges.

Figure 11. Result summary of question 8

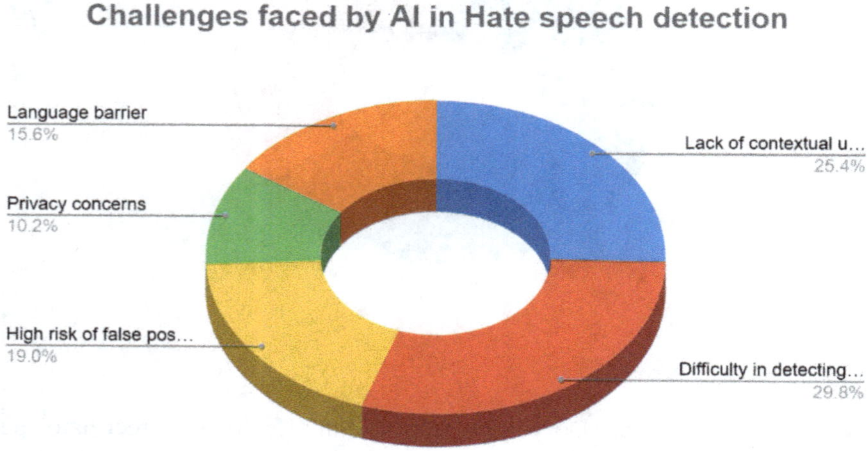

The next question was "Do you think real-time detection of hate speech by AI should lead to immediate consequences (e.g., content removal, account suspension)?". Over 50% of respondents are in favour of immediate consequences such as derogatory content removal. This question was to understand the perception of people regarding punitive actions taken against perpetuation of online Hate speech.

Figure 12. Result summary of question 9

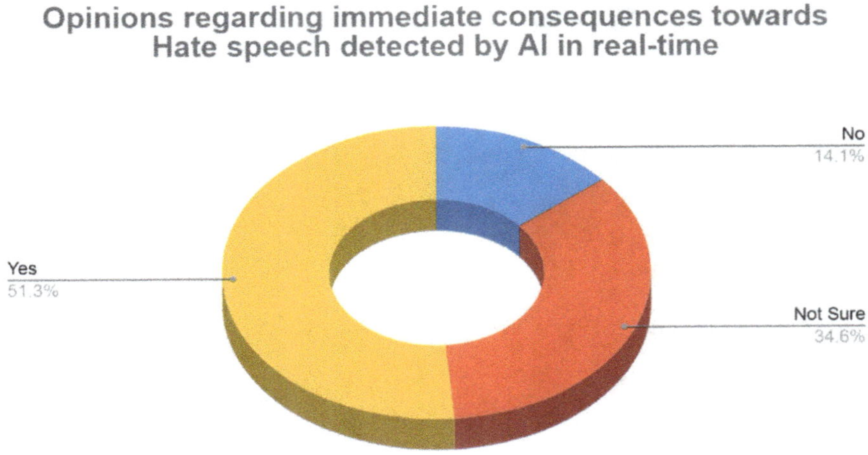

The next section deals with Legal Framework and Policy Recommendations. Under this section the first question was "Are existing laws are sufficient to address Hate speech in the online space". Figure 13 shows the inadequacy of legal frameworks in regulating online Hate speech as an overwhelming percentage (64.1%) of responders had a negatory response.

Figure 13. Result summary of question 10

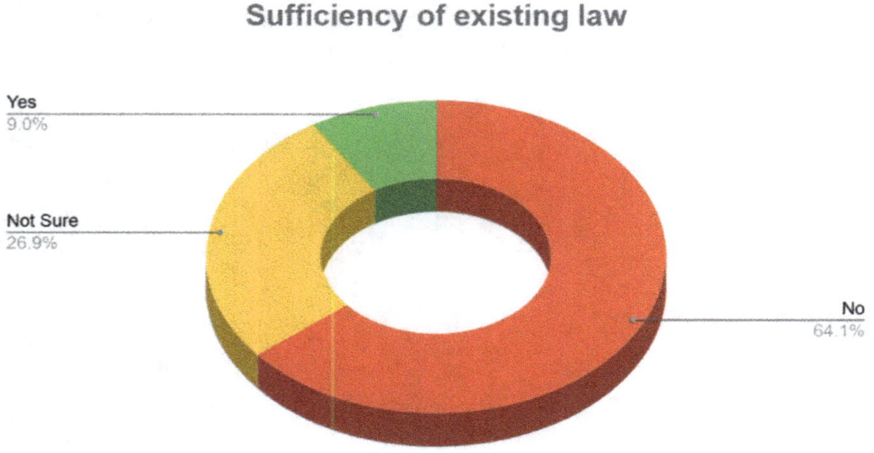

The following question was "Should AI-generated data pertaining to hate speech be admissible in legal proceedings?". This question was to understand whether the responders consider AI generated data to be reliable enough for legal proceedings, 64.1% agree with this notion. It is to be noted that AI generated data in this context is simply the predictive results of the model.

Figure 14. Result summary of question 11

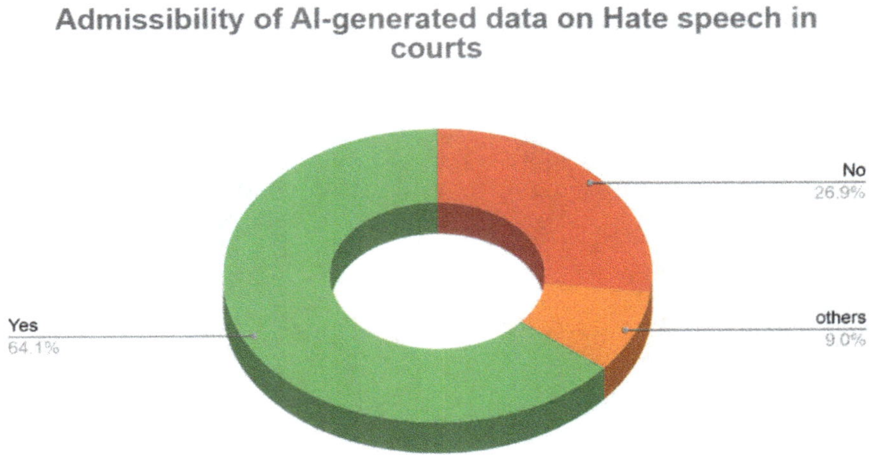

The subsequent question "What additional measures can enhance the legal framework for combating hate speech through AI?" was asked in the hopes of gaining perspective on the shortcomings of existing legal frameworks in combating online Hate speech. Figure 15 shows the distribution of recommendations from the responders.

Figure 15. Result summary of question 12

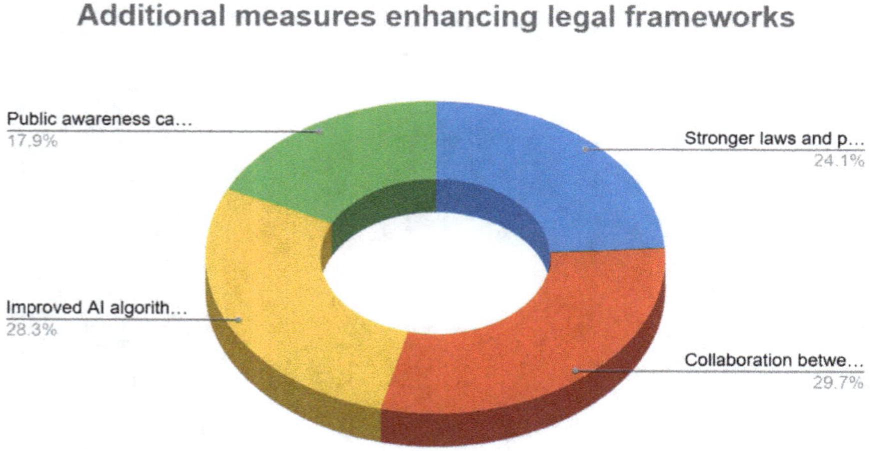

The question “Do you think AI-based hate speech detection aligns with freedom of speech?” was asked to gain the viewpoint of responders whether AI based detection of Hate speech infringe on their fundamental right of freedom of speech under Article 19(1)(a) of the Constitution. It must be noted that majority (48.7%) feels that AI based detection would align with their right to freedom of speech.

Figure 16. Result summary of question 13

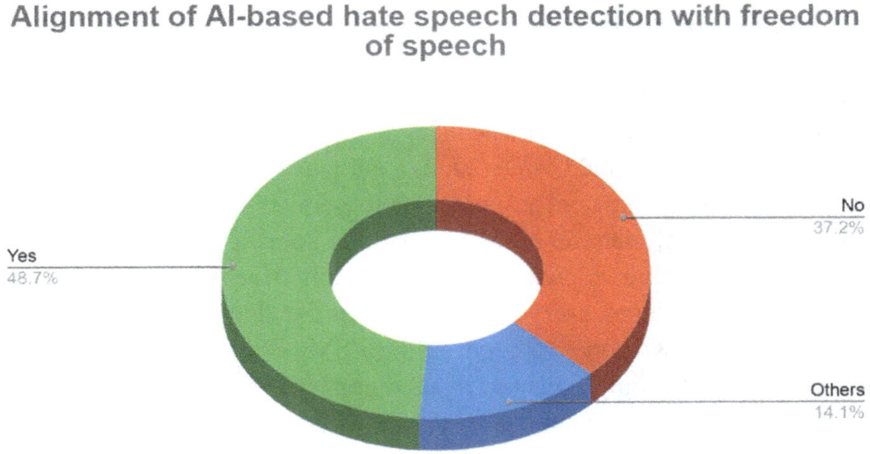

SUMMARY OF FINDINGS

The survey highlights the prevalence of online hate speech, mostly perpetrated on social media platforms. Women tend to report facing hate speech more, suggesting some degree of gender bias in online interactions. There is no universal definition of hate speech, as some people regard it as targeting specific groups while others see it as general negativity toward anyone. There appears to be some awareness among respondents concerning AI-implemented hate speech detection mechanisms, although they suspect that contextual misinterpretation, sarcasm detection, and false positives/negatives are some of the challenges that undermine the efficacy of AI-based learning algorithms. Many respondents accept AI-generated evidence in courts but remain sceptical about its bias and implications for free speech; thus, stronger regulations, enhanced AI capability, and collaboration between governments and tech firms are required. Public education campaigns might help to promote responsible online behaviour. The findings indicate that while AI can ultimately be an ally against hate speech, it needs to be backed by ethics, law, and technological development to be fully implementable.

SCOPE OF ARTIFICIAL INTELLIGENCE (AI)

In this digitized era, social media platforms (SMPs) have become the prime medium for communication, information as well as entertainment. Adhering to strict regulatory requirements are compulsory to avoid paying steep fine amounts. Therefore, SMPs take the approach of "better safe than sorry" for content moderation, (United Nations Office on Drugs and Crime, 2006). As Llanso notes, the sheer amount of online communication and content posted on these platforms is so massive that it is impossible and inefficient for human moderators to review all content. The task of flagging any problematic material is further complicated by the sheer volume of online content produced every second of every day to satiate our social media addiction, (Bartlett & Krasodomski-Jones, 2016). SMPs therefore turned to artificial intelligence (AI) as the only way to navigate regulatory pressures and the technical problems associated with content scale and quantity. Artificial intelligence-proactive or reactive mechanism is employed by SMPs to address entirely problematic content quite good, including hate speech. AI is therefore a simple tool "to police an enormous and ever-increasing flow of information – which comes in handy in the implementation of content policies," (Richards & Calvert, 2000).

To understand the scope of AI in detecting hate speech especially in Indian context we first must have a rudimentary understating of natural language processing. In the below image we have given a schematic diagram of a generic pipeline for speech detection model training.

Figure 17. Pipeline schematic diagram (Richards & Calvert, 2000)

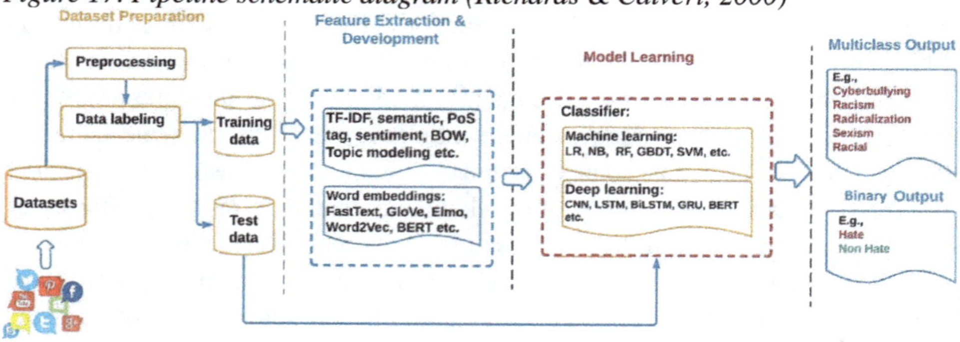

If we are to actively looking to flag hate speech in India this generic model need to be adapted according to Indian context. We are a diverse country with more than 30+ languages in 100+ dialects. A Speech Detection Model will have to encompass all these languages along with scripts and grammatical understanding.

Datasets

Our first aim should be to make a multilingual dataset containing words written in their original script. There are two publicly available hate speech datasets in Indian context are the Hostility Detection Dataset (A collection of 8000+ posts from various social media platforms) (Express Web Desk, 2017) and HASOC fire dataset (An Indo-European Dataset with 5983 posts in Hindi) (Lal, 2018). However, for all these instances the only Indian language they have managed to incorporate is Hindi language and script.

The create a robust software capable of flagging hate content in real -time, the model in question must be trained in the language itself as most of the models currently in practice first translate the given input in English before applying speech detection algorithms. Alternatively, we can create a multilingual dataset by creating pairs of data points (the actual hate speech and the corresponding counter narrative in English properly translated), (Alkiviadou, 2022). This might appear laborious but later we can use the human-in-the-loop (HITL) method to produce more data points. In this method the algorithm is iteratively processed along with human feedback to generate more data.

Data Annotation

Data labelling or annotating is the next crucial step. Annotation bias is very common and ends up creating a biased model, which has very dangerous repercussions. Minority community often gets underrepresented during the process of annotation. Slurs like "Bhangi" or "Chamar" which are caste insults often don't get flagged as the annotators themselves are unaware of the existence of the slur. The result is that often minority communities get unnecessary or wrongfully flagged when saying something against the majority community.

Feature Extraction

The feature extraction is the core structure of hate speech detection modelling through which raw text data is transformed into a vector format so that natural Language Processing algorithms can process the data. One of the most widely used techniques is word embeddings in NLP, where words get represented as multi-dimensional vectors. These word embeddings always carry along the biases that exist in the training or raw dataset. As far as India is concerned, the dominance of English and Hindi in the training data causes marginalization of other regional languages and dialects.

For instance, when training word embeddings using news articles or social media posts, words affiliated to certain communities get marked with negative connotations as there historical and social biases in the data, likely because the human annotator also suffers from the same bias. Words such as "Dalit" or "Adivasi" might get coined with negative sentiments more frequently because of the systematic discrimination. This means the model might mistakenly flag neutral or even positive statements about these communities as hate speech while ignoring actual caste-oppressive slurs due to their underrepresentation in mainstream datasets. On the other hand, caste-oppressive slurs like that of "Bhangi" or "Chamar" are often undetected because the model was not trained appropriately as regards to the cultural significance of these words. It shows that feature extraction can amplify discrimination amplification rather than mitigation when it is not relevant to the Indian language and contextual social features.

Sentiment Analysis

Sentiment analysis a "obvious choice as a way to filter what is usually negative connotations out, the determination of speech as correspondingly positive, negative or neutral," (Llansó, 2020), hence making is a crucial step toward hate speech detection. However, the existing algorithmic biases from feature extraction can easily trickle down into sentiment analysis, exacerbating cultural and gender biases.

Considering the following example, the term "Shakti,"(usually translated as power in English), normally is associated with positive sentiments, but when it appears in feminist discourses like "Nari Shakti" (women empowerment in English), a model trained on a male-dominant dataset may classify it as aggressive or confrontational. Similarly, even constructive critique on patriarchal norms may be tagged as "hate speech" as the software fails to distinguish between legitimate criticism and targeted harassment.

Yet another form of the algorithmic bias is in cases where the tweets demanding rights for the LGBTQ+ community are flagged as "inappropriate," while allowing the use of homophobic slurs. The model learnt to associate words "queer" and "gay" with negative sentiment because of annotation bias in the training data.

Semantic Analysis

Semantic analysis enables models to learn the contextual meaning of words rather than their surface representation. However, linguistic bias occurs when a model is trained on English or Hindi datasets that are primarily used, thereby ignoring other

Indian languages and scripts. This results in over-reliance on literal translation, because of the absence of multilingual dataset which is prone to misinterpreting the intended meaning.

For example, in Tamil, "Pandi" is used to refer to a caste in a derogatory sense, even though the word literally means only "pig." A model that has been trained only on English or Hindi corpora would probably not know its derogatory application in Tamil language. Similarly, in Bengali, the word "Chhotolok"(means little guy when translated in English) is used derogatorily as a classist slur for economically deprived people, even though a literal translation would not capture its social implications.

Contextual bias also becomes prominent during semantic analysis, as both politically and religiously loaded statement like "Muslims should go back to Pakistan", will not be banned as the model is unaware of "Pakistan" being used as religious slur.

Another tactic used by users is Adversarial Misspelling one of the evasion tactics to confuse NLP algorithms. In this tactic users modify spellings or using character substitutions to bypass AI moderation and avoid detection of flagged words. The word "rape" therefore can be spelled as "r@pe", "r*pe", "repee", and "*rape*" (Unicode trick).

Another linguistic issue is a result of the evolution of a language such as "Hinglish"(A digital language combining both English and Hindi). Translations become different as grammartical rules often overlap.

The development of an Indian-specific hate speech model that is strong requires a shift in paradigm in terms of methodology. Instead of relying solely on English translations, one needs to develop context-sensitive annotated multilingual datasets. The annotators must possess diverse linguistic and social backgrounds in order to effectively minimize bias. Word embeddings must be refreshed periodically to include the shift in social discourse, and sentiment analysis must be fine-tuned to detect power relations as opposed to simply picking up overt negativity.

By resolving the biases in feature extraction, sentiment analysis, and linguistic interpretation, it is possible to build a system that actually comprehends and identifies hate speech on social media platforms in real time, especially in the case of India.

CONCLUSION

With the continuous caste and communal tensions in India, hate speech is a major issue. Powerful speakers who have the ability to encourage violence are able to escape punishment, and the government frequently fails to stop it. This is partly due to institutional shortcomings in the law's execution and partly to remedies and solutions made possible by the law. Since the law is frequently abused by the government or utilised by third-party organisations to intimidate speakers, it has a negative effect on the right to free speech. Therefore, research on the law's second-order effects on hate speech is equally as important as its immediate effects.

An developing issue that is similar to India's offline hate speech problems is hate speech online. According to Indian news reports, social media instigation to violence is a major issue. The Indian government has decided to shut down the Internet in order to avoid incitement, following years of negotiations with web companies in other jurisdictions. Legitimate speech is disproportionately impacted by this blunt-instrument tactic. Other tactics, such counter-speech, are also employed, but their efficacy is unknown. This is due to the fact that independent academics who would examine the relationship between speech and violence are not given access to data on the rate at which hate speech and rumours spread on social media, (Union of India, 1973). Hence, in an ever-evolving landscape of communication, the problem of hate speech becomes a challenge insurmountable and irretrievably embedded within the roots of society. Recognizing the multifarious aspects of hate speech makes it pretty evident that this pervasive problem is to be dealt with through a holistic and an integrative approach. The repercussions of hate speech dig deep into the fabric of society and leaves lasting scars in the community. marking the erosion of social harmony and degrading the very foundation on which civilized society is built on. The politicians and the society continue to choose a delicate path between that of freedom of speech and that of preventing harm. Education remains a very potent weapon in the war on hate speech. It provides the much-needed mechanism with which empathy, critical thinking, and an understanding of the negative consequences of discriminatory language can be instilled in people. Media literacy, values education, and legal awareness formed part of that educational armoury.

Global events and conflicts, all firmly intertwined into the fabric of modern world, have demonstrated their capacity to exacerbate hate speech via social media. This very bridge of global accessible communication may have helped in propagating hate speech, while also providing avenues for international cooperation aimed at addressing this global challenge.

For hate speech to be curtailed, there is a necessity for cohesive participation of individuals, communities, governments, and international organizations. There is an urgent need to develop an environment where mutual respect, understanding, and dialogue will can be conducted. legal, educational, and international schemes, when integrated together can help us build a world an inclusive world devoid of hate speech. The path henceforth shall be one of constant vigilance, adaptability, and unwavering commitment to create a safe place based on unity and collective harmony.

REFERENCES

ADL. (2021). *Online Hate and Harassment: The American Experience 2021*. ADL. www.adl.org

Alkiviadou, N. (2022). *Artificial Intelligence and Online Hate Speech Moderation*, SUR 32. https://sur.conectas.org/en/artificial-intelligence-and-online-hate-speech-moderation/

Bajoria, J. (2016, May 24). *How India's archaic laws have a chilling effect on dissent*. Scroll.in. https://scroll.in/article/808641/how-indias-archaic-laws-have-a-chilling-effect-on-dissent

Banks, J. (2010). Regulating hate speech online. *International Review of Law Computers & Technology*, *24*(3), 233–239. DOI: 10.1080/13600869.2010.522323

Bartlett, J., & Krasodomski-Jones, A. (2016). Counter-speech on Facebook. *Demos (Mexico City, Mexico)*.

Brown-Sica, M., & Beall, J. (1999). Library 2.0 and the Problem of Hate Speech Library 2.0 and the Problem of Hate Speech. *The Electronic Journal of Academic and Special Librarianship Summer, 1*. https://digitalcommons.unl.edu/cgi/viewcontent.cgi?article=1098&context=ejasljournal

Chakrapani, N. (2025). *Hate Speech Laws in India: Examining Legal and Constitutional Challenges*. The Legal Quorum.

Citizens for Justice and Peace. (2022, February 1). *Speak up against hate | Safoora Zargar*. YouTube. https://www.youtube.com/watch?v=BjL0itmo0gU

Das, D. (2024). Hate speech in India: Contemporary legal challenges and responses. *LAW&PASS: International Journal of Law. Public Administration and Social Studies*, *1*(2), 250–264.

Das, S., & Das, S. (2021, October 25). *Caste-Based Discrimination Rampant In Higher Educational Institutions, Affirms Study*. Feminism in India. https://feminisminindia.com/2021/10/26/caste-based-discrimination-rampant-in-higher-educational-institutions-affirms-study/

Dictionary, C. (2019, December 4). *HATE SPEECH | meaning in the Cambridge English Dictionary*. Cambridge.org. https://dictionary.cambridge.org/dictionary/english/hate-speech

Express Web Desk. (2017). *What is the not in my name protest?* Indian Express, https://indianexpress.com/article/what-is/what-is-the-not-in-my-name-protest-lynching-junaid-khan-4725668/

Facebook (n.d.). *Community Standards,* Facebook. https://www.facebook.com/communitystandards/hate_speech

Facebook (n.d.). *Facebook Transparency Report | Community Standards.* Transparency.facebook.com. https://transparency.facebook.com/community-standards-enforcement#hate-speech

FBI. (2022). *FBI Releases 2022 Crime in the Nation Statistics | Federal Bureau of Investigation.* Federal Bureau of Investigation. https://www.fbi.gov/news/press-releases/fbi-releases-2022-crime-in-the-nation-statistics

Free Word Centre. (2018). Responding to 'hate speech' with positive measures: A case study from six EU countries 2018 report. https://www.article19.org/wp-content/uploads/2018/06/Responding-to-%E2%80%98hate-speech%E2%80%99-with-positive-measures-A-case-study-from-six-EU-countries-.pdf

Gagliardone, I., Gal, D., Alves, T., & Martinez, G. (2015). *Countering Online Hate Speech (PDF).* Paris: UNESCO Publishing. pp. 7–15. ISBN 978-92-3-100105-5. Archived from the original on 13 March 2022. Retrieved 27 March 2025.

Fowler, G.A., & Harwell, D. (2018). *2018 was the year of online hate. Meet the people whose lives it changed,* The Washington Post.

Gillespie, T. (n.d.). *Custodians of the Internet platforms, content moderation, and the hidden decisions that shape social media.* https://tarletongillespie.org/Gillespie_CUSTODIANS_print.pdf

Gnanith, A. (2015). *Shreya Singhal v. Union Of India AIR 2015 SC 1523.* Legalserviceindia.com. https://www.legalserviceindia.com/legal/article-10124-shreya-singhal-v-union-of-india-air-2015-sc-1523.html

Gupta, N., & Gupta, K. (2020). *Do Indian Courts Face A Dilemma in Interpreting Hate Speech?* Economic and Political Weekly. https://www.epw.in/engage/article/do-indian-courts-face-dilemma-interpreting-hate

Guterres, A. (2019). *UNITED NATIONS STRATEGY AND PLAN OF ACTION ON HATE SPEECH* (pp. 1–5). https://www.un.org/en/genocideprevention/documents/UN%20Strategy%20and%20Plan%20of%20Action%20on%20Hate%20Speech%2

Hatano, A. (23 October 2023). Regulating Online Hate Speech through the Prism of Human Rights Law: The Potential of Localised Content Moderation. *The Australian Year Book of International Law Online*. 41 (1):127–156. doi:. ISSN 2666-0229. DOI: 10.1163/26660229-04101017

hate-alert. (2019). *Hate-Speech-Reading-List/README.md at master · hate-alert/ Hate-Speech-Reading-List*. GitHub. https://github.com/hate-alert/Hate-Speech -Reading-List/blob/master/README.md

Herz, M. E., & Molnár, P. (2012). *The content and context of hate speech: rethinking regulation and responses*. Cambridge University Press ; New York.

Hunt, C. (2016). *"It's just a joke": the subtle effects of offensive language*. The University of Sydney. https://www.sydney.edu.au/news-opinion/news/2016/07/20/ _it_s-just-a-joke--the-subtle-effects-of-offensive-language.html

Hyman, T. (2021). *The Harms of Racist Online Hate Speech in the Post-COVID Working World: Expanding Employee Protections – Fordham Law Review*. Fordhamlawreview.org. https://fordhamlawreview.org/issues/the-harms-of-racist-online -hate-speech-in-the-post-covid-world-expanding-employee-protections/

Kanalstein, E. (n.d.). *Hate speech and incitement to hatred in the electoral context*. https://www.ohchr.org/sites/default/files/2024-05/information-note-hate-speech -incient-hatred-in-electoral-context.pdf

Kinney, T.A. (5 June 2008). *Hate Speech and Ethnophaulisms*. The International Encyclopedia of Communication. doi:DOI: 10.1002/9781405186407.wbiech004

Lal, N. (2018). *#Notinmyname: Celebrities join protesters in Delhi, Mumbai*, Times of India. https://timesofindia.indiatimes.com/city/delhi/notinmyname-celebrities -join-protesters-in-delhi-mumbai/articleshow/63786171.cms

Lehning, S. (2021). *Hate Speech Laws in Democratic Countries*. JSU Digital Commons. https://digitalcommons.jsu.edu/compass/vol5/iss1/2/

Lepoutre, M. (2017). Hate Speech in Public Discourse. *Social Theory and Practice*, *43*(4), 851–883. DOI: 10.5840/soctheorpract201711125

Levin, B. (2002). Cyberhate: A Legal and Historical Analysis of Extremists' Use of Computer Networks in America. *The American Behavioral Scientist*, *45*(6), 958–988. DOI: 10.1177/0002764202045006004

Llansó, E. J. (2020). No Amount of AI in Content Moderation Will Solve Filtering's Prior-Restraint Problem. *Big Data & Society*, *7*(1).

Meta. (n.d.). *Hate Speech, Community Standards Enforcement Report*, Meta/com. https://transparency.meta.com/reports/community-standards-enforcement/hate-speech/facebook/

Mirchandani, M. (2019, February 12). *The Parliamentary Panel Will Reinforce Bias on Twitter, Not Fix It*. Maya Mirchandani. https://mayamirchandani.com/2019/02/12/the-parliamentary-panel-will-reinforce-bias-on-twitter-not-fix-it/

Mirchandani, M. (n.d.). *Fighting Hate Speech, Balancing Freedoms: A Regulatory Challenge*. Retrieved September 11, 2025, from https://jils.blog/wp-content/uploads/2025/01/maya-mirchandani_9.pdf

Müller, K., & Schwarz, C. (2020). Fanning the Flames of Hate: Social Media and Hate Crime. *Journal of the European Economic Association, 19*(4). Advance online publication. DOI: 10.1093/jeea/jvaa045

Narayanan, M. K. (2019, June 25). *The future of parliamentary democracy*. The Hindu. https://www.thehindu.com/opinion/lead/the-future-of-parliamentary-democracy/article28138347.ece

Narendrakumar, N. & Fnu, H. (2023, May 1). *International Journal of Engineering Technology Research & Management from legacy to digital: How AI and cloud computing is changing health insurance*. https://www.researchgate.net/publication/389633691_International_Journal_of_Engineering_Technology_Research_Management_FRO

National Law University Delhi. (2024). *Centre for Communication Governance at NLU Delhi - National Law University Delhi*. National Law University Delhi. https://nludelhi.ac.in/research/centre-for-communication-governance-at-nlu-delhi/

Nayak, M. (2025). Analyzing the Integration of Artificial Intelligence in Fostering 21st-Century Competencies and Socio-Emotional Learning in Education: Opportunities and Challenges. *International Journal for Multidisciplinary Research, 7*(3). Advance online publication. DOI: 10.36948/ijfmr.2025.v07i03.47449

Negi. (2024). The Rise of Hate Speech Around the World. SSRN *Electronic Journal*. https://doi.org/DOI: 10.2139/ssrn.4719266

Olsen, R., Courtney, L., Warnberg, C., & Samuels, J. (n.d.). *How Prosecutors Are Collecti ng and Using Data for Decisionmaking Findings from the 2018 National Survey of State Prosecutors' Offi ces*. Retrieved September 11, 2025, from https://www.urban.org/sites/default/files/2018/09/25/prosecutor_fact_sheet.pdf

Omar, A., & Hashem, M. E. (2022). An Evaluation of the Automatic Detection of Hate Speech in Social Media Networks. *International Journal of Advanced Computer Science and Applications, 13*(2). Advance online publication. DOI: 10.14569/ijacsa.2022.0130228

Paterson, J. L., Brown, R., & Walters, M. A. (2018). The Short and Longer Term Impacts of Hate Crimes Experienced Directly, Indirectly, and Through the Media. *Personality and Social Psychology Bulletin, 45*(7), 994–1010. https://journals.sagepub.com/doi/full/10.1177/0146167218802835 PMID: 30400746

Press Trust of India. (2016, March 19). *EC takes up issue of hate speech, provocative ads with parties.* The Indian Express. https://indianexpress.com/article/india/india-news-india/election-commission-nasim-zaidi-hate-speech-provocative-ads/

Richard, N. (2018). *Facebook's new Rosetta AI system helps detect hate speech.* CNET. https://www.cnet.com/tech/tech-industry/facebooks-new-rosetta-ai-system-helps-detect-hate-speech/

Richards, R. D., Calvert, C. (2000). Counterspeech 2000: A New Look at the Old Remedy for Bad Speech, *BYU L. Rev*. 585.

Saldanha, A. (2017, December 28). *2017, a year of hate crimes in India: Number of violent incidents related to cows, religion is rising-India News, Firstpost.* Firstpost. https://www.firstpost.com/india/2017-a-year-of-hate-crimes-in-india-number-of-violent-incidents-related-to-cows-religion-is-rising-4278751.html

Schulze, E. (4 February 2019). *EU says Facebook, Google and Twitter are getting faster at removing hate speech online*. CNBC. Retrieved 25 March 2025.

SELMA Partners. (2019, April 8). *The consequences of online hate speech – a teenager's perspective | SELMA Hacking Hate*. Hackinghate.eu. https://hackinghate.eu/news/the-consequences-of-online-hate-speech-a-teenager-s-perspective/

Simpson, R. M. (2012). Dignity, Harm, and Hate Speech. *Law and Philosophy, 32*(6), 701–728. DOI: 10.1007/s10982-012-9164-z

Singhari, S., & Madheswaran, S. (2016). Social exclusion and caste discrimination in public and private sectors in India: A decomposition analysis. Bangalore: Institute for Social and Economic Change.

Space, C. (2018). *Self-Regulation and 'Hate Speech' on Social Media Platforms*, ARTICLE 19, https://www.article19.org/resources/self-regulation-hate-speech-social-media-platforms/

Staff, F. P. (2013, September 12). *Muzaffarnagar riots: The inciteful speeches that fanned rioters' fury*. Firstpost. https://www.firstpost.com/politics/muzaffarnagar-riots-the-inciteful-speeches-that-fanned-rioters-fury-1103789.html

Stefancic, J., & Delgado, R. (n.d.). *A Shifting Balance: Freedom of Expression and Hate-Speech Restriction Essay*. The University of Alabama.

Suroor, J. (2012) *You can't read this book*, The Hindu. https://www.thehindu.com/books/you-cant-read-this-book/article2953626.ece

The Indian Express. (2018). *The mob that hates*. Harsh Mander.

The YouTube Team. (2019). *Our Ongoing Work to Tackle Hate*, Official YouTube Blog, https://youtube.googleblog.com/2019/06/our-ongoing-work-to-tackle-hate.html

Twitter (n.d.). *Hateful Conduct Policy*, Twitter, https://help.twitter.com/en/rules-and-policies/hateful-conduct-policy

Union of India. (1951). *The Representation of the People Act, 1951*. Kanoon.

Union of India. (1973). *The Code of Criminal Procedure, 1973*. Kanoon.

United Nations Office on Drugs and Crime. (2006). *Handbook on Restorative justice programmes*. https://www.unodc.org/pdf/criminal_justice/Handbook_on_Restorative_Justice_Programmes.pdf

U.S. Department of Justice. (2023, October 30). *Community Relations Service | 2022 FBI Hate Crimes Statistics*. Www.justice.gov. https://www.justice.gov/crs/highlights/2022-hate-crime-statistics

Venkataramanan, K. (2022). *Explained | What is "hate speech," and how is it treated in Indian law?* The Hindu. https://www.thehindu.com/news/national/explained-what-is-hate-speech-and-how-is-it-treated-in-indian-law/article64851585.ece

Vergani, M. (2024, January 29). *New Study Explores the Impact of Hate Crimes on Victims - Tackling Hate*. Tackling Hate. https://tacklinghate.org/blogs/new-study-explores-the-impact-of-hate-crimes-on-victims/

Waldron, J. (2012). The Harm in Hate Speech. In *JSTOR*. Harvard University Press., https://www.jstor.org/stable/j.ctt2jbrjd

Walker, S. (1994). *Hate Speech: The History of an American Controversy*. University of Nebraska Press.

Webb, T.J. (2011). *Verbal Poison - Criminalizing Hate Speech: A Comparative Analysis and a Proposal for the American System*. 50 Washburn L.J. 445.

WIPO. (2009). *Cable Television Networks Rules, 1994 (as amended up to February 27, 2009), India*.int. https://www.wipo.int/wipolex/en/legislation/details/13628

Yadav, A. (n.d.). *Countering hate speech in india: Looking for answers beyond the law*. https://ili.ac.in/pdf/csi.pdf

Zapata, J., & Deroy, O. (2023). Ordinary citizens are more severe towards verbal than nonverbal hate-motivated incidents with identical consequences. *Scientific Reports*, *13*(1). Advance online publication. DOI: 10.1038/s41598-023-33892-8 PMID: 37130915

Chapter 10
AI for a Greener Tomorrow:
Harnessing Artificial Intelligence for Environmental Sustainability

Md Mehedi Hasan Emon
https://orcid.org/0000-0002-6224-9552
American International University-Bangladesh, Bangladesh

Avishek Nath
https://orcid.org/0009-0006-9466-1425
American International University-Bangladesh, Bangladesh

Meherun Nisa Nipa
https://orcid.org/0009-0005-7810-0970
National University, Bangladesh

ABSTRACT

This chapter explores the transformative role of artificial intelligence in advancing environmental sustainability amid escalating climate challenges. It examines how AI-driven technologies optimize resource management, enhance climate monitoring, and promote green innovations across sectors such as energy, agriculture, and waste management. Through predictive analytics, machine learning, and real-time data integration, AI supports more precise climate modeling, disaster early warning systems, and efficient energy use. The chapter also addresses ethical and practical concerns, including algorithmic bias, data privacy, and the digital divide, emphasizing the need for inclusive and responsible AI deployment. By highlighting real-world applications and offering policy recommendations, it underscores the potential of

DOI: 10.4018/979-8-3373-2387-9.ch010

AI to balance technological progress with ecological stewardship. Finally, this work advocates for interdisciplinary collaboration and equitable governance to ensure AI contributes meaningfully to a sustainable and just environmental future.

INTRODUCTION

As the world faces more climate change, less biodiversity and the overuse of natural resources, everyone is at a crucial moment. The environmental sustainability actions we have traditionally used are not enough to solve the big challenges facing the environment today. Now, artificial intelligence (AI) is more than something expected in the future; it is necessary for us right now. This chapter explores how AI can assist in environmental protection, though not in place of human role, providing better, faster and more adjustable assistance. At the beginning of the chapter, authors place AI into the broader context of sustainable development and environmental policy. It investigates the ways in which machine learning; computer vision and predictive analytics are changing our ability to manage and study nature. In this chapter, a sectoral analysis introduces AI applications in various areas, including electricity production, agriculture, waste processing, use of water resources and supervision of biological diversity, showing how smart algorithms help resource use, cut pollution and control threats to natural ecosystems. The chapter clearly moves past describing technology solely as progress. It studies the ways in which AI might affect sustainability, asking major questions on issues such as data governance, algorithmic impartiality and helping the digital divide grow. AI also points out the need for many fields combining forces and for policies to be consistent. It considers that promoting environmental goals through AI requires inclusive design, tight oversight and equal access. The chapter uses reports, specific case studies and theory to give a fair assessment of how AI affects environmental sustainability. The study concludes with recommendations for the use of science and highlights areas where learning could continue, all aimed at creating responsible innovation that matches the goals of environmental justice and long-term resilience. This chapter helps address the issues regarding inclusive and equitable development by making clear that AI is important for working together to make the world greener, fairer and more sustainable.

AI APPLICATIONS IN ENVIRONMENTAL MONITORING AND MANAGEMENT

Modern environmental monitoring doesn't rely only on manual data collection and scattered data. Now, advanced AI techniques can help environmental scientists and policy-makers handle, predict and manage risks to the environment more easily. Incorporating AI into tracking the environment marks a crucial step forward for how we connect with the world around us, matching precision and ability unreachable by previous approaches. Satellite tracking of climate and rapid reaction to disasters are now possible largely because of AI. AI has greatly improved the way we study information from remote sensing instruments. For a long time, understanding satellite imagery meant waiting for experts to study the data and perform manual interpretation, making the process uneven and not easy to scale. Conventional image classification methods have been replaced by powerful CNNs. They can notice features in visual images, helping to determine land use, note unusual factors in the environment and track changes in ecosystems with a high rate of precision. Furthermore, Peng et al., (2024) showed that CNNs achieved a high level of reliability by distinguishing urban sprawl, forest damage and agricultural expansion in real time.

In addition, using AI in remote sensing is now common for tracking and stopping deforestation in places such as the Amazon and Southeast Asia. Global Forest Watch and similar projects are using machine learning to find and report illegal logging right as it takes place, so that governments and NGOs can take immediate action (Causevic et al., 2024). AI algorithms are also being used to keep a better watch on glacial retreat and track how it relates to climate change. New technologies help us grasp how climate works and contribute to fine-tuning the model's governments depend on for making decisions. Moreover, using AI in situations besides understanding visual information. Today, warning systems that use AI are key to lowering risks from disasters. Floods, wildfires, hurricanes and earthquakes, as natural disasters, are very complex situations that depend on using a wide range of sources. Prediction of such events with improved accuracy and a lead time benefit has been noted in AI systems that use both ensembles learning and RNNs. Furthermore, combining data from the weather, satellite, topographic maps and social media with AI enables models to forecast flash floods up to six hours in advance, much better than traditional hydrological models (Debata & Elango, 2024).

In California, wildfire prediction demonstrates the development of the field. Today, AI uses historical burn data, up-to-date measures of plants and grasses, wind speed and temperature to issue warnings and set up the best logistics for emergency response teams (Albahri et al., 2024). Forecasting weather changes means we can save lives, lessen the effect on the economy and manage cities and areas more wisely over the long run. AI systems are also being used now on drones and ground-level sensors in risky zones to support visibility during ongoing blazes. AI is now being used to keep an eye on air and water quality as part of environmental studies. In urban and rural environments, environmental sensors collect a lot of data about pollutants and particulates. Data analysis is happening using AI, especially SVMs and decision tree models, to look for traffic and chemical contamination sources, spot unusual situations and predict future issues. For example, using machine learning, Liu et al., (2021) monitored air quality in Beijing real time and helped authorities predict levels of PM2.5, so they could take effective action.

AI is also playing a role in keeping an eye on pollution in the ocean and on groups who fish illegally. Using satellite data with AI helps detect abnormal vessel moves and discover how marine waste is dispersing, supporting laws and environmental conservation (Alloghani, 2024). AI works in these fields by facilitating diagnosis and providing helpful data for regulators to enforce environmental laws. Predictive analytics from AI are being used widely for climate policy and to lower carbon emissions. Companies across all kinds of industries are now using AI to model how their activities impact the environment. The tools use energy, transportation and supply chain figures to give a detailed picture of the sources of emissions. Microsoft and Google are among those that have established AI technology for sustainability, providing ongoing overview of their emissions and energy use to help them move closer to being net-zero (Ferdaus et al., 2024). City planners at the municipal level are using AI models to develop areas of low emissions and to arrange public transport routes that produce less carbon. The spatial analysis and scenario testing offered by AI support the shift of cities toward ecological infrastructure. AI is used in city planning to study heat-retaining areas and estimate the impact of green spaces, so important changes can be made in urban landscaping.

Moreover, bringing AI to environmental monitoring comes with its own set of problems. The quality and ready availability of data are still major challenges, mainly due to the lack of environmental sensor systems in developing nations. In addition, it is very important to be able to see how data is processed by algorithms and to reproduce the results. All major environmental decisions regarding enforcement and safety should be supported by interpretable and auditable models. Deep learning systems that work like "black boxes" face problems with public trust and accountability if action is not taken (Hassija et al., 2024). They are only as effective as the information they are fed. Data that is unfinished, biased or dated can create incorrect results and worsen problems of environmental fairness. In practice, building AI methods for disaster planning by using few samples from specific regions might unfairly influence how those systems help marginalized people (Zolkafli et al., 2024). Ethics in AI should therefore be an important part of discussions about AI in environmental use.

All things considered, AI has greatly improved how we keep an eye on the environment and manage it. Modern sustainability science depends greatly on the ability of big data science to handle wide datasets, notice patterns and produce predictions. Technological advancements require us to update AI governance so that it supports environmental protection, ethics and the participation of all people around the world. There is a lot that AI can accomplish here, but it should only be developed if we take care, work with others and make sure it promotes equity.

AI IN ENERGY AND RESOURCE OPTIMIZATION

As people demand more action on climate change, making better use of resources is now a main goal in the global effort to reduce emissions. Since energy sector activities make up about three-quarters of worldwide GHG emissions, adding AI to the mix isn't only about being more efficient but is also a necessary move for sustainable growth. Energy generation and consumption can be thoroughly transformed because AI helps manage huge sets of data, spot system shifts and automate control tasks. This part of the content describes how AI is making a major difference in how we manage our energy and use resources, mainly through smart grids, including more renewable energy, improved industrial results and changing to a circular economic approach. A smart grid is the result of IT and energy infrastructure coming together. Smart grids work differently from old grids which run on set plans and are managed centrally, by being dynamic, decentralized and more adaptive. In this transformation, AI is necessary since it monitors energy use, helps predict future needs and keeps energy flow managed in real time. Deep learning models are now widely used to forecast electricity demand using information such as the days' time, the weather outside and how consumers behave. Predicting energy use allows the best use of resources which means less fossil fuel use at peak times and reduced emissions (Wang & Azam, 2024).

In addition, the fact that solar and wind energy is not always available has kept them from being fully used in the nation's power grids. AI overcomes this trouble by helping to make renewable energy forecasts more accurate. Analyzing historical data on the weather, forms of energy used and pictures from space with machine learning algorithms helps improve forecasting of changes in renewable resources. It has now been shown that using AI in solar forecasting lowers the error rate by more than 30% when compared to standard statistical techniques (T. Khan et al., 2020; Kumar & Katiyar, 2024). The advancements protect the power grid and at the same time, keep expenses and negative effects on the environment low by avoiding both under and overproduction of energy. API plays a key role in how renewable energy systems are built and operated. AI helps to smoothly link renewable products that individuals and homes may have such as rooftop solar panels, electric vehicles and home batteries, to general energy networks. Algorithms are used to oversee the trading of energy between users, to control the batteries in home energy storage and to avoid overwhelming the power grid. AI is changing the way industry manages its resources, apart from what it does in the power sector. Engineering and heavy industries use AI analytics to show where production wastes arise, optimize the use of raw materials and help create better products. Reinforcement learning ensures that machine parameters are always adjusted, depending on feedback, so the machine saves energy and delivers the required output. AI is also used for predictive maintenance, spotting changes in equipment before they turn into problems that require a lot of energy to repair or stop (Ravichandra et al., 2024). They enable the practical adoption of circular economic rules which stress less waste and more resource reuse.

AI technology looks at the flow of materials, product life and waste to locate places where waste can be given new life in the production process. Textile factories make use of AI algorithms to neatly separate post-consumer textiles by the type of fiber and their colors during recycling (Sahu & Rath, 2025). In food processing, AI systems can find any issues in goods which raises sorting efficiency and supports better management of goods. AI is also making a big difference in optimizing uses of water. Algorithms in AI analyze soil levels, predict the weather and track crop progress, to properly water plants on farms. AI in urban regions helps regularly estimate water demand, detect pipeline leaks and ensure the most efficient management of treating wastewater. There is no doubt about what AI can do in energy and resources, but it's not free from challenges. The challenges of data quality and easy access remain serious, mainly because low- and middle-income countries have limited digital resources. In addition, the high energy demands linked to training large machine learning models call for additional attention. According to VanGessel et al., (2023), the energy necessary to train a single large natural language processing model can be similar to flying across the Atlantic multiple times, so we must carefully consider how much energy is used. Moreover, reliance on AI in energy areas causes questions about how transparent, accountable and controllable the use of AI becomes. Black-box AI models are very useful but remain hard for regulators and interested parties to understand how they reach their decisions. The difficulty caused by this opacity becomes serious when AI influences energy pricing or regulates who gets access to important utilities. In order to stop AI from adding to inequality issues, making it fair and easy to understand is most important.

Balancing security with convenience means we also need to address cybersecurity. When AI starts being used in critical infrastructure, energy systems are more at risk from cyberattacks. It's possible that AI used to manage our power supply could be hacked to shut off service and possibly cause major damage. Strengthening these systems needs both strong technical measures and support from the law and from other countries. Although it hasn't always been easy, AI for improving energy and resource use shows a mainly positive trend. There is growing realization within governments and at the international level that AI can help with reaching climate targets. AI-driven energy efficiency projects are strongly supported in the European Commission's Horizon Europe initiative and the International Renewable Energy Agency (IRENA) sees AI as crucial to achieving a global transition to renewable energy.

AI FOR GREEN TECHNOLOGIES AND CIRCULAR ECONOMY

Ecosystem degradation and the challenges of linear models have led the world to switch to a circular economy. Its goal is to create systems that maintain the worth of products for a long time which supports the environment and lowers waste. In this changing landscape, AI acts less as a tool and more as a thinking partner that updates how sustainability is done. Its use of data, pattern detection, prediction abilities and ability to operate on its own is why it helps achieve green technologies and supports the circular economy. The chapter studies AI's use with various sustainability objectives, including waste management, greater use of resources and pollution control, as well as the effects this technology has on the wider community. AI is especially useful in circular economy when it comes to dealing with waste management. Traditional waste sorting practices are usually slow, not very accurate and can expose workers to dangerous materials. In comparison, computer vision systems in AI-enabled technologies help identify and dispose of plastics, metals, glass and organic substances in waste with high accuracy and in a very short time. Moreover, combined with robotic arms, these systems walk along conveyor belts and manage objects more efficiently than any human team could do (Dmytriyev et al., 2024). Platforms such as those by AMP Robotics, powered by AI, help to spot logos and understand packaging types so that recycling can be accomplished in a complete circle for selected manufacturers and with less risk of contamination. AI makes recyclables of a higher quality which means less waste ends up in landfills or is burned. Apart from waste sorting, AI is used for other logistics tasks in circular waste systems. In this way, predictive algorithms make waste collection schedules better by reviewing real-time data collected by sensor-integrated bins. It decreases the amount of fuel these services use, lowers operation costs and lessens greenhouse gas emissions from the vehicles involved (Sacchi et al., 2022). Dynamic pricing strategies in recovery facilities are now possible using AI which adjusts the approach based on changes in demand and materials.

AI makes a big difference in creating and managing sustainable supply chains. Supply chains in a circular economy are responsible for delivering goods and for gathering used products for recovery, remaking, recycling or reuse. AI plays a role by predicting which products need to be returned, choosing the best pickup areas and controlling how secondary materials are handled (Shi, 2022). In addition, AI makes it possible for companies to automate how they gather and interpret environmental data from the beginning of the product's life all the way to when it is recycled or discarded. As a result, companies can find the most harmful parts of their business and create new strategies to create less environmental damage. Process optimization in manufacturing is led by AI. Machine learning models can identify places where energy is wasted, suggest the best settings for production and forecast when equipment should be maintained to reduce slowdowns and wastage. In doing so, Siemens uses AI in factories to efficiently change production as each new material arrives which helps reduce scrap and save resources (Waltersmann et al., 2021). In addition, generative design tools, driven by AI, help engineers produce products that require less material without compromising their stability. It both cuts back on the use of resources and allows the product to be more easily taken apart and recycled once it reaches its end of life.

A central part of the circular economy is product-as-a-service (PaaS) where the goods belong to the provider and people rent their use. Airline, electronics, fashion and mobility sectors are among those now using this model, powered by AI for operational purposes. Predictive analytics tracks how assets are being used, helps design the best asset spread and oversee when maintenance should be carried out. AI on mobility-as-a-service (MaaS) platforms plans how electric vehicles are grouped which paths are taken by drivers and how often to charge them (Servou et al., 2023). The result is increased reliability for assets and a reduction in the environmental damage that comes from making too many things and leaving them unused.

AI is also making big differences in water conservation and controlling pollution. Smart irrigation in agriculture is built around AI technologies that analyze weather data, what crops require and the moisture of the soil, so water is delivered only when and where needed. Smart monitoring solutions spot abnormalities in the use of water in factories and thus help identify leaks or problems with machines, making it easy to do repairs promptly. Measuring and regulating water quality is as important an area for AI. A variety of sensors are installed in rivers, reservoirs and treatment plants to collect lots of information about pH, turbidity, oxygen in the water and potential contamination. Real-time processing of data by AI models allows them to find where pollution originates, to estimate upcoming contamination issues and to suggest ways to deal with them. For example, systems that use machines to help predict HABs use satellite imagery, historic records and current water quality to report harmful changes ahead of time, so authorities and officials can act swiftly (T. Khan & Emon, 2024; Leape et al., 2023). To make the circular economy work, consumers need to participate and AI helps by providing better user interfaces that nudge people toward doing the right thing. Promoting sustainability, giving advice on product repair and offering rewards for resale and recycling are all possible with e-commerce recommendation systems. Because of AI, consumers are now able to see their activity's environmental consequences, learn more about green living and become more responsible about protecting the environment (M. S. Khan et al., 2020). Since more people are asking for corporate sustainability and laws are now focusing on producer responsibility such systems are growing in importance.

Furthermore, there are obstacles to successful AI use in eco-friendly and closed-loop economic approaches. We must recognize how much energy AI uses. Teaching large machine learning models consumes a great deal of energy. That's why working towards greener AI algorithms and data centers using renewable energy is required to achieve its original sustainability goals (Yigitcanlar et al., 2021). In addition, because the gap in technology across the world stops many in poorer areas from using AI for sustainability, existing environmental injustices and difficulties getting resources may increase. For AI-driven circular economy models to work well, they should be accessible, open and controlled by the people they serve.

Privacy of data is an important concern, mainly because of AI's use with consumer information in sustainability-related tasks. The log of personal data is collected and analyzed with ethics, with each person agreeing and having strong protection from misuse. AI, in short, is central to pushing for a circular economy and supporting new environmentally friendly technologies. Green technology touches every part of the process, from developing clever products, building sustainably, handling waste, regenerating resources, to working with consumers. If stakeholders want to realize the best outcomes, they should use systems-thinking to include responsible technology, social inclusion and concern for the environment. The circular economy is shaping up to include both better technology and better decisions, so we can work together to improve and heal the world instead of only lessening its harm.

AI IN CLIMATE CHANGE MITIGATION AND ADAPTATION

As the entire world is facing growing problems from climate change, there is greater urgency for strong solutions to help us adapt and respond. The key focus is on gaining deep knowledge of climate systems and changing those findings into useful policy and technology options. AI's power to look at many types of data and learn patterns hidden from people has made it very important in helping both fight and adjust to climate change. This section examines how AI assists climate modeling, supports more effective planning for adaptation and encourages innovative strategies to lower emissions with carbon capture and storage. Good climate policy is based on correct forecasts of future climate changes. Computational restraints and limited access to all the data needed make it hard for traditional climate models to accurately show small differences in geography and time. AI adds value to these models by including different types of data, including observations from space, historical climate data, atmospheric information and social and economic statistics, in advanced learning algorithms. The models use neural networks, combining them with many techniques and deep learning methods to improve predictions of temperature changes, changes in rainfall and the occurrence of hurricanes, droughts and floods (Haggag et al., 2021). According to Peng et al., (2024), CNNs have successfully cut down the data from large global climate models so that communities can plan better ways to adapt to climate change. This improved prediction enables governments and urban planners to see climate risks more clearly. AI makes it possible to bring model outcomes together with real-time environmental data so help the process of adjusting measures. AI can be used in coastal regions that might suffer from sea-level rise by connecting information about terrain, tide measurements and the way land is used to predict flooding and help suggest how to build and set up early alarm systems (Bahari et al., 2023). In agricultural zones, predictions made with AI help determine strong drought crops and plan the best planting periods which are important for food security when the climate changes (Delfani et al., 2024).

AI is helping to address major causes of greenhouse gas emission from across several sectors. Efficiency in energy consumption and production is one of the main achievements of these industries. AI makes power grids more efficient because it forecasts use, helps balance demand and mixes renewables in the best way. Apart from managing energy systems, AI can handle smart transportation management, cut down emissions by arranging traffic well, help electric vehicles choose their fastest routes and promote shared mobility models (Suganya et al., 2025). In addition to helping the environment such apps improve city life for everyone by lowering air pollution and traffic congestion. It is widely believed that achieving net-zero goals relies greatly on CCS technologies which can be greatly improved by using AI. Industrial emissions of carbon dioxide can be captured and sent underground by CCS to keep them from causing air pollution. Even though CCS has been designed, its practical use has been blocked by the high costs and complexity of its operations. AI uses ongoing monitoring to check how the plant is doing and changes operational features, allowing more carbon to be captured and less overall energy and maintenance costs (Manikandan et al., 2025). Reinforcement learning has been used to set pressure and temperature in absorption columns, so the capture can improve and there is no threat to safety. Moreover, AI is able to spot ideal CO_2 storage sites by examining seismic activity, the chemical makeup of soil and water movements. Risk assessment by machine learning involves potential leaks or seismic problems, allowing storage sites to meet tough safety and environmental guidelines. The use of data in selecting sites speeds up projects and increases the confidence of all involved

AI-based inventions are now arising in the field of negative emissions technologies (NETs), including bioenergy with carbon capture and storage (BECCS) and direct air capture (DAC). AI models ensure that biomass feedstocks are grown optimally in BECCS, weighing the environment for yield, the ability to remove carbon and land use. In DAC systems, AI runs operations and checks the energy use by monitoring both the amount of CO_2 in the air and the system performance (Ozkan, 2024). Although AI shows a lot of potential for responding to climate change, we should place these developments in bigger socio-technical and ethical categories. A major problem is the power consumption needed to both train and implement advanced AI models. It has been shown through studies that the energy usage of certain deep learning applications is similar to the emissions from a small vehicle over its entire life. Hence, companies should pay attention to efficiency in AI, start using renewable energy in data centers and ensure fair sharing of information about AI's effect on the environment. Along with these applications, there are questions about equity and justice to be dealt with. Climate change hits people from marginalized and low-income communities harder, mainly because such groups are unable to use the AI-powered information and tools on offer. It is very important to make sure everyone is involved in AI to avoid adding to existing imbalances. Ensuring that data and AI services are open to all residents, supporting local skills development and making tools suitable for each community are all important (Goralski & Tan, 2020). The use of AI also makes data privacy and security concerns more important, mainly because AI depends on data collected by sensors, satellites and our personal equipment. If climate AI is to benefit the public, sensitive data must be covered and suited ethical practices are put in place to ensure the public is not jeopardized. AI is a critical tool for helping us protect against and adapt to climate change. By enhancing climate models, offering tailored policy help and optimizing innovation in emissions, AI makes it possible for us to face the many problems related to climate change. Nevertheless, it needs to be developed through a combined process that looks after technology, the environment, social needs and ethical values. Researchers and policymakers must work on developing AI systems that are clear, effective, fair and support the main aim of getting to a safe and just climate future.

CHALLENGES AND ETHICAL CONSIDERATIONS

AI has incredible potential in helping with tough environmental issues yet using it in sustainability is often complicated. Challenges in AI are caused by factors within our society, as well as in ethics and government, that influence each step of AI solutions. As people in both academic and practice start relying on AI for better environmental, energy and climate outcomes, we must pay attention to the potential challenges and ethical problems associated with these advances. The chapter analyzes the issues, ethical problems and policy holes linked to AI in environmental sustainability to inspire responsible and equal implementation. Everyone in the field is concerned about how algorithmic biases impact environmental sustainability. The results from machine learning models depend on the data they were taught from and if this data contains existing inequalities, those inequalities could be strengthened. If AI disaster response solutions rely more on data from rich regions, their function in low-income or rural places which are the most likely to suffer from climate change, may be heavily reduced (Balogun et al., 2020). As a result, AI tools work less effectively, and the topic of distributive justice and environmental equity becomes very challenging. There will not be fair use of AI unless we use diverse methods to source data and get a range of perspectives during the design process.

Additionally, deep learning models made with algorithms can be very hard for people to explain because their work is so complex. Black box models prevent easy access to information and stop people from holding agencies accountable in environmental care. In some cases, when AI helps in making resource decisions or choosing which regions require evacuation, that conscious may not understand the process clearly, nor may officials (Alqahtani et al., 2024; Emon & Khan, 2025). Lack of transparency in AI decreases the public trust and hinders democratic review of actions when AI systems can have a serious impact on people's livelihoods, the distribution of resources or risks to the environment. Both personal data privacy and the risk of being monitored are very related to these concerns. A growing number of devices for environmental monitoring depend on remote sensing, IoT gadgets and mobile tech and these technologies often collect data in places people visit. Although these technologies reveal useful information about environmental issues, they might sometimes pick up private information about individuals' actions, their land or how often they travel. A lack of data security regulations in some countries leads to big privacy problems. In addition, environmental monitoring tools in authoritarian countries might be turned into methods for political monitoring or repression (Zhu et al., 2023). Therefore, top-quality security is required to guarantee that data gathering honors privacy and follows human rights rules.

There is also a major challenge from the worldwide digital divide. Despite the idea of AI being widely transformative, there are big differences in who can use AI infrastructure, skills and resources globally. In AI, research is mainly done and products created by high-income and multinational firms, whereas the technical, financial or policy support needed by poorer countries is lacking. This situation not only keeps the Global South from fully using AI to fight climate change, but it might also boost inequality in decision making about the environment worldwide (Goralski & Tan, 2020). Fixing the digital divide requires answering technological needs as well as investing in schools, laboratories and inclusive laws. In addition, people are starting to doubt how sustainable AI can be. The training process for large and deep learning models uses plenty of both computing power and energy. According to V. Liu & Yin, (2024), there is a good chance that training just one natural language processing model may produce the greenhouse gas equivalent of five American cars driving all the way through their lifetimes. AI should only be suggested as a response to environmental degradation when the environmental impact is both recognized and controlled. Beliefs can be broken down like this: Make data centers run on renewable energy, improve algorithms to use the least amount of effort and avoid overcomplicating models.

Incorporating AI into environmental work requires that those involved include a wide range of voices. Frequently, new AI solutions are made in a technocratic way, without seeking help from Indigenous or marginalized communities who have great ecological understanding. As a result, AI interventions could stand discredited, and the algorithms themselves will not benefit from a range of cultural perspectives and beliefs. This area needs dedicated interaction with different parties, including those on the ground and higher-level policymakers and a strong standard for procedural justice. Collaboration with different expert groups plays an important role in solving ethical and practical problems. AI governance in the field of environmental sustainability should connect technology firms, researchers, policymakers and civil groups. Ecological systems, rules and what communities find useful can be understood more clearly by combining several fields of expertise. Moreover, such collaborations are important for writing guidelines on responsible AI use, covering how data is managed, how algorithms are explained and how society should be held accountable. Furthermore, overseeing financial organizations continues to be a continuing challenge. Because AI is advancing faster than the law can update, many countries do not have full rules for common issues such as AI-related discrimination, blame for errors and environmental consequences of using technology. A lack of global coordination is serious because both the problems and the supply chains that manage AI technology cross international lines. The United Nations and ITU are good candidates to help establish worldwide ethical standards and tools for working together (von Ingersleben-Seip, 2023).

CASE STUDIES AND REAL-WORLD APPLICATIONS

Artificial intelligence is now being applied to environmental protection, supporting real actions while also revealing the benefits and downsides of its use. Examining real-world AI case studies from different environmental and economic zones helps us identify how environmental management is being transformed, the benefits it brings and the difficulties that arise. The actual cases show both what AI can do and the ways in which society affects how and why it is used. Many studies celebrate Google's innovation in making its data centers more efficient in their energy use. Data centers worldwide use up a lot of energy which often means having a significant impact on the environment. Google realized this problem and used deep reinforcement learning to manage cooling systems, a major user of energy in these facilities. According to Yan et al., (2021), the AI intervention reduced cooling energy usage by a stunning 40% which cut both expenses and the building's effect on the environment. The platform is able to react to weather changes outside and server loads inside, keeping its power use low and delivering top performance. This case demonstrates that AI can be used to achieve scalability and sustainability at the same time, and it provides a repeated example for other industries with high energy needs.

The Amazon rainforest, a difficult ecosystem to protect, has become easier to guard because of the benefits AI brings to biodiversity conservation. Biodiversity, the lives of indigenous peoples and climate regulation are all at risk from constant illegal logging, since forests help control carbon. Ball et al., (2022) showed how CNNs and satellite images are used to identify deforestation in the current period. The automatic nature of the system means authorities can detect law violations quickly, thus redirecting security forces to solve the problem. Also, drones using computer vision are sent out to scan the forest, giving detailed results on forest conditions and animal populations. The demonstration showed better environmental results as well as clearer and more accountable management, making it easier for government bodies, NGOs and local people to work together. The use of AI has made big improvements in the agriculture industry which cares greatly about environmental sustainability. AI models connected to precision farming technology look at readings from soil, weather stations and satellite pictures to help with irrigation, feeding plants and pest control. An AI platform called AgroSense was developed in India. It predicts pest problems and suggests livelihood management methods that substantially cut down on chemicals (Sharada et al., 2025). Practicing this way raises farmers' earnings and strengthens soil and water, keeping runoff within acceptable limits. All of these cases confirm that using AI helps achieve balanced use of land by giving practical, field-tailored suggestions for productivity and conservation.

Artificial intelligence promises to play an important role in making cities more environmentally friendly. AI is being used in smart cities to enhance how traffic moves, decrease emissions and enhance waste management. For example, in Barcelona, AI is used to review the speed and flow of traffic near busy areas and adjust the city's traffic signals in real time. The traffic congestion fell by 25% as well as the number of pollutants from motor vehicles which made the air healthier (Rodriguez-Rey et al., 2022). Additionally, automated material separation is used in Amsterdam and other European cities with AI to improve recycling and reduce waste sent to landfills while cutting greenhouse gas emissions from waste disposal (Satpathy et al., 2024).

Artificial intelligence helps make cities greener and more comfortable for residents by guiding city policies toward eco-friendly and safe city environments. While AI is gaining success, various studies point out that both being aware of the environment and including stakeholders is very important in any AI project. In many parts of Sub-Saharan Africa, it was noticed that AI projects for water management ran into issues thanks to low community participation and unclear information on how the data was collected (Adom & Simatele, 2025). As communities had concerns about AI watching them or using their data, few were interested and therefore AI did not make much difference. They show how ignoring social and political realities and local knowledge leads to problems with technology-based reading initiatives. Effective actions in these communities involved building trust, designing widely for all and investing in improvement. As a result, anyone who works in AI needs to focus on social justice and empowering their community too.

A further problem is scaling AI systems and supporting them where resources are limited. In Southeast Asia, using AI to predict floods worked well, but the systems could not be used much because of a lack of both infrastructure and trained staff to act on them (Munawar et al., 2022). It demonstrates that cooperation between AI and building the right public agencies and policies is necessary to deal with environmental problems immediately and effectively. How public and private actors cooperate is a main feature of AI's role in the environment. Cooperative efforts of governments, technology businesses and non-profit organizations have usually fostered progress in the field. Yet, these teams sometimes face challenges involving data, who controls it and share benefits equally. Microsoft's AI for Earth program gives support to initiatives all over the world that address water problems, protect wildlife populations and control pollution. Although the initiative has supported many expanding projects, there are concerns that giving these strategies to corporations may decrease transparency and ensure top priority is given to business purposes instead of benefiting the public (Wirba, 2023). Encouraging inventions in AI while being open about how it is used is still a major challenge in promoting good use of AI. Furthermore, integrated models that rely on both AI and skilled and trusted community groups are likely the path with the greatest promise. At the Great Barrier Reef, computer-aided image viewing goes hand in hand with knowledge shared by local Indigenous people to observe changes in coral and diversity among marine life. Ecological knowledge improves by working together which supports Indigenous communities as stewards of their natural environments. These approaches imply that AI will play a major role in saving the environment by improving technology and by connecting scientists and those in practice. In essence, AI is proving its ability to transform environmental sustainability, for example through efficient data centers, detecting unauthorized logging, agriculture technology and city sustainability plans. At the same time, these examples demonstrate some of the various issues connected to deploying AI, for example, adapting to local needs, including everyone in decisions, boosting skills and ensuring transparency with data. The knowledge gained points out that simply introducing new technology will not improve the environment unless moral, social and political factors work to support justice, fairness and inclusion. A real difference in sustainability will only be made when AI is used this way.

POLICY RECOMMENDATIONS AND FUTURE DIRECTIONS

As artificial intelligence is increasingly used to protect the environment, it is necessary to make strong policies to make sure its pros are reached, and cons are managed. AI can significantly support sustainability in energy, resources, modeling and conservation, yet taking advantage of these benefits needs more than installing new technology. A responsible approach to AI means a policy that promotes ethical, responsible development and works to eliminate differences between wealthy and poor, resolve complicated ethical problems and tackle issues in how AI is governed. This section looks at recent discoveries and new best approaches, proposing recommendations to support the integration of AI in sustainability planning.

Regulatory Frameworks for Responsible AI Development

A major focus in policy should be to make sure that the development and use of AI along with strict environmental rules are steadfast. These regulations should place greater attention on openness, reliability and doing what is right when making decisions with results on the environment or people who might be harmed. Algorithmic biases may increase environmental problems for those already facing social and economic disadvantages (Akter et al., 2022). As a result, confined use of AI in environmental fields is only possible with additional bias audits and fairness examinations being required by regulatory bodies. AI needs to allow explorations of processes so stakeholders can question outcomes when necessary. Ensuring the right use of data is also very significant. The need for big datasets in AI could affect people's privacy and it matters most when monitoring the environment also leads to involvement with people. Laws built to safeguard personal privacy should not slow down new inventions. It focuses on blending projects that make data public for research and transparency with rules to protect the data. Transparent policies that explain who has data, what individuals can do with it and how it is processed are vital for AI technologies to benefit everyone and restore public trust (Agrawal, 2024).

Promoting Interdisciplinary Research and Inclusive Innovation

AI works in sustainability on both technical and social, economic and cultural levels. As a result, policies should encourage research that combines computer science, environmental science, social sciences and ethics. With an integrated process, solutions can be both advanced and appropriate to each society's values and needs. Financial organizations and universities ought to reward work that encourages different groups to come together, including locals, policy experts and business leaders. Blending climate adaptations guided by AI models with local information and group participation improves the results (Jain et al., 2023). Encouraging health services and education to collaborate will lead to new solutions that fit the area, are supported by the community and continue to have a positive impact in the future. In addition, creating AI by teaming social scientists and ethicists with developers can allocate together to solve any challenges regarding ethics and respect for human values.

Bridging the Digital Divide Through Investment in Infrastructure and Education

Even though AI has great potential, some people will likely miss out because there are still large differences in digital tools and skills. A big problem for low- and middle-income countries as well as marginalized areas in wealthy nations is the digital divide. AI-powered initiatives to help the environment may not do their job properly because infrastructure and technical abilities need to be improved (Emon et al., 2025; Gundeti et al., 2023). Experts should place more emphasis on letting lots of people benefit from high-speed internet, online computing resources and affordable AI resources to join in AI efforts for sustainability. The main approach is for public funds to be dedicated to remote and neglected regions, with international aid playing a possible additional part. Educational programs and building up people's capacities are needed alongside improvement to infrastructure. Curriculums must prepare current and future generations for AI, data science and environmental matters so they are ready to manage and use AI in sustainability applications. Teaching policymakers, practitioners and community leaders about AI will improve how they take decisions and adjust their policies. This way of teaching allows a larger group to design and ensure AI tools which helps to give all involved a say and helps avoid decisions being made just by the technical field experts.

Fostering Public-Private Partnerships for Innovation and Knowledge Sharing

AI-powered answers for environmental problems are commonly developed by working closely together with governments, private businesses and community groups. The government should help form PPPs that encourage each side to make the most of their strengths. Private companies usually have leading technology and resources, but public agencies provide rules, public interest and reach into communities and ecosystems. When organizations join forces for AI, they speed up the growth and use of smart grids, more accurate agriculture and systems for tracking pollution by using resources from all parties. Microsoft demonstrates this through its AI for Earth program which helps to build global innovation hubs, test new ideas and strengthen the capacity of many (van der Vlist et al., 2024). But, for PPPs to succeed, there must be clear rules for sharing the benefits, preserving data and ensuring everyone knows what is happening. A policy should explain who owns what and who can do what with intellectual property through data and should also include plans for splitting revenue, so that individuals and organizations do not take advantage of each other. In addition, open systems of supervision and interaction with stakeholders are necessary for trust and accountability to endure.

Enhancing Adaptive and Resilient Governance Models

Government strategies are required to be flexible because the environmental situation and technology keep progressing. It's possible that the existing approach to regulation cannot flex enough to suit the speed of AI progress. Consequently, those making policies should consider adaptive systems that allow for repeated checking, input from the public and quick policy modifications. Using foresight and scenario planning in government policies helps us to expect what can go wrong with AI use and allows us to plan ways to solve problems ahead of time. For example, regularly observing how the system operates and what impact it has in society, plus reporting on these matters, helps engineers detect and handle challenges such as unconscious bias or issues with system status as they arise. In addition, global teamwork will play a key role because environmental issues and advanced AI spread over different countries. When nations foster similarity in their regulation, exchange good ideas and coordinate investigation, they can build better AI for sustainability and avoid divided or inconsistent rules (ÓhÉigeartaigh et al., 2020).

Encouraging Ethical AI Design and Sustainability-Centered Innovation

Moving forward, new policies should support AI that puts ethics and sustainability at the center already from the start. Therefore, AI systems that lower energy use, use fewer resources and benefit the environment, but do not worsen social inequality, should be rewarded. Awards and public money could be given to AI advancements that prove they help the circular economy, protect animal and plant life or make things more resilient to climate change. Developers should use standardized environmental assessments right from the start to make technology accountable. At the same time as regulations, companies creating AI can work voluntarily, using codes of conduct and certifications, to give confidence to their customers and investors regarding the responsibility of their products and services.

CONCLUSION

Blending artificial intelligence with environmental sustainability actions is a significant change in how we handle some of the biggest issues we face today. Throughout the chapter explored how, when used wisely and ethically, AI can change energy systems, improve efficiency in resource management, support circular economic ideas, strengthen climate change preparation and advise decision makers. Although technology promises much now, these applications also demonstrate our growing shared obligation to care for the planet. The strength of AI is that it can review huge and intricate data very fast, finding information that was once outside human grasp. AI provides tools to predict energy needs, track pollution locations and manage transportation more effectively, each very important when ecological challenges arise. Therefore, this gives businesses additional ethical, social and political duties. The risks related to biased algorithms, strong surveillance and digital isolation are major, but especially so as these tools reach groups with different technological resources and government control. One thing becomes very clear: AI only helps the environment through sustainability when other factors are considered, too. A proper regulatory system ought to ensure transparency and responsibility, disciplines must engage ecologists, social justice advocates and ethics experts and governance should provide a platform for representation of all groups. Besides, making sure that AI benefits everyone, including different countries, business sectors and groups, will be a main challenge for upcoming policies. Recently, AI could help turn the economy away from linear, take-and-throw practices to recycling and regenerate natural resources. It all depends on the ways these technologies are chosen, developed, managed and implemented by everyone. The decisions people make about designing and using AI will decide if it becomes part of ecological restoration or adds to pollution problems in the environment. An environmentally safe tomorrow depends less on technology and more on being thoughtful, interdisciplinary and constantly dedicated to fairness and justice. AI on its own is not a goal, but a way to reach other objectives. Its role in sustainability discussions should be as an enabler and this must be led by morally responsible leaders, the People and people who are aware of how much we can use. If sustained by careful use, creativity and fair thinking, artificial intelligence can be a key tool for shaping a fair and healthy planet.

REFERENCES

Adom, R. K., & Simatele, M. D. (2025). Enhancing water management in South Africa: The need for efficiency in monitoring and evaluation programmes. *Environmental Systems Research*, *14*(1), 9. DOI: 10.1186/s40068-025-00400-y

Agrawal, G. (2024). *Accountability*. Trust, and Transparency in AI Systems From the Perspective of Public Policy., DOI: 10.4018/979-8-3693-7452-8.ch009

Akter, S., Dwivedi, Y. K., Sajib, S., Biswas, K., Bandara, R. J., & Michael, K. (2022). Algorithmic bias in machine learning-based marketing models. *Journal of Business Research*, *144*, 201–216. DOI: 10.1016/j.jbusres.2022.01.083

Albahri, A. S., Khaleel, Y. L., Habeeb, M. A., Ismael, R. D., Hameed, Q. A., Deveci, M., Homod, R. Z., Albahri, O. S., Alamoodi, A. H., & Alzubaidi, L. (2024). A systematic review of trustworthy artificial intelligence applications in natural disasters. *Computers & Electrical Engineering*, *118*, 109409. DOI: 10.1016/j.compeleceng.2024.109409

Alloghani, M. A. (2024). Using AI to Monitor Marine Environmental Pollution. *Systematic Reviews*, **•••**, 87–97. DOI: 10.1007/978-3-031-45214-7_5

Alqahtani, A., Alsubai, S., & Bhatia, M. (2024). Applied artificial intelligence framework for smart evacuation in industrial disasters. *Applied Intelligence*, *54*(11–12), 7030–7045. DOI: 10.1007/s10489-024-05550-7

Bahari, N. A. A. B. S., Ahmed, A. N., Chong, K. L., Lai, V., Huang, Y. F., Koo, C. H., Ng, J. L., & El-Shafie, A. (2023). Predicting Sea Level Rise Using Artificial Intelligence: A Review. *Archives of Computational Methods in Engineering*, *30*(7), 4045–4062. DOI: 10.1007/s11831-023-09934-9

Ball, J. G. C., Petrova, K., Coomes, D. A., & Flaxman, S. (2022). Using deep convolutional neural networks to forecast spatial patterns of Amazonian deforestation. *Methods in Ecology and Evolution*, *13*(11), 2622–2634. DOI: 10.1111/2041-210X.13953

Balogun, A.-L., Marks, D., Sharma, R., Shekhar, H., Balmes, C., Maheng, D., Arshad, A., & Salehi, P. (2020). Assessing the Potentials of Digitalization as a Tool for Climate Change Adaptation and Sustainable Development in Urban Centres. *Sustainable Cities and Society*, *53*, 101888. DOI: 10.1016/j.scs.2019.101888

Causevic, A., Causevic, S., Fielding, M., & Barrott, J. (2024). Artificial intelligence for sustainability: Opportunities and risks of utilizing Earth observation technologies to protect forests. *Discover Conservation*, *1*(1), 2. DOI: 10.1007/s44353-024-00002-2

Debata, S., & Elango, S. (2024). Empowering flood forecasting through meteorological and social media data. *International Journal of Information Technology : an Official Journal of Bharati Vidyapeeth's Institute of Computer Applications and Management, 16*(6), 3757–3770. DOI: 10.1007/s41870-024-01961-4

Delfani, P., Thuraga, V., Banerjee, B., & Chawade, A. (2024). Integrative approaches in modern agriculture: IoT, ML and AI for disease forecasting amidst climate change. *Precision Agriculture, 25*(5), 2589–2613. DOI: 10.1007/s11119-024-10164-7

Dmytriyev, Y., Carnevale, M., & Giberti, H. (2024). Enhancing flexibility and safety: Collaborative robotics for material handling in end-of-line industrial operations. *Procedia Computer Science, 232*, 2588–2597. DOI: 10.1016/j.procs.2024.02.077

Emon, M. M. H., & Khan, T. (2025). The mediating role of attitude towards the technology in shaping artificial intelligence usage among professionals. *Telematics and Informatics Reports, 17*, 100188. DOI: 10.1016/j.teler.2025.100188

Emon, M. M. H., Khan, T., Rahman, M. A., Hamid, A. B. A., & Yaakub, N. I. (2025). GreenTech Revolution: Navigating Challenges and Seizing Opportunities. In *AI and Green Technology Applications in Society* (pp. 63–90). IGI Global Scientific Publishing. https://doi.org/DOI: 10.4018/979-8-3693-9879-1.ch003

Ferdaus, M. M., Dam, T., Anavatti, S., & Das, S. (2024). Digital technologies for a net-zero energy future: A comprehensive review. *Renewable & Sustainable Energy Reviews, 202*, 114681. DOI: 10.1016/j.rser.2024.114681

Goralski, M. A., & Tan, T. K. (2020). Artificial intelligence and sustainable development. *International Journal of Management Education, 18*(1), 100330. DOI: 10.1016/j.ijme.2019.100330

Gundeti, R., Vuppala, K., & Kasireddy, V. (2023). *The Future of AI and Environmental Sustainability.*, DOI: 10.4018/979-8-3693-0892-9.ch017

Haggag, M., Siam, A. S., El-Dakhakhni, W., Coulibaly, P., & Hassini, E. (2021). A deep learning model for predicting climate-induced disasters. *Natural Hazards, 107*(1), 1009–1034. DOI: 10.1007/s11069-021-04620-0

Hassija, V., Chamola, V., Mahapatra, A., Singal, A., Goel, D., Huang, K., Scardapane, S., Spinelli, I., Mahmud, M., & Hussain, A. (2024). Interpreting Black-Box Models: A Review on Explainable Artificial Intelligence. *Cognitive Computation, 16*(1), 45–74. DOI: 10.1007/s12559-023-10179-8

Jain, H., Dhupper, R., Shrivastava, A., Kumar, D., & Kumari, M. (2023). AI-enabled strategies for climate change adaptation: Protecting communities, infrastructure, and businesses from the impacts of climate change. *Computational Urban Science*, *3*(1), 25. DOI: 10.1007/s43762-023-00100-2

Khan, M. S., Saengon, P., Alganad, A. M. N., Chongcharoen, D., & Farrukh, M. (2020). Consumer green behaviour: An approach towards environmental sustainability. *Sustainable Development*, *28*(5), 1168–1180. DOI: 10.1002/sd.2066

Khan, T., & Emon, M. M. H. (2024). Exploring the Potential of the Blue Economy: A Systematic Review of Strategies for Enhancing International Business in Bangladesh in the context of Indo-Pacific Region. *Review of Business and Economics Studies*, *12*(2), 55–73. DOI: 10.26794/2308-944X-2024-12-2-55-73

Khan, T., Rahman, S. M., & Hasan, M. M. (2020). Barriers to growth of renewable energy technology in Bangladesh: case of solar home system in rural regions. *Proceedings of the International Conference on Computing Advancements*, 1–6.

Kumar, N., & Katiyar, A. (2024). *Ompal.* Artificial Intelligence and the Future of Renewable Energy., DOI: 10.4018/979-8-3693-1954-3.ch001

Leape, J., Abbott, M., Sakaguchi, H., Brett, A., Cao, L., Chand, K., Golbuu, Y., Martin, T., Mayorga, J., & Myksvoll, M. S. (2023). Technology, Data and New Models for Sustainably Managing Ocean Resources. In *The Blue Compendium* (pp. 185–211). Springer International Publishing., DOI: 10.1007/978-3-031-16277-0_6

Liu, G., Dong, X., Kong, Z., & Dong, K. (2021). Does national air quality monitoring reduce local air pollution? The case of PM2.5 for China. *Journal of Environmental Management*, *296*, 113232. DOI: 10.1016/j.jenvman.2021.113232 PMID: 34246901

Liu, V., & Yin, Y. (2024). Green AI: Exploring carbon footprints, mitigation strategies, and trade offs in large language model training. *Discover Artificial Intelligence*, *4*(1), 49. DOI: 10.1007/s44163-024-00149-w

Manikandan, S., Kaviya, R. S., Shreeharan, D. H., Subbaiya, R., Vickram, S., Karmegam, N., Kim, W., & Govarthanan, M. (2025). Artificial intelligence-driven sustainability: Enhancing carbon capture for sustainable development goals– A review. *Sustainable Development*, *33*(2), 2004–2029. DOI: 10.1002/sd.3222

Munawar, H. S., Mojtahedi, M., Hammad, A. W. A., Kouzani, A., & Mahmud, M. A. P. (2022). Disruptive technologies as a solution for disaster risk management: A review. *The Science of the Total Environment*, *806*, 151351. DOI: 10.1016/j.scitotenv.2021.151351 PMID: 34740667

ÓhÉigeartaigh, S. S., Whittlestone, J., Liu, Y., Zeng, Y., & Liu, Z. (2020). Overcoming Barriers to Cross-cultural Cooperation in AI Ethics and Governance. *Philosophy & Technology*, *33*(4), 571–593. DOI: 10.1007/s13347-020-00402-x

Ozkan, M. (2024). Atmospheric alchemy: The energy and cost dynamics of direct air carbon capture. *MRS Energy & Sustainability : a Review Journal*, *12*(1), 46–61. DOI: 10.1557/s43581-024-00091-5

Peng, M., Liu, Y., Khan, A., Ahmed, B., Sarker, S. K., Ghadi, Y. Y., Bhatti, U. A., Al-Razgan, M., & Ali, Y. A. (2024). Crop monitoring using remote sensing land use and land change data: Comparative analysis of deep learning methods using pre-trained CNN models. *Big Data Research*, *36*, 100448. DOI: 10.1016/j.bdr.2024.100448

Ravichandra, T., Murugeswari, P., Revathi, M., Senthilkumar, S., Rathore, D. S., & Sudhakar, M. (2024). *The Future of Machine Learning and Robotics in Digital Technology for Hospitality*., DOI: 10.4018/979-8-3693-9586-8.ch014

Rodriguez-Rey, D., Guevara, M., Linares, M. P., Casanovas, J., Armengol, J. M., Benavides, J., Soret, A., Jorba, O., Tena, C., & García-Pando, C. P. (2022). To what extent the traffic restriction policies applied in Barcelona city can improve its air quality? *The Science of the Total Environment*, *807*, 150743. DOI: 10.1016/j.scitotenv.2021.150743 PMID: 34634347

Sacchi, R., Bauer, C., Cox, B., & Mutel, C. (2022). When, where and how can the electrification of passenger cars reduce greenhouse gas emissions? *Renewable & Sustainable Energy Reviews*, *162*, 112475. DOI: 10.1016/j.rser.2022.112475

Sahu, D. K., & Rath, G. (2025). Innovative Approaches to Recover Waste in the Textile Sector. In *Nanotechnology-Assisted Recycling of Textile Waste* (pp. 129–169). Wiley., DOI: 10.1002/9781394175017.ch5

Satpathy, I., Nayak, A., & Jain, V. (2024). *The Green City*., DOI: 10.4018/979-8-3693-6854-1.ch009

Servou, E., Behrendt, F., & Horst, M. (2023). Data, AI and governance in MaaS – Leading to sustainable mobility? *Transportation Research Interdisciplinary Perspectives*, *19*, 100806. DOI: 10.1016/j.trip.2023.100806

Sharada, K., Choudhary, S. L., Harikrishna, T., Dixit, R. S., Suman, S. K., Ayyappa Chakravarthi, M., & Bhagyalakshmi, L. (2025). GeoAgriGuard: AI-Driven Pest and Disease Management with Remote Sensing for Global Food Security. *Remote Sensing in Earth Systems Sciences*, *8*(2), 409–422. DOI: 10.1007/s41976-025-00192-w

Shi, J. (2022). Research on Optimization of Cross-Border e-Commerce Logistics Distribution Network in the Context of Artificial Intelligence. *Mobile Information Systems*, *2022*, 1–11. DOI: 10.1155/2022/3022280

Suganya, R., Joseph, L. M. I. L., & Kollem, S. (2025). *Integrating Artificial Intelligence in Electric Vehicles and Optimizing Logistics for Sustainable Transportation.*, DOI: 10.4018/979-8-3693-7483-2.ch014

van der Vlist, F., Helmond, A., & Ferrari, F. (2024). Big AI: Cloud infrastructure dependence and the industrialisation of artificial intelligence. *Big Data & Society*, *11*(1). Advance online publication. DOI: 10.1177/20539517241232630

VanGessel, F. G., Perry, E., Mohan, S., Barham, O. M., & Cavolowsky, M. (2023). Natural language processing for knowledge discovery and information extraction from energetics corpora. *Propellants, Explosives, Pyrotechnics*, *48*(11). Advance online publication. DOI: 10.1002/prep.202300109

von Ingersleben-Seip, N. (2023). Competition and cooperation in artificial intelligence standard setting: Explaining emergent patterns. *The Review of Policy Research*, *40*(5), 781–810. DOI: 10.1111/ropr.12538

Waltersmann, L., Kiemel, S., Stuhlsatz, J., Sauer, A., & Miehe, R. (2021). Artificial Intelligence Applications for Increasing Resource Efficiency in Manufacturing Companies—A Comprehensive Review. *Sustainability*, *13*(12), 6689. DOI: 10.3390/su13126689

Wang, J., & Azam, W. (2024). Natural resource scarcity, fossil fuel energy consumption, and total greenhouse gas emissions in top emitting countries. *Geoscience Frontiers*, *15*(2), 101757. DOI: 10.1016/j.gsf.2023.101757

Wirba, A. V. (2023). Corporate Social Responsibility (CSR): The Role of Government in promoting CSR. *Journal of the Knowledge Economy*, *15*(2), 7428–7454. DOI: 10.1007/s13132-023-01185-0 PMID: 40479158

Yan, B., Hao, F., & Meng, X. (2021). When artificial intelligence meets building energy efficiency, a review focusing on zero energy building. *Artificial Intelligence Review*, *54*(3), 2193–2220. DOI: 10.1007/s10462-020-09902-w

Yigitcanlar, T., Mehmood, R., & Corchado, J. M. (2021). Green Artificial Intelligence: Towards an Efficient, Sustainable and Equitable Technology for Smart Cities and Futures. *Sustainability*, *13*(16), 8952. DOI: 10.3390/su13168952

Zhu, X., Qiu, T., & Liu, D. (2023). Resisting public monitoring in authoritarian regimes: Evidence from local environmental litigation in China. *Governance: An International Journal of Policy, Administration and Institutions*, *36*(2), 459–477. DOI: 10.1111/gove.12675

Zolkafli, A., Mansor, N. S., Omar, M., Ahmad, M., Ibrahim, H., & Yasin, A. (2024). *AI for Smart Disaster Resilience among Communities*., DOI: 10.1007/978-3-031-67317-7_22

KEY TERMS AND DEFINITIONS

Algorithmic Bias: Systems driven by AI can create unjust discrimination due to the way the data used to train them is biased.

Artificial Intelligence (AI): The use of machines such as computer systems, to imitate human thinking processes that help them handle learning, reasoning and solving problems.

Circular Economy: An approach that works to prevent waste and keep using materials by recycling, reusing and regenerating them.

Climate Change Mitigation: Activities designed to tackle emissions of greenhouse gases to control global warming.

Digital Divide: The term describes the inequality that happens when people, communities or regions use technology for information or communication differently.

Environmental Sustainability: Handling the environment properly to stop using up natural resources and support healthy conditions for future generations.

Predictive Analytics: Using the past to predict what will most likely occur in the future using data, statistics and machines.

Smart Grid: A Smart Grid is an electricity system that uses advanced communications and AI to handle changes in energy use locally and increase both energy efficiency and the trustworthiness of the electricity supply.

Chapter 11
Addressing Algorithmic Bias: Legal Challenges and Solutions

Abhishek Benedict Kumar
https://orcid.org/0000-0002-3998-3150
Symbiosis Law School, Symbiosis International University, Pune, India

Karun Sanjaya
https://orcid.org/0009-0005-1647-1549
Symbiosis Law School, Symbiosis International University, Pune, India

ABSTRACT

As artificial intelligence (AI) systems increasingly make decisions in areas such as justice, health, and finance, issues related to algorithmic biases have risen to prominence when discussing equity and inclusion. This chapter investigates how prejudices are built into data and model specifications, and how they can contribute to further entrenching social disparities. From a legal and ethical perspective, it examines the shortcoming that current anti-discrimination laws face when confronted with AI-generated harm. The chapter provides examples of actual cases, such as COMPAS risk assessment tool, to illustrate the real-life implications of biased algorithms. It calls for holistic approaches that include legal remedies, algorithmic transparency, participatory governance, and anti-discrimination data practices. By integrating the development of AI into fair, accountable, and human rights respecting principles, the chapter emphasize the immediate necessity of ensuring that technological development is aligned with just and inclusive development.

DOI: 10.4018/979-8-3373-2387-9.ch011

INTRODUCTION

AI is now a pervasive and transformative force in modern society. From banking to health care, education to criminal justice, artificial intelligence systems are being used to automate decisions that affect the lives of humans in profound ways. These systems sift through huge data sets to reveal patterns, to forecast outcomes and, in theory at least, to make rational decisions more rapidly and even more neutrally than humans. The AI race and companies and states alike are applying AI to help streamline workflow, eliminate humans making mistakes, and make things bigger. For countries such as India, artificial intelligence offers a unique opportunity to address some of the technology gaps, plug infrastructure holes, and make public services more efficient and promote inclusive economic growth (Gipson, 2024).

But as the reach of AI systems extends, the question of how fairly and equitably these systems work gains importance is unclear. Although AI is commonly lauded as impartial and neutral, that is not completely accurate enough. There have been many, cases and studies showing how AI systems can re-create, manifest, and even enshrine social inequalities and discriminatory practices. This is what is known as algorithmic bias, when AI systems produce systematically and unintentionally skewed outputs, yielding unfair results for particular groups frequently based on race, gender, class or ethnicity (Min, 2023).

The cause of algorithmic bias is embedded within the foundation of AI itself through data and algorithms. It is not a perfect system since AI systems are trained on historical data, and this data may reflect ingrained societal biases and structurally perpetuated inequalities. Unaddressed, these biases in data and model design can percolate into discriminatory AI behavior. A facial recognition system that has been primarily trained on Caucasian faces may be challenged to accurately recognize individuals of color, resulting in misidentification or exclusion. In the same way, a credit scoring algorithm might unfairly discriminate against people from minority groups if it is trained on data that exhibits historic disparities in financial access.

The outcomes of algorithmic bias are not just technical glitches, they have tangible impacts on people's lives, livelihoods, freedom, and their human rights. Biased AI systems have already been accused of being responsible for various forms of discrimination like job-seekers eliminated on the basis of gendered language by machines that sort resumes, racial bias in predictive policing programs that result in over-patrolling minority communities and health care algorithms that assign priority based on biased cost-benefit calculations, disfavoring the underinsured.

These issues are exacerbated by the 'black box' nature of plenty of AI systems. The problem is that complex machine learning models, like deep neural networks, are famously opaque they can be black boxes in the sense that even their developers and users have only a limited understanding of how decisions are reached (Savaşan,

2024). This opacity seriously hinders accountability and redress. When biased algorithms harm people, it can be difficult to determine who is to be blamed, the engineer, the data supplier or the company that uses them? The complexity of the technology needed to audit and read these systems is also a hurdle for many impacted communities, leaving the question as to who gets to access justice in a better manner.

But as AI starts to be woven into governance and public administration, the risks of unmitigated algorithmic bias become even more pressing. In countries working towards balanced development and digital inclusivity, these risks have the potential to counteract a balanced and just society to be achieved in such efforts. Picture an AI-run government welfare distribution program that unintentionally leaves certain vulnerable populations behind because the data used to train it were biased. This would not only weaken the efficiency of the program, but also further undermine people's confidence in technology and institutions.

Addressing these challenges will require a multifaceted approach that combines technical innovation with ethical design, organizational responsibility, and most crucially, strong legal frameworks. While some jurisdictions have started to make policies and laws to consider AI and the risks related to it there is a substantial dearth in rules focusing precisely on algorithmic bias. It is true that existing anti-discrimination laws, privacy rules and consumer protection rules offer some recourse, but they are typically inadequate to suit in handling the new questions posed by AI systems. For example, demonstrating that an AI system discriminates according to conventional legal rules can be nearly impossible without transparency about how the algorithm works or access the proprietary data.

This issue is not unique to Europe, though other parts of the world have similar problems catching up with the speed of AI's acceleration. The European Union's proposed AI Act aims to differentiate AI systems according to risk and apply commensurate obligations, such as obligation for transparency and human oversight in relation to high-risk applications (Chandra & Sanjaya, 2023). There is something of a patchwork of state-based efforts emerging in the United States to address algorithmic accountability, but comprehensive federal legislation has yet to emerge. In India, AI has been declared as a strategic priority, but there is no comprehensive legal or regulatory framework yet to regulate the ethical use of AI (Kordzadeh & Ghasemaghaei, 2021). The Digital India initiative and NSAI on the way forward for AI in India indicate government plans to leverage AI for inclusive growth however there is need for more work in implementation, oversight and redress mechanisms.

How then, do we address this issue of the legal and regulatory framework as part of the overall mandate to harness AI for more inclusive and equitable development? Law is far from just preventing harm and is needed to set the norms that encourage developers to act responsibly. Regulation, transparency requirements, impact analysis, and the opportunities for public participation are some of the ways to make certain that that AI systems serve the public good and not just solidify an already unequal world. Furthermore, a regulatory environment that encourages fairness and accountability can help to build confidence for members of the public in AI technologies and ensure that there is more uptake and innovation (Kumar et al., 2025).

Designing effective legal responses to algorithmic bias is not, however, without its challenges. Policymakers face tough technical challenges, and balancing competing interests, risks and benefits as well as finding their way through ambiguities about how the future is likely to unfold for AI. The law must be flexible enough to adapt to innovation yet solid enough to defend civil liberties. They should also be enforceable, with clear definitions of liability and accessible avenues for individuals to seek redress.

This chapter discusses these layered issues further, seeking to provide clarity homing in on legal aspects of algorithmic bias and actionable opportunities. It starts by deconstructing the multiple inputs and forms in which bias shows up in AI systems and the implications it has across several sectors. It goes on to analyze the legal framework as it stands, looking at the shortcomings and difficulties of regulating discriminatory algorithms (Kumar & Sanjaya, 2025). Using domestic case studies and insights from legal systems the chapter investigate what might be possible in remedial terms, including policy or legal interventions to address algorithmic discrimination. Finally, it proposes a set of India-specific recommendations that emphasise the country's distinctive socio-economic diversity and its aspirations for AI-led growth.

By considering algorithmic bias as a legal issue, this chapter aspires to contribute to the larger project of ensuring that AI operates as a force of empowerment rather than exclusion (Cheong, 2024). At a time when access to resources, opportunities, and rights are increasingly mediated by algorithms, the pursuit of fairness and accountability in AI is not a purely technical challenge it is a question of justice, equity, and democratic governance.

UNDERSTANDING ALGORITHMIC BIAS

As artificial intelligence (AI) systems make more and more decisions that affect people's lives, so does the risk run high that theoretical fairness and non-discrimination may not in practice become a reality, as bias gets amplified and auto-catalytic, where these biased systems could reflect or even exacerbate existing societal biases. At the heart of the matter is the problem of algorithmic bias, where AI systems generate consistently skewed outputs as a result of bad data, architecture, or context. In order to mitigate algorithmic bias in practice, it is important to comprehend its origins, flavor and real-world consequences (Jain & Menon, 2023).

What is Algorithmic Bias?

Algorithmic bias is when an AI system consistently and unfairly privileges one group over others. Bias does not cause errors of random direction, which might be symmetric; instead, it generates consistent errors that fall on one side or another, typically affecting certain people (often those who are already disadvantaged) more than others. While it is the data that upholds AI which carries the bias, bias in AI is not itself intentional nor is it necessarily malevolent either; it is a byproduct of the data, assumptions, and values upon which the design and teaching of AI systems are based.

So, if an AI hiring tool is trained on data from the past showing that male candidates were hired more often than female candidates, it might learn to connect certain gendered traits to the fitness to fulfill a job, even if this relationship is based on sexist discrimination rather than actual performance. The system might continue to perpetuate that bias by excluding qualified women from the talent pipeline.

Sources of Algorithmic Bias

Understanding the root causes of algorithmic bias is paramount for devising preventative or remedial measures. Widely known sources are:

i. Data Bias: AI models are developed using historical or observational data. If this data is biased because of underrepresentation or structural discrimination, then it is guaranteed to result in biased models.
ii. Sampling Bias: If the training data does not include the full range of diversity in the population, the AI can do a good job for majority groups, but a terrible job for minority groups. For instance, medical diagnostic technologies, that are trained largely on data from lighter-skinned patients can overlook conditions in people with darker skin.
iii. Historical Bias: Some biases are not mistakes, they are part of the real-world data due to historical inequalities. A predictive policing application based on arrest data could entrench racial profiling, as it reflects past over-policing of specific communities.
iv. Label Bias: If human annotators have implicit biases, labels for the supervised task (labeling successful applicant or fraudulent transaction) can be biased themselves.
v. Measurement Error: Inaccuracies can occur when complex social phenomena are substituted with proxies. For instance, relying on zip codes to represent creditworthiness can replicate redlining policies.

Design and Development Bias

Bias can also be added in the formulation of algorithm and feature selection. Developers face numerous choices like what data is fed in, which outcomes are optimized, and how relationships are modelled (Fazelpour & Danks, 2021). The reasoning behind those decisions frequently mirrors the views, assumptions, and constraints of the team cooperating on the project:

i. Feature Selection Bias: The selection of other features on which the inferred label can depend, the selection of those features that correlate with a protected characteristic (e.g., race or gender) can cause discriminatory outputs, although the protected feature is not explicitly given.
ii. Objective Function Bias: The objective function used (maximizing profit or minimizing error) might not match to fairness or equity needs. A hiring algorithm could be designed to be fast and cheap, but not very good at creating a diverse and inclusive workplace.
iii. Development teams are homogeneous: Homogeneous teams cannot be expected to have the cultural or contextual awareness that would enable them to foresee the impact of an algorithm on marginalized populations.

Feedback Loop Bias

Indeed, some AI procedures are adaptive and work from actual interactions. Should these interactions be biased, the system may fall into a feedback circle and the discrimination would be constantly reinforced.

i. Reinforcement bias: Recommendation engines that recommend content similar to an observation can form echo chambers and exaggerate stereotypes.
ii. Outcome Bias: Prediction systems within the criminal justice system can act as self-fulfilling prophecies. For instance, if a location is designated a high-crime zone, it will get more police presence, and more arrests, thus proving the model's assumption.

Contextual Bias

Even well-designed algorithms can be biased if they are applied in the wrong circumstances. AI systems designed in one cultural or jurisdictional context may not work fairly when used elsewhere:

i. Cross-context failures: A speech recognition system is trained on American English, but does not perform well for Indian English speakers not because the system is badly designed, but because the context is different.
ii. Policy Recommendations: A failure of even the smallest type of algorithm could cause significant harm in countries without robust data governance or consumer protection regimes (Obermeyer et al., 2021).

TYPES OF ALGORITHMIC BIAS

There are many ways to be biased in AI. These include:

i. Pre-existing Bias: Due to underlying societal and structural inequalities that are mirrored in the data.
ii. Technical Bias: Arising from constraints or assumptions in the model.
iii. Latent Bias: Is evolved through a learned relationship of the system with users and its context.

Fairness in algorithmic decision-making has been classified in a different categorization from various other frameworks by researchers and ethicists:

i. Disparate Impact: When the results disproportionately hurt a protected group, even though there is no intent in the matter.
ii. Discriminatory Treatment: When protected attributes are taken into account in decision making by the system.
iii. Group Fairness: All groups are treated similarly.
iv. Single Fairness: The similar individuals should be treated similarly.

Impacts of Algorithmic Bias

Algorithmic bias is not just a theoretical problem, it is literally affecting people's lives (Edenberg & Wood, 2023).

Such effects are most pronounced in high-stakes fields:

i. Criminal Justice: Predictive police and risk assessment tools have both been found to overestimate recidivism risks for Black defendants and underestimate those risks for white defendants. This can result in unjust bail, sentencing and parole determinations.
ii. Healthcare: AI systems deployed in triage, diagnosis, and planning treatment could fare worse for underrepresented populations. One frequently cited example

was an algorithm deployed to distribute health care resources that systematically gave lower risk scores to Black patients than to white patients with similar health problems.

iii. Finance: The systems used for scoring and approving loans could unfairly punish some applicants based on their demographic. Historical income, employment and residential disparities can be baked into models that purport to be neutral but which are really discriminatory in effect.
iv. Employment and Hiring: AI software used to screen resumes or analyze interview performance have demonstrated gender and racial biases. Occasionally women received lower scores because their resumes did not look like those of previous successful hires, most of whom had been men.
v. Education: Algorithms to predict student success or to evaluate applications can incorporate biases around class and race. Poor students also could be unfairly identified as under-performing, closing doors to them.

Why Bias is Hard to Detect

Bias is frequently opaque and is not easily observed and detected without scrutiny. Compounding this issue include:

i. Proprietary Algorithms: Most algorithms are not public, making it difficult for third-party evaluators to test for fairness.
ii. Absence of Data Accessibility: Both individuals and regulators frequently lack access to the data needed to demonstrate that biased outcomes are occurring.
iii. Opaque Models: Deep learning systems can contain millions of parameters, and even the authors of a model may not understand the reasons behind a model decision.

Additionally, what it means to be 'biased' is not always a technical judgment; it is also a social judgment and an ethical one. What is fair, what trade-offs are acceptable, and whose values we prioritize are inherently political decisions. Al bias is a problem with multiple dimensions caused not only by historical inequalities, but also design decisions and societal conditions. Those effects are not only real but potentially self-reinforcing unless remedied. Understanding the impacts of bias is the first step towards building AI systems that are more fair and accountable, in line with efforts to foster inclusive development (Simon et al., 2020). Legal, technical and organizational interventions should come next but they all start with a nuanced understanding of exactly what algorithmic bias is and why it matters.

LEGAL CHALLENGES IN ADDRESSING ALGORITHMIC BIAS

With AI systems in widespread use across key domains, including criminal justice, employment, health care, finance, and the delivery of public services, concerns about fairness, transparency, and accountability have been brought to the forefront. Algorithmic bias is one of the most urgent problems; it leads to discriminatory and harmful outcomes for the individuals and communities it works against, particularly those who are already marginalized (Lopes, 2025).

Although the technical community has focused on ways to identify and mitigate bias in algorithms and the maintenance of data, law and regulation have few resources to confront legal issues such as those GDPR and MMD raise (Ebers & Sein, 2024). Conventional legal paradigms, tailored for human agents, frequently break down when they are applied to automatic and semi-automatic agents. This part then outlines the primary legal issues regarding the regulation of algorithmic bias, concentrating on the inadequacy of existing laws, enforcement obstacles, transparency and accountability, and the challenge of translating existing antidiscrimination norms into the AI era.

Absence of AI-Specific Legislation

While the inherent problem of algorithmic bias is the dearth of AI-specific sets of regulations in most countries. Few countries, including India, have laws to regulate the design, deployment and surveillance of AI systems. As a result, regulators need to work with patchwork legal tools say privacy laws, consumer protection laws, a smattering of general anti-discrimination rules that were not really built for AI.

Although these laws constitute a foundation, they are inadequate to account for the complications associated with automated decision making. For instance, the norm of equality before the law expressed in constitutions and civil rights statutes cannot automatically translate into algorithmic results when its decision-making logic is opaque, indirect, or probabilistic.

This has led to a legal vacuum. The ones we might want to be worried about are the organizations deploying AI to discriminate, or those with business models that create little incentive to test for fairness who may not know what, if any, standards they have to live up to, and those who have been harmed by bias in algorithms, with no clear legal path to justice. In much of the developing world, the deficiency of AI regulation is compounded by resource constraints, poor institution-building, and lackluster enforcement.

Inadequacy of Existing Anti-Discrimination Laws

The vast majority of countries already have long-established laws that outlaw discrimination based on skin colour, sex, caste, religion, disability and other protected status. Yet such laws are generally aimed at intentional discrimination on the part of human beings. Algorithmic discrimination is unintentional and it is not usually perpetrated by a direct act of humanness like shooting.

For instance, an algorithm used to hire workers may not directly take gender as a feature, but may instead use proxies (for instance, time periods when a candidate was not employed or particular verbs that appear in applications) that disproportionately penalize women. In these instances, traditional legal tests that measure discriminatory intent are very difficult to establish (S. et al., 2024).

Besides, it is hard to regulate statistical discrimination, where the algorithm acts on generalizations about groups rather than behavior of individual participants, with our current set of tools. Judges and regulators may have trouble sorting out the extent to which unfair results are due to permissible, data-fueled optimization or impermissible discrimination.

In order to make matters worse, anti-discrimination laws are generally reactive, not primitive, in not requiring the evaluation or audit of decision-making tools before their use. This reactive stance also makes it difficult to prevent bias, and to stop systemic harms from building up unnoticed.

Transparency and the 'Black Box' Problem

One of the features of many AI systems particularly those that rely on machine learning or deep learning is their opaqueness. These systems are commonly called black boxes, because the processes by which they make decisions are indecipherable even to those who create them (Mougdir, 2023).

This opacity presents several legal problems:

Due Process and Explanation Right

Those harmed by an autodidactic algorithm may be entitled bylaw to an explanation to why a decision was reached. But for an opaque or proprietary AI model, it is often infeasible to obtain a valid explanation.

Burden of Proof of Discrimination

Plaintiffs who believe an algorithm discriminated against them face an almost impossible burden of proof. They do not have access to the model, the data that was fed into the model, and the decision logic, so how can they show it was biased?

Trade Secret Provisions

Even when there are legal provisions for a right to explanation, such as the GDPR's right to explanation, firms often claim intellectual property/ trade secret protections to insulate their algorithms from inspection.

Such opacity threatens the very notion of accountability. In the model of the traditional legal institution there is someone who is the person that is accountable for discriminatory action. Responsibility is diffused among developers, data providers, and end users in the AI world, which leads to a gap in the liability (Chaudhary, 2024).

Ambiguity Around Liability and Accountability

Artificially intelligent systems upend conventional ideas of legal responsibility. In typical circumstances, harm can be attached to an identifiable human ator who could also be made accountable in a civil or criminal process. But what when the choices are made by an AI system. According to whom is the result biased, the programmer that wrote the algorithm? The organization it was set up in? Who was the data provider for the training dataset? Or the AI system itself?

What, then, transpires when the decisions themselves are autonomous? Say an AI system trained with machine learning changes over time and starts producing biased outputs that were not anticipated during its development, would its designers still have to face the music?

These are questions which the Legal Order has not yet embraced. A handful of jurisdictions have advanced a 'chain of accountability' architecture to apportion responsibility across the AI lifecycle, from data collection through model deployment, but they've barely begun to take shape.

Cross-Border Jurisdiction and Enforcement

AI technologies are also often developed, trained, and implemented in multiple jurisdictions, creating questions about which laws and enforcement provisions apply. A hiring platform built in the United States with European-trained algorithms and adopted by a company in India creates a web of conflicting legal responsibilities (AllahRakha, 2025).

The global nature of AI poses challenges in:

i. Jurisdiction in Algorithmic Harm.
ii. Harmonizing standards across borders.
iii. Safeguarding consumers' rights when the liable party is in another country.

Without internationally harmonized regulation of AI, corporations may engage in regulatory arbitrage, developing and deploying AI systems in jurisdictions with less oversight and protection.

Regulatory Capacity and Expertise

Even in cases where there are adequate legal frameworks, they go unenforced because regulatory bodies are simply not qualified to do so. Artificial Intelligence systems are intricate and effective, oversight involves specialized knowledge of statistics, data science, algorithm design, and ethics.

Many, particularly low- and middle-income countries, lack the resources to:

i. Conduct algorithmic audits.
ii. Assessability to fair use compliance.
iii. Examine allegations of bias in automated systems.

This lack of capacity makes it hard even to enforce good laws, and undermines trust in the regulation.

Limited Public Awareness and Access to Justice

Public exposure to and understanding of algorithmic bias is also low. Many people are already clueless to the fact that a decision involving them whether it is a rejected loan, job offer or lower score on a school admission test was determined by an AI system. When they do have knowledge, the road to challenging the rulings they face is hardly direct.

Barriers include:

i. The absence of legal literacy regarding AI and data rights.
ii. Legal assistance or counsel experienced in tackling algorithmic bias is hard to come by.
iii. Procedural difficulty in establishing offences or being victimized.

For marginalized communities who were already acutely experiencing systemic exclusion, these barriers render justice even more out of reach. The legal difficulties to be navigated in addressing algorithmic bias are complex and stem from the particular newness of AI systems themselves, as well as the inadequacies of current legal frameworks. The absence of AI-centric legislation, insufficiency of anti-discrimination regimes in place, black-box nature of code, wide-spread responsibility and enforcement capacity deficiencies all add up to hamper the law's capability to provide effective redress (Mohamed et al., 2024).

These impediments will only fall when the fundamental maxims of law are reconsidered, in combination with institutional competence-building and the articulation of appropriate digital-era rights and obligations. It also calls for a forward-looking, human-centric strategy around technology regulation, one that makes fairness, transparency, and accountability a focal point of AI governance.

In the following section, we consider potential legal and policy responses to these challenges, through a comparative lens, and within the framework of the broader objective to harness AI for the benefit of inclusive and equitable development.

CASE STUDY: THE COMPAS ALGORITHM AND ALGORITHMIC BIAS IN CRIMINAL JUSTICE

Among the most widely cited and studied examples of algorithmic bias in practice is the use of the Correctional Offender Management Profiling for Alternative Sanctions (COMPAS) algorithm for decision-making. This case also offers important case studies as to how automated systems can entrench historical injustices and contravene principles of just transparency and accountability, particularly when put into practice in high-stake applications such as criminal sentencing (Kawamleh, 2024).

We delve into the history of COMPAS and examine how it works, identify the results of some of the most important investigations into its biases, discuss the legal and ethical disputes it has generated, and draw out broader lessons for AI governance and policy reform (Cordella & Gualdi, 2024).

Background: What is COMPAS?

COMPAS, created by a for-profit company called Northpointe Inc. (now Equivant), is a risk assessment system purportedly developed to help judges, parole boards, and others in the criminal justice system make decisions about sentencing, bail, and parole. It assesses the probability that a defendant will commit further crimes (recidivate), and stratifies people into low, medium or high risk (Kawamleh, 2024).

The algorithm relies on answers to a questionnaire, which include more than 130 items about criminal history, substance use, employment, family background and attitudes. It crunches these inputs, producing scores for recidivism risk, violent recidivism risk and pretrial failure risk.

The ProPublica Investigation

In May of 2016, the investigative journalism organization ProPublica reported on how COMPAS was being used in Florida in a piece titled 'Machine Bias'. They also examined those who were assessed as high-risk but did not reoffend as well as those deemed low-risk who did reoffend in the two years after the forecast was made.

The findings were alarming, black defendants were almost twice as likely as white defendants to be incorrectly classified as high risk but no more likely to actually reoffend. White defendants, as it turned out, were falsely declared low risk more often than black defendants.

The algorithm could only beat a toss of a coin and achieved an average predictive accuracy of approximately 61%. ProPublica found that COMPAS showed clear racial bias, disproportionately mislabeling black defendants as being at a higher risk of committing a future crime that COULD result in harsher sentencing or denial of bond (Engel et al., 2024).

The Company's Defense and Technical Debate

Northpointe responded to ProPublica's findings by asserting that the algorithm had sought to achieve predictive parity that is, to attain roughly the same level of accuracy for each racial group. They argued that the false positive and false negative rates had to be different across groups because of differences in the base rate of recidivism across populations (Van Woerkom et al., 2024). This difference underscores a fundamental problem in algorithmic fairness, different notions of fairness are not all satisfiable at once. For COMPAS, striving to balance one fairness statistic (predictive parity) created imbalances for others (false positive rates) and disproportionately hurt disadvantaged populations.

The debate was a watershed moment in public conversations regarding the fairness of AI and showed that, firstly fairness in AI is not only a technical problem, but fundamentally normative and juridical and secondly designers need to determine which fairness metric is the most important in a particular situation and make that choice based on the law, ethics and a dose of public accountability.

Legal Challenges and the Loomis Case

Use of COMPAS in the criminal justice system was addressed in the Wisconsin Supreme Court in State v. Loomis (2016). The defendant in the case, Eric Loomis, argued that his sentencing was influenced by use of COMPAS:

i. The violation of his due process rights because he was unable to understand or challenge the variables fed into the algorithm.
ii. Relied on proprietary, non-transparent model, giving him no opportunity to challenge its findings.
iii. Might have to do with sexist and racist reasons, thereby making the judgment unfair.

The court did eventually rule that COMPAS was admissible, but it warned against using risk assessment tools in a wholesale way, without taking the crime-specific context into account. The ruling mandated courts to tell defendants about the tool's limitations and explicitly forbade judges from relying on scores alone (Ray, 2024).

The decision was a compromise; it allowed risk assessment to continue without announcing the death of COMPAS, but it underscored the mounting conflict between algorithm-driven decision-making and constitutional guarantees, including the right to a fair trial and access to justice.

Implications for Legal Accountability

The COMPAS case illustrates many legal conundrums that extend beyond the U.S.

Opacity and Proprietary Models

Courts and defendants cannot usually inspect the proprietary algorithms. Without transparency, pending litigation and legal challenges have no place to go anathema to the notion of an open justice system.

Disparate Impact sans Discriminatory Intent

COMPAS-type algorithms need not have the intent to discriminate but may still generate disparate effects. The traditional legal concepts of having to prove intent do not apply here. Due Process and Right to Explanation: Fundamental questions have been raised about the extent to which individuals should understand and be able to challenge opaque AI-system decisions that have substantial implications on their freedom.

These are the precise reasons we are in dire need of legislation that compels the explainability, auditability, and human-overseen administration of these algorithms, especially in heavily biased downstream applications like criminal justice.

Broader Policy Lessons and Global Relevance

The lessons here, from COMPAS, apply universally as governments and companies around the world incorporate AI tools into public administration and social services. Similar risk-assessment tools are being considered for everything from policing and surveillance to welfare allocation in many parts of the Global South.

Lessons for policy development are as follows:

i. No risk assessment instrument should be used in isolation. Above all, decision-making must be based on human judgment, with AI acting as an assisting tool not as a substitute.
ii. Algorithm audits performed by an independent organization need to be considered mandatory, at least for systems used in public decision making. These audits must evaluate disparate impact, accuracy, transparency, and adherence to fairness norms.
iii. Government procurement and use of AI tools in both public sector institutions should include participatory governance, civil society oversight, community engagement and legal review.

It is necessary that ethical principles are actionable, not merely aspirational (Engel et al., 2024. Without a law that carries teeth, principles of fairness and responsibility would be toothless.

LOOKING AHEAD: REFORM AND THE PATH FORWARD

In the wake of the public outcry over COMPAS and the academic analysis that case prompted, broader reforms to the system have been proposed or enacted in the United States and in other countries:

i. A few states and territories are forsaking proprietary systems in favor of open-source models of risk assessment for criminal decisions, which are more transparent.

ii. Lawyers and advocacy organizations have been urging lawmakers to pass algorithmic accountability legislation that, among other things, would require explanation, contestability and fairness audits.
iii. One approach is through multidisciplinary collaboration; AI developers working with ethics experts, legal scholars and community advocates to co-design more equitable systems.

The COMPAS case has demonstrated that machines cannot relieve us of the requirement of accountability. Legal and ethical standards should adapt to the reality of automated decision-making and technological innovation must be subject to democratic, legal, and ethical norms. The COMPAS case is not just a tale of a faulty algorithm, it is a warning of the hazards of implementing AI without sufficient processes for oversight, transparency and fairness. It demonstrates that existing legal frameworks have their limitations and that we need a reform agenda based on human dignity, justice and fairness.

As countries around the world, including India, roll out AI in their public services, the lessons learned from COMPAS are a timely reminder that technology must serve people and not the other way around. It is in the combination of regulation, institution-building, community participation, and legal empowerment that we ensure AI contributes to a fairer, more inclusive future.

CONCLUSION

As AI becomes more and more infused in systems of governance, finance, health care, criminal justice, education, and social welfare, it has the potential to remake societies for the better and for worse. The value of AI is its power to increase productivity, to scale effectiveness and to spot previously invisible patterns. However, as this chapter has documented, AI can also reinforce (if not amplify) current social disparities by reproducing algorithmic bias.

The legal, ethical, and social concerns of algorithmic bias are not speculative or future-bound, rather they are pressing. Biased algorithms are already shaping who gets credit, a job, a house, health care or justice. Such impacts frequently go unchallenged, due to the opaqueness of algorithmic systems, the dearth of legal protections, and even our lack of comprehension as users and sometimes, regulators. If left unchecked, such algorithmic systems will skew trust in governance and erode democratic values, causing harm, which will fall disproportionately on the most vulnerable (Goswami & Verma, 2024).

The conclusion is based on the critical insights to be gained by this chapter and sketches an interconnected roadmap for dealing with algorithmic bias through law, technology, and participatory governance. It also meditates on implications for philosophy and development and also how society can moderate and reconcile innovation with inclusion, rights, and justice.

Bias is Not Just a Bug: It is a Mirror of Society

One of the most valuable things we have learned from studying algorithmic bias is that algorithms do not generate bias on their own. They mirror the data they are trained on, the biases inherent in their design, and the social systems in which they are used. So algorithmic bias is not just some error in code, it is a symptom of a much more profound social injustice.

If historical records encode biases based on race, gender, caste or class, then machine learning models trained on these records will ultimately reproduce these biases. Similarly, when developers do not take into account the social circumstances of an AI system or do not include multiple perspectives in its design, a biased result frequently skews in favor of the ruling category.

This is the insight that changes everything. Rather than something to be patched as a technological glitch, we need to address bias as a social phenomenon that demands societal responses inclusive data governance, anti-discrimination protections and systems of democratic oversight.

Legal Reform Must Match Technological Change

Current legal regimes cannot keep up with the pace and intricacy of AI systems. Many species of anti-discrimination laws are creatures of the analog age and deal with intention-based discrimination, by humans. But while algorithms can, of course, be discriminatory without meaning, they can also be based on statistical correlations, not on explicit prejudice.

If, as this chapter has argued, legal orders have to develop to:

i. Identify Algorithmic Discrimination: Make Definitions Actionable.
ii. Replace the emphasis on discriminatory intent with consideration of disparate impacts.
iii. Guarantee the rights to explanation, rectification and accountability in the context of automated decision-making.
iv. Govern the use of AI in high-stakes areas including criminal justice, health care, finance and public services.

The European Union's AI Act or Canada's Directive on Automated Decision-Making are examples of progressive legal tools that could be seen in the future as early versions of risk-based, rights-respecting AI regulation. But countries in the Global South need to work out their own constitutionally-sensitive legal systems based upon the foundational jurisprudential values of equality, dignity, and social justice.

Technical Solutions Must Be Paired with Ethical Design

Fairness is not something you can 'bolt on' after you have deployed an algorithm. It needs to be architected in from the start. This involves incorporating notions of fairness, transparency, and accountability at every step in the AI lifecycle, starting with data collection and model development to deployment and iteration.

Also, there are promising other technical approaches such as:

i. Regarding bias remedies for machine learning (pre-in and post-processing).
ii. Algorithmic auditing to measure disparate impact by demographic category.
iii. Explainable AI (XAI) in order to increase transparency and trust.
iv. Strong validation and testing in ethnically and racially diverse populations.

But there are limits on technical fixes. They tend to involve normative choices as to which definition of fairness to use, which outcomes to weigh more heavily, whose harms to measure. These are not merely engineering questions, but ethical and political ones. This is why technical innovation needs to go hand-in-hand with interdisciplinary work, community involvement, and regulatory monitoring.

Public Sector AI Requires Higher Standards

AI systems are being used by governments and public institutions in applications such as law enforcement, welfare assessment, school admission, and taxation. Such applications are commonly presented as delivering efficiency, objectivity and financial saving. But when algorithmic decisions influence people's rights, freedoms and livelihoods, the standard of accountability should be higher.

Public sector AI deployment should be aligned with the constitutional principles of openness, fairness, equity, and due process. Governments should:

i. Carry out algorithmic impact assessments prior to implementation.
ii. Openly share decisions made with AI.
iii. Invest in distinct monitoring and auditing instruments.
iv. Guarantee means of public redress and appeal.

Such policies should also mandate that vendors adhere to high ethical and legal standards. The public interest should not be subcontracted to closed, proprietary systems owned by private tech companies.

Inclusive Development Requires Inclusive Governance

Algorithmic bias is not just about harm, it is about fairness and opportunity. In a world where algorithms are increasingly serving as gatekeepers to jobs, loans, health insurance and education, prejudiced systems can cement societal exclusion.

As such, the governance of AI should be participatory and inclusive. This means:

i. Engaging affected communities in the development and implementation of AI systems.
ii. Backing civil society groups in tracking down algorithmic harms and working toward fairness.
iii. Empowering citizens with legal and digital literacy solutions.
iv. Building forums for public discussion and democratic deliberation of AI policy.

In order to make AI development inclusive in countries with caste, racial or gender discriminatory pasts, we need to respond to historic injustices and actively work towards social justice.

International Cooperation and South-South Dialogue Are Crucial

Algorithmic bias is a global problem, yet most of the research, regulation and policy tools have been developed in the Global North. With urgent necessity to build capabilities in the Global South for participating in AI governance and co-creating global standards inclusive of diverse legal systems, cultural values, and developmental priorities.

This South-South collaboration may:

i. Spread policy innovations for low and middle income settings.
ii. Combine tech expertise to develop fair AI technology on an open-source basis.
iii. Promote fair governance of data at the international level.
iv. Form coalitions to resist AI-enabled digital colonisation by big tech companies.

Global collaboration has to be horizontal and democratic, rather than top-down. AI governance must be open to all voices, including marginalized and underrepresented communities.

Building Ethical AI Futures

Ultimately, the goal is not just to 'fix' algorithmic bias, but to reimagine the digital future. A future in which AI upholds human rights, strengthens democratic institutions, and promotes social justice. A future where technological development serves the collective good of all people and not just the interests of a few. This calls for a shift in our perception of innovation, no longer as a competition to conquer, but as a quest to share. Not as a matter of convenience, but a matter of conscience.

In order to create ethical AI futures, we need to:

i. Root technology development in human dignity and constitutional principles.
ii. Legally liable both public and private for the damage inflicted by AI.
iii. Prioritize the needs and voices of those most impacted by algorithmic decisions.
iv. Bake ethics, equity, and empathy into the very design of technology.

As this chapter has demonstrated, algorithmic bias is not inevitable but avoidable. But prevention is about vigilance, regulation, education, and solidarity. It means understanding, that technology is never neutral, and that each layer in every system reflects the political, social, economic, and ethical decisions of its designers and implementers and the culture that brings it into existence. Unless we act decisively, we risk losing over the course of just one generation the tools and technology available to our society that have recovered millions of our sick and dying kin in a frightful gale of suffering and grief. Not exclusion, but inclusion not injustice but justice. The challenges are immense in going forward but the opportunity are too. We should take this opportunity to design AI systems that are both intelligent and wise, powerful and just, efficient and equitable.

REFERENCES

AllahRakha, N. (2025). Cross-Border E-Crimes: Jurisdiction and Due Process Challenges. *ADLIYA Jurnal Hukum Dan Kemanusiaan, 18*(2), 153–170. https://doi.org/DOI: 10.15575/adliya.v18i2.38633

Chandra, R., & Sanjaya, K. (2023). Punishing the Unpunishable: A Liability Framework for Artificial Intelligence Systems. *Springer Nature Link*, 55–64. https://doi.org/DOI: 10.1007/978-3-031-29860-8_6

Chaudhary, G. (2024). Unveiling the Black Box: Bringing Algorithmic Transparency to AI. *Masaryk University Journal of Law and Technology, 18*(1), 93–122. https://www.ceeol.com/search/article-detail?id=1287954

Cheong, B. C. (2024). Transparency and accountability in AI systems: Safeguarding wellbeing in the age of algorithmic decision-making. *Frontiers in Human Dynamics, 6*. Advance online publication. DOI: 10.3389/fhumd.2024.1421273

Cordella, A., & Gualdi, F. (2024). Algorithmic formalization: Impacts on administrative processes. *Public Administration*. Advance online publication. DOI: 10.1111/padm.13030

Ebers, M., & Sein, K. (2024). Data-driven Technologies. *Routledge EBooks*, 3–37. https://doi.org/DOI: 10.4324/9781003502791-2

Edenberg, E., & Wood, A. (2023). *Disambiguating Algorithmic Bias: From Neutrality to Justice*. https://doi.org/DOI: 10.1145/3600211.3604695

Engel, C., Linhardt, L., & Schubert, M. (2024). Code is law: How COMPAS affects the way the judiciary handles the risk of recidivism. *Artificial Intelligence and Law*. Advance online publication. DOI: 10.1007/s10506-024-09389-8

Fazelpour, S., & Danks, D. (2021). Algorithmic bias: Senses, sources, solutions. *Philosophy Compass, 16*(8). Advance online publication. DOI: 10.1111/phc3.12760

Gipson, S. M. (2024). MITIGATING ALGORITHMIC BIAS. *Scitech Lawyer, 20*(4), 26–32. https://www.proquest.com/docview/3070768938?pq-origsite=gscholar&fromopenview=true&sourcetype=Scholarly%20Journals

Goswami, D., & Verma, B. (2024). The Intersection of Ethics and Big Data. *Advances in Web Technologies and Engineering Book Series*, 269–285. https://doi.org/DOI: 10.4018/979-8-3693-1762-4.ch013

Jain, L. R., & Menon, V. (2023). *AI Algorithmic Bias: Understanding its Causes*. Ethical and Social Implications., DOI: 10.1109/ictai59109.2023.00073

Kawamleh, S. (2024). *Algorithmic evidence in U.S criminal sentencing*. Springer Nature Link., DOI: 10.1007/s43681-024-00473-y

Kordzadeh, N., & Ghasemaghaei, M. (2021). Algorithmic bias: Review, synthesis, and Future Research Directions. *European Journal of Information Systems, 31*(3), 388–409. DOI: 10.1080/0960085X.2021.1927212

Kumar, A. B., & Sanjaya, K. (2025). Ethics, Algorithms, and the Rules of Evidence. *Forensic Intelligence and Deep Learning Solutions in Crime Investigation*, 103–124. https://doi.org/DOI: 10.4018/979-8-3693-9405-2.ch006

Kumar, A. B., Sanjaya, K., & Saleem, M. (2025). Justice in the Age of Algorithms. *Advances in Computational Intelligence and Robotics*, •••, 191–210. DOI: 10.4018/979-8-3693-9395-6.ch009

Lopes, G. P. (2025). Bias in Adjudication and the Promise of AI: Challenges to Procedural Fairness. *Law. Technology and Humans*, *7*(1), 47–67. DOI: 10.5204/lthj.3812

Min, A. (2023). Artifical Intelligence and Bias: Challenges, Implications, and Remedies. *Journal of Social Research*, *2*(11), 3808–3817. DOI: 10.55324/josr.v2i11.1477

Mohamed, E., Quteishat, A., Qtaishat, A., & Mohammad, A. (2024). Exploring the Role of AI in Modern Legal Practice: Opportunities, Challenges, and Ethical Implications. *J. Electrical Systems, 20*(6), 3040–3050. https://pdfs.semanticscholar.org/7828/77a8679e1811ad00094d934faee36c23ea1a.pdf

Mougdir, S. (2023). *What is in the black box: The ethical implications of algorithms ...: Ingenta Connect*. Ingentaconnect.com; Ingentaconnect. https://www.ingentaconnect.com/content/hsp/airwa/2024/00000003/00000001/art00010

Obermeyer, Z., Nissan, R., Stern, M., Eaneff, S., Bembeneck, E., & Mullainathan, S. (2021). Algorithmic Bias Playbook. In *Algorithmic Bias Playbook*. Algorithmic Bias Playbook. https://ic3.center.ufl.edu/wordpress/files/2022/08/algorithmic-bias-playbook.pdf

Ray, S. (2024). Ile constitutional review volume iii and issue i of 2024 code and court: a case study on the impact of algorithmic decisions on legal principles and precedents" best citation -dr sanchita ray, code and court: a case study on the impact of algorithmic decisions on legal principles and precedents". In *Ile Constitutional Review*. Institute of Legal Education. https://cr.iledu.in/wp-content/uploads/2024/08/V3I14.pdf

Savaşan, Z. (2024). Data Bias and Discrimination in AI: Addressing Social Justice Concerns through Legal Reform. *Mayo Communication Journal, 1*(1), 73–82. https://www.researchcorridor.org/index.php/mcj/article/view/149

Simon, J., Wong, P.-H., & Rieder, G. (2020). Algorithmic bias and the Value Sensitive Design approach. *Internet Policy Review*, *9*(4). Advance online publication. DOI: 10.14763/2020.4.1534

Van Woerkom, W., Grossi, D., Prakken, H., & Verheij, B. (2024). A Case-Based-Reasoning Analysis of the COMPAS Dataset. *Frontiers in Artificial Intelligence and Applications*. https://doi.org/DOI: 10.3233/faia241244

Chapter 12
Artificial Intelligence and Financial Stability Risks in Nigeria

Peterson K. Ozili
https://orcid.org/0000-0001-6292-1161
Central Bank of Nigeria, Nigeria

Kingsley Obiora
International Monetary Fund, USA

Chinwendu Onuzo
https://orcid.org/0009-0005-1805-8600
Central Bank of Nigeria, Nigeria

ABSTRACT

Artificial intelligence is disrupting the financial sector globally. Artificial intelligence will also affect financial regulation and financial system stability in several ways. Little is known about how artificial intelligence might affect the stability of the financial system. Using a contextual framework and discourse analysis methodology, this article identifies some risks that artificial intelligence could pose to financial system stability in Nigeria. The study focused on how AI risks affect those directly involved in financial stability work in Nigeria. If these risks are mitigated, the adoption of AI for financial stability work will yield positive benefits for financial stability in Nigeria.

DOI: 10.4018/979-8-3373-2387-9.ch012

INTRODUCTION

The purpose of the article is to explore some risks that artificial intelligence could pose for those involved in financial stability work in Nigeria. Financial stability is a condition in which the financial system which comprises of financial institutions, financial markets and financial infrastructures are functioning well, allocating financial resources efficiently and are able to withstand shocks of any kind (Brunnermeier *et al.*, 2009; Sarlin and Peltonen, 2013). In simple terms, financial stability refers to the absence of financial crisis.

Several factors or determinants help to preserve financial stability. The academic literature identified several determinants of financial stability, such as competition (Kasman and Carvallo, 2014; Berger *et al.*, 2017), leverage (Alessi and Detken, 2018), bank profitability (Xu *et al.*, 2019), nonperforming loans (Makri *et al.*, 2014) and institutional quality (Ozili, 2018). But the literature has not considered artificial intelligence to be a determinant of financial stability in Nigeria.

Artificial intelligence is disrupting many industries including the financial services industry. In terms of definition, there is no universal definition of artificial intelligence. However, artificial intelligence is commonly viewed as the use of appropriate computer algorithms to perform routine and non-routine tasks, and to make decisions which are usually done by humans. Artificial intelligence has become an important topic in economics and finance, and its effect on financial stability is attracting a lot of attention among policymakers and central banks around the world. Many academic economists acknowledge the important role of AI for financial stability (Remolina, 2023; Gensler and Bailey, 2020; Li, 2021; Ozili, 2024). But these scholars have not explored how artificial intelligence might affect financial stability in Nigeria or how artificial intelligence risks could affect those involved in financial stability work in Nigeria.

Artificial intelligence has some advantages which should be acknowledged. The most important advantages are cost savings, its ability to improve the quality and efficiency of financial services delivery, and its ability to improve financial intermediation processes across the financial ecosystem (Remolina, 2023; Gensler and Bailey, 2020). Artificial intelligence also poses some risks. These include the risks that arise when artificial intelligence systems replace the humans or bank examiners who are involved in financial regulation and banking supervision work. Such replacement or partial replacement could expose the financial system to financial stability risks.

Therefore, the purpose of the article is to explore some risks that artificial intelligence could pose to financial stability in Nigeria particularly the AI risks that could affect those directly involved in financial stability work in Nigeria. This study seeks to answer the following research questions: Does AI pose any risk for those involved in financial stability work in Nigeria? Can regulatory personnel use AI inappropriately in Nigeria? Can Nigerian financial regulators be misinformed by AI? Can the use of AI for financial stability work give rise to false positives in Nigeria? Are there any accountability problems associated with using AI for financial stability work in Nigeria? Can AI worsen an existing financial crisis in Nigeria? Are there sufficient crisis data to support regulatory AI-based decision making in Nigeria? Is the Nigerian regulator ready to join the AI-finance revolution in Nigeria?

The insight gained from this study will guide the Central Bank of Nigeria in understanding the potential impact of artificial intelligence on financial stability in Nigeria, and to determine whether the financial system regulator is ready for the artificial intelligence disruption that is unfolding before our eyes in the world today. The study found that the potential risks that could be encountered include the inappropriate use of artificial intelligence by personnel involved in financial stability work, the risk of being misinformed by artificial intelligence systems, the potential for false positives and over-reliance on artificial intelligence decisions, heightened accountability risks without a clear accountability framework, the potential for artificial intelligence systems to worsen an existing financial crisis, limited crises data to support artificial intelligence decision making, and the risk that regulators will be left behind in the AI-finance revolution in Nigeria.

The study contributes to the financial stability literature that examines the determinants of financial stability, but which has not considered artificial intelligence to be a factor that affect financial stability in Nigeria. Such studies include Adelmann *et al.* (2020), Cecchetti *et al.* (2020), Clayton and Schaab (2022) and Elsayed *et al.* (2023).

The rest of the article is structured in the following way. Review of the prior literature and contextual framework are presented in section 2. The methodology is stated in section 3. The risks of AI to financial stability work are presented in section 4. The conclusion is reported in section 5.

CONTEXTUAL FRAMEWORK AND REVIEW OF LITERATURE

Contextual Framework

In the last decade, the Nigerian financial sector has undergone disruptive digital transformation. The most recent digital transformation in the Nigerian financial sector is the use of artificial intelligence (AI) tools to deliver essential financial services. Some financial institutions have deployed AI tools to improve their internal processes and to serve customers better. The most popular application of AI in the Nigerian financial system today are the use of AI-powered chatbots, virtual assistants, and robo advisors to deliver quality customer services, and the use of AI-based process automation to automate repetitive processes in risk management and cyber security. The benefit they offer to Nigerian financial institutions include 24/7 customer service accessibility, multi-lingual support for non-English speaking customers, instant responses to customer queries, customized product recommendations, reduction in labor cost and improved security for customers. Several real-world AI use cases exists. For example, Zenith Bank has launched an AI chatbot called ZiVA which enables the bank's customers to perform financial transactions seamlessly. The AI chatbot also responds to chats or queries made by customers on WhatsApp and Facebook platforms, and it enables customers to open new accounts and receive instant notifications. Sparkle, which is a payment service bank, has launched an AI customer experience platform called 'Proto' that is equipped with an automated chatbot interface, a third-party ticketing system, and multi-language support for customers. United Bank for Africa also launched its AI chatbot named 'Leo' which assists customers to perform fund transfers, check account balances and purchase airtime through social messaging apps like Facebook and WhatsApp. Access bank also launched the chatbot 'Ada' which assists customers in finding the closest bank branch, and in checking their transaction history and account balances. Guaranty Trust Bank launched the 'GTCrea8' Chatbot that helps customers to perform very basic banking services on Facebook. With regards to financial stability, financial institutions are considering the use of AI-based RegTech tools to enhance their regulatory reporting capability. Meanwhile, among the regulators, there is presently no known use case of AI for financial stability work in Nigeria by the central bank or other regulators. This might be due to lack of clarity about the benefits of AI for financial stability work or due to lack of interest in using AI for financial stability work or it might be due to concerns about the risks that AI pose for financial stability work.

Review of Literature

There are very few studies on the effect of artificial intelligence on financial stability. For example, Danielsson *et al.* (2022) argued that artificial intelligence is risky to the financial system because it would change how the financial system operate, it would take over established finance functions, and it would displace the workers doing repetitive financial processes. They further argued that artificial intelligence would create new risks that have not been seen before, and it would amplify existing risks in unprecedented ways. Notwithstanding, they identified some benefits of artificial intelligence which includes cost savings and increase in operational efficiency. Ozili (2024) was concerned about how artificial intelligence would affect central banking. The author showed that even though artificial intelligence would motivate central banks to invest in data science and improve their ability to detect financial stability risks, the author called for caution in the use of artificial intelligence by pointing out some important risks to watch out for which includes the potential for violation of data privacy, embedded bias risk and cybersecurity risk. Remolina (2023) also examined how artificial intelligence use cases could lead to financial stability risks. The author showed that the lack of artificial intelligence governance and oversight by financial regulators will trigger risks to financial stability. The author called for increased trustworthiness, transparency, explainability and fairness in the use of artificial intelligence to promote financial stability. Buckley *et al.* (2021) focused on the regulation of artificial intelligence in the financial sector. The authors suggest the need for artificial intelligence regulation that oppose the independent operation of artificial intelligence systems in the financial services sector due to the ability of artificial intelligence systems to go rogue and to generate misleading output that lead to harmful decision-making in the financial sector. They describe this to be the black-box of artificial intelligence. Li (2021) also identified some risks of artificial intelligence for financial stability based on the report of the financial stability Council (FSB). The report identified several risks which include the potential for breach of data privacy and operational risk failures.

Other studies examine how AI may affect the financial sector. Goodell *et al.* (2021) considered the development of artificial intelligence and machine learning in the finance literature. They conducted a literature survey and showed that there is growing interest in the application of AI in investment portfolio construction and valuation, understanding investor behavior, assessing financial fraud, assessing financial distress, and in sentiment analyses and inference. Max *et al.* (2021) raised some ethical concerns about the use of AI in the financial sector. They first highlight some benefits of AI which include cost saving, efficiency benefits, improvement in regulatory compliance capability and improved service delivery. They also point out that AI raises concerns about ethical responsibility, legal accountability, data ownership, data security, loss of jobs, unwarranted personalization of service offerings, and systemic risk in the financial sector. Königstorfer and Thalmann (2020) considered the application of AI in commercial banks. They focused on how AI could change the way customers and business processes interact with AI systems. They found that commercial banks use AI to minimize credit losses, increase payment processing, automate regulatory compliance processes, and deliver personalized services to the customers of commercial banks.

Sadok *et al.* (2022) showed that AI models could make new sources of information available for the purpose of assessing the creditworthiness of bank borrowers. Banks can also use AI to aid credit analysis so that more bank customers can have access to credit using non-traditional credit information. But the use of AI for credit worthiness analysis could lead to bias as well as ethical, legal and regulatory issues. Mhlanga (2021) also acknowledge that AI will affect the assessment of credit risk because alternative data sources can be used by AI systems to reduce the information asymmetry, adverse selection, and moral hazard problems associated with credit assessment. Mhlanga (2021) further acknowledge that AI will enable rigorous analysis of credit risk, and will enable loan repayment when due, and improve access to credit for people who cannot obtain credit using traditional means. Ashta and Herrmann (2021) admitted that AI is risky for the financial sector and that it will be a major disruption since its major point of attraction is in AI's ability to reduce cost and offer customization benefits for consumers. They however argued that AI risks will emerge from issues surrounding the use of nonrepresentative data, the bias inherent in representative data, inappropriate choice of algorithms, and the issues surrounding the interpretation of AI data. Rahman *et al.* (2023) assessed the factors affecting the intention of consumers to adopt AI in banking services in Malaysia. They conducted interviews of bank officials in Malaysia. They also collected 302 questionnaires from Malaysian bank customers. They found that many bank officials consider AI to be useful in detecting fraud and to prevent risk. They also show that lack of regulatory requirements for AI, data privacy issues, security risks, and lack of relevant skills are some impediments to AI adoption among Malaysian bank customers. In their quantitative analysis, they show that customers' attitude towards AI, the perceived usefulness, risk, and trust limit the intention of customers to adopt and use AI in banking services. Milana and Ashta (2021) in a literature survey also show that the literature acknowledge that AI can improve efficiency, create new data sources and improve risk mitigation.

In summary, the literature showed some benefits of AI and the challenges associated with using AI in the financial sector and for financial stability. The benefits include cost savings, increase in operational efficiency, improvement in regulatory compliance capability, improved service delivery, reduction in credit losses, fast payment processing, regulatory compliance process automation, and the personalization of customer service (see, Königstorfer and Thalmann, 2020; Max *et al.,* 2021; Danielsson *et al.,* 2022). The challenges include the displacement of workers doing repetitive financial processes, the potential for data privacy violation, embedded bias risk, cybersecurity risk, the potential for AI to generate misleading output that lead to harmful decision-making in the financial sector, operational risk failures, and unwarranted personalization of service offerings (see Max *et al.,* 2021; Li, 2021; Buckley *et al.,* 2021; Danielsson *et al.*, 2022; Ozili, 2024). These identified benefits and challenges were derived from the experience of developed countries and non-African countries. Yet, little is known about the benefits and risks of AI in the financial sector in developing countries like Nigeria. There is no documented knowledge on how AI might affect those involved in financial stability work in Nigeria. This study fills this gap in the literature by identifying the potential risks that artificial intelligence could pose to financial stability in Nigeria and with particular focus on how AI risks could affect those directly involved in financial stability work in Nigeria.

METHODOLOGY

The study was undertaken using the discourse analysis methodology. The discourse analysis methodology involves postulating a relationship between two or more concepts based on real-world observations and validating the relationship with the existing literature. It also involves using the existing literature to reach conclusions about the relationship between two or more concepts. The discourse analysis methodology is an exploratory research design in which the existing literature is analyzed using thematic engagement.

AI RISKS TO FINANCIAL STABILITY: RISK TO WATCH OUT FOR

This section discusses the potential risks posed by artificial intelligence system to those involved in financial stability work in Nigeria.

Inappropriate Use of Artificial Intelligence Systems by Personnel Involved in Financial Stability Work

Luxton (2014) and Zhai *et al.* (2021) show that artificial intelligence systems can be used inappropriately by users. The biggest challenge of using artificial intelligence systems for financial stability work in Nigeria is its ability to be used inappropriately, and without detection, by personnel involved in banking supervision and financial regulation work in Nigeria. The personnel using the AI system may unintentionally bypass AI-based controls and introduce new algorithm-based instructions into the AI system used by regulators. This could lead the AI system to generate inaccurate analyses, and recommend policy decisions that are misleading, and which could lead to financial instability if implemented.

Risk of Being Misinformed by Artificial Intelligence Systems

Monteith *et al.* (2024), Bewersdorff *et al.* (2023) and Kaur *et al.* (2022) acknowledge that artificial intelligence systems can increase misinformation if they are fed with incorrect or bias data. The soundness of the decisions or output generated by data-driven artificial intelligence systems depend largely on the quality of the data fed into the artificial intelligence system. Since AI systems strongly depend on the data fed into it, bank supervisors and financial regulators are faced with the risk of unknowingly importing incorrect data or bias data into the AI-systems they use for financial stability work. The risk is that incorrect or biased data may be used to make forecasts about future industry nonperforming loans, future loan growth and future deposit base of the banking sector for stress testing purposes. The danger here is that the artificial intelligence system could generate misleading stress test results based on incorrect or bias data and give financial regulators the impression that the financial system is safe, when in fact, it is not safe.

Risk of Over-Reliance on AI Decisions and False Positives

Mytnyk *et al.* (2023) point out that over-reliance on artificial intelligence systems increases the likelihood of obtaining false positives. In Nigeria, data-driven artificial intelligence systems know little or nothing about the principles of financial stability, but they can generate recommendations with high statistical accuracy. Their statistical accuracy can tempt financial regulators and bank supervisors to accept the recommendations of AI systems without probing the underlying assumptions on which the recommendations are made. This risk can be avoided if bank supervisors and financial regulators do not over-rely on artificial intelligence systems for financial stability recommendations. To be safe, bank supervisors and financial regulators should only use artificial intelligence systems to analyse financial stability data, but they should not over-rely on AI system to generate financial stability recommendations. They should treat AI-based financial stability recommendations with caution and subject the recommendations to internal review and peer evaluation.

Heightened Accountability Risks and the Absence of a Clear Accountability Framework

Novelli *et al.* (2023) argued that accountability is a serious challenge when using artificial intelligence systems in organisations. Accountability is also a serious challenge when using artificial intelligence systems to do financial stability work in Nigeria. This is because the use of artificial intelligence for financial stability work raises a number of questions. Who should be held responsible for any implemented AI-based decisions that turn out to have an adverse effect on the Nigerian financial system? Should the information technology (IT) staff or the banking supervision staff manning the AI system be held responsible and disciplined? Or, should their superiors be penalised instead of the operational employees? Or, should the AI-system be discarded for producing a bad result that everyone relied on and implemented? Is it fair to discipline the staff manning the AI system? Is it fair to discipline their superiors who relied completely on the recommendations generated by the AI system? Who exactly should take the fall for faulty AI-based financial stability decisions? These questions point to the issue of artificial intelligence accountability in Nigeria. This issue needs to be addressed before using artificial intelligence systems for financial stability work in Nigeria. Accountability frameworks must be established that specify who will be held responsible when implemented AI-based decisions turn out to have adverse effects on the Nigerian financial system.

Artificial Intelligence Decisions Could Worsen an Existing Financial Crisis

Chen *et al.* (2023) and Lin (2019) demonstrate that artificial intelligence systems can be used by financial institutions during financial crisis but there is no guarantee that the AI based decision will make a significant difference during the financial crisis. During a financial crisis, banks and other financial institutions will make careful financial decisions and adopt a wait-and-see posture towards investment until there is some stability in the financial system (Lin, 2019). However, during a financial crisis, AI systems can generate quick actionable insights that can lead financial institutions to quickly sell off investments, hoard liquidity and decrease lending during a financial crisis. The adoption and reliance on artificial intelligence systems by financial institutions during a financial crisis can lead banks and other financial institutions to make hasty financial decisions during a financial crisis. Such hasty financial decisions could lead to panic in financial markets, trigger a credit crunch in the interbank market or trigger a bank run in the banking system. Such panic, induced by AI-based decision making, will further worsen the existing financial crisis, and complicate the financial stability responsibility of the central bank during a financial crisis.

Limited Crises Data to Support Artificial Intelligence Decision Making

Hilpisch (2020) points out that insufficient historical data is a challenge faced by data-driven artificial intelligence systems. Artificial intelligence systems often rely on long historical data to generate reliable forecast for the present and the future. However, using artificial intelligence systems to forecast the likelihood of a future financial crisis is difficult because data about past financial crises in Nigeria is limited. This is because the occurrence of financial crisis in Nigeria is infrequent and when a financial crisis occurs in Nigeria, it is often short-lived. Financial crisis in Nigeria occurs once in every 12 years. This makes it difficult to obtain a long historical financial crisis data that could be fed into an artificial intelligence system for the purpose of financial crisis stress testing. The scarce nature of financial crisis data makes it difficult to rely on artificial intelligence systems for financial stability purposes and considering the fact that it is inappropriate to rely on short historical data to make forecast about present and future crises.

Risk That Regulators Will be Left Behind in the AI-Finance Revolution in Nigeria

Nwosu (2018) and Elegunde and Osagie (2020) acknowledge that the use of artificial intelligence tools by regulated financial institutions is increasing in Nigeria. Some financial institutions are already using AI tools to simplify their regulatory reporting to the central bank to comply with micro prudential regulatory requirements. As more Nigerian financial institutions and fintech operators adopt and use artificial intelligence tools and systems to improve their functions, the central bank and other regulators will have no option but to follow and join the artificial intelligence revolution. Else, they stand the risk of being left behind in the on-going AI-finance revolution. Some regulators may find it difficult to follow and join the artificial intelligence revolution because they have rigid legacy systems which are not easy to overhaul while other regulators may find it much easier to adapt. Regulators should prepare for the transition to AI-led regulation to avoid being left behind in the AI-finance revolution which is taking place in the Nigerian financial sector.

CONCLUSION

This study identified some of the risks that may be encountered when using artificial intelligence to do financial stability work in Nigeria. The study focused on the risks that bank supervisors and financial regulators may encounter when using artificial intelligence to undertake financial stability work in Nigeria. The identified risks include the inappropriate use of artificial intelligence by personnel involved in financial stability work, the risk of being misinformed by artificial intelligence systems, the over-reliance on artificial intelligence decisions and false positives, heightened accountability risks without a clear accountability framework, the potential for artificial intelligence system to worsen an existing financial crisis, limited crises data to support artificial intelligence decision making and the risk that regulators will be left behind in the AI-finance revolution in Nigeria.

The insight gained from the identified risks can help financial regulators and bank supervisors to understand how the use of artificial intelligence can amplify fragilities in the Nigerian financial system if care is not taken when using artificial intelligence for financial stability work in Nigeria. The insight gained from this study will also help the central bank to understand the full implication of artificial intelligence for financial stability work. It is recommended that financial regulators and bank supervisors should be vigilant to detect other threats that artificial intelligence systems may pose for financial stability which have not been highlighted in this article.

Finally, the use of artificial intelligence for financial stability work in Nigeria should not be opposed, rather the authors recommend the cautious use of artificial intelligence systems for financial stability work in Nigeria. Every technology has good and bad effects, so also does artificial intelligence. There is a need to harness the good benefits of artificial intelligence, understand the risks that may be encountered when using artificial intelligence systems to do financial stability work in Nigeria, and work out possible risk mitigants to ensure the safe use of artificial intelligence systems for financial stability work in Nigeria.

REFERENCES

Adelmann, F., Ergen, I., Gaidosch, T., Jenkinson, N., Khiaonarong, M. T., Morozova, A., Schwarz, N., & Wilson, C. (2020). *Cyber risk and financial stability: It's a small world after all.* International Monetary Fund.

Alessi, L., & Detken, C. (2018). Identifying excessive credit growth and leverage. *Journal of Financial Stability, 35*, 215–225.

Ashta, A., & Herrmann, H. (2021). Artificial intelligence and fintech: An overview of opportunities and risks for banking, investments, and microfinance. *Strategic Change, 30*(3), 211–222.

Berger, A. N., Klapper, L. F., & Turk-Ariss, R. (2017). Bank competition and financial stability. In *Handbook of competition in banking and finance* (pp. 185–204). Edward Elgar Publishing.

Bewersdorff, A., Zhai, X., Roberts, J., & Nerdel, C. (2023). Myths, mis-and preconceptions of artificial intelligence: A review of the literature. *Computers and Education: Artificial Intelligence, 4*, 100143.

Brunnermeier, M., Crockett, A., Goodhart, C. A., Persaud, A., & Shin, H. S. (2009). *The fundamental principles of financial regulation* (Vol. 11). ICMB, Internat. Center for Monetary and Banking Studies.

Buckley, R. P., Zetzsche, D. A., Arner, D. W., & Tang, B. W. (2021). Regulating artificial intelligence in finance: Putting the human in the loop. *The Sydney Law Review, 43*(1), 43–81.

Cecchetti, S. G., Mancini-Griffoli, T., Narita, M., & Sahay, R. (2020). US or domestic monetary policy: Which matters more for financial stability? *IMF Economic Review, 68*(1), 35–65.

Chen, M., DeHaven, M., Kitschelt, I., Lee, S. J., & Sicilian, M. J. (2023). Identifying financial crises using machine learning on textual data. *Journal of Risk and Financial Management, 16*(3), 1–28.

Clayton, C., & Schaab, A. (2022). Multinational banks and financial stability. *The Quarterly Journal of Economics, 137*(3), 1681–1736.

Danielsson, J., Macrae, R., & Uthemann, A. (2022). Artificial intelligence and systemic risk. *Journal of Banking & Finance, 140*, 106290.

Elegunde, A. F., & Osagie, R. (2020). Artificial intelligence adoption and employee performance in the Nigerian banking industry. *International Journal of Management and Administration*, *4*(8), 189–205.

Elsayed, A. H., Naifar, N., & Nasreen, S. (2023). Financial stability and monetary policy reaction: Evidence from the GCC countries. *The Quarterly Review of Economics and Finance*, *87*, 396–405.

Gensler, G., & Bailey, L. (2020). "Deep learning and financial stability", *Available at SSRN* 3723132.

Goodell, J. W., Kumar, S., Lim, W. M., & Pattnaik, D. (2021). Artificial intelligence and machine learning in finance: Identifying foundations, themes, and research clusters from bibliometric analysis. *Journal of Behavioral and Experimental Finance*, *32*, 100577.

Hilpisch, Y. (2020). *Artificial Intelligence in Finance*. O'Reilly Media.

Kasman, A., & Carvallo, O. (2014). Financial stability, competition and efficiency in Latin American and Caribbean banking. *Journal of Applied Econometrics*, *17*(2), 301–324.

Kaur, D., Uslu, S., Rittichier, K. J., & Durresi, A. (2022). Trustworthy artificial intelligence: A review. *ACM Computing Surveys*, *55*(2), 1–38.

Königstorfer, F., & Thalmann, S. (2020). Applications of Artificial Intelligence in commercial banks–A research agenda for behavioral finance. *Journal of Behavioral and Experimental Finance*, *27*, 100352.

Li, C. (2021). "The application of artificial intelligence and machine learning in financial stability", In *The 2020 International Conference on Machine Learning and Big Data Analytics for IoT Security and Privacy: SPIoT-2020,* Vol. 1 (pp. 214-219). Springer International Publishing.

Lin, T. C. (2019). Artificial intelligence, finance, and the law. *Fordham Law Review*, *88*(2), 531–551.

Luxton, D. D. (2014). Recommendations for the ethical use and design of artificial intelligent care providers. *Artificial Intelligence in Medicine*, *62*(1), 1–10. PMID: 25059820

Makri, V., Tsagkanos, A., & Bellas, A. (2014). Determinants of non-performing loans: The case of Eurozone. *Panoeconomicus*, *61*(2), 193–206.

Max, R., Kriebitz, A., & Von Websky, C. (2021). "Ethical considerations about the implications of artificial intelligence in finance", *Handbook on ethics in finance*, pp. 577-592.

Mhlanga, D. (2021). "Financial inclusion in emerging economies: The application of machine learning and artificial intelligence in credit risk assessment", *International journal of financial studies*, Vol. *9 No.* 3, pp. 1-17.

Milana, C., & Ashta, A. (2021). Artificial intelligence techniques in finance and financial markets: A survey of the literature. *Strategic Change*, *30*(3), 189–209.

Monteith, S., Glenn, T., Geddes, J. R., Whybrow, P. C., Achtyes, E., & Bauer, M. (2024). Artificial intelligence and increasing misinformation. *The British Journal of Psychiatry*, *224*(2), 33–35. PMID: 37881016

Mytnyk, B., Tkachyk, O., Shakhovska, N., Fedushko, S., & Syerov, Y. (2023). Application of artificial intelligence for fraudulent banking operations recognition. *Big Data and Cognitive Computing*, *7*(2), 93.

Novelli, C., Taddeo, M., & Floridi, L. (2023). Accountability in artificial intelligence: What it is and how it works. *AI & Society*, •••, 1–12.

Nwosu, J. N. (2018). An investigation into the extent of the use of artificial intelligence in nigeria banks. *IAA Journal of Applied Sciences*, *4*(1), 105–111.

Ozili, P. K. (2018). Banking stability determinants in Africa. *International Journal of Managerial Finance*, *14*(4), 462–483.

Ozili, P. K. (2024). "Artificial intelligence in central banking: benefits and risks of AI for central banks", In *Industrial Applications of Big Data, AI, and Blockchain* (pp. 70-82). IGI Global.

Rahman, M., Ming, T. H., Baigh, T. A., & Sarker, M. (2023). Adoption of artificial intelligence in banking services: An empirical analysis. *International Journal of Emerging Markets*, *18*(10), 4270–4300.

Remolina, N. (2023). Interconnectedness and financial stability in the era of artificial intelligence. In *Artificial Intelligence in Finance* (pp. 350–367). Edward Elgar Publishing.

Sadok, H., Sakka, F., & El Maknouzi, M. E. H. (2022). Artificial intelligence and bank credit analysis: A review. *Cogent Economics & Finance*, *10*(1), 2023262.

Sarlin, P., & Peltonen, T. A. (2013). Mapping the state of financial stability. *Journal of International Financial Markets, Institutions and Money*, *26*, 46–76.

Xu, M. T., Hu, K., & Das, M. U. S. (2019). *Bank profitability and financial stability*. International Monetary Fund.

Zhai, X., Chu, X., Chai, C. S., Jong, M. S. Y., Istenic, A., Spector, M., Liu, J. B., Yuan, J., & Li, Y. (2021). A Review of Artificial Intelligence (AI) in Education from 2010 to 2020. *Complexity, Vol., 2021*(1), 8812542.

Chapter 13
Farmers Rights vis-à-vis Plant Breeder Privilege:
Exploring the Issues and Challenges

Ananya Pandey
https://orcid.org/0000-0002-2419-6314
Christ University, India

Achyutananda Mishra
https://orcid.org/0000-0002-4113-0974
Christ University, India

ABSTRACT

This chapter highlights the conflict between technical advancement and socioeconomic inequality by examining the complex relationship between biotechnology, farmers' rights, and human rights. Although biotechnology has the potential to improve food security, sustainability, and agricultural production, its use frequently marginalizes smallholder farmers due to seed monopolies and stringent intellectual property laws. The chapter looks critically at how national patent laws, TRIPS, UPOV, and other international legal frameworks disproportionately favor agribusinesses at the expense of traditional knowledge, seed sovereignty, and the right to survive. A more inclusive and equitable governance model that empowers farmers as stewards of food systems and biodiversity is advocated in this chapter by contrasting the techno-economic agenda of agricultural biotechnology with the human rights imperative.

DOI: 10.4018/979-8-3373-2387-9.ch013

INTRODUCTION

A transformative shift has been witnessed in the agricultural sector that is driven by the biotechnological revolution such as the introduction of genetically modified plant varieties and crops. The introduction of innovation in the field of agriculture has introduced deep socio-economic concerns, particularly for smallholder and traditional farmers who form the backbone of agriculture in the Global South. While biotechnology offers the potential to increase productivity and secure food systems, it simultaneously raises questions of equity, access, and agency, placing farmers at a crossroads between innovation and vulnerability. The adoption of biotechnology has often been controlled by powerful transnational corporations, primarily based in the Global North, that dominate the seed and agrochemical markets through extensive patent regimes and plant varieties by the breeders (Shiva, 2016). This corporate consolidation of genetic resources, protected through intellectual property rights (IPRs), has limited the ability of farmers to save, exchange, or modify seeds—practices that have historically been vital to agrobiodiversity and cultural identity (Kloppenburg, 2010). The imposition of restrictive legal mechanisms such as UPOV 1991 and the WTO's TRIPS Agreement has resulted in the erosion of seed sovereignty of farmers, replacing it with a model of proprietary control and commercial dependence. As farmers increasingly rely on patented biotechnologies, they face mounting risks: indebtedness due to high input costs, reduced biodiversity from monoculture practices, and criminalization for alleged intellectual property violations (De Schutter, 2009). Biotechnology is creating a paradox lies the dual-edge nature of agricultural biotechnology: one side holds the promise of scientific progress and improved livelihoods, while the other brings forth precarity, legal exclusion, and dependency. An under-edge privilege granted to the breeders over the farmers rights with respect to the plant variety rights and biotechnological innovation of seeds puts the farmers in unequitable condition to access, save, sell and exchange the seeds.

The scope of this chapter is thus interdisciplinary and critical. It begins with a technical overview of key biotechnological advances and their role in transforming agriculture, particularly in the Global South. This is followed by a detailed analysis of how these innovations have disrupted traditional agricultural practices and affected farmers' socio-economic rights, drawing on case studies from India, Africa, and Latin America. The third section of the chapter unpacks the human rights dimensions of biotechnology, focusing on legal instruments and ethical principles that underscore the rights of farmers to access, control, and benefit from genetic resources. The fourth section addresses the problem of power asymmetries, corporate monopolies, and regulatory failures that exacerbate inequality within biotechnological regimes. It critiques the current intellectual property paradigm and explores alternative legal and policy tools that can democratize innovation while safeguarding farmers' autonomy and biodiversity.

In light of the above perspective, this chapter also delves into ethical and legal challenges such as informed consent, biosafety, liability for biotechnological failures, and the marginalization of indigenous knowledge systems. It evaluates whether existing legal frameworks provide adequate protections or whether new, hybrid models—such as open-source biotechnology and community seed banks—are needed to achieve justice. The conclusive section proposes a rights-based innovation framework that integrates farmers' voices into biotechnological research and policy, ensuring that technological advancements serve public goods rather than private interests. Policy recommendations are then offered to guide governments, civil society, and international organizations in building inclusive and resilient food systems that protects the rights of the farmers.

BIOTECHNOLOGY, AGRICULTURAL TRANSFORMATION AND TRIPS

Biotechnology has emerged as a transformative force in modern agriculture, reshaping the production, processing, and distribution of food at an unprecedented scale. Central to this transformation are four key technological innovations namely,

a. Genetically Modified Organisms (GMOs), GMOs were among the earliest breakthroughs, involving the direct manipulation of an organism's genome to express desirable traits—most notably pest resistance, herbicide tolerance, and drought resilience. Since the 1990s, GM crops such as Bt (Bacillus thuringiensis) cotton, glyphosate-resistant soybeans, and Golden Rice have been introduced in various parts of the world, with significant adoption in countries like the United States, Brazil, India, and China (Qaim, 2020).
b. Gene-editing Tools such as Clustered Regularly Interspaced Short Palindromic Repeat (CRISPR-Cas9) (CRISPR-Cas9 is a gene editing technology that allows scientists to precisely alter an organism's DNA. It's based on a natural bacterial immune system that can be adapted to target and modify specific DNA sequences in any organism). CRISPR-Cas9, a more recent and precise gene-editing tool, has allowed scientists to edit plant genomes with unprecedented accuracy, efficiency, and affordability. Unlike traditional GMOs, CRISPR can introduce specific edits without foreign DNA insertion, leading to regulatory debates over whether such products fall under existing GMO frameworks (Jinek et al., 2012; Ishii & Araki, 2016).

c. Synthetic Biology, i.e., the potential of biotechnology by designing and constructing new biological parts, devices, and systems that do not exist in nature. It enables the creation of novel plant metabolic pathways and engineered microbes to enhance nitrogen fixation or degrade pesticides in the soil (Khalil & Collins, 2010).
d. Bioinformatics, i.e., the application of computational tools to understand biological data—has accelerated genomic research, enabling precision breeding, molecular diagnostics, and predictive analytics for crop management. The integration of large-scale genomic datasets with AI and machine learning further enables the identification of gene-trait relationships, thus facilitating targeted innovation in seed development and stress tolerance (Varshney et al., 2021).

Agricultural Transformation with Biotechnology

Collectively, all the above-mentioned biotechnological advancements have significantly contributed to enhancing agricultural productivity, especially in the context of growing global food insecurity, climate change, and ecological degradation. For instance, biotech crops have demonstrated yield increases of 20–25% in certain developing regions, reduced pesticide use by 37%, and increased farmer profits by 68% on average (Klümper & Qaim, 2014). Genetic engineering has enabled crops to withstand biotic and abiotic stresses such as drought, salinity, and disease, thus offering potential solutions to climate-induced yield variability. Golden Rice, engineered to combat Vitamin A deficiency, and drought-tolerant maize (DTMA), developed for sub-Saharan Africa, are emblematic of the promise biotechnology holds in addressing malnutrition and food scarcity (Beyer et al., 2002; Cairns et al., 2013). Moreover, the technology facilitates reduced post-harvest losses, enhances shelf-life, and supports biofortification, thereby improving food quality alongside quantity.

Beyond the farm, biotechnology is deeply integrated into global agribusiness and food chains. Multinational corporations such as Bayer-Monsanto, Syngenta, and Corteva dominate the biotech seed and agrochemical markets, controlling proprietary seed technologies through robust intellectual property regimes. These entities not only produce biotech seeds but also develop linked agro-input packages, including herbicides and data-driven farm management systems. As a result, agriculture has become increasingly digitized, consolidated, and commodified. Corporate mergers and acquisitions in the sector have led to a significant concentration of market power, with just four firms controlling over 60% of the global seed and pesticide markets (Howard, 2015). This corporate-driven model promotes economies of scale and standardization but often sidelines smallholder farmers and diverse, local farming practices.

The rapid spread of biotechnology in agriculture, while promising, also poses considerable socio-economic and ethical risks—particularly for smallholder farmers in the Global South. One of the primary concerns is the emergence of technological dependency. Many biotech seeds are protected by patents and licensing agreements, restricting farmers from saving or reusing seeds—a traditional practice integral to seed sovereignty. This has led to the replacement of diverse, farmer-saved seed varieties with proprietary hybrids, reducing genetic diversity and increasing vulnerability to market volatility and climate change (Shiva, 2016). Furthermore, the high costs associated with biotech seeds and their required chemical inputs often create financial burdens for smallholders. In India, for example, the introduction of Bt cotton led to both increased yields and higher input costs, with mixed outcomes for farmer livelihoods and reports linking financial stress to rural indebtedness and even farmer suicides (Gruère & Sengupta, 2011).

TRIPS and Agricultural Innovation

Additionally, the legal and institutional frameworks governing biotechnology are often skewed in favor of corporate rights rather than farmers' rights. The Agreement on Trade-Related Aspects of Intellectual Property Rights (TRIPS) under the World Trade Organization, along with UPOV 1991, promote the protection of plant varieties and biotechnology innovations through patents and breeders' rights. These instruments prioritize commercial innovation but often fail to recognize the informal innovation systems of indigenous and local farming communities. Consequently, farmers may find themselves entangled in complex legal disputes over seed use, especially when patent infringement claims are made against unintended cross-pollination—a scenario that has occurred in both developed and developing countries (Lacy, 2017). The reliance on a narrow set of biotech traits and crop varieties also poses ecological risks. For instance, the widespread cultivation of herbicide-tolerant crops has led to the emergence of "superweeds" resistant to common herbicides like glyphosate, prompting a pesticide treadmill that requires ever-stronger chemical solutions (Benbrook, 2012). This undermines sustainable farming practices and raises environmental health concerns. Furthermore, the techno-centric approach to agricultural transformation may marginalize agroecological approaches and traditional ecological knowledge, which emphasize biodiversity, soil health, and community-based resource management.

Despite these challenges, the future of biotechnology in agriculture need not be exclusionary. A more inclusive approach—integrating public-sector research, participatory breeding, open-source biotech platforms, and farmer-led innovation—can harness the potential of these technologies while minimizing socio-economic inequities. Regulatory frameworks must evolve to ensure transparency, accountability, and equitable benefit-sharing, particularly with marginalized farming communities. Moreover, ethical deliberations on the direction of agricultural biotechnology must include diverse voices from civil society, indigenous groups, and smallholder farmers, ensuring that innovation aligns not only with economic growth but also with social justice and environmental sustainability (Leach et al., 2020).

BIOTECHNOLOGY AND HUMAN RIGHTS OF FARMERS

Biotechnology in agriculture has ushered in transformative innovations with the potential to address global hunger, climate change, and resource scarcity. Yet, it also presents deep human rights dilemmas for farmers, particularly concerning the right to food, the right to livelihood, and the right to culture, all of which are enshrined in international human rights law.

International Covenant on Economic, Social and Cultural Rights (ICESCR)

The right to food, as recognized in Article 11 of the International Covenant on Economic, Social and Cultural Rights (ICESCR), asserts that every individual is entitled to "adequate food" and the "fundamental right to be free from hunger" (UN General Assembly, 1966). However, the increasing control of agricultural biotechnology by transnational corporations has created barriers to this right. By patenting genetically modified seeds and controlling input chains, these corporations limit farmers' autonomy, especially in the Global South, where access to proprietary technologies is cost-prohibitive (De Schutter, 2009). This restriction not only undermines food sovereignty but also constrains smallholder farmers' capacity to make independent decisions about seed saving, planting, and exchange—an essential component of agricultural biodiversity and cultural continuity. The right to livelihood is similarly affected. Biotechnology has led to the displacement of traditional agricultural practices and the erosion of informal seed systems. For example, contract farming arrangements tied to biotech inputs often bind farmers into cycles of debt and dependency, threatening their economic security (Shiva, 2016). Additionally, the entry of biotechnology into rural spaces without adequate consultation or safeguards disproportionately impacts communities with limited legal and financial resources. The right to culture, understood as the right to enjoy one's cultural heritage and practices—including indigenous agricultural knowledge—is undermined when traditional seed varieties are replaced by genetically uniform crops (Daes, 2001). These uniform crops often fail to adapt to local ecological conditions, resulting in ecological vulnerability and the loss of cultural identity embedded in indigenous farming systems.

The United Nations Declaration on the Rights of Peasants and Other People Working in Rural Areas (UNDROP)

The United Nations Declaration on the Rights of Peasants and Other People Working in Rural Areas (UNDROP), adopted in 2018, provides a comprehensive framework to evaluate biotechnology through a human rights lens. UNDROP explicitly recognizes peasants' rights to seeds, biodiversity, land, and traditional knowledge (UN Human Rights Council, 2018). Article 19 of the Declaration affirms the right to save, use, exchange, and sell farm-saved seed and propagating material, and emphasizes the need for states to support and promote biodiversity as maintained by peasants. This provision directly challenges the intellectual property (IP) regimes promoted under agreements like TRIPS and UPOV 1991, which restrict farmers' traditional seed-saving practices in favor of breeder and corporate rights (Brahmi et al., 2018). UNDROP's holistic framing of human rights—including economic, social, cultural, and environmental dimensions—serves as a counter-narrative to the dominant techno-centric and market-driven approach to agricultural innovation. Yet, glaring disparities exist in access to and control over biotechnology between the Global North and the Global South. In high-income countries, biotechnology is often subsidized, protected through robust intellectual property regimes, and supported by advanced infrastructure and institutional capacity. In contrast, many low- and middle-income countries struggle with underfunded agricultural research institutions and lack regulatory oversight, which leaves them vulnerable to corporate influence and external dependency (Scoones, 2002). The technological imbalance results in asymmetric negotiations where countries in the Global South adopt biotechnologies under pressure from trade agreements or development aid, without fully understanding or negotiating their long-term social and ecological implications (Stone, 2011). Moreover, donor-driven biotech projects often prioritize export-oriented cash crops over local food crops, further marginalizing subsistence farmers and threatening local food systems (Glover, 2010). These disparities reproduce colonial patterns of control over land, knowledge, and biological resources, reinforcing geopolitical hierarchies within global agricultural governance.

Convention on Biological Diversity (CBD) and the Nagoya Protocol

Biopiracy exemplifies how biotechnology, when unchecked, can facilitate the exploitation of indigenous and local communities. Biopiracy refers to the appropriation of genetic resources and traditional knowledge without fair compensation or consent, often through patenting by corporations or researchers in the Global North (Robinson, 2010). This phenomenon violates the principles of prior informed consent and equitable benefit-sharing outlined in the Convention on Biological Diversity (CBD) and the Nagoya Protocol (CBD, 2011). Notable cases such as the patenting of basmati rice and neem by foreign companies have spotlighted the unjust commodification of traditional knowledge systems in India, leading to international outcry and eventual legal reversals (Shiva, 2001). These instances illustrate how biotechnological innovation can become a vehicle for cultural and biological appropriation, reducing centuries-old knowledge systems to patentable commodities. For indigenous communities, whose identities and livelihoods are deeply intertwined with biodiversity, such practices are not just exploitative—they are existential threats. Moreover, the legal architecture that enables such appropriation often excludes indigenous worldviews and values. Western intellectual property regimes emphasize individual inventiveness and market-driven innovation, while indigenous knowledge is typically communal, spiritual, and ecologically embedded (Posey & Dutfield, 1996). As a result, indigenous and local knowledge systems face epistemic marginalization in global governance frameworks, including those related to biotechnology. The challenge, therefore, is not only to protect these knowledge systems from theft but also to recognize and elevate them as legitimate, co-equal systems of innovation.

To address these injustices, a shift is needed from a corporate-centered model of biotechnology governance to a rights-based approach that prioritizes equity, participation, and ecological sustainability. Such a framework must uphold the principles of the UNDROP and other human rights instruments, while also integrating local voices in decision-making processes. It must challenge the monopolization of biotechnology by private actors and create spaces for community-led innovation and agroecological alternatives. Only then can biotechnology fulfill its promise of contributing to food security and sustainable development—without compromising the rights and dignity of the very communities it seeks to serve.

FARMERS RIGHTS IN THE AGE OF AGRICULTURAL BIOTECHNOLOGY

The emergence of biotechnology in agriculture has profoundly reshaped the dynamics of seed access, ownership, and innovation, challenging long-standing agrarian traditions and customary rights. Historically, farmers have played a central role in conserving, developing, and sharing plant genetic resources. This informal innovation system—anchored in seed sovereignty, indigenous practices, and traditional knowledge—has sustained agrobiodiversity and food systems across generations (Andersen, 2008). Seed sovereignty, defined as the right of farmers to save, use, exchange, and breed seeds without external interference, has been foundational to agricultural resilience and cultural identity, especially in the Global South. Indigenous agricultural systems, often managed communally, ensured the free flow of genetic materials, knowledge, and farming techniques across communities. However, with the advent of modern biotechnology and the imposition of intellectual property regimes, these practices have come under increasing pressure, leading to a systematic erosion of customary rights.

The global expansion of patent laws and plant variety protection mechanisms has prioritized proprietary innovation over communal knowledge systems. Biotechnology companies, through patents and plant breeders' rights (PBRs), have secured monopolistic control over genetically engineered seeds, thereby restricting farmers' traditional freedoms. Under these regimes, saving or reusing patented seeds becomes a legal infringement, effectively criminalizing age-old practices. The Agreement on Trade-Related Aspects of Intellectual Property Rights (TRIPS), administered by the World Trade Organization (WTO), played a pivotal role in this transformation by mandating member states to provide intellectual property protection for plant varieties, either through patents or an effective sui generis system (WTO, 1994). This requirement catalyzed the global diffusion of the International Union for the Protection of New Varieties of Plants (UPOV) Convention, especially its 1991 Act, which significantly curtailed farmers' rights in favor of breeders. Unlike the 1978 Act, which allowed for limited seed saving and exchange, the 1991 Act grants breeders exclusive rights over the production, reproduction, and commercialization of protected varieties, including stricter controls on farm-saved seeds (Leskien & Flitner, 1997).

Simultaneously, the International Treaty on Plant Genetic Resources for Food and Agriculture (ITPGRFA) introduced in 2001 by the Food and Agriculture Organization (FAO) aimed to rebalance these developments by formally recognizing farmers' rights. Article 9 of the ITPGRFA affirms farmers' rights to save, use, exchange, and sell farm-saved seeds, as well as their participation in decision-making and benefit-sharing mechanisms (FAO, 2009). Yet, the implementation of this provision has been uneven and non-binding, leaving it subordinates to national intellectual property laws influenced by UPOV and TRIPS standards. Many countries, particularly those in the Global South, face conflicting obligations between honoring farmers' rights under the Treaty and adhering to trade and intellectual property commitments under WTO agreements (De Schutter, 2009). The result is a fragmented legal landscape where multinational corporations dominate seed markets, and traditional farming communities are pushed to the margins of innovation and access.

Empirical evidence highlights how biotechnology has deepened inequities in seed access, often displacing subsistence and smallholder farmers. In India, the introduction of Bt cotton, a genetically modified (GM) crop engineered for pest resistance, initially increased yields but also led to rising costs due to the dependency on proprietary seeds and associated inputs (Gruère, Mehta-Bhatt, & Sengupta, 2008). Farmers were required to purchase new seeds each season due to contractual restrictions and the non-viability of saved GM seeds. Cases of crop failure, debt, and farmer suicides in some regions have been linked, though contentiously, to the biotech seed model's socio-economic burdens (Shiva, 2004). Similarly, in Latin America, traditional maize varieties have been threatened by the unregulated spread of transgenic crops, undermining indigenous seed systems and food sovereignty (Cleveland, Soleri, & Smith, 2000). In Africa, concerns have been raised about the Gates Foundation and biotech firms promoting genetically modified organisms through philanthropic-agribusiness partnerships, which may inadvertently compromise local seed autonomy (Patel, 2013).

Moreover, biotech-driven legal regimes have facilitated land dispossession and contractual dependencies. Contract farming arrangements often require the exclusive use of company-owned seeds and agrochemicals, limiting farmers' freedom and pushing them into cycles of dependency. Such dynamics have been witnessed in countries like Brazil and the Philippines, where biotechnology has fueled land consolidation and market monopolization by a handful of corporations (Howard, 2009). Furthermore, indigenous communities' seed knowledge has often been appropriated without proper consent or compensation, a practice known as biopiracy. The case of the neem tree in India and the patenting of its medicinal properties by Western companies exemplifies how traditional knowledge can be commodified without recognizing its custodians (Shiva, 2001).

The intersection of biotechnology, intellectual property, and farmers' rights reflects a deeper tension between privatized innovation and communal agricultural heritage. While biotechnology holds immense promise for addressing food security and climate resilience, its current governance structure tends to exclude the voices and rights of farmers, particularly those from indigenous and marginalized communities. As such, there is a pressing need to revisit and reform international legal frameworks to ensure that farmers are not only beneficiaries of biotechnology but also its co-creators and rights-holders. National governments must be encouraged to adopt and implement robust sui generis systems that prioritize farmers' rights, align with the ITPGRFA, and resist the restrictive impulses of UPOV 1991. Legal pluralism, community participation, and the recognition of customary law should form the backbone of a more equitable biotechnology regime—one that bridges innovation with justice and rights-based agricultural development.

FARMERS RIGHTS UNDER CORPORATE CONTROL

The biotechnology revolution in agriculture, while heralded for its transformative potential, has simultaneously catalyzed the consolidation of power in the hands of a few multinational corporations (MNCs), thereby exacerbating global inequalities and threatening the sovereignty of national agricultural systems. The most prominent firms—such as Bayer-Monsanto, Syngenta-ChemChina, BASF, and Corteva—dominate the global agro-biotech landscape, controlling vast portfolios of patented seeds, pesticides, and gene-editing technologies (Howard, 2021). This oligopolistic concentration restricts farmers' choices and undermines seed sovereignty by displacing traditional practices of seed saving, exchange, and reuse. Such dominance has been enabled through the global expansion of intellectual property (IP) regimes, especially the WTO's Trade-Related Aspects of Intellectual Property Rights (TRIPS) Agreement and the 1991 revision of the International Convention for the Protection of New Varieties of Plants (UPOV 1991), which prioritize breeders' rights over farmers' customary rights (Gonzalez, 2020). By securing exclusive rights over genetically modified organisms (GMOs) and related technologies, corporations enforce rigid contractual agreements that criminalize the unauthorized saving or replanting of seeds, pushing smallholders into cycles of dependency and legal precarity.

This corporate control directly impacts national sovereignty, particularly in the Global South, where states often lack the regulatory strength or political leverage to counterbalance the power of biotech conglomerates. When countries adopt biotech innovations—frequently under pressure from international trade agreements or development aid conditionalities—they often do so at the expense of their autonomy over agricultural policy (Shiva, 2016). For instance, in India and several African nations, the introduction of Bt cotton and other genetically engineered crops has proceeded despite contested biosafety concerns and strong resistance from farmer organizations and civil society (Stone, 2022). Such developments erode local seed systems and indigenous knowledge networks, leading to genetic erosion, cultural displacement, and the weakening of local agro-biodiversity. In many cases, states have facilitated these shifts through regulatory harmonization measures that align domestic seed laws with UPOV standards, thereby criminalizing farmers who operate outside formalized, certified seed channels (Calo, 2020). These legal shifts are not just technical adjustments; they reflect deeper ideological commitments to market-driven development models, often promoted by donor agencies, multinational firms, and global financial institutions.

Contract Farming

Contract farming—a key mechanism through which biotech firms and agribusinesses penetrate rural economies—has become a central conduit of control. Under these arrangements, farmers are bound by pre-determined agreements to produce specific crops using prescribed inputs, including patented seeds, fertilizers, and agrochemicals provided by the contracting corporation. Although contract farming is promoted as a model for integrating smallholders into global value chains and improving incomes, it frequently results in economic dependency and the erosion of autonomy. Farmers face steep input costs, fluctuating market prices, and exploitative terms that often lead to debt accumulation and, in severe cases, land loss or suicide (Patel, 2013; Ramaswamy & Gulati, 2021). Additionally, contract disputes are typically resolved under corporate arbitration mechanisms rather than through public legal institutions, thereby depriving farmers of impartial redress mechanisms. This contractual asymmetry reflects a broader neoliberal logic wherein corporate efficiency is privileged over community resilience and agrarian justice.

Compounding these challenges is the expanding role of public-private partnerships (PPPs) in biotechnology research, seed development, and agricultural extension services. While PPPs are often justified as innovative responses to underfunded public research and rural development needs, they frequently serve as vehicles for legitimizing corporate interests under the guise of public good. For instance, entities like the Alliance for a Green Revolution in Africa (AGRA) and CGIAR have increasingly partnered with biotech firms to promote genetically engineered crops and IP-intensive solutions, sidelining agroecological and farmer-led approaches (Bezner Kerr et al., 2019). These partnerships often lack transparency and accountability, especially when it comes to the governance of seed systems and benefit-sharing arrangements. The prioritization of proprietary technologies in PPP agendas reflects a commodification of agricultural innovation, whereby public resources are channeled into private gains without sufficient safeguards for equitable access, farmer consultation, or long-term sustainability (Jansen, 2020). Moreover, these partnerships blur the lines of responsibility, making it difficult to hold either public agencies or private actors accountable for socio-environmental harms resulting from biotech deployment.

In this context, power asymmetries between corporations, states, and farming communities not only widen inequalities but also challenge the democratic governance of food systems. The rise of corporate control over biotechnology has profound implications for distributive justice, particularly for smallholder farmers, indigenous groups, and women, who often rely on informal seed systems and are excluded from decision-making platforms. While corporations claim to innovate for the benefit of food security and climate resilience, their model of innovation is primarily extractive—targeting high-value crops for commercial markets rather than staple crops needed by marginalized communities. As a result, the social contract between innovation and equity is being renegotiated in ways that privilege corporate epistemologies over farmer wisdom and community-led science (Kloppenburg, 2014). Ultimately, the entrenchment of corporate power in biotechnology raises urgent questions about who controls the means of agricultural production, what types of knowledge are valued, and whose rights are protected or sacrificed in the name of progress. Without robust legal and ethical frameworks that foreground farmers' rights, cultural sovereignty, and ecological sustainability, the biotech revolution risks deepening rather than bridging the chasm between innovation and inequality. A rights-based approach that prioritizes pluralism, justice, and democratic control is essential to redirect the trajectory of biotechnology toward truly inclusive and sustainable futures.

BIOTECHNOLOGY IN AGRICULTURE: A NEED FOR REGULATION

The intersection of biotechnology and agriculture presents profound regulatory and ethical challenges, particularly in developing countries where legal and institutional infrastructures remain underdeveloped. One of the foremost concerns lies in biosafety governance, which refers to the regulation and management of risks associated with genetically modified organisms (GMOs) and other biotechnological innovations. Although international frameworks such as the Cartagena Protocol on Biosafety under the Convention on Biological Diversity (CBD) provide guidance for the safe handling and transboundary movement of GMOs, implementation remains uneven and often weak in many Global South countries (CBD, 2000). National biosafety laws frequently lack comprehensive risk assessment protocols, trained personnel, and public engagement processes. This regulatory lacuna becomes more troubling in light of rapid advancements in gene-editing technologies like CRISPR, whose long-term ecological and socio-economic impacts are still uncertain (Jasanoff et al., 2015). Compounding this is the absence of robust liability and redress mechanisms to hold developers accountable for potential environmental or socio-economic harms. Most legal regimes struggle to assign liability when GMO contamination affects non-GMO crops or indigenous seed systems, leaving smallholder farmers and indigenous communities with little recourse (Patterson, 2006).

A closely related concern is access to justice. Marginalized farming communities, especially in the Global South, often lack the legal literacy, institutional support, or financial capacity to seek redress in cases of harm caused by biotechnological products. Even where legal avenues exist, the dominance of multinational corporations and the complexity of patent regimes make litigation protracted and prohibitively expensive (Shiva, 2000). In such contexts, traditional mechanisms of justice—customary dispute resolution or community-based adjudication—are often sidelined in favor of formal legal systems that are distant, inaccessible, or non-responsive to local realities. Moreover, while human rights frameworks like the UN Declaration on the Rights of Peasants (UNDROP) emphasize access to justice and the right to participate in technological decision-making (United Nations, 2018), their legal enforceability at the national level remains limited.

Another significant challenge is enforcing benefit-sharing obligations, particularly under the International Treaty on Plant Genetic Resources for Food and Agriculture (ITPGRFA) and the Nagoya Protocol. These treaties call for equitable sharing of benefits arising from the utilization of genetic resources and associated traditional knowledge. However, practical enforcement mechanisms remain ambiguous. Many companies utilizing genetic resources from indigenous or local communities fail to enter into Access and Benefit-Sharing (ABS) agreements or do so under coercive or opaque conditions (Morgera, 2015). In several cases, the documentation of traditional knowledge is weak or non-existent, making it difficult to establish provenance and claim rights. This results in what is often termed "biopiracy"—the unauthorized commercial use of indigenous biological resources without fair compensation or acknowledgment. The failure to operationalize benefit-sharing thus exacerbates historical injustices and widens the gap between innovation and equity.

The precautionary principle, enshrined in various international environmental and health agreements, suggests that the lack of full scientific certainty should not be used as a reason for postponing cost-effective measures to prevent environmental degradation (Rio Declaration, 1992). However, in biotechnology regulation, this principle is often undermined by commercial and political pressures to fast-track approvals of new technologies in the name of food security or economic growth. In many jurisdictions, regulatory authorities lack the autonomy or capacity to rigorously assess long-term environmental and social risks, resulting in a bias toward short-term productivity gains (Levidow et al., 2005). Moreover, risk assessments typically focus on technical and biological parameters, neglecting socio-economic, ethical, and cultural considerations that are equally important in the context of agricultural biotechnology.

Participatory technology assessment (PTA) offers a promising ethical framework by involving farmers, civil society, indigenous groups, and other stakeholders in the evaluation and governance of biotechnologies. Yet, in practice, participation is often tokenistic or occurs too late in the innovation process to influence outcomes meaningfully (Stirling, 2008). True participatory governance demands not only inclusive consultation but also redistributive power in decision-making, something that current technocratic and market-driven models of innovation rarely accommodate.

To be effective, PTA must be institutionalized within national regulatory frameworks and be guided by principles of transparency, accountability, and procedural justice. Without such measures, the promise of biotechnology as a tool for inclusive and sustainable development will remain unfulfilled, deepening existing inequalities and undermining the human rights of those who feed the world.

INNOVATION IN AGRICULTURE: A RIGHT AND EQUITY BASED APPROACH FOR FARMERS

The rapid advancement of biotechnology in agriculture offers significant potential to address global food insecurity and climate challenges, yet its benefits have not been equitably distributed. As innovation accelerates, the need for a rights-based framework becomes increasingly urgent—one that not only promotes scientific advancement but also upholds the dignity, autonomy, and participation of farmers, especially those in the Global South. Bridging the gap between innovation and equity necessitates addressing systemic disparities in access to technology, resources, and decision-making power. A rights-based framework insists that innovation should be evaluated not merely on technical efficacy but on its capacity to enhance social justice, economic inclusion, and ecological sustainability (De Schutter, 2009). This begins by ensuring that farmers are not passive recipients of biotechnology but active participants in shaping its development and governance.

Farmers' participation is critical in making biotechnological innovation more democratic and contextually appropriate. Historically, dominant models of innovation have prioritized top-down approaches that marginalize indigenous knowledge systems and traditional agricultural practices (Chaudhary et al., 2018). Participatory technology development, which involves farmers at every stage—from research design to field testing and policy formulation—has been shown to yield more socially acceptable and ecologically grounded outcomes. Mechanisms such as community seed banks, participatory plant breeding, and farmer-led innovation networks exemplify inclusive models that prioritize local autonomy and sustainability. Embedding farmers' voices within biotechnology governance structures—such as regulatory boards, biosafety committees, and seed certification systems—can counterbalance the influence of multinational corporations and ensure that innovations reflect local realities and ethical concerns (Andersen & Winge, 2013). Moreover, respecting the principle of free, prior, and informed consent (FPIC) is essential to uphold farmers' rights, especially in indigenous and tribal communities.

Another pillar of equitable innovation lies in reimagining intellectual property regimes to better align with human rights and distributive justice. Current intellectual property laws, rooted in the TRIPS Agreement and UPOV 1991, tend to privilege corporate patents over communal and traditional knowledge, often criminalizing practices like seed saving, sharing, and exchange (Rajagopal, 2003). This legal asymmetry exacerbates power imbalances and threatens farmers' autonomy and seed sovereignty. A rights-based reconfiguration of intellectual property should incorporate safeguards that recognize the collective contributions of farming communities to agrobiodiversity and agricultural knowledge. The International Treaty on Plant Genetic Resources for Food and Agriculture (ITPGRFA) and the Nagoya Protocol on Access and Benefit Sharing offer models for integrating benefit-sharing and community rights into intellectual property frameworks. Such reforms could include sui generis systems that permit seed reuse, community ownership over traditional knowledge, and obligations for companies to contribute to biodiversity conservation (Brush, 2005). Aligning intellectual property laws with human rights principles means ensuring that the right to food, the right to culture, and the right to development are not subordinated to commercial interests.

Promoting open-source biotechnology and community-led innovation can further democratize access and disrupt monopolistic control over agricultural technologies. Open-source models—akin to those in software development—enable collaborative innovation while ensuring transparency and freedom to operate. Initiatives like the Open-Source Seed Initiative (OSSI) exemplify how seeds can be shared and improved upon without proprietary restrictions, fostering innovation within ecological and social boundaries (Kloppenburg, 2014). These models support a paradigm shift from competitive, market-driven biotech development to cooperative, commons-based innovation that respects community knowledge and ecological integrity. Community-led research initiatives, especially those housed within universities, public agricultural institutes, or civil society organizations, have a critical role in co-producing technologies with farmers rather than for them. Such approaches nurture local innovation ecosystems that are resilient, inclusive, and sustainable, offering a credible alternative to the corporate-led biotechnology pipeline.

A rights-based framework for equitable innovation must be multidimensional—addressing structural inequalities, legal asymmetries, and participation deficits simultaneously. It must recognize farmers not merely as beneficiaries but as co-creators of agricultural knowledge and technology. By fostering inclusive governance, revising exclusionary intellectual property regimes, and scaling open-access models, biotechnology can be reoriented toward justice rather than just yield. This transformation demands political will, institutional reform, and a fundamental rethinking of the purposes and beneficiaries of innovation. Ultimately, aligning biotechnology with the imperatives of human rights and equity is not just a normative goal—it is a practical necessity for achieving truly sustainable development and food sovereignty.

CONCLUSION AND SUGGESTIONS

Biotechnology in agriculture stands at a critical juncture—celebrated for its transformative potential yet critiqued for deepening existing socio-economic divides. This chapter has traced how modern biotechnological interventions, while enhancing productivity and resilience in agriculture, simultaneously disrupt traditional farming systems, marginalize smallholder farmers, and consolidate power within a narrow cluster of multinational corporations. It has highlighted how the expansion of intellectual property regimes and seed patents curtail farmers' centuries-old rights to save, share, and cultivate their own seeds. As a result, biotechnology emerges not merely as a technical field, but as a contested terrain shaped by the competing forces of innovation and inequality.

The issues discussed above underscores the urgent need for a paradigm shift—a move away from corporate-centric innovation models toward governance frameworks that place farmers' rights and human dignity at their core. A rights-based approach to biotechnology recognizes farmers not only as beneficiaries or consumers of innovation but as active custodians of biodiversity, traditional knowledge, and food systems. Such an approach must be pluralistic and inclusive, embracing diverse epistemologies and ensuring that indigenous practices and local contexts inform technological development and policy.

Looking ahead, the future of agricultural innovation must be recalibrated toward justice and sustainability. This entails reimagining biotechnological research and governance through participatory mechanisms, transparent benefit-sharing, and legal safeguards that empower rural communities. By centering the agency of farmers and aligning technological advancement with human rights principles, biotechnology can evolve from a tool of exclusion to an instrument of empowerment. Only through inclusive, accountable, and ecologically sound innovation can the promise of biotechnology be fully realized in service of global food security, environmental sustainability, and the equitable flourishing of all farming communities.

Policy Recommendations

To address the growing disjunction between agricultural biotechnology and farmers' rights, a robust policy framework is essential. First, strengthening national and international legal protections for farmers is critical. Countries must align their laws with human rights instruments like the UN Declaration on the Rights of Peasants (UNDROP), while ensuring domestic legislation—such as plant variety protection acts—respects farmers' traditional rights to save, use, exchange, and sell seeds. International treaties like the ITPGRFA should be enforced with binding benefit-sharing mechanisms to counteract the exploitative tendencies of global intellectual property regimes.

Second, there is an urgent need to mandate corporate accountability and transparency in biotech deployment. Biotech corporations must be compelled to disclose research data, environmental impacts, and socio-economic implications of their technologies. Transparent licensing arrangements and fair contracts are essential to prevent exploitative practices in seed distribution and genetically modified crop promotion, especially among smallholders.

Third, enhancing legal literacy and institutional support for rural communities must be prioritized. Farmers often lack awareness of their rights under international and domestic legal frameworks. Establishing grassroots legal aid services, farmer education programs, and participatory rural governance mechanisms will empower communities to assert their rights and negotiate fairer terms with agribusiness entities.

Finally, supporting agroecological and rights-based research as alternatives to corporate-led biotechnology is a key step toward sustainability. Public investment in non-proprietary, community-driven innovation—rooted in traditional knowledge and ecological resilience—offers a democratic and equitable path forward. Policymakers must create enabling environments for such research by redirecting subsidies, incentivizing public sector innovation, and integrating local knowledge systems into agricultural R&D agendas. These recommendations collectively seek to realign innovation with justice, ensuring that biotechnological advancement serves the long-term interests of farmers, food systems, and society at large.

REFERENCES

Andersen, R. (2008). *Governing Agrobiodiversity: Plant Genetics and Developing Countries*. Routledge.

Andersen, R., & Winge, T. (2013). *Realising Farmers' Rights to Crop Genetic Resources: Success Stories and Best Practices*. Earthscan.

Benbrook, C. M. (2012). Impacts of genetically engineered crops on pesticide use in the U.S.—The first sixteen years. *Environmental Sciences Europe*, *24*(1), 24. DOI: 10.1186/2190-4715-24-24

Beyer, P., Al-Babili, S., Ye, X., Lucca, P., Schaub, P., Welsch, R., & Potrykus, I. (2002). Golden Rice: Introducing the β-carotene biosynthesis pathway into rice endosperm by genetic engineering. *Science*, *287*(5451), 303–305. PMID: 11880581

Bezner Kerr, R., Snapp, S., Chirwa, M., Shumba, L., & Msachi, R. (2019). Participatory, agroecological and gender-sensitive approaches to improved nutrition: A case study from Malawi. *Agriculture & Food Security*, *8*(1), 1–13. DOI: 10.1186/s40066-019-0273-4

Brahmi, P., Saxena, S., & Dhillon, B. S. (2018). Intellectual property rights in agriculture: Implications for food security and farmers' rights. *Journal of Intellectual Property Rights*, *23*(2), 64–71.

Brush, S. B. (2005). Protecting Traditional Agricultural Knowledge. *Washington University Journal of Law and Policy*, *17*, 59–109.

Cairns, J. E., Hellin, J., Sonder, K., Araus, J. L., MacRobert, J. F., Thierfelder, C., & Prasanna, B. M. (2013). Adapting maize production to climate change in sub-Saharan Africa. *Food Security*, *5*(3), 345–360.

Calo, M. (2020). Scaling Agroecology from the Bottom-Up: Six Domains of Transformation. *Agriculture and Human Values*, *37*, 355–369. DOI: 10.1007/s10460-019-09951-w

CBD. (2000). *Cartagena Protocol on Biosafety to the Convention on Biological Diversity*. Secretariat of the Convention on Biological Diversity.

CBD. (2011). *Nagoya Protocol on Access to Genetic Resources and the Fair and Equitable Sharing of Benefits Arising from their Utilization to the Convention on Biological Diversity*. Secretariat of the CBD.

Chaudhary, S., McGregor, A., Houston, D., & Chettri, N. (2018). Reconceptualizing participation in conservation: Towards resilience through engaged political ecology. *Biological Conservation, 218*, 242–251.

Cleveland, D. A., Soleri, D., & Smith, S. E. (2000). A biological framework for understanding farmers' plant breeding. *Economic Botany, 54*(3), 377–394.

Daes, E.-I. A. (2001). *Protection of the heritage of indigenous people: Final report.* UN Sub-Commission on the Promotion and Protection of Human Rights.

De Schutter, O. (2009). *Seed policies and the right to food: Enhancing agrobiodiversity and encouraging innovation.* United Nations.

FAO. (2009). *International Treaty on Plant Genetic Resources for Food and Agriculture.* Food and Agriculture Organization of the United Nations.

Glover, D. (2010). The corporate shaping of GM crops as a technology for the poor. *The Journal of Peasant Studies, 37*(1), 67–90.

Gonzalez, C. G. (2020). International economic law and the right to food. In Andreassen, B., & Ulfstein, H. (Eds.), *Research Handbook on Human Rights and Poverty* (pp. 201–220). Edward Elgar.

Gruère, G. P., Mehta-Bhatt, P., & Sengupta, D. (2008). Bt cotton and farmer suicides in India: Reviewing the evidence. *International Food Policy Research Institute (IFPRI) Discussion Paper 00808.*

Gruère, G. P., & Sengupta, D. (2011). Bt cotton and farmer suicides in India: An evidence-based assessment. *The Journal of Development Studies, 47*(2), 316–337. PMID: 21506303

Howard, P. H. (2009). Visualizing consolidation in the global seed industry: 1996–2008. *Sustainability, 1*(4), 1266–1287.

Howard, P. H. (2015). Intellectual property and consolidation in the seed industry. *Crop Science, 55*(6), 2489–2495.

Howard, P. H. (2021). *Concentration and Power in the Food System: Who Controls What We Eat?* (2nd ed.). Bloomsbury Publishing.

Ishii, T., & Araki, M. (2016). Consumer acceptance of food crops developed by genome editing. *Plant Cell Reports, 35*(7), 1507–151. PMID: 27038939

Jansen, K. (2020). The debate on public–private partnerships and their implications for agricultural development and food sovereignty. *The Journal of Peasant Studies, 47*(4), 805–832. DOI: 10.1080/03066150.2020.1743065

Jasanoff, S., Hurlbut, J. B., & Saha, K. (2015). CRISPR democracy: Gene editing and the need for inclusive deliberation. *Issues in Science and Technology*, *32*(1), 25–32.

Jinek, M., Chylinski, K., Fonfara, I., Hauer, M., Doudna, J. A., & Charpentier, E. (2012). A programmable dual-RNA–guided DNA endonuclease in adaptive bacterial immunity. *Science*, *337*(6096), 816–821. PMID: 22745249

Khalil, A. S., & Collins, J. J. (2010). Synthetic biology: Applications come of age. *Nature Reviews. Genetics*, *11*(5), 367–379. PMID: 20395970

Kloppenburg, J. (2010). Impeding dispossession, enabling repossession: Biological open source and the recovery of seed sovereignty. *Journal of Agrarian Change*, *10*(3), 367–388.

Kloppenburg, J. (2014). *First the Seed: The Political Economy of Plant Biotechnology, 1492–2000* (2nd ed.). University of Wisconsin Press.

Klümper, W., & Qaim, M. (2014). A meta-analysis of the impacts of genetically modified crops. *PLoS One*, *9*(11), e111629. DOI: 10.1371/journal.pone.0111629 PMID: 25365303

Lacy, W. B. (2017). The paradox of agricultural biotechnology. In Koushik, K. O. (Ed.), *Agriculture, food and biodiversity* (pp. 141–162). Springer.

Leach, M., Scoones, I., & Stirling, A. (2020). Governing epidemics in an age of science and uncertainty. *Social Studies of Science*, *50*(4), 610–638.

Leskien, D., & Flitner, M. (1997). *Intellectual property rights and plant genetic resources: Options for a sui generis system*. IPGRI.

Levidow, L., Carr, S., & Wield, D. (2005). European Union regulation of agri-biotechnology: Precautionary links between science, expertise and policy. *Science & Public Policy*, *32*(4), 261–276.

Morgera, E. (2015). The Need for an International Legal Concept of Fair and Equitable Benefit Sharing. *European Journal of International Law*, *27*(2), 353–383.

Patel, R. (2013). *Stuffed and Starved: The Hidden Battle for the World Food System*. Melville House.

Patterson, L. A. (2006). Agricultural biotechnology and intellectual property: Seeds of change or an uneven playing field? *The Drake Journal of Agricultural Law*, *11*(2), 239–258.

Posey, D. A., & Dutfield, G. (1996). *Beyond Intellectual Property: Toward Traditional Resource Rights for Indigenous Peoples and Local Communities*. IDRC.

Qaim, M. (2020). *Genetically Modified Crops and Agricultural Development.* Palgrave Macmillan.

Rajagopal, B. (2003). *International Law from Below: Development, Social Movements and Third World Resistance.* Cambridge University Press.

Ramaswamy, N. S., & Gulati, A. (2021). *Contract farming in India: Enhancing farmer income. Indian Council for Research on International Economic Relations.* ICRIER.

Robinson, D. F. (2010). *Confronting Biopiracy: Challenges, Cases and International Debates.* Earthscan.

Scoones, I. (2002). *Science, policy and regulation: Challenges for agricultural biotechnology in developing countries.* IDS Working Paper 147.

Shiva, V. (2001). *Protect or Plunder? Understanding Intellectual Property Rights.* Zed Books.

Shiva, V. (2004). The suicide economy of corporate globalization. *The Ecologist, 32*(6), 28–31.

Shiva, V. (2016). *The Violence of the Green Revolution: Third World Agriculture, Ecology and Politics.* University Press of Kentucky.

Stirling, A. (2008). "Opening up" and "closing down": Power, participation, and pluralism in the social appraisal of technology. *Science, Technology & Human Values, 33*(2), 262–294.

Stone, G. D. (2011). Field versus farm in Warangal: Bt cotton, higher yields, and larger questions. *World Development, 39*(3), 387–398.

UN General Assembly. (1966). *International Covenant on Economic.* Social and Cultural Rights.

UN Human Rights Council. (2018). *United Nations Declaration on the Rights of Peasants and Other People Working in Rural Areas.*

Varshney, R. K., Bohra, A., Yu, J., Graner, A., Zhang, Q., & Sorrells, M. E. (2021). Designing future crops: Genomics-assisted breeding comes of age. *Trends in Plant Science, 26*(6), 631–649. PMID: 33893045

WTO. (1994). *Agreement on Trade-Related Aspects of Intellectual Property Rights.* Retrieved from https://www.wto.org/

Chapter 14

Bridging the Digital Divide and Improving Access for Students With Disabilities in Higher Education

Marubini Christinah Sadiki
https://orcid.org/0009-0001-3655-9610
University of South Africa, South Africa

Nthabiseng Istorina Mahetlana
University of South Africa, South Africa

ABSTRACT

The digital divide continues to be a significant barrier to education, disproportionately affecting students with disabilities. This chapter explores the challenges these students face in accessing digital resources and the strategies necessary to create a more inclusive digital learning environment. Key areas of focus include accessible technology, assistive devices, inclusive design principles, and policy frameworks that support equitable access. By integrating universal learning design (UDL) and leveraging advances in assistive technologies, educational institutions can bridge the digital divide and foster a more inclusive learning experience. The chapter highlights best practices, case studies, and recommendations for policymakers, educators, and technology developers to enhance accessibility and ensure that all students, regardless of ability, have equal opportunities to succeed in a digital world.

DOI: 10.4018/979-8-3373-2387-9.ch014

INTRODUCTION

In an increasingly digital world, access to technology and online learning has become essential for success in higher education (Alenezi, 2023). However, students with disabilities often face significant barriers that hinder their ability to participate fully in digital learning environments. Higher education institutions must prioritise inclusive and accessible education by implementing policies, technologies, and teaching strategies that ensure equitable student access (Yadav, 2024). This includes providing assistive technologies, developing universally designed learning materials, and ensuring compliance with digital accessibility standards (Sanderson et al., 2022). Additionally, financial constraints, lack of awareness, and institutional challenges further exacerbate the difficulties faced by students with disabilities in accessing digital learning (Matsieli & Mutula, 2024). This chapter explores the challenges and opportunities associated with bridging the digital divide for students with disabilities in higher education. It examines the role of technology, institutional policies, and pedagogical approaches in fostering an inclusive learning environment.

The rapid shift to digital learning has transformed higher education, offering flexibility, accessibility, and new opportunities for students worldwide (Mohamed Hashim et al., 2022). However, for students with disabilities, the digital divide remains a significant barrier to full participation in academic life (Johansson et al., 2021). The digital divide refers to disparities in access to technology, internet connectivity, and digital literacy, which disproportionately impact marginalised groups, including individuals with disabilities (Raihan et al., 2024). Without intentional efforts to bridge this gap, higher education institutions risk excluding students who require accessible learning environments (Smith, 2024). Bridging the digital divide in higher education is essential to promote inclusivity and ensure equal opportunities for students with disabilities (Memon & Memon, 2025). By implementing accessible technology, inclusive teaching strategies, and institutional policies, universities can create a learning environment where all students, regardless of ability, can thrive (Ngqunguza et al., 2024). Moving toward a more inclusive digital education system is a legal and ethical responsibility and a step toward more significant social equity in higher education (Lambert, 2020). In an era where digital education is rapidly becoming the norm, ensuring inclusivity in higher education is both a legal and ethical obligation and a crucial step toward more significant social equity (Brighouse & McPherson, 2022). The shift to online learning has created new opportunities for accessibility, but it has also exposed and intensified existing inequalities, particularly for students with disabilities and those of marginalised backgrounds. Students with disabilities face barriers such as limited access to technology, inaccessible digital platforms, and lack of institutional support, which prevent them from fully engaging in academic opportunities (Ersoy,2023).

A genuinely inclusive digital education system goes beyond mere compliance with accessibility regulations. It requires a commitment to equitable access, adaptive learning strategies, and institutional transformation (Sato et al., 2023). By prioritising universal design, assistive technologies, and inclusive policies, higher education institutions can create learning environments where all students, regardless of ability or background, can thrive (Oyedokun, 2025). This chapter explores the significance of digital inclusion in higher education, highlighting its impact on social equity and proposing strategies to ensure that online learning is accessible and empowering for all. The digital transformation of higher education has created new opportunities for learning, collaboration, and academic success. However, for students with disabilities, the digital divide and the gap in access to technology, digital literacy, and inclusive learning resources continue to pose significant challenges (Afzal et al., 2023). Without targeted interventions, these students' risk being excluded from the full benefits of digital education, reinforcing systemic inequalities in higher learning institutions (Salmi & D'Addio, 2021).

THE DIGITAL DIVIDE AND ITS IMPACT ON STUDENTS WITH DISABILITIES

The concept of the digital divide has been a subject of growing concern in the context of higher education, particularly as it pertains to students with disabilities. The rapid adoption of digital technologies in academic settings has the potential to offer students new opportunities for learning and engagement. However, for students with disabilities, accessing these opportunities can be challenging due to a variety of barriers that inhibit their ability to participate in digital learning environments fully. The digital divide refers to the gap between those with access to modern information and communication technologies (ICTs) and those without (Hankerson & Brown, 2020).

In the context of higher education, the digital divide can manifest in various ways, including disparities in access to digital devices, internet connectivity, digital literacy, and the availability of accessible digital content (Van Dijk, 2020). While the digital divide originally referred to general disparities in technology access, it has become increasingly relevant in education due to the integration of digital learning tools, online courses, and virtual classrooms in academic institutions. As higher education institutions increasingly rely on digital platforms for course delivery, assessments, and communication, students lacking access to these technologies are disadvantaged significantly (Burgstahler, 2015). For students with disabilities, the digital divide is not solely about access to technology but also the accessibility of the technologies themselves. Digital platforms and content are often designed with a one-size-fits-all approach that does not consider the diverse needs of students with disabilities, creating additional barriers to academic participation and success (Seale, 2013). The digital divide in this context involves both the physical availability of technology and the ability to use that technology effectively and inclusively.

EXPLORING THE UNIQUE BARRIERS FACED BY STUDENTS WITH DISABILITIES IN ACCESSING DIGITAL RESOURCES

Digital resources in higher education face technological barriers that hinder accessibility for students with disabilities. For example, students with visual impairments often struggle with digital content incompatible with screen readers, while those with hearing impairments may find multimedia content without captions challenging (Kimogol, (2023). Furthermore, students with mobility impairments may struggle to navigate websites requiring precise movements. In addition to these technological issues, pedagogical barriers exist. Faculty may lack training in creating accessible digital content and utilising assistive technologies, leading to inadequate course materials and assessments (Seale, 2013). Online course structures may also fail to accommodate diverse learning styles, limiting meaningful engagement for students with disabilities. Social barriers further compound these challenges, as using assistive technologies can lead to stigma and isolation among students. This self-consciousness can hinder participation in public and virtual learning environments (Al-Azawei et al., 2016). Moreover, there is often a scarcity of peer support networks or mentorship programs to assist these students in navigating their educational experiences.

EXAMINING THE DISPARITIES IN ACCESS TO TECHNOLOGY AND INTERNET CONNECTIVITY THAT AFFECT STUDENTS WITH DISABILITIES

Access to technology and reliable internet connectivity is essential for participation in modern higher education. Students with disabilities often encounter disparities in accessing these resources, which can adversely affect their academic success. Students lack access to necessary technology, such as specialised devices (e.g., braille displays and adaptive keyboards), which can be costly and unavailable to all (Kyei, 2023). Additionally, students may not have standard devices like computers or smartphones, which are needed for accessing course materials. Reliable internet access is equally important, as students with disabilities live in areas with limited high-speed internet options or face financial barriers, hindering their ability to engage with online courses and resources (Van Dijk, 2020). Consequently, these challenges can widen the gap between students with disabilities and their peers significantly when reliance on specific online tools is affected by poor connectivity.

THE SOCIO-ECONOMIC FACTORS CONTRIBUTING TO THE DIGITAL DIVIDE FOR STUDENTS WITH DISABILITIES

The socio-economic status of students with disabilities significantly impacts their access to digital resources in higher education, with income disparities and geographic location being key factors (Van Dijk, 2020). Students from lower-income backgrounds often struggle to afford necessary technology and high-speed internet, which is exacerbated for those needing specialised assistive technologies (Burgstahler, 2015). Additionally, students in rural or remote areas may encounter barriers due to inadequate infrastructure and limited local support services, making obtaining and maintaining essential digital tools challenging (Van Dijk, 2020). The level of institutional support for students with disabilities can also significantly influence their access to digital resources. Higher education institutions may offer robust programs that provide assistive technologies, digital literacy training, and technical support for students with disabilities. However, other institutions may lack the resources or commitment to provide these services, exacerbating the digital divide (Seale, 2013). Students at institutions with limited support may find themselves further marginalised in digital learning environments.

THE ROLE OF ASSISTIVE TECHNOLOGY IN BRIDGING THE DIGITAL DIVIDE

Assistive technology (AT) is essential for bridging the digital divide for students with disabilities and facilitating their participation in increasingly digital higher education environments (Jackson, 2023). These technologies ensure equal access to educational resources for students with disabilities. Common forms of AT include:

- *Screen Readers*: These software applications convert text to speech or braille, allowing visually impaired students to access digital content. Notable screen readers include JAWS, NVDA, and Voice Over (Burgstahler, 2015).
- *Voice Recognition Software*: This technology lets users control devices and input text via voice, providing a hands-free option for students with physical impairments. Dragon NaturallySpeaking is a prominent example (Al-Azawei et al, 2016).

- *Adaptive Keyboards and Mice*: Designed for mobility impairments, these devices feature customisable layouts and alternative input methods, enabling effective engagement with digital platforms (Seale, 2013).
- *Braille Displays:* These devices translate digital text into braille, allowing visually impaired students to read digital content through touch, thus providing access to essential academic materials (Burgstahler, 2015).

HOW ASSISTIVE TECHNOLOGY CAN SUPPORT STUDENTS WITH DISABILITIES IN DIGITAL LEARNING ENVIRONMENTS

Assistive technology (AT) is crucial in fostering an inclusive learning environment in higher education by providing essential tools that enhance academic achievement for students with disabilities. Key benefits include enhanced access to digital content, as tools like screen readers and voice recognition software enable students with visual and mobility impairments to interact effectively with educational materials (Jackson, 2023). Additionally, AT promotes independence by empowering students to perform tasks autonomously, such as using adaptive keyboards and Braille displays, which boosts their confidence and academic performance (Burgstahler, 2015). It also facilitates communication and collaboration, allowing students with disabilities to participate in group discussions and virtual classrooms through tools like speech-to-text software (Seale, 2013). Moreover, AT supports diverse learning styles by providing customisable options, such as text-to-speech tools for those with dyslexia and Braille formats for visually impaired students, ensuring that all learners can engage with content in a manner that suits their needs (Al-Azawei et al., 2016).

ACCESSIBILITY OF ASSISTIVE TECHNOLOGY IN HIGHER EDUCATION AND HOW INSTITUTIONS CAN SUPPORT ITS IMPLEMENTATION

Assistive technology (AT) has significant potential to enhance accessibility for students with disabilities in higher education, but its practical implementation is not always assured. To promote equitable access, institutions should provide a range of AT tools, such as screen readers and adaptive keyboards, and ensure these tools are compatible with digital platforms (Burgstahler, 2015). Training is crucial; faculty and students need education on the effective use of AT and accessible digital content design, with dedicated support available for troubleshooting (Seale, 2013). Furthermore, institutions must establish policies prioritising digital accessibility and integration of AT, ensuring compliance with standards like the Web Content

Accessibility Guidelines (WCAG). Financial assistance for AT through aid packages or grants can also enhance accessibility for needy students (Al-Azawei et al., 2016).

CHALLENGES RELATED TO THE AFFORDABILITY AND AVAILABILITY OF ASSISTIVE TECHNOLOGIES

Despite the clear benefits of assistive technologies, there are challenges related to their affordability and availability, which can impede their widespread use in higher education. One of the most significant barriers to the widespread use of assistive technologies is their cost. Assistive technologies, such as Braille displays, screen readers, and adaptive keyboards, can be expensive, often costing hundreds to thousands of dollars. For students from low-income backgrounds, this financial burden can prevent them from acquiring the necessary tools to succeed in higher education (Seale, 2013). While institutions may offer these tools for free or at a reduced cost, the lack of comprehensive funding options can limit accessibility for students with disabilities. The availability of specialised assistive technology equipment may also be limited, particularly in under-resourced institutions. Smaller or less-funded institutions may not have the necessary budget to provide assistive technologies to all students who need them. Additionally, students may face difficulties accessing specialised AT equipment in remote areas or countries with limited access to technology (Al-Azawei et al., 2016). The lack of infrastructure to support the distribution and maintenance of AT tools can further exacerbate disparities in access. Even when institutions provide access to assistive technologies, students may encounter compatibility and integration issues with digital platforms used in higher education. Digital tools may not be fully compatible with screen readers, voice recognition software, or other assistive devices, making it difficult for students to access course content and participate in online activities. Ensuring that digital platforms and content are fully accessible requires ongoing collaboration between IT departments, faculty, and disability support services to ensure that accessibility standards are met (Burgstahler, 2015).

UNIVERSAL DESIGN FOR LEARNING (UDL) AND DIGITAL ACCESSIBILITY

Universal Design for Learning (UDL) is an educational framework that provides equitable learning opportunities for all students, irrespective of their abilities or disabilities. Grounded in neuroscience, UDL advocates for flexible learning environments that remove barriers through varied instructional strategies, materials, and assessments (CAST, 2018). It highlights the importance of engaging students through multiple means, recognising that different individuals are motivated by various stimuli, whether visual, interactive, or practical (Mansell, 2023). UDL also emphasises presenting information in diverse formats to accommodate students with disabilities, ensuring all learners can access content (CAST, 2018). Furthermore, it allows students to demonstrate their learning in varied ways, fostering equity by aligning assessments with individual strengths (Saborío-Taylor & Rojas-Ramírez, 2024). In digital environments, UDL principles promote accessibility, integrating elements like alternative text, keyboard navigation, and screen reader compatibility to support all learners (CAST, 2018).

THE IMPORTANCE OF DESIGNING DIGITAL CONTENT, WEBSITES, AND PLATFORMS THAT ARE ACCESSIBLE TO ALL STUDENTS, INCLUDING THOSE WITH DISABILITIES

The digital transformation of higher education has introduced new opportunities for students to engage with content innovatively. However, this shift also challenges students with disabilities, who may face barriers to accessing digital materials if not designed with accessibility in mind. Designing accessible digital content, websites, and platforms is crucial for fostering inclusivity and ensuring that all students can participate fully in their learning experiences, regardless of their abilities. Students with disabilities often rely on specific assistive technologies like screen readers or voice recognition software to access digital content. If educational materials, websites, or platforms are not designed to be compatible with these tools, students with disabilities may be unable to engage with the content effectively. For instance, images without alternative text (alt text) prevent screen reader users from understanding visual content, and videos without captions or transcripts exclude students with hearing impairments from accessing auditory information. By incorporating accessibility features, such as alt text, captions, and accessible navigation, digital content becomes usable for a broader range of students (Burgstahler, 2015).

In countries like the United States, higher education institutions are legally required to provide accessible learning environments for students with disabilities. Legislation such as the Americans with Disabilities Act (ADA) mandates that institutions ensure digital resources, including websites and learning management systems, are accessible to all students (Seale, 2013). By designing accessible digital content, institutions comply with legal requirements and are committed to inclusivity and equity in education. The digital divide, which refers to disparities in access to technology, is a significant issue for students with disabilities. Without accessible digital content, these students may be excluded from online courses, digital libraries, or interactive learning modules. Ensuring that digital platforms are designed with accessibility helps bridge this divide and creates a more equitable learning environment. It allows students with disabilities to participate fully in educational experiences, just as their peers do, which promotes a sense of belonging and inclusion (Burgstahler, 2015).

CREATING INCLUSIVE DIGITAL LEARNING ENVIRONMENTS

Creating accessible online courses is essential for fostering an inclusive digital learning environment. Key practices include using clear and consistent layouts, which benefit students with disabilities by promoting easy navigation and organisation (Seale, 2013). Providing text alternatives for non-text content, such as alt text for images and captions for videos, is crucial for students with visual and auditory impairments (Burgstahler, 2015). Moreover, ensuring that all course documents follow best design practices such as structured headings and readable fonts enhances accessibility and compatibility with assistive technologies (Seale, 2013). Offering multimodal learning resources aligns with the Universal Design for Learning (UDL) framework, as it accommodates various learning preferences by providing content in multiple formats (CAST, 2018). Lastly, incorporating interactive and engaging elements, such as accessible quizzes and discussions, promotes a more inclusive learning atmosphere while encouraging student participation (Al-Azawei et al., 2016).

The Importance of Accessible Digital Platforms (e.g., Learning Management Systems, Video Conferencing Tools) for Students with Disabilities

Accessible digital platforms are essential for inclusive digital learning environments, mainly through Learning Management Systems (LMS) and video conferencing tools. LMS platforms like Canvas, Moodle, and Blackboard must support screen readers, keyboard navigation, and customisable interfaces to ensure equitable access for students with disabilities. Features such as video captioning and text-to-speech tools are also vital, with adherence to Web Content Accessibility Guidelines (WCAG) being crucial in creating inclusive settings (Burgstahler, 2015). Regarding video conferencing, tools such as Zoom and Microsoft Teams must incorporate live captioning, sign language interpretation, and screen reader compatibility. Zoom's automatic captioning serves students with hearing impairments well, and providing transcripts enhances accessibility for all students (Burgstahler, 2015). Moreover, mobile accessibility is critical as learners access content via mobile devices; thus, features like adjustable text size and responsive design must be prioritised to ensure that all students can participate fully (Seale, 2013).

Strategies for Instructors to Accommodate Diverse Learning Needs in Digital Education Settings

Instructors are crucial in accommodating the diverse learning needs of students in digital education, especially for those with disabilities. To create an inclusive environment, they should provide clear, step-by-step instructions for assignments and utilise written and visual aids to enhance understanding (Seale, 2013). Flexible assessment methods, such as offering alternative formats and extended deadlines, can support diverse learning styles and help manage workloads for students with specific disabilities (Al-Azawei et al., 2016). Encouraging assistive technologies like screen readers and voice recognition software can further enhance accessibility and support (CAST, 2018). Additionally, fostering a sense of community through peer interaction and collaboration is essential for all students, particularly those with disabilities, as it helps them feel connected to their peers and learning environment (Al-Azawei et al., 2016).

The Role of Digital Course Design in Fostering an Inclusive and Equitable Educational Experience

Digital course design is essential for creating an inclusive and equitable educational environment, particularly by considering the needs of students with disabilities from the start. Applying Universal Design for Learning (UDL) principles helps ensure accessibility by allowing flexibility in how students engage with content, which includes providing materials in various formats (CAST, 2018). Additionally, building accessible content from the outset, such as clear navigation and alternative text for images, helps prevent barriers to learning (Burgstahler, 2015). Furthermore, engaging diverse learners through interactive technologies, like discussion boards and collaborative tools, enhances participation and allows students to demonstrate their knowledge in various ways, promoting inclusivity (Al-Azawei et al., 2016).

POLICY FRAMEWORKS FOR SUPPORTING DIGITAL ACCESSIBILITY IN HIGHER EDUCATION

The Americans with Disabilities Act (ADA) and Section 508 in the United States

In the U.S., the *Americans with Disabilities Act* (ADA) of 1990 is a cornerstone legislation to ensure that individuals with disabilities have equal access to public services, including education. Title II of the ADA mandates that public colleges and universities must provide digital resources and services accessible to students with disabilities. Section 508 of the *Rehabilitation Act of 1973* further complements the ADA by requiring federal agencies and educational institutions that receive federal funding to ensure their electronic and information technology is accessible to people with disabilities (U.S. Department of Justice, 2020).

The European Accessibility Act (EAA)

In Europe, the *European Accessibility Act* (EAA), implemented in 2019, is a significant policy that mandates the accessibility of a wide range of services, including e-learning platforms and online education tools. The act stipulates that higher education institutions within the European Union must ensure that their digital platforms, websites, and educational content comply with accessibility standards (European Commission, 2019). It promotes equal access to digital education by mandating that institutions take concrete actions to make their online environments accessible to all learners, including those with disabilities.

UNESCO's *Convention on the Rights of Persons with Disabilities (CRPD)* and Global Educational Policies

Internationally, UNESCO's *Convention on the Rights of Persons with Disabilities* (CRPD), adopted by the United Nations in 2006, provides a global framework for promoting inclusive education. Article 24 of the CRPD emphasises the right to inclusive education for students with disabilities and calls on governments to ensure accessibility to information, including digital resources, in educational settings. This convention has been instrumental in shaping educational policies that support digital accessibility in countries worldwide (UNESCO, 2006).

The Web Content Accessibility Guidelines (WCAG)

While not a policy per se, the *Web Content Accessibility Guidelines* (WCAG) developed by the World Wide Web Consortium (W3C) have become a global standard for digital accessibility. These guidelines provide recommendations for making web content, including e-learning platforms, accessible to people with disabilities. Countries, including the U.S. and European Union members, use WCAG as the technical basis for national accessibility laws (W3C, 2018).

South African Policies that Address Digital Accessibility in Higher Education Reflect a Broader Commitment to Inclusivity and Social Justice in Education

The White Paper on Post-School Education and Training (2013) establishes a framework for inclusive education in South Africa, particularly emphasizing the need to improve access for marginalized groups, including students with disabilities. It calls for the development of inclusive systems and accessible digital learning environments (Department of Higher Education and Training, 2013). Similarly, the Disability Framework for Higher Education (2016) provides guidelines for higher education institutions to enhance accessibility for students with disabilities, advocating for the adoption of assistive technologies and training for faculty (Department of Higher Education and Training, 2016). The National Integrated ICT Policy White Paper (2016) promotes the use of Information and Communication Technologies (ICT) to advance socio-economic development and calls for accessible digital infrastructure, specifically benefiting students with disabilities (Department of Telecommunications and Postal Services, 2016). The National Development Plan (NDP) 2030 outlines broader education goals that support inclusive education systems and access to digital resources for all students, including those with disabilities (National Planning Commission, 2012). Finally, the South African Disability Act (1998), though older, emphasizes the elimination of barriers that inhibit participation in education, reinforcing the need for inclusivity within educational institutions.

The Role of Governmental and Educational Policies in Promoting Accessible Digital Education

Governmental and educational policies are essential for promoting accessible digital education by establishing legal standards and providing guidance for implementation. Legal frameworks such as the ADA and Section 508 mandate accessibility, ensuring institutions are accountable for creating inclusive digital environments through regular assessments and staff training (Burgstahler, 2015).

While government policies set the legal foundation, institutions must actively integrate these regulations into their digital infrastructures, conduct accessibility audits, and foster collaboration among stakeholders like IT departments and disability support services (Seale, 2013). Additionally, financial support for digital accessibility initiatives is crucial, as it enables funding for assistive technologies and training resources (National Centre on Disability and Access to Education, 2020). Finally, governmental efforts to raise awareness and build institutional capacity can shift the perspective on accessibility from mere compliance to viewing it as a benefit for all students (Burgstahler, 2015).

The Need for Stronger Enforcement of Digital Accessibility Laws and Standards

Despite advancements in digital accessibility policies, stronger enforcement is essential for effective implementation, ensuring students with disabilities receive the necessary support. Current enforcement efforts are insufficient; institutions do not adhere to standards, and minimal penalties for non-compliance leave significant accessibility barriers unaddressed (Seale, 2013). To enhance enforcement, it is recommended that governments mandate regular accessibility audits for educational platforms and incorporate accessibility into accreditation processes, thus incentivizing institutions to prioritize these issues (Burgstahler, 2015). Additionally, advocacy and litigation have been pivotal in advocating for stronger enforcement. Legal actions against non-compliant universities have heightened awareness and prompted action, fostering accountability and encouraging comprehensive digital accessibility policies (U.S. Department of Justice, 2020).

TRAINING FACULTY AND STAFF TO SUPPORT STUDENTS WITH DISABILITIES IN DIGITAL LEARNING

In the context of digital learning, faculty and staff must have the necessary knowledge and tools to support students with disabilities effectively. Professional development is vital in enhancing educators' understanding of the barriers faced by these students, as they may be unaware of the specific challenges that hinder access to online content and participation in virtual classrooms (Burgstahler, 2015). Key aspects of professional development include raising awareness of various disabilities and fostering empathy among educators, ensuring they recognize that accessibility is an ongoing process (Seale, 2013). Additionally, understanding legal and ethical responsibilities, such as compliance with the Americans with Disabilities Act (ADA) and Section 508, is essential for making digital materials accessible. Finally, providing hands-on training with accessibility tools can bolster faculty confidence and encourage engagement in inclusive practices, improving support for students with disabilities (Seale, 2013).

Practical Strategies for Faculty and Staff to Incorporate Accessibility Features into Digital Learning Environments

Integrating accessibility features into digital learning environments is crucial for enhancing the learning experience for students with disabilities. Faculty and staff can apply practical strategies to make course materials more accessible, such as using appropriate file formats, providing alternative text for images, and ensuring videos have closed captioning (Boettcher & Conrad, 2021). Learning management systems (LMS) must also be designed with accessibility in mind. Training for faculty should cover the use of LMS features that support accessibility, ensuring that content is navigable for all students (Seale, 2013). Interactive tools and platforms also require attention; for instance, features like closed captioning in video conferencing tools should be utilized, and discussions should be structured to accommodate diverse communication needs (Burgstahler, 2015). Lastly, assessments must be flexible and inclusive, allowing for various forms of expression and providing accessible feedback mechanisms to support all learners (Seale, 2013).

Addressing the Digital Literacy of Educators in Making Content and Platforms Accessible

A major barrier to accessibility in digital learning environments is educators' digital literacy, as they lack the technical skills to create accessible content and utilize accessibility tools effectively. To address this, faculty development programs should provide comprehensive digital literacy training focused on accessibility, including assistive technologies and content creation tools (Seale, 2013). Additionally, fostering self-directed learning among faculty members can empower them to improve their content continuously, using resources like accessibility checklists and tutorials (Burgstahler, 2015).

Creating a Culture of Inclusivity Within Higher Education Institutions to Support Students with Disabilities

Higher education institutions must create a culture of inclusivity to support students with disabilities, which involves leadership, collaboration, and a commitment to accessibility. Institutional leaders should prioritize digital accessibility in policies and allocate resources for training and standards integration, signalling to the community that inclusivity is a core value (Seale, 2013). Collaboration between faculty, staff, IT, and disability services is essential, and providing dedicated accessibility support can assist faculty in making courses more inclusive (Treve, 2021). Additionally, faculty development programs should promote inclusive pedagogy, emphasizing that accessibility enhances learning for all students, not just a legal obligation (Seale, 2013).

LEVERAGING ARTIFICIAL INTELLIGENCE (AI) FOR ACCESSIBILITY

Artificial Intelligence (AI) has the potential to significantly improve accessibility in education for students with disabilities through innovative tools and technologies. Automatic transcription services, such as Otter.ai and Google Live Transcribe, convert spoken language into written text in real-time, benefiting students with hearing impairments by allowing them to follow lectures and engage in discussions more effectively (Meyer, 2020). Additionally, smart assistive technologies like voice recognition software and eye-tracking devices enhance access for students with physical disabilities by enabling them to interact with digital content through non-traditional input methods (Cox, 2021). Furthermore, AI-powered text-to-speech (TTS) tools, such as Microsoft's Immersive Reader, support students with visual impairments or reading disabilities by reading course materials aloud, while speech-to-text technologies assist those with writing difficulties in expressing their thoughts efficiently (Lindsay et al., 2021). Overall, these AI tools not only enhance accessibility but also pave the way for personalized learning experiences, although ethical considerations regarding bias and inclusivity remain crucial in their implementation.

The Potential of AI to Create Personalized Learning Experiences for Students with Disabilities

AI has significant potential to enhance learning experiences for students with disabilities by personalizing educational materials and methods. Adaptive learning platforms like Knewton and Smart Sparrow can tailor content delivery to meet individual learning styles and needs, providing features such as visual aids or interactive components for those who require them (Slater et al., 2020). Additionally, AI can facilitate personalized learning paths by analyzing student interactions with content, ensuring that students with specific challenges, such as dyslexia or motor impairments, receive appropriate accommodations that promote their autonomy and pace of learning (Bryson et al., 2021). Furthermore, AI can support students with cognitive disabilities, like ADHD or ASD, by offering tools that provide reminders, simplify tasks, and deliver real-time feedback, ultimately fostering greater engagement and success in their educational pursuits (Lindsay et al., 2021).

Ethical Considerations of AI in Education and Its Potential for Unintended Biases or Inaccessibility

AI has significant potential to improve accessibility in education, but its implementation entails notable ethical challenges. One major issue is bias in AI algorithms, as these systems can inadvertently reflect biases from the datasets they are trained on, potentially misrepresenting or excluding certain groups, particularly students with disabilities (Eubanks, 2018). Additionally, privacy and data security concerns arise when sensitive student information is collected to personalize learning experiences; schools must establish transparent policies to protect this data (Cox, 2021). Moreover, while AI can aid students, there are risks that different groups may struggle with these technologies due to a lack of familiarity or access to necessary devices and connectivity. Therefore, AI tools should be designed with universal accessibility (Lindsay et al., 2021). To address these challenges, educational institutions must create ethical frameworks that ensure transparency and inclusivity and minimize bias in AI implementation. Engaging with students, educators, and advocacy groups is essential to ensure these technologies meet the diverse needs of all students and promote fairness and equity in education (Bryson et al., 2021).

PROMOTING DIGITAL LITERACY FOR STUDENTS WITH DISABILITIES

Digital literacy is crucial in enabling students with disabilities to access and engage with online educational content. It is essential to utilize digital resources like online textbooks and multimedia tools, as these students often rely on accessibility features such as screen readers and closed captions to navigate educational materials (Tohara et al., (2021). Additionally, proficiency in navigating learning management systems (LMS) is vital; students with disabilities need training to effectively use these platforms, which allows them to complete assignments and advocate for necessary accommodations (Orkin, 2020). Ultimately, enhancing digital literacy fosters empowerment and independence, enabling students with disabilities to seek information, interact with peers and instructors, and contribute meaningfully to their academic communities (Reich, 2020).

Offering Training on How to Use Assistive Technologies and Digital Tools for Academic Success

Assistive technologies are crucial for supporting students with disabilities in higher education by enhancing their access to academic content and engagement. However, for these tools to be effective, students require comprehensive training to use them proficiently (Lyman, 2020). This includes understanding tools like screen readers and adaptive keyboards, which can significantly improve their educational experiences. Additionally, incorporating digital tools such as note-taking apps and task management systems can further aid organization and collaboration, particularly for students with mobility impairments (Shaw, 2020). It is also vital that faculty and staff receive training on these technologies to ensure they are equipped to support students effectively, necessitating ongoing professional development workshops focused on accessibility tools and best practices (Botelho, 2021).

Tailored Digital Literacy Programs Designed for Students with Disabilities

A one-size-fits-all approach to digital literacy training is ineffective for students with disabilities due to their diverse needs. Institutions should provide tailored programs with personalized instruction, such as training on screen reader software for students with visual impairments and captioning tools for those with hearing impairments (Orkin, 2020). Adaptive learning pathways are also essential, offering simplified lessons for students with cognitive impairments and practical instruction for those with physical disabilities (Burgstahler & Cory, 2019). Continuous support and mentoring, including access to workshops and one-on-one assistance, are vital for helping students effectively use assistive technologies (Desmarais, 2023).

However, barriers to digital literacy persist, including inadequate training opportunities, lack of access to assistive technologies, and insufficient institutional support. Institutions fail to provide adequate resources for training on assistive technologies, hindering students' academic progress. Institutions must invest in accessible training programs and ongoing professional development (Reich, 2020). Additionally, the high cost of assistive technologies limits access, so institutions should offer these tools at no cost or at a subsidized rate to meet students' diverse needs (Burgstahler & Cory, 2019). Lastly, strong institutional support is necessary to create inclusive learning environments, equipping faculty and staff to develop accessible course materials and effectively support students with disabilities in navigating online learning (Botelho, 2021).

Ensuring Equity in Access to Digital Resources

Ensuring equitable access to digital resources is essential for creating an inclusive and supportive learning environment for all students, including those with disabilities. As education increasingly moves into digital platforms, students with disabilities face unique challenges in accessing necessary technologies and resources. Disparities in access to hardware, software, and reliable internet connections compound these challenges. Addressing these issues is essential to ensure that students with disabilities can fully participate in and benefit from digital education. This discussion will explore the disparities in access to computers, the internet, and other digital resources, the importance of providing equitable access to hardware and software in educational institutions, and how to address the gap in digital access between affluent and less affluent regions or countries. Access to digital resources is a foundational element of modern education, yet students with disabilities face significant barriers to accessing these resources. A major disparity lies in the availability of assistive technologies and adaptive devices, such as screen readers, adaptive keyboards, and Braille displays, essential for students with visual, auditory, and physical impairments (Jackson, 2023). For example, students with visual impairments rely heavily on-screen readers to access digital content. These students cannot use the same resources as their peers without these tools, leading to educational inequities (Mason, 2020).

Additionally, internet access is often a critical issue for students with disabilities. The COVID-19 pandemic has highlighted the stark disparities in digital access, with students in underserved communities lacking reliable internet connections. Students with disabilities may also struggle to use the Internet in environments that are not designed to meet their needs, further exacerbating inequalities (Chen et al., 2020). As such, students with disabilities often face a double disadvantage, lacking both the general resources required for digital learning and the specialized tools and support necessary for equal participation. Furthermore, educational content is not always accessible. Websites, learning management systems (LMS), and educational videos must be compatible with assistive technologies so students can access them fully. Unfortunately, educational platforms are not designed with accessibility in mind, leading to a situation where students with disabilities must navigate barriers that their peers do not (Sweeney, 2019). Institutions must prioritize digital accessibility in both the design and implementation of educational resources to level the playing field for all students.

THE IMPORTANCE OF PROVIDING EQUITABLE ACCESS TO BOTH HARDWARE AND SOFTWARE IN EDUCATIONAL INSTITUTIONS

Equitable access to hardware and software is crucial to ensure that all students, including those with disabilities, can participate in the digital learning environment. Educational institutions must provide students with the necessary tools, such as computers, adaptive devices, and software applications, which are effective and tailored to their needs. While computers and internet access form the basic infrastructure for digital learning, assistive technologies such as screen magnifiers, voice recognition software, and Braille displays are essential for students with visual and physical impairments (Sharma & Raskin, 2020).

Beyond hardware, software plays a key role in digital accessibility. Institutions must ensure that software used in academic settings is compatible with assistive technologies. Educational tools, websites, and LMS platforms should adhere to accessibility standards such as the Web Content Accessibility Guidelines (WCAG), ensuring they are compatible with screen readers and other assistive devices. Moreover, software programs that provide alternative formats, such as text-to-speech or captioning services, are crucial for students with learning disabilities or hearing impairments (Jansma, 2020). Equitable access also means institutions should offer students with disabilities personalised support when using these technologies. Training sessions or workshops that teach students how to use assistive software and devices can empower them to become more independent in their learning. By providing the necessary hardware, software, and training, educational institutions can create an environment where students with disabilities have the tools and resources to succeed academically.

ADDRESSING THE GAP BETWEEN STUDENTS IN MORE AFFLUENT AND LESS AFFLUENT REGIONS OR COUNTRIES REGARDING ACCESS TO DIGITAL RESOURCES

The disparity in access to digital resources is even more pronounced when comparing students in affluent regions with those in less affluent areas. In developing countries, students with disabilities face compounded barriers to accessing both general and specialised digital tools. For example, countries lack the infrastructure needed to provide consistent internet access, which hinders students' ability to participate in digital learning (Chen et al., 2020). Additionally, the availability of assistive technologies is often limited in less affluent regions due to the high cost of these devices and the lack of government funding for specialised resources.

The economic divide between affluent and less affluent regions also means that educational institutions in wealthier countries can offer students with disabilities a greater variety of digital resources. In these regions, students may have access to various assistive technologies, from screen readers to adaptive keyboards, high-speed internet and reliable technical support (Jackson, 2023). In contrast, students in less affluent regions may have to rely on outdated technology or may not have access to assistive technologies at all, further exacerbating the educational divide. In addition to technological disparities, the digital literacy gap between affluent and less affluent regions must also be addressed. Students in wealthier areas may receive better training in digital literacy, including the use of general technologies and assistive technologies. Conversely, students in less affluent regions may not have the same opportunities for digital literacy education, which can limit their ability to use digital resources effectively (Sweeney, 2019). Addressing these disparities requires targeted local, national, and international efforts. Governments and educational institutions must prioritise digital accessibility as part of their broader equity agendas. This may involve ensuring that assistive technologies are available at subsidised rates, investing in internet infrastructure in underserved areas, and effectively training students and educators on using these resources (Mason, 2020). International collaborations and partnerships can also help bridge the gap. Organisations such as the World Bank and UNESCO can play a pivotal role in promoting the adoption of accessible digital learning resources in developing countries. Through these partnerships, resources can be shared, and best practices for creating equitable access to digital education can be disseminated globally (Sharma & Raskin, 2020).

CHALLENGES IN IMPLEMENTING DIGITAL ACCESSIBILITY SOLUTIONS

In recent years, digital accessibility has become an essential component of inclusive education. However, implementing accessibility solutions in higher education institutions remains challenging due to various factors. These challenges include limited funding, resistance to change, lack of stakeholder awareness, technical difficulties, and legal and institutional barriers. Addressing these challenges is crucial to ensuring that students with disabilities have equal access to digital resources and learning environments. This section discusses the key challenges in implementing digital accessibility solutions and suggests strategies for overcoming them.

Limited Funding

One of the most significant barriers to implementing digital accessibility solutions is inadequate funding. Developing accessible digital content, adopting assistive technologies, and providing necessary training require substantial financial resources. Institutions, especially those with limited budgets, may struggle to allocate sufficient funds for these initiatives. The cost of purchasing assistive devices, software licenses, and training programs can be prohibitively expensive, and without external funding or support, y institutions may prioritise other initiatives over accessibility (Botelho, 2021).

Resistance to Change

Another challenge is the resistance to change among faculty, administrators, and IT staff. Educators and staff are accustomed to traditional teaching methods and may be unfamiliar with the tools and strategies required to create accessible digital content. Additionally, they perceive implementing digital accessibility measures as time-consuming or unnecessary, especially if they are unaware of the legal requirements and the benefits of inclusive education. This resistance can delay the adoption of best practices for digital accessibility and hinder the overall progress toward inclusivity (Burgstahler, 2020).

Lack of Awareness Among Stakeholders

A lack of awareness and understanding of digital accessibility issues among faculty, administrators, and students can further exacerbate the problem. Stakeholders may not recognise the barriers students with disabilities face when accessing digital content and resources. Moreover, there is often insufficient training or education about the legal obligations that institutions must adhere to, such as the Americans with Disabilities Act (ADA) or Section 508 of the Rehabilitation Act, which requires that educational institutions provide equal access to online resources (Desmarais, 2023). Without a widespread understanding of these challenges, institutions may struggle to implement effective accessibility solutions.

Addressing Technical Difficulties in Ensuring that All Digital Content is Universally Accessible

One of the significant technical challenges in implementing digital accessibility solutions is ensuring that all digital content is universally accessible. Educational content, including websites, online course materials, videos, and multimedia resources, must be designed with accessibility. This includes adhering to guidelines such as the Web Content Accessibility Guidelines (WCAG), which provide a framework for making digital content accessible to users with various disabilities (W3C, 2018). However, not all faculty members are trained in these guidelines, and creating accessible digital content requires specialised knowledge of web development, design principles, and assistive technologies.

For instance, ensuring that multimedia content (such as videos and images) includes alternative text, captions, and audio descriptions can be complex and time-consuming for instructors. Institutions may lack the resources to support faculty in creating accessible materials, leading to inconsistencies across courses and platforms. As such, institutions need to invest in professional development for faculty, provide templates and guidelines for accessible content creation, and support using tools that can automate or simplify the process (Shaw, 2020).

Technical Barriers to Assistive Technologies

Another technical challenge is the integration of assistive technologies into existing digital platforms. Assistive technologies such as screen readers, speech-to-text software, and alternative input devices must be compatible with the digital content used in higher education. However, platforms or systems may not support these technologies, requiring significant modifications or updates. Additionally, not all assistive technologies are universally compatible with every type of content, which can create a fragmented experience for students. Ensuring that all digital platforms and content work seamlessly with various assistive technologies is a complex, ongoing process that requires collaboration between IT departments, accessibility specialists, and faculty members (Reich, 2020).

Ensuring Compatibility Across Devices

Another technical challenge is ensuring that digital content is accessible across various devices and operating systems. Students with disabilities may use various devices, such as smartphones, tablets, and desktop computers, along with assistive technologies that may not be universally compatible with all devices. Ensuring compatibility and consistency across devices and platforms can be resource-intensive and challenging, as it requires testing and modification of digital content and systems to work across multiple formats. Institutions must prioritise universal design principles and develop solutions that allow students to access content regardless of their device (Desmarais, 2023)

OVERCOMING BARRIERS RELATED TO LEGAL AND INSTITUTIONAL OBSTACLES TO IMPLEMENTING DIGITAL ACCESSIBILITY POLICIES

Legal Barriers and Compliance

Legal requirements play a central role in driving the adoption of digital accessibility policies. In the United States, laws such as the ADA and Section 508 of the Rehabilitation Act require that educational institutions provide equitable access to digital resources for students with disabilities. However, compliance with these laws can be complicated. Institutions lack clear guidelines on ensuring digital content meets accessibility standards, and there is often a lack of enforcement mechanisms to ensure adherence. As a result, institutions may only make minimal efforts to comply with accessibility laws rather than striving for comprehensive, institution-wide accessibility (Botelho, 2021).

Institutional Obstacles and Resistance to Policy Change

At the institutional level, implementing digital accessibility policies can face resistance due to a lack of organisational commitment or competing priorities. Institutional leadership may not fully understand the importance of accessibility or may not prioritise it in the face of other budgetary and operational concerns. Sometimes, there may also be a lack of expertise or dedicated staff to oversee digital accessibility initiatives. Institutions that fail to integrate accessibility into their broader strategic planning may struggle to create a cohesive and sustainable accessibility policy (Burgstahler, 2020).

Developing Institutional Support for Accessibility

Overcoming these institutional barriers requires strong leadership, commitment to inclusivity, and the development of clear policies and procedures. Institutions should establish dedicated offices or committees focused on digital accessibility, with a mandate to ensure compliance with legal requirements and best practices for accessible content. They should also invest in accessibility training for all staff, ensure ongoing technical support for accessible content creation, and allocate sufficient funding to support the implementation of accessibility policies. Additionally, institutions should establish transparent processes for monitoring compliance, collecting feedback from students with disabilities, and continuously improving accessibility (Reich, 2020).

Lack of Accountability and Enforcement

A critical barrier to the effective implementation of digital accessibility policies is the lack of accountability and enforcement. While institutions create accessibility policies, these policies are not always effectively enforced. Without clear consequences for non-compliance or systematic monitoring of accessibility standards, departments or faculty members may continue to overlook accessibility requirements. Institutions must develop mechanisms for monitoring the accessibility of digital content, including regular audits, faculty evaluations, and feedback systems, to ensure that accessibility remains a priority (Shaw, 2020).

Ethical and Legal Considerations in Digital Accessibility

Digital accessibility in higher education has become an essential concern, with legal and ethical implications for institutions. As technology plays a pivotal role in educational settings, institutions must ensure that digital environments and resources are accessible to all students, including those with disabilities. Failure to do so can lead to serious legal consequences, ethical dilemmas, and challenges in promoting equitable education. This section explores the legal implications of failing to provide digital accessibility, ethical considerations, and the role of standards such as the Web Content Accessibility Guidelines (WCAG) and Section 508 of the Rehabilitation Act in promoting inclusivity.

THE LEGAL IMPLICATIONS OF FAILING TO PROVIDE DIGITAL ACCESSIBILITY IN HIGHER EDUCATION

One of the primary legal risks institutions face when they fail to provide accessible digital environments is the potential for lawsuits. In countries, including the United States, students with disabilities have the legal right to access educational resources and digital content under laws like the Americans with Disabilities Act (ADA) and Section 504 of the Rehabilitation Act of 1973. These laws mandate that educational institutions ensure equal access to programs and services, extending to digital resources. Failure to meet these legal obligations can result in lawsuits from students or advocacy groups. In recent years, there has been an increase in legal action against universities for not providing accessible websites, online courses, and digital materials (Lindsay, 2020).

Regulatory Fines and Penalties

In addition to lawsuits, institutions may face regulatory fines and penalties for failing to meet digital accessibility requirements. Under Section 508 of the Rehabilitation Act, federal agencies and educational institutions receiving federal funds must ensure that electronic and information technology is accessible to individuals with disabilities. Non-compliance can lead to investigations by the Department of Education's Office for Civil Rights (OCR), which can impose corrective actions, including fines and withholding federal funding. Other regulatory bodies, including the Equal Employment Opportunity Commission (EEOC) and state-level human rights commissions, may also enforce compliance (Burgstahler, 2020).

Ethical Considerations in Designing Inclusive Digital Experiences for Students with Disabilities

Promoting Equal Access and Social Justice

Beyond the legal implications, there are crucial ethical considerations surrounding digital accessibility. At its core, digital accessibility promotes fairness, equity, and social justice. Educational institutions are ethically responsible for providing equal opportunities for all students, regardless of their abilities. Failing to provide accessible digital environments marginalises students with disabilities, limiting their ability to participate fully in their educational experience. This is an issue of legal compliance and upholding ethical standards in education (Jansma, 2018).

An inclusive digital experience allows students with disabilities to engage with the same educational content, technologies, and resources as their peers. Designing accessible online learning platforms, multimedia content, and course materials ensures that students with disabilities are not excluded from the digital learning environment. Ethical design requires careful consideration of how content is presented, the technologies used, and how students interact with them. For instance, providing alt text for images, video captions, and compatible tools for screen readers are ethical choices that ensure students with visual, auditory, and cognitive impairments can fully access digital content (Burgstahler, 2020).

Respecting the Rights and Dignity of Students with Disabilities

Ethical considerations also involve respecting the dignity and autonomy of students with disabilities. Institutions must acknowledge the rights of students with disabilities to have equal access to education, just as their peers without disabilities do. This includes respecting students' needs for assistive technologies, accommodations, and individualised support, crucial to their success in digital learning environments. Ethical design goes beyond simply meeting legal requirements; it involves proactively identifying barriers that might hinder students' ability to access or engage with digital content and taking steps to remove them (Jansma, 2018). Furthermore, there is an ethical obligation to ensure privacy and security for students with disabilities using assistive technologies that collect or store personal data. Institutions should adopt best practices to protect these students' data privacy and security, ensuring that their sensitive information is not exposed through digital tools (Schroeder, 2020).

Collaboration Between Technology Developers, Educators, and Disability Advocacy Groups

In the evolving landscape of higher education, the need for inclusive digital learning environments has never been more critical. Technology developers, educators, and disability advocacy groups must collaborate effectively to create accessible and equitable educational solutions for students with disabilities. By combining expertise from diverse fields, these stakeholders can address the technological and social barriers that impede digital accessibility. This discussion explores the importance of collaboration among these groups, provides examples of successful partnerships, and discusses how these collaborations can address both the technological and social aspects of digital accessibility.

Leveraging Expertise Across Fields

The development of accessible educational technologies requires the collaboration of stakeholders, including educational institutions, technology developers, and disability advocacy groups. Each group brings distinct expertise essential to creating effective and inclusive solutions. Educational institutions, especially those with expertise in pedagogy, can provide insight into the specific needs of students and the best practices for integrating accessible technologies into learning environments. Technology developers contribute technical knowledge, providing tools that can be customised to meet these needs. Disability advocacy groups play a crucial role in ensuring that the solutions developed are genuinely inclusive, advocating for the needs of individuals with disabilities and ensuring that products are user-friendly and effective (Jackson, 2023).

Collaborative efforts between these groups can ensure that technologies are not only designed with accessibility in mind but also implemented in a way that maximises their impact. Disability advocacy groups, for example, can ensure that assistive technologies are designed in ways that meet the diverse needs of students with disabilities. At the same time, educators can provide feedback on how these tools are integrated into the learning environment (Jansma, 2020). This partnership helps ensure that technologies are innovative and effective in fostering an inclusive educational experience.

Creating Holistic, Sustainable Solutions

Collaboration between educators, technology developers, and disability advocacy groups can create holistic solutions that address both the technological and social aspects of digital accessibility. While technology developers focus on technical aspects such as coding, interface design, and compatibility with assistive technologies, educators are better equipped to consider the pedagogical and practical implications of technology use in educational settings. Disability advocacy groups, meanwhile, can ensure that social and attitudinal barriers to access are identified and addressed (Sweeney, 2019). Together, these groups can advocate for policies and practices that not only encourage the development of accessible technologies but also promote a culture of inclusion within educational institutions. Such collaborations can lead to the development of digital tools and learning platforms that support diverse learners while fostering social change within academic communities to ensure greater acceptance and understanding of students with disabilities (Sharma & Raskin, 2020).

HOW PARTNERSHIPS CAN ADDRESS BOTH THE TECHNOLOGICAL AND SOCIAL ASPECTS OF DIGITAL ACCESSIBILITY

Tackling Technological Barriers

Technological barriers to digital accessibility include issues related to website design, software compatibility with assistive technologies, and inadequate digital content formatting. Through collaboration, technology developers can design products that meet established accessibility standards, such as the Web Content Accessibility Guidelines (WCAG). Collaboration with educators ensures that these tools meet the practical needs of students in real-world classroom settings (Chambers, 2019).). For example, technology companies may collaborate with educators to develop learning management systems (LMS) that are fully compatible with screen readers and provide alternatives for multimedia content, such as captions and transcripts (Jackson, 2023).

Addressing Social Barriers

While technological solutions are essential, social and attitudinal barriers often hinder the full integration of students with disabilities into the learning environment. Disability advocacy groups play a key role in advocating for the social inclusion of students with disabilities, ensuring that they are treated with respect and dignity in both digital and physical environments. Collaborations between disability advocacy groups, educators, and technology developers help raise awareness about the importance of digital accessibility and promote inclusive attitudes within academic institutions. Educators, for instance, can be trained to use assistive technologies and adopt inclusive teaching practices that accommodate a wide range of learning needs (Sharma & Raskin, 2020). Moreover, such partnerships can help reduce the stigma around disability in educational settings. When educators and developers understand the value of inclusive digital learning environments, they are more likely to promote positive attitudes toward students with disabilities. Disability advocacy groups can help ensure that digital accessibility is not just a technical feature but part of a broader cultural shift towards inclusion (Jansma, 2020).

CONCLUSION

The digital divide poses significant challenges in higher education, especially for students with disabilities who face unique barriers to accessing digital resources. This chapter highlights their obstacles and emphasises the need for inclusive strategies, such as accessible technology and assistive devices, to create a more equitable online learning environment. It stresses the importance of integrating Universal Design for Learning (UDL) principles and advanced assistive technologies to support diverse learning needs. The chapter also offers best practices and recommendations for policymakers, educators, and technology developers to improve accessibility. Ultimately, a concerted effort is required from higher education institutions to foster inclusion and empower students with disabilities to thrive in a digital world.

REFERENCES

W3C. (2018). *Web Content Accessibility Guidelines (WCAG) 2.0*. W3C. Retrieved from https://www.w3.org/WAI/WCAG21/

Afzal, A., Khan, S., Daud, S., Ahmad, Z., & Butt, A. (2023). Addressing the Digital Divide: Access and use of technology in education. *Journal of Social Sciences Review*, *3*(2), 883–895.

Al-Azawei, A., Parslow, P., & Lundqvist, K. (2016). The impact of universal design for learning on student engagement and academic achievement in higher education. *The Journal of Scholarship of Teaching and Learning*, *16*(3), 1–19.

Alenezi, M. (2023). Digital learning and digital institution in higher education. *Education Sciences*, *13*(1), 88.

Boettcher, J. V., & Conrad, R. M. (2021). *The online teaching survival guide: Simple and practical pedagogical tips*. John Wiley & Sons.

Botelho, F. H. (2021). Accessibility to digital technology: Virtual barriers, real opportunities. *Assistive Technology, 33*(sup1), 27-34.

Brighouse, H., & McPherson, M. (2022). *Ethics in Higher Education: Promoting equity and inclusion through case-based inquiry*. Harvard Education Press.

Bryson, J. R., Castelnovo, W., & Eubanks, V. (2021). *The role of artificial intelligence in education: An overview*. Springer.

Burgstahler, S. (2015). *Universal design in higher education: From principles to practice*. Harvard Education Press.

Burgstahler, S. (2020). Legal and institutional challenges to implementing digital accessibility policies in higher education. *Journal of Postsecondary Education and Disability*, *33*(3), 100–115.

Burgstahler, S., & Cory, R. (2019). Inclusive instruction: Digital literacy for all students. *Journal of Postsecondary Education and Disability*, *32*(2), 125–138.

CAST. (2018). *Universal Design for Learning Guidelines version 2.2*. Retrieved from https://www.cast.org/

Chambers, D. (2019). Assistive technology to enhance inclusive education. In *Oxford research encyclopedia of education.*

Chen, X., Zhang, J., & Yang, C. (2020). Digital accessibility and educational equity: Bridging the gap for students with disabilities. *Journal of Educational Technology, 38*(4), 115–127.

Cox, A. (2021). AI in education: Ethical concerns and opportunities for students with disabilities. *Journal of Educational Technology, 58*(2), 127–141.

Department of Higher Education and Training. (2013). *White Paper on Post-School Education and Training*. Pretoria: Department of Higher Education and Training.

Department of Higher Education and Training. (2016). *Disability Framework for Higher Education*. Department of Higher Education and Training.

Department of Telecommunications and Postal Services. (2016). *National Integrated ICT Policy White Paper*. Pretoria: Department of Telecommunications and Postal Services.

Desmarais, M. É. (2023). How to Engage Students with Universal Design for Learning. *Transformative Inclusive Education*, 213.

Eubanks, V. (2018). *Automating inequality: How high-tech tools profile, police, and punish the poor*. St. Martin's Press.

Hankerson, D. L., & Brown, L. X. (2020). Technology as a civil right and a move toward disability justice: Ensuring digital access for disabled students in the pandemic. *Drexel L. Rev., 13*, 869.

Jackson, A. K. (2023). *Closing the Digital Divide: Understanding Organizational Approaches to Digital Accessibility in Higher Education* (Doctoral dissertation, University of South Dakota).

Jansma, J. (2018). The ethical imperatives of inclusive digital design in higher education. *Ethics and Education, 13*(2), 105–118.

Jansma, J. (2020). Improving access for students with disabilities in digital environments: The role of technology and accessibility standards. *International Journal of Inclusive Education, 24*(7), 709–721.

Johansson, S., Gulliksen, J., & Gustavsson, C. (2021). Disability digital divide: The use of the Internet, smartphones, computers, and tablets among people with disabilities in Sweden. *Universal Access in the Information Society, 20*(1), 105–120.

Kimogol, S. S. (2023). *Accessibility of digital teaching materials. Identifying barriers faced by students with visual impairment in digital teaching materials* (Master's thesis, Oslomet-story universitetet).

Kyei, A. K. (2023). *Experiences of students with visual impairment in studying Information, Communication and Technology at the University of Education, Winneba* (Doctoral dissertation, University of Education, Winneba).

Lambert, S. R. (2020). Do MOOCs contribute to student equity and social inclusion? A systematic review 2014–18. *Computers & Education*, *145*, 103693.

Lindsay, S. (2020). The legal implications of digital accessibility in higher education. *International Journal of Educational Law*, *38*(1), 33–49.

Lindsay, S., Sussman, T., & Northway, M. (2021). Artificial intelligence and its impact on accessibility in higher education: A critical review. *International Journal of Educational Technology*, *12*(3), 45–59.

Lyman, R. (2020). Empowering students with disabilities: The role of assistive technology in higher education. *Assistive Technology Journal*, *22*(3), 143–157.

Mansell, W. L. (2023). Perceptions of Applying Universal Design for Learning to Quaver's Marvelous World of Music to Increase Engagement of Students with Autism.

Mason, A. (2020). Digital literacy in the context of students with disabilities. *Journal of Education and Technology*, *15*(3), 152–167.

Matsieli, M., & Mutula, S. (2024). COVID-19 and digital transformation in Higher Education Institutions: Towards inclusive and equitable access to quality education. *Education Sciences*, *14*(8), 819.

Memon, F. N., & Memon, S. N. (2025). Digital Divide and Equity in Education: Bridging Gaps to Ensure Inclusive Learning. In Impact of Digitalisation on Education and Social Sustainability (pp. 107-130). IGI Global.

Meyer, K. (2020). Transcribing technology in the classroom: Enhancing accessibility for students with hearing impairments. *Journal of Assistive Technologies*, *22*(1), 56–65.

Mohamed Hashim, M. A., Tlemsani, I., & Matthews, R. (2022). Higher education strategy in digital transformation. *Education and Information Technologies*, *27*(3), 3171–3195. PMID: 34539217

National Planning Commission. (2012). *National Development Plan 2030: Our Future - Make it Work.* National Planning Commission.

Ngqunguza, A., Seleke, Z., & Makhoba, T. I. (2024). Digital Transformation in Higher Education: Leadership Strategies for ensuring equity and inclusion in digital learning environments. [JPADA]. *Journal of Public Administration and Development Alternatives*, *9*(2), 101–114.

Orkin, A. (2020). The importance of digital literacy for students with disabilities in higher education. *Journal of Educational Technology*, *58*(2), 215.

Oyedokun, T. T. (2025). Assistive Technology and Accessibility Tools in Enhancing Adaptive Education. In *Advancing Adaptive Education: Technological Innovations for Disability Support* (pp. 125-162). IGI Global Scientific Publishing.

Raihan, M. M., Subroto, S., Chowdhury, N., Koch, K., Ruttan, E., & Turin, T. C. (2024). *Dimensions and barriers for digital (in) equity and digital divide: A systematic integrative review*. Digital Transformation and Society.

Reich, J. (2020). Navigating the digital divide: Legal frameworks and barriers to digital accessibility in higher education. *Journal of Digital Education*, *39*(4), 245–259.

Saborío-Taylor, S., & Rojas-Ramírez, F. (2024). Universal Design for Learning and artificial intelligence in the digital era: Fostering inclusion and autonomous learning. *International Journal of Professional Development, Learners and Learning, 6*(2).

Salmi, J., & D'Addio, A. (2021). Policies to achieve inclusion in higher education. *Policy Reviews in Higher Education*, *5*(1), 47–72.

Sanderson, N. C., Kessel, S., & Chen, W. (2022). What do faculty members know about universal design and digital accessibility? A qualitative study in computer science and engineering disciplines. *Universal Access in the Information Society*, *21*(2), 351–365. PMID: 35370532

Sato, N. N., Condes Moreno, E., Rubio-Zarapuz, A., Dalamitros, A. A., Yaez-Sepulveda, R., Tornero-Aguilera, J. F., & Clemente-Suárez, V. J. (2023). Navigating the new normal: Adapting online and distance learning in the post-pandemic era. *Education Sciences*, *14*(1), 19.

Schroeder, P. (2020). Digital accessibility in higher education: Legal, ethical, and institutional challenges. *Journal of Disability Policy Studies*, *30*(4), 258–273.

Seale, J. (2013). *E-learning and disability in higher education: Accessibility research and practice*. Routledge.

Sharma, M., & Raskin, S. (2020). The digital divide: Addressing the accessibility gap for students with disabilities in global education. *International Journal of Educational Development*, *49*, 57–68.

Shaw, R. (2020). Overcoming barriers to digital accessibility: Strategies for improving compliance and support. *Disability Studies Quarterly*, *40*(2), 85–98.

Shaw, R. (2020). Supporting students with disabilities through digital literacy training: Strategies for success. *Disability Studies Quarterly*, *40*(4), 60–72.

Slater, S., Taylor, R., & Green, P. (2020). The impact of AI on personalised learning in higher education. *Educational Research Review, 15*(2), 189–202.

Smith, D. G. (2024). *Diversity's Promise for Higher Education: Making it work.* Jhu Press.

Sweeney, M. E. (2019). Digital assistants.

Tohara, A. J. T., Shuhidan, S. M., Bahry, F. D. S., & Nordin, M. N. B. (2021). Exploring digital literacy strategies for students with special educational needs in the digital age. *Turkish Journal of Computer and Mathematics Education, 12*(9), 3345–3358.

Treve, M. (2021). What COVID-19 has introduced into education: Challenges facing higher education institutions (HEIs). *Higher Education Pedagogies, 6*(1), 212–227.

UNESCO. (2006). *Convention on the Rights of Persons with Disabilities (CRPD).* Retrieved from https://www.un.org/disabilities/convention/conventionfulltext.shtml

U.S. Department of Education. (2020). *Section 508 of the Rehabilitation Act: Accessibility requirements for electronic and information technology.* Retrieved from https://www.ed.gov

U.S. Department of Justice. (2020). *Americans with Disabilities Act (ADA).* Retrieved from https://www.ada.gov

Van Dijk, J. A. G. M. (2020). *The digital divide: The internet and social inequality in international perspective* (3rd ed.). Sage Publications.

World Wide Web Consortium. (W3C). (2018). *Web Content Accessibility Guidelines (WCAG) 2.1.* Retrieved from https://www.w3.org/WAI/WCAG21/

Yadav, A. K. (2024). Challenges facing visually impaired students in inclusive higher education. *Educating for Societal Transitions*, 27.

Chapter 15
Cogs and Code:
Understanding AI's Societal Impact in the Digital Era

Valisher Sapayev
https://orcid.org/0000-0002-6751-5864
Mamun University, Uzbekistan

Noor Hayat
https://orcid.org/0000-0003-2726-2847
University of Central Punjab, Pakistan

Iroda Abdullaeva
Urgench State University, Uzbekistan

Munir Ahmad
https://orcid.org/0000-0003-4836-6151
Survey of Pakistan, Pakistan

ABSTRACT

This chapter explores Artificial Intelligence (AI) as a transformative force in the era of digital transformation, highlighting its impact beyond technical innovation to include deep societal and institutional shifts. AI not only automates and optimizes systems but also redefines decision-making, assessment, and service delivery across sectors. The chapter critically examines challenges such as bias, transparency, and accountability, while also exploring AI's potential to promote social good. Emphasizing ethical responsibility and democratic values, it offers a framework for integrating AI in ways that ensure inclusive and equitable digital futures.

DOI: 10.4018/979-8-3373-2387-9.ch015

INTRODUCTION

We live in the age of digital transformation, which is characterized by the emergence of technological innovation that transforms both industries but also institutions, economies, and even human relations in their daily lives. Big data, robotics, blockchain, and cloud computing, among others, have reshaped the production, processing, and usage of information in the last 20 years, with a sweeping effect on the field (Hsien et al., 2021; Muheidat et al., 2022; Nair & Tyagi, 2023; Peng, 2021). Among them, artificial intelligence (AI) can be distinguished as a game changer that can make decisions automatically, enable customization of experiences at scale and pace as never before possible (Iyer, 2021; Mana et al., 2024; Miao et al., 2021; Rajpurkar et al., 2022; Rana et al., 2025). Nonetheless, digital transformation cannot only be that of the implementation of new tools; it is a complete rearrangement of working processes, value chains, and the corporate governance system. The AI integration into such systems is not an addition but a catalyst - it makes organizations and societies re-evaluate how to work, as well as what it is to be a human in a world created by machines.

The emergence of AI has so far extended beyond the virtual walls of data science research centers and business software into the larger societal trends, decision-making systems, job arenas, and even ethical principles. In contrast to other similar technological spurts in the past, AI systems respond to social data, take probabilistic decisions that impact the lives of human beings, and reflect and even amplify current societal prejudices (Anderljung et al., 2024; Farina et al., 2024; Molfino et al., 2024; Sharma, 2024). Therefore, the proliferation of AI in the field of public services (Kulal et al., 2024), healthcare (Maleki Varnosfaderani & Forouzanfar, 2024), education (Imran & Almusharraf, 2024), law enforcement (Sachoulidou, 2024), and media (Owsley & Greenwood, 2024) are not just a technical improvement, it is a cultural step, which requires critical thinking and a democratic discussion. How AI is created, implemented, and also managed is far-reaching in terms of equity, privacy, accountability, and democracy. The digital transformation that is led by AI needs to be perceived not only as efficient and innovative but also be seen through an aspect of social responsibility and ethics.

This chapter reflects on the complex character that AI in the way that it serves as the causal agent of digital transformation, and its implications for society. It explores the way in which AI technologies are transforming regimes of evaluation, decision, and service provision through critical areas. The chapter opens with a conceptual introduction to digital transformation, then presents a task on how AI contrasts with previous technologies both in form and in operation. In further parts, the problems with AI that it brings forth are addressed, especially concerning bias, determination, and accountability, as well as the potential to enhance human potential and social welfare. Last, but not least, the chapter provides a roadmap, laying out the way forward towards adopting AI in such a manner that it will help to advance the interests of a democratic society.

AI IN DAILY LIFE

AI is today the unseen driver of most parts of our social media life. AI algorithms are essential to platforms, such as Facebook, Instagram, TikTok, and YouTube, to filter what people see in their social media feeds, recommend new acquaintances, and promote viral content. Such systems monitor user behavior, e.g., likes, shares, comments, watch time, and scroll patterns, to observe future strategies of content delivery and engagement strategies. AI allows a hyper-personalized experience, where every user would get the content that appeals to their interests and patterns. At the same time, these algorithms drive micro-targeted advertising by examining the demographic data, online behavioral activity, and guessing the interests, thus providing a highly profitable digital marketing model. But the trade-off is that personalization may create an echo chamber, as algorithms reflect personal biases, and contribute to filter bubbles, and engagement efforts on the part of social sites may lead to renationalization and biased information. Therefore, the role of AI in the context of social media is not only to affect digital experiences but to distort the societal course and opinion on a large scale.

AI in Education

In the education industry, AI is transforming learning among students and teaching among educators (Ahmad et al., 2025; Ali et al., 2024; Imran & Almusharraf, 2024; Labadze et al., 2023; Maqsood et al., 2025). Machine learning and natural language processing are underlying technologies of intelligent tutoring systems that offer adaptive learning conditions based on the specific needs of students. To give an example, services such as Duolingo employ AI to automatically increase or decrease the level of difficulty by learning how well a person performs (Kazu & Kuvvetli, 2025). Khan Academy incorporates AI as a way of suggesting review activities and returning feedback in real-time (Li et al., 2024). Another very significant strength of AI is that it automates administrative tasks, including grading assignments, monitoring student progress, and identifying at-risk students, so that educators are able to spend a little more time on pedagogy. Besides, AI-based teaching assistants support the educational process in massive online classes, performing routine tasks and content delivery. Such developments have created possibilities of more accessible and broad-based education, especially in outlying or deprived locations. Nevertheless, they also contend issues of privacy, fairness in algorithms, and that they may perpetuate existing educational disparities in a biased model or non-access to AI-amplified services.

AI in Healthcare

In healthcare, AI is revolutionizing the process of clinical work, diagnostics, and management of patients (Bangash et al., 2025; Joseph et al., 2024; Kaul et al., 2023; Rajpurkar et al., 2022; Trocin et al., 2023; Zhang & Kamel Boulos, 2023). The algorithms trained on the large repositories of medical images like X-rays, MRIs, and CT scans now may recognize anomalies as accurately as human radiologists, in some cases even more. Artificial intelligence also applies in predictive analytics to determine the likelihood of patients developing an illness such as diabetes, sepsis, or heart failure so that they can be intervened in early. The purpose of technologies, such as IBM Watson Health (Chow et al., 2023), is to assist clinicians so that they are presented with evidence-based treatment suggestions based on analyses of large volumes of medical literature and patient data. Telemedicine systems need AI chatbots that could conduct initial examinations, triage patients, and direct them towards the right care paths. In addition, AI-fueled wearable devices track real-time vital signs and health trends that allow preventive care and personal health data (Almathami et al., 2020; Doniec et al., 2023; Vasileiou & Maglogiannis, 2022). Although the incorporation of AI increases efficiency and decision-making, it is also associated with problems associated with explainability, liability in clinical errors, and the moral use of sensitive health information.

AI in Finance

The financial sector is one of the industries that has embraced AI quickly to improve security, efficiency, and customer interaction (Cao, 2022; Zhou et al., 2022). AI can be used in fraud detection systems to identify atypical transactions, assuming the abnormal behavior of a user, which may be in real time (Qatawneh, 2024). The use of more traditional data sources, such as mobile phone usage, online activity, or e-commerce behaviour is being added to the credit scoring models so as to determine credit worthiness more comprehensively and not without some discussion on fairness and non-transparency. Robo-advisors such as Betterment and Wealthfront apply AI (Di, 2023; Kaur et al., 2024)to deliver individual investment approaches that match the aims, hazard tolerance, and market conditions of specific customers and make financial planning services more available to people. With algorithmic systems, high-frequency transactions are traded by interpreting market condition signs faster than is possible by human beings, maximizing profits and liquidity.

Artificial intelligence also has a hand in customer service, where chatbots address account management, loan applications, and insurance claims questions. Nevertheless, the fact that AI with respect to the financial sector is becoming more reliant also prompts the significance of sound monitoring, explainable AI frameworks, and ways to address systemic risk due to fully automated decision-making.

Influence of Algorithms on Behavior and Decision-Making

In addition to apparent capabilities, the AI systems may have a hidden, significant impact on human actions and decision-making (Herath Pathirannehelage et al., 2024; Storey et al., 2024). An example of such influence can be the social media algorithms, which do not simply resonate with user preferences; they construct them. Short-sighted algorithms maximize content that elicits extreme responses and, as a result, could even increase polarization of extremes or misinformation. In the retail business, the role of AI recommendation engines is obvious because they push the customers to make decisions in favor of particular products even when they are not aware of such manipulations. Likewise, it is possible to see an automated system come into play in education and job hiring, where opportunities could be whittled down by mostly unenforceable rules. Even medical decisions themselves (previously solely the subject of manual judgement by human clinicians) come to be informed by algorithmically estimated risk and prognosis. The technologies are not neutral and give a place to definite logics, prejudices, and priorities, inducing the activity of the users to reproduce the definite habits, perceptions of the world, and lines of decisions. This shows that it is urgent to learn that algorithmic influence is more than a technical optimization; rather, it is a sociotechnical effect with some moral implications.

Benefits and Dependencies in Digital Life

Massive use of AI has indeed come with tremendous advantages-efficiency, convenience, and personalization, to mention but a few. Individual learning conditions promote the elimination of achievement differences. The use of AI in finance makes budgeting and investing easy. In healthcare, AI eliminates the number of diagnostic mistakes and improves predictive care. These systems improve human potential, mechanical repetitive activities, and make services more reactive and flexible. Nevertheless, we are getting more and more dependent due to the increase in AI reliance. People are usually unaware of the decisions taken in their favor and what data are being gathered and processed. And the comfort of predictive text, or a smart assistant, or the AI-curated news feed will make you less creative, less critical, and less of an agent. In addition, systemic reliance on black-box AI systems may become problematic when algorithms are on the verge of breakdown, breakage, or continue to perpetuate the bias. This being the two-sidedness of AI as an accelerator and a potential dependency, philosopher requires, we pay close attention to design, transparency, and education so as to create the autonomous and informed digital citizen.

Whether it is in the initial moments of the day as we scroll through our smartphone devices or it is at the end of the week as we have to overdose on a given TV series nestled in someone's recommendation, Artificial Intelligence, or AI, is sitting in the middle of most of our lives. Siri, Alexa, Google Assistant, etc. are examples of virtual assistants that understand voice instructions with the help of natural language processing and organize daily schedules. IoT-enabled Smart homes adapt to the preferences learned by the lighting, security, and climate-practicing systems. Applications Google Maps and ride-sharing algorithms of Uber or Careem utilize AI in urban mobility by creating fast routes and prices. AI can be used by e-commerce platforms to forecast demand, stock distribution, as well as to target individualized offers. Industry example: Streaming services like Netflix and Spotify base their recommendations regarding mood, genre preferences, and watch history via AI. This omnipresence in day-to-day interactions displays to what extent these systems have become entrenched in our lives, not by being flashy, futuristic, but rather subtle and constant facilitation of our experiences in the world that continues to shape them.

AI is not only transforming modes of service interaction but also modes of self and others' perception since it is extending the self in digital environments. Consumers start to be constructed into a social identity, consumer persona, and even professional opportunities based on digital profiles, based on algorithmic interpretation of our behavior. On the one hand, the digital lives of people are becoming more algorithmically mediated, hence the boundaries between choice and manipulation become unclear. As an example, the social media networks have the "echo chamber" phenomena that restrict exposure to various perspectives, which is a passive way to affect political views and social attitudes. In the meantime, AI-based health and fitness applications create data-related stories over wellness, productivity, or self-worth. To learn more about the place of AI in people's lives, one has to go above and beyond the usefulness of this technology and focus on its impact on human principles, interactions, and social systems. As citizens and communities, but also as humans, there is no longer a choice in whether we learn to be AI-literate; it is imperative that we need to protect our agency and learn how a more inclusive and reflective digital future can be achieved.

CHALLENGES AND RISKS

Algorithmic Bias and Discrimination

Algorithmic bias may be one of the most tenacious and recalcitrant issues in AI systems, since it can happen when machine learning algorithms incorporate/or exacerbate pre-existing socially discriminating patterns or patterns baked into their training data (Akter et al., 2021; Kordzadeh & Ghasemaghaei, 2022; Makanadar et al., 2024). These prejudices may be neither implicit nor systematic, and they are based on the historical data of the past that denotes disparate treatment in such areas as policing, lending, healthcare, or employment. As an example, facial recognition systems possess an elevated rate of errors in identifying people with darker skin tones, which has a practical implication in the form of erroneous arrests or denial of service to individuals. On the same note, when hiring an algorithm, it might unintentionally give preferences over candidates based on the history of hiring, which reinforces the gender or race bias in terms of employment opportunities. The opaqueness and size of algorithmic bias are what make the subject so concerning. Biased AI systems do not respond well to humans because they are run out of black boxes, and unlike human decision-makers, who can be accountable and argued with, one cannot know why biased AI systems show what or how they do. Besides, after implementation, such systems will generate biased decisions thousands or millions of times, which introduces discrimination into seemingly neutral or efficient processes. To resolve this dilemma, the design of the algorithm must be transparent, the training data must be diverse, as well as continue to be audited AI systems to identify and resolve biased patterns. Nevertheless, due to the growing deployment of AI in such sensitive areas as justice, financial services, and public services, the threat of algorithmic impairment has become a topic of primary concern related to social equity and human rights.

Data Privacy and Surveillance Concerns

The spread of AI has tremendously expanded the volume and extent of data gathering to the point where privacy and surveillance are becoming of concern (Yang et al., 2024). The AI systems rely on massive amounts of personal data to operate efficiently, either in the form of search records, biometrics, audio recordings, geolocation data, or shopping habits. This information is easily and secretly collected, and at times without consent. As states, as well as companies, use AI as a means to observe behavior, monitor movement, or profile their users, citizens are becoming more vulnerable to some form of digital surveillance, which may selectively violate rights to privacy. In authoritarian regimes, it is possible to use

AI-powered surveillance tools, including facial recognition, predictive policing, or social credit score, to silence the opposition and strengthen control. In democracies, personal information is gathered by the data brokers and tech firms that have been exploiting consumer data, often based on a form of consent, with terms that are unclear or complicated. The increasing application of AI in civic spheres, including the infrastructure of smart cities or surveillance in the field of public health, continues to dilute the border between safety and surveillance. The use of AI-supported surveillance will damage trust, freedom of expression, and democratic existence without strong safety regulations, ethics, and methodologies to control the user. The reinforcement of legal regulations such as the GDPR or data minimization and the use of privacy-enhancing solutions in the area of AI (such as federated learning) may be the necessary steps to protect civil liberties in the digital world.

Economic Disruption and Labor Displacement

AI systems are quickly rendering pointless activities that used to be done by humans, leading to great unemployment in the labor market (George, 2024; Occhipinti et al., 2025; Ramarajan et al., 2024). By leaving the routine, analytical, or repetitive tasks to AI systems, the ordinary work sectors (manufacturing, transportation, customer service, and even professional spheres such as law or journalism) will experience a change. As an example, the chatbots that utilize machine learning and answer customer questions are already offered by AI-driven applications, autonomous vehicles promise to replace truck and taxi drivers, and natural language processing tools can create a legal document or even analyze a financial report. This automation can be quite beneficial to the organization, as it provides efficiency and lowers costs, but at the same time causes fear among people who are not sure about their jobs and long-term employment. Labor displacement AI is not evenly distributed. There are greater chances that the low-skilled and middle-tier jobs will be automated, leading to a widening of income inequality and polarized economies. Furthermore, the positive impact of AI is usually available to the people who can access higher education, digital infrastructure, and capital, resulting in a digital gap between the users of AI and others who are excluded. Implementation of an AI-driven economy will therefore necessitate some active policy response: skilling up initiatives, social insurance flows, inclusive innovation, and ethical AI adoption within workplaces. In the absence of such interventions, the economic opportunities of AI may herald mass dislocation in the labor market and a destabilized society.

Mental Health and Misinformation

The finding of the applications of AI on mental health is gaining more attention, particularly due to how the use of algorithm-based systems impacts how a person interacts with others, how they pay attention, and how they view themselves (Baeza-Yates et al., 2024; Ogunwale et al., 2024). AI enhancement of social media platforms aims at increasing engagement by maximizing which content provokes the strongest emotional response in a user, which tends to be outrage, envy, or fear. All these various filtered realities, algorithm-chosen news, attention-hacking reminders, can cause stress, feelings of loneliness, sleep disturbance, and even depression. Probably associated with the appearance of AI-curated content, there is also a set of studies on a number of issues that have emerged in connection with the phenomenon: an increase in body image problems among adolescents, polarization both in culture and in a civic sense, and a decline in digital well-being. Going hand in hand with this is the issue of AI propagating the information of misinformation and disinformation. Generative AI functions allow creating fake content that can trick people into believing it, even as realistic fake videos (deepfakes) or fake news (synthetic articles). The promotion of conspiracy theories or other falsehoods through AI algorithms used on such platforms as YouTube and Facebook is possible because AI algorithms focus on those items that are the most engaging without considering how correct/accurate they might be. When crises occur, like a pandemic or an election, the dynamics can be dramatic with potentially disastrous results, weakening or destroying the health response or destabilizing electoral processes. It is necessary to fight against these issues by adopting more vigorous content moderation tools, media literacy, ethical algorithm design, and open processes that ignore or de-rank damaging content. The overlap of AI, information ecosystems, and mental health is a hot spot in terms of technical progress as well as social responsibility.

POLICIES AND REGULATIONS

Major Policy Efforts

With the growing power of Artificial Intelligence in sectors and international borders, governments and global institutions have started developing regulatory policies in order to see to it that the technologies applied in AI are developed and implemented responsibly. It may be considered one of the most comprehensive legislative ventures as the European Union introduces the AI Act that classifies the AI applications according to the risk groups, such as those with low, substantial, or unacceptable risk, and provides strict requirements on the high-risk systems. These comprise transparency requirements, human oversight mandates, and restrictions on the application of AI capabilities in one of the forms, like biometric surveillance or social scoring. The act is not just trying to safeguard the rights of EU citizens, but also tries to establish a global framework of rights-based, trusted governance of AI.

Intergovernmental organizations have made a big step outside the EU as well. Outside of the OECD AI Principles, which are recognized by more than 40 countries, uphold human-centered principles like transparent, robust, and accountable AI design and implementation. The focus of these guidelines is international collaboration, investment in R&D, and the significance of data governance. In the same manner, the recommendation from UNESCO on the ethics of AI urges the creation of inclusive policies, environmental sustainability, and protection against the harms of algorithms. Although these efforts have varying degrees of legal binding, it appears that there is an increasing consensus amongst the community about the necessity of having a common moral ground and a system of organizing AI governance.

Gaps in Regulation

Nevertheless, many deficiencies exist in terms of global governmental regulation of AI despite these encouraging signals. Nations, especially those found in the Global South, have no national AI plans or legal framework to regulate AI applications, and as such, the citizens of these nations are at the mercy of technology experimentation. In addition, in developed countries, already established data protection or consumer safety legislation may tend to be poorly equipped to deal with the particular risks of AI as they are currently identified, exemplified by algorithmic discrimination, unintelligible decision-making, and autonomous systems. Forces of rapid innovation gain an advantage over law and policy, and overcome regulatory controls, thus leading to what some term a governance lag, whereby potential ill applications may proliferate well prior to being regulated by valid law.

The problem is also complicated by the fact that international regulation is broken and inconsistent. AI is not a geopolitical technology, but the governance initiatives are mostly confined to a region or sector. This poses a threat of regulatory arbitrage, wherein firms relocate to locations where regulation is less tough. There are also geopolitical strains to consensus-building: on one hand, the EU focuses on rights-based forms of regulation; on the one hand, nations, such as the U.S., insist on regulation based on the promotion of innovation and light-touch regulation; on the other, other nations, such as China, favours greater forms of state-led hegemony of control and surveillance. The vision of a harmonized, global AI governance regime can only become a reality in the absence of international coordination mechanisms, e.g., a treaty, multilateral standards, or some framework of joint enforcement. To fill these gaps, it will be necessary to encourage an open dialogue, cross-border data standards, and interoperability frameworks to make sure that AI is developing in a way that works in the interest of everyone.

Ethics vs. Enforceable Law in AI Governance

The main conflict related to AI governance is the separation of ethical principles and legal regulations. Ethics frameworks, which may be done by research institutions or NGOs, can clearly express such laudable values as fairness, accountability, transparency, and non-maleficence. These guidelines are excellent guidelines for ethically responsible innovation, particularly in the case of a lack of official governmental regulation. Nevertheless, they are usually not enforceable; thus, the company is free to use ethical phrasing without using much in terms of concrete action, which can be collectively known as ethics washing. Consequently, voluntary codes of conduct may be insufficient to safeguard the interests of the population where economic factors or commercial forces encourage more risk-taking behaviour.

Conversely, legal structures are binding, though they tend to lag behind the rapidity and the intricacy of the development of technologies. The complexity of abstract terms related to explainability (or algorithmic harm), such as these definitions, presents a problem to lawmakers who may struggle to define such concepts in terms that can be acted upon by the legal system. Moreover, it is a fine line between controlling AI and suppressing innovation: most laws can restrict or block positive research, and loose legislation can allow some potentially dangerous applications. Governance of AI should therefore be a hybrid of both: unrealistic idealism of ethical philosophy and the binding statute of the law. This entails incorporation of ethical values into regulatory design, reinforcement of accountability by application of audits and impact assessments, and development of laws based on inclusive policies and in an evidence-based manner. The future of AI governance boils down to whether we can develop shared values that we can recognize in long-lasting institutions and legal protection.

BUILDING RESPONSIBLE AI

Responsible Innovation and Inclusive Design

Responsible AI should be built by instilling good ethics at all phases of the innovation lifecycle, i.e. fairness, transparency, accountability, etc. By responsible innovation, we have to look at the social and ethical impacts of AI systems in advance, and we must make sure that they can only serve the public good, but not commercial or state interests. It means that we have to extend beyond such performance measures as accuracy or efficiency and ask: Who will be helped by this AI system? Who can be injured? And what are the assumptions in its logic? Inclusive design is critical at this point, where the consideration of the different users, communities, and perspectives should also be reflected during design and testing. The lack of this inclusion can result in the recreation of already established social disparities or the deprivation of existing groups who are not well-represented in the digital realm of benefits.

The idea of inclusive AI also implies designing accessibility, which is the possibility to have people of various backgrounds in terms of language and literacy, abilities, and socio-economics, use and employ AI-driven services effectively. This could include voice interface design for low-literacy users, the construction of diverse datasets and algorithms that can be audited for fairness to different population groups. Inclusive design must not be a check-the-box or a second thought, but rather a trust, ease of use, and ethical resiliency to AI systems. Institutions, developers, and funders should carry these principles and apply them at the level of design review, hiring patterns, and community-based IDE reviews.

Public Engagement and Digital Literacy

An active public engagement is one of the foundations of responsible AI that extends beyond informing the users of AI, but includes them in decisions regarding how AI should be subject to governance and use. Time and again, the design of AI systems remains a secretive affair, and the systems are foisted on the masses with neither consultation nor comprehension. This technocratic method creates distrust and exposes society to destructive effects. Authentic participation implies establishing mechanisms of discussion between developers, policymakers, and citizens, particularly the most interested and at-risk groups that should become most affected by automated decisions. Some examples of how the voice of the people can build responsible AI are participatory design workshops, open consultations, citizen juries, and digital ethics forums.

Digital literacy accompanies engagement as another key to empowering individuals to explore the AI-based systems. Since AI is gradually taking over every sector, including education, employment, health, and government, business owners and end-users should be aware of how it functions, what rights they possess, and how to appeal wrong or false results. Digital literacy is not only mastering the usage of apps but also the process of studying topics like the algorithmic decision-making process, data privacy, consent versus digital security. The responsibilities to foster AI literacy also lie with governments, schools, media, and civil society organizations, in terms of bringing it to the curriculum, national awareness campaigns, and making concrete learning materials available. Another necessity is a digitally literate population, which allows not only holding the AI in check but also keeping its evolution at the level that is consistent with democratic principles and social imperatives.

AI as a Tool for Empowerment

In its accessible forms, AI can become a potent empowerment instrument: assuring people to make better decisions, gain access to necessary services, and play a more active role in society. In common examples, AI could be used to help farmers in remote areas with crop projections and weather information, provide people with disability with voice recognition and real-time translation services, and provide access to credit to low-resource populations by developing alternative credit scores. It is also possible to improve the levels of civic engagement, including natural language processing to facilitate readership of policy texts or the use of chatbots to make government and agency connections easier. Used in the service of the common good, AI is an enabling multiplier of inclusion, equity, and development.

But the promise of it is usually dominated by the idea of AI as a means of control rather than liberation: invasive surveillance systems, biased predictive policing, murky social scoring systems. These apps degrade human dignity and limit freedom, especially in authoritarian settings or in impoverished societies that are placed under top-down automation. Whether AI should be an empowerment or a control is simply up to our approach in solving and regulating the use of the technology. The future of AI should be institutionalized, and its safeguards should protect its rights, as well as invest efforts in applications that bridge inequality gaps, and ensure that AI supplements rather than supplants human agency. In order to serve humanity, AI should serve people and not them.

Since AI technologies keep on transforming societies, economies, and systems of governance, policymakers need to make sure that the development of these technologies is based on democratic principles, human rights, and social inclusion. The proposed policy recommendations are intended to pursue the development of responsible, transparent, and equitable AI ecosystems that empower individuals and communities instead of maintaining control over them.

Recommendations for Responsible AI Development

The use of ethical principles of AI design should be required by policymakers in both public and privately sponsored operations. This will mean that algorithm developers must pass an algorithmic impact assessment (AIA) before their deployment, at least in high-consequence applications like healthcare, education, policing, or the provision of any kind of welfare payments. Governments can present an inclusivity check to guarantee that datasets are diverse in terms of demographics and that AI systems can be employed by individuals with varying capabilities, language, and levels of literacy. The enforceable design protocols that meet national standards should be established by national standards bodies in collaboration with the civil society and academia so that transparency, explainability, and fairness are built into the development process a priori.

There must be official channels of citizen engagement in policymaking regarding AI. It involves citizen assemblies, community co-design, and online portals of consultation to make sure that the marginalized or unsuspecting population is also heard. These platforms are not just supposed to inform, but they should also make decisions on the use and governance of AI. Also, ethicists, social scientists, law specialists, and community representatives should form regulatory and research oversight advisory councils to enhance multidisciplinary research.

The governments must include AI and digital literacy in national curricula, teacher education programs, and public awareness initiatives to develop informed citizenry's interaction with AI. It is a sort of education that must not be limited to technical knowledge but also embraces the skill of thinking critically about AI ethics, data rights, algorithmic transparency, and digital safety. Lifelong learning on AI could be developed around public libraries, local community facilities, and media.

Although ethics are good provisions, the securities of rights must be enforced lawfully in an AI-driven world. Governments ought to come up with fully established legal frameworks that govern the use of AI in surveillance, hiring, credit scoring, health, and law enforcement. Among them are a ban or the strict constriction of the high-risk application of facial recognition in the general areas, predictive policing, and the social scoring made through AI. Data protection rules should also be extended to AI-related damages, such as automated decision-making, profiling, and manipulation of consent. Such laws must be in conformance with global human rights standards and must have robust mechanisms for ensuring enforcement and remedy.

Governments and international donors must create funding adjustment opportunities to enable projects that focus on the greater good in ethics of application, accessibility, and social good of AI. These can be AI in affordable education, rural health, agricultural resilience, disaster response, and civic engagement. The requirements proposed on funding calls must be interdisciplinary and include community partnerships so that the co-creation of solutions is through mutual testing with the intended beneficiaries.

Since AI is not a nation-specific technology, governments should act together to create interoperable rules, a common ground to oversee, and international principles of responsible AI. The third point towards a greater role in these international forums, like the OECD AI Policy Observatory, UNESCO, and UN AI For Good, needs to be pushed by Pakistan and other developing countries, as it should be a more inclusive process for the developing world. The presence of regional blocks, mainly of the Global South countries, can magnify the voice on concerns relating to equity, development, and cultural contexts in AI governance.

CONCLUSION

Since expanding and developing artificial intelligence has become a part of almost all aspects of contemporary lives, the impact it might have on society has gained a lot of depth. Whether it is determining how to engage in a social media platform, a diagnostic technique, determining medical procedures or protocols, AI is not an out-of-reach or theoretical technology but is a current and active presence in our households, learning institutions, places of work, and in the streets. The current chapter has examined how AI is embedded into everyday life and provides both the scale of opportunities never seen before and new kinds of risk. Although AI could be used to increase efficiency, personalization, and scale-up of problems, the unregulated application of AI also creates alarming issues related to fairness, privacy, transparency, and human well-being.

Some of the most urgent issues include anti-bias in algorithms, surveillance of data, misinformation, and loss of jobs. The latter are not just technical shortcomings, but indicators of the values, assumptions, and priorities that are at the base of the design and use of AI systems. Therefore, such cannot be dealt with by engineering solutions only. Instead, they require a change in our governance, evaluation, and involvement in AI development. Another aspect that was indicated in the chapter is that the existing regulatory initiatives, including the EU AI Act and OECD AI Principles, are an important step to accountability, although there is still little coordination across the world and enforceable legal tools. Moreover, the distance between ethical ideals and their realization persists to grow; that is why the bridge between the aspirational framework and the enforceable right should be reinforced.

The only way to develop an AI that is indeed responsible, non-discriminatory, and reflects democratic ideals is to use a multi-pronged strategy. These covers integrate notions of fairness and inclusivity in the design processes, meaningful participation of people, and the spread of AI literacy. It also asks that legal safeguards be instituted that not only protect individuals but also enable them to comprehend and contest the result of algorithmic decision-making. Notably, AI cannot be a controlling or commercial commodity instrument; rather, it can be used as an opportunity-opener to increase human agency and social equity. This needs governments, technology firms, scientists, and civil society to be partners in the development of AI ecosystems that serve the common good rather than personal interests.

The question then should be not whether we can make more powerful artificial intelligence systems--but whether we will be able to make them responsibly, equitably, and ethically. It requires an explicit responsibility on the part of technological improvement to conform to fundamental human principles: dignity, freedom, equity, justice, and the common good. AI cannot be perceived as just the toolset, but rather the project of the society that shows what type of future we would like to create. It is the challenge that needs foresight, humility, and cooperation among disciplines and nations as well as between communities.

The way ahead should therefore be steered by inclusive innovation and sound governance as we are at this crossroads. That is the only way in which AI may be an uplifting power that benefits people and makes people stronger instead of dividing and weakening them. It is in this light that AI might be a technology that may serve people, as opposed to a technology that dominates or takes the place of people. The decisions that we make nowadays will define not only the future of AI but also the future of society.

REFERENCES

Ahmad, M., Ho, W. Y., Goyes Robalino, A. P., Maqsood, M., Ahmad, M., Ho, W. Y., Goyes Robalino, A. P., & Maqsood, M. (2025). Theoretical Implications of Generative AI for Content Generation in Geoinformatics Training. In A. Anna A. (Ed.), *Integration Strategies of Generative AI in Higher Education* (pp. 101–130). IGI Global Scientific Publishing. https://doi.org/DOI: 10.4018/979-8-3693-5518-3.CH005

Akter, S., Dwivedi, Y. K., Biswas, K., Michael, K., Bandara, R. J., & Sajib, S. (2021). Addressing Algorithmic Bias in AI-Driven Customer Management. *Journal of Global Information Management*, *29*(6). Advance online publication. DOI: 10.4018/JGIM.20211101.oa3

Ali, M. H., Kainat, M., Maqsood, M., Fernandez, S. F., Ali, S., & Ahmad, M. (2024). Chatbots in Academic Literacy Exploring AI in Education. In *Enhancing Higher Education and Research With OpenAI Models* (pp. 37–59). IGI Global.

Almathami, H. K. Y., Than Win, K., & Vlahu-Gjorgievska, E. (2020). Barriers and facilitators that influence telemedicine-based, real-time, online consultation at patients' homes: Systematic literature review. In *Journal of Medical Internet Research* (Vol. 22, Issue 2). https://doi.org/DOI: 10.2196/16407

Anderljung, M., Hazell, J., & von Knebel, M. (2024). Protecting society from AI misuse: When are restrictions on capabilities warranted? *AI & Society*, *40*(5), 3841–3857. DOI: 10.1007/S00146-024-02130-8/FIGURES/2

Baeza-Yates, R., Fayyad, U. M., & Fayyad, U. (2024). Responsible AI: An Urgent Mandate. *IEEE Intelligent Systems*, *39*(1), 12–17. DOI: 10.1109/MIS.2023.3343488

Bangash, S. A., Shah, S. S., Adam, M. A., Khan, M. F. I., & Ahmad, M. (2025). Chatbots in Telemedicine: Exploring Ethical Dimensions of AI in Healthcare. In Duygu, Ç. E., & Atilla, E. (Eds.), *Multifaceted Uses of Cutting-Edge Technologies and Social Concerns* (pp. 33–60). IGI Global Scientific Publishing., DOI: 10.4018/979-8-3693-9591-2.CH002

Cao, L. (2022). AI in Finance: Challenges, Techniques, and Opportunities. *ACM Computing Surveys*, *55*(3). Advance online publication. DOI: 10.1145/3502289

Chow, J. C. L., Wong, V., Sanders, L., & Li, K. (2023). Developing an AI-Assisted Educational Chatbot for Radiotherapy Using the IBM Watson Assistant Platform. *Healthcare (Switzerland)*, *11*(17). Advance online publication. DOI: 10.3390/healthcare11172417 PMID: 37685452

Di, X. (2023). Regulatory leadership in struggling–the US path in robo-advisors governance. *Law and Financial Markets Review, 17*(2), 116–135. DOI: 10.1080/17521440.2024.2313473

Doniec, R. J., Piaseczna, N. J., Szymczyk, K. A., Jacennik, B., Sieciński, S., Mocny-Pachońska, K., Duraj, K., Cedro, T., Tkacz, E. J., & Glinkowski, W. M. (2023). Experiences of the Telemedicine and eHealth Conferences in Poland—A Cross-National Overview of Progress in Telemedicine. In *Applied Sciences (Switzerland)* (Vol. 13, Issue 1). https://doi.org/DOI: 10.3390/app13010587

Farina, M., Zhdanov, P., Karimov, A., & Lavazza, A. (2024). AI and society: A virtue ethics approach. *AI & Society, 39*(3), 1127–1140. DOI: 10.1007/S00146-022-01545-5/METRICS

George, Dr. A. S. (2024). Bracing for the Coming AI Tsunami: Preparing the Global Workforce for Displacement and Inequality in the Age of Accelerating Technological Advancement. *Partners Universal Innovative Research Publication, 2*(3), 126–146. DOI: 10.5281/ZENODO.11668571

Herath Pathirannehelage, S., Shrestha, Y. R., & von Krogh, G. (2024). Design principles for artificial intelligence-augmented decision making: An action design research study. *European Journal of Information Systems*. Advance online publication. DOI: 10.1080/0960085X.2024.2330402;PAGE:STRING:ARTICLE/CHAPTER

Hsien, K., Chung, Y., Adriaens, P., Han, H., Liu, Z., Wang, X., & Li, S. (2021). Research of the Relations Among Cloud Computing, Internet of Things, Big Data, Artificial Intelligence, Block Chain and Their Application in Maritime Field. *Journal of Physics: Conference Series, 1927*(1), 012026. DOI: 10.1088/1742-6596/1927/1/012026

Imran, M., & Almusharraf, N. (2024). Google Gemini as a next generation AI educational tool: A review of emerging educational technology. *Smart Learning Environments, 11*(1), 1–8. DOI: 10.1186/S40561-024-00310-Z/METRICS

Iyer, L. S. (2021). AI enabled applications towards intelligent transportation. *Transportation Engineering, 5*. Advance online publication. DOI: 10.1016/j.treng.2021.100083

Joseph, S., Ul-Ain, Q., Nosheen, S., Ahmad, M., & Fatima, R. (2024). Navigating the Promise and Perils of Generative AI in Healthcare. In *Revolutionizing the Healthcare Sector with AI* (pp. 91–110). IGI Global.

Kaul, R., Ossai, C., Forkan, A. R. M., Jayaraman, P. P., Zelcer, J., Vaughan, S., & Wickramasinghe, N. (2023). The role of AI for developing digital twins in healthcare: The case of cancer care. *Wiley Interdisciplinary Reviews. Data Mining and Knowledge Discovery, 13*(1). Advance online publication. DOI: 10.1002/widm.1480

Kaur, A., Kaur, H., & Tanwar, A. (2024). *Are Robo-Advisors Revolutionizing Portfolio Management for Enhanced Returns Over Human Advisors?* 165–191. https://doi.org/: Kazu, İ. Y., & Kuvvetli, M. (2025). Digital language learning with Duolingo: assessing its impact on listening, speaking, reading, and writing skills. *Journal of Computers in Education*, 1–27. https://doi.org/DOI: 10.4018/979-8-3693-2185-0.CH008

Kordzadeh, N., & Ghasemaghaei, M. (2022). Algorithmic bias: review, synthesis, and future research directions. In *European Journal of Information Systems* (Vol. 31, Issue 3). https://doi.org/DOI: 10.1080/0960085X.2021.1927212

Kulal, A., Rahiman, H. U., Suvarna, H., Abhishek, N., & Dinesh, S. (2024). Enhancing public service delivery efficiency: Exploring the impact of AI. *Journal of Open Innovation, 10*(3), 100329. DOI: 10.1016/J.JOITMC.2024.100329

Labadze, L., Grigolia, M., & Machaidze, L. (2023). Role of AI chatbots in education: Systematic literature review. *International Journal of Educational Technology in Higher Education, 20*(1), 56.

Li, Z., Pardos, Z. A., & Ren, C. (2024). Aligning open educational resources to new taxonomies: How AI technologies can help and in which scenarios. *Computers & Education, 216*, 105027. DOI: 10.1016/J.COMPEDU.2024.105027

Makanadar, A., Shahane, S., & Patil, U. (2024). Tracing Algorithmic and AI-biased Data. *Economic and Political Weekly, 59*(7).

Maleki Varnosfaderani, S., & Forouzanfar, M. (2024). The Role of AI in Hospitals and Clinics: Transforming Healthcare in the 21st Century. *Bioengineering 2024, Vol. 11, Page 337, 11*(4), 337. https://doi.org/DOI: 10.3390/BIOENGINEERING11040337

Mana, A. A., Allouhi, A., Hamrani, A., Rahman, S., el Jamaoui, I., & Jayachandran, K. (2024). Sustainable AI-based production agriculture: Exploring AI applications and implications in agricultural practices. *Smart Agricultural Technology, 7*. Advance online publication. DOI: 10.1016/j.atech.2024.100416

Maqsood, M., Butt, H. H., Ali, M. A., Chinedu, C. C., Ahmad, M., Maqsood, M., Butt, H. H., Ali, M. A., Chinedu, C. C., & Ahmad, M. (2025). Chatbots as Learning Companions Exploring Ethical Dimensions of AI in Education. In Jean-Éric, P. (Ed.), *Architecting the Digital Future: Platforms, Design, and Application* (pp. 311–348). IGI Global Scientific Publishing., DOI: 10.4018/979-8-3693-2973-3.CH012

Miao, F., & Holmes, W. (2021). *AI and education: A guidance for policymakers*. Unesco Publishing.

Molfino, R., Cepolina, F. E., Cepolina, E., Cepolina, E. M., & Cepolina, S. (2024). Robots trends and megatrends: Artificial intelligence and the society. *The Industrial Robot*, *51*(1), 117–124. DOI: 10.1108/IR-05-2023-0095/FULL/PDF

Muheidat, F., Patel, D., Tammisetty, S., Tawalbeh, L. A., & Tawalbeh, M. (2022). Emerging Concepts Using Blockchain and Big Data. *Procedia Computer Science*, *198*, 15–22. DOI: 10.1016/J.PROCS.2021.12.206

Nair, M. M., & Tyagi, A. K. (2023). AI, IoT, blockchain, and cloud computing: The necessity of the future. *Distributed Computing to Blockchain: Architecture, Technology, and Applications*, 189–206. https://doi.org/DOI: 10.1016/B978-0-323-96146-2.00001-2

Occhipinti, J. A., Prodan, A., Hynes, W., Buchanan, J., Green, R., Burrow, S., Eyre, H. A., Skinner, A., Hickie, I. B., Heffernan, M., Song, Y. J. C., Ujdur, G., & Tanner, M. (2025). Artificial intelligence, recessionary pressures and population health. *Bulletin of the World Health Organization*, *103*(2), 155. DOI: 10.2471/BLT.24.291950 PMID: 39882489

Ogunwale, A., Smith, A., Fakorede, O., & Ogunlesi, A. O. (2024). Artificial intelligence and forensic mental health in Africa: A narrative review. *International Review of Psychiatry (Abingdon, England)*, *37*(1), 3–13. DOI: 10.1080/09540261.2024.2405174;WGROUP:STRING:PUBLICATION PMID: 40035373

Owsley, C. S., & Greenwood, K. (2024). Awareness and perception of artificial intelligence operationalized integration in news media industry and society. *AI & Society*, *39*(1), 417–431. DOI: 10.1007/S00146-022-01386-2/METRICS

Peng, S. (2021). *Blockchain for Big Data : AI, IoT and Cloud Perspectives*. Blockchain for Big Data., DOI: 10.1201/9781003201670

Qatawneh, A. M. (2024). The role of artificial intelligence in auditing and fraud detection in accounting information systems: Moderating role of natural language processing. *The International Journal of Organizational Analysis*, *33*(6), 1391–1409. DOI: 10.1108/IJOA-03-2024-4389/FULL/XML

Rajpurkar, P., Chen, E., Banerjee, O., & Topol, E. J. (2022). AI in health and medicine. In *Nature Medicine* (Vol. 28, Issue 1). https://doi.org/DOI: 10.1038/s41591-021-01614-0

Ramarajan, M., Dinesh, A., Muthuraman, C., Rajini, J., Anand, T., & Segar, B. (2024). AI-Driven Job Displacement and Economic Impacts. 216–238. https://doi.org/: DOI: 10.4018/979-8-3693-2643-5.CH013

Rana, P., Ahmad, M., Stephen, T., & Chemingui, H. (2025). Agricultural Intelligence (AI)'s Impact on Society 5.0 Farming. In Rajiv, P. (Ed.), *Open AI and Computational Intelligence for Society 5.0* (pp. 109–128). IGI Global Scientific Publishing., DOI: 10.4018/979-8-3693-4326-5.CH005

Sachoulidou, A. (2024). Harnessing AI for law enforcement: Solutions and boundaries from the forthcoming AI Act. *New Journal of European Criminal Law*, *15*(2), 117–125. DOI: 10.1177/20322844241260114;PAGEGROUP:STRING:PUBLICATION

Sharma, S. (2024). Benefits or concerns of AI: A multistakeholder responsibility. *Futures*, *157*, 103328. DOI: 10.1016/J.FUTURES.2024.103328

Storey, V. C., Hevner, A. R., & Yoon, V. Y. (2024). The design of human-artificial intelligence systems in decision sciences: A look back and directions forward. *Decision Support Systems*, *182*, 114230. DOI: 10.1016/J.DSS.2024.114230

Trocin, C., Mikalef, P., Papamitsiou, Z., & Conboy, K. (2023). Responsible AI for Digital Health: A Synthesis and a Research Agenda. *Information Systems Frontiers*, *25*(6). Advance online publication. DOI: 10.1007/s10796-021-10146-4

Vasileiou, M. V., & Maglogiannis, I. G. (2022). The Health ChatBots in Telemedicine: Intelligent Dialog System for Remote Support. *Journal of Healthcare Engineering*, *2022*. Advance online publication. DOI: 10.1155/2022/4876512

Yang, L., Tian, M., Xin, D., Cheng, Q., & Zheng, J. (2024). AI-driven anonymization: Protecting personal data privacy while leveraging machine learning. *Applied and Computational Engineering*, *67*(1), 273–279. DOI: 10.54254/2755-2721/67/2024MA0053

Zhang, P., & Kamel Boulos, M. N. (2023). Generative AI in Medicine and Healthcare: Promises, Opportunities and Challenges. In *Future Internet* (Vol. 15, Issue 9). https://doi.org/DOI: 10.3390/fi15090286

Zhou, J., Chen, C., Li, L., Zhang, Z., & Zheng, X. (2022). FinBrain 2.0: when finance meets trustworthy AI. In *Frontiers of Information Technology and Electronic Engineering* (Vol. 23, Issue 12). https://doi.org/DOI: 10.1631/FITEE.2200039

Compilation of References

14 biggest healthcare data breaches [Updated 2024] | UpGuard. (n.d.). https://www.upguard.com/blog/biggest-data-breaches-in-healthcare

Adanma, U. M., & Ogunbiyi, E. O. (2024). Artificial intelligence in environmental conservation: Evaluating cyber risks and opportunities for sustainable practices. *Computer Science & IT Research Journal*, *5*(5), 1178–1209.

Adekunle, A. (2024). Application of Artificial Intelligence and Digital Technologies in Fashion Design and Innovation in Nigeria. *International Journal of Fashion and Design*, *3*(1). Advance online publication. DOI: 10.47604/ijfd.2389

Adeleye, O. O., Eden, C. A., & Adeniyi, I. S. (2024). Innovative teaching methodologies in the era of artificial intelligence: A review of inclusive educational practices. *World Journal of Advanced Engineering Technology and Sciences*, *11*(2). Advance online publication. DOI: 10.30574/wjaets.2024.11.2.0091

Adelmann, F., Ergen, I., Gaidosch, T., Jenkinson, N., Khiaonarong, M. T., Morozova, A., Schwarz, N., & Wilson, C. (2020). *Cyber risk and financial stability: It's a small world after all.* International Monetary Fund.

ADL. (2021). *Online Hate and Harassment: The American Experience 2021*. ADL. www.adl.org

Adom, R. K., & Simatele, M. D. (2025). Enhancing water management in South Africa: The need for efficiency in monitoring and evaluation programmes. *Environmental Systems Research*, *14*(1), 9. DOI: 10.1186/s40068-025-00400-y

Adu-Gyamfi, B., Ariyaningsih, A., Zuquan, H., Yamazawa, N., Kato, A., & Shaw, R. (2024). Reflections on science, technology and innovation on the aspirations of the Sendai framework for disaster risk reduction. *International Journal of Disaster Resilience in the Built Environment*, *15*(2). Advance online publication. DOI: 10.1108/IJDRBE-06-2022-0062

Afzal, A., Khan, S., Daud, S., Ahmad, Z., & Butt, A. (2023). Addressing the Digital Divide: Access and use of technology in education. *Journal of Social Sciences Review*, *3*(2), 883–895.

Agrawal, G. (2024). *Accountability*. Trust, and Transparency in AI Systems From the Perspective of Public Policy., DOI: 10.4018/979-8-3693-7452-8.ch009

Ahmad, I., Sharma, S., Singh, R., Gehlot, A., Gupta, L. R., Thakur, A. K., Priyadarshi, N., & Twala, B. (2024). Inclusive learning using industry 4.0 technologies: addressing student diversity in modern education. In *Cogent Education* (Vol. 11, Issue 1). https://doi.org/DOI: 10.1080/2331186X.2024.2330235

Ahmad, M., Ho, W. Y., Goyes Robalino, A. P., Maqsood, M., Ahmad, M., Ho, W. Y., Goyes Robalino, A. P., & Maqsood, M. (2025). Theoretical Implications of Generative AI for Content Generation in Geoinformatics Training. In A. Anna A. (Ed.), *Integration Strategies of Generative AI in Higher Education* (pp. 101–130). IGI Global Scientific Publishing. https://doi.org/DOI: 10.4018/979-8-3693-5518-3.CH005

Ahmad, S., Zeb, B., Ditta, A., Alam, K., Shahid, U., Shah, A. U., & Alqurashi, M. (2023). Morphological, mineralogical, and biochemical characteristics of particulate matter in three size fractions (PM10, PM2. 5, and PM1) in the urban environment. *ACS Omega*, *8*(35), 31661–31674. PMID: 37692244

Ahmar, A. S., Singh, P. K., Ruliana, R., Pandey, A. K., & Gupta, S. (2023). Comparison of ARIMA, SutteARIMA, and holt-winters, and NNAR models to predict food grain in India. *Forecasting*, *5*(1), 138–152.

Ahmed, K., Mahmood, A., & Irfan, M. (2021). AI-driven environmental monitoring for smart cities: A systematic review. *Environmental Science & Policy*, *122*, 1–12.

Akindele, N., Taiwo, R., Sarvari, H., Oluleye, B. I., Awodele, I. A., & Olaniran, T. O. (2024). A state-of-the-art analysis of virtual reality applications in construction health and safety. *Results in Engineering*, *23*, 102382. DOI: 10.1016/j.rineng.2024.102382

Akter, S., Dwivedi, Y. K., Biswas, K., Michael, K., Bandara, R. J., & Sajib, S. (2021). Addressing Algorithmic Bias in AI-Driven Customer Management. *Journal of Global Information Management*, *29*(6). Advance online publication. DOI: 10.4018/JGIM.20211101.oa3

Akter, S., Dwivedi, Y. K., Sajib, S., Biswas, K., Bandara, R. J., & Michael, K. (2022). Algorithmic bias in machine learning-based marketing models. *Journal of Business Research*, *144*, 201–216. DOI: 10.1016/j.jbusres.2022.01.083

Al-Azawei, A., Parslow, P., & Lundqvist, K. (2016). The impact of universal design for learning on student engagement and academic achievement in higher education. *The Journal of Scholarship of Teaching and Learning*, *16*(3), 1–19.

Albahri, A. S., Khaleel, Y. L., Habeeb, M. A., Ismael, R. D., Hameed, Q. A., Deveci, M., & Alzubaidi, L. (2024). A systematic review of trustworthy artificial intelligence applications in natural disasters. *Computers & Electrical Engineering*, *118*, 109409.

Alenezi, M. (2023). Digital learning and digital institution in higher education. *Education Sciences*, *13*(1), 88.

Alessi, L., & Detken, C. (2018). Identifying excessive credit growth and leverage. *Journal of Financial Stability*, *35*, 215–225.

Ali, M. H., Kainat, M., Maqsood, M., Fernandez, S. F., Ali, S., & Ahmad, M. (2024). Chatbots in Academic Literacy Exploring AI in Education. In *Enhancing Higher Education and Research With OpenAI Models* (pp. 37–59). IGI Global.

Al-Khasawneh, A. (2015). A method for classification using data mining technique for diabetes: A study of Health care Information system. *International Journal of Healthcare Information Systems and Informatics*, *10*(3), 1–23. DOI: 10.4018/ijhisi.2015070101

Alkiviadou, N. (2022). *Artificial Intelligence and Online Hate Speech Moderation,* SUR 32. https://sur.conectas.org/en/artificial-intelligence-and-online-hate-speech-moderation/

AllahRakha, N. (2025). Cross-Border E-Crimes: Jurisdiction and Due Process Challenges. *ADLIYA Jurnal Hukum Dan Kemanusiaan, 18*(2), 153–170. https://doi.org/DOI: 10.15575/adliya.v18i2.38633

Alloghani, M. A. (2024). Using AI to Monitor Marine Environmental Pollution. *Systematic Reviews*, •••, 87–97. DOI: 10.1007/978-3-031-45214-7_5

Almathami, H. K. Y., Than Win, K., & Vlahu-Gjorgievska, E. (2020). Barriers and facilitators that influence telemedicine-based, real-time, online consultation at patients' homes: Systematic literature review. In *Journal of Medical Internet Research* (Vol. 22, Issue 2). https://doi.org/DOI: 10.2196/16407

Almeida, D. V., Kolinjivadi, V., Ferrando, T., Roy, B., Herrera, H., Gonçalves, M. V., & Van Hecken, G. (2023). The "greening" of empire: The European Green Deal as the EU first agenda. *Political Geography*, *105*, 102925.

Alnaser, A. A., Maxi, M., & Elmousalami, H. (2024). AI-Powered Digital Twins and Internet of Things for Smart Cities and Sustainable Building Environment. *Applied Sciences (Basel, Switzerland)*, *14*(24), 12056.

Alqahtani, A., Alsubai, S., & Bhatia, M. (2024). Applied artificial intelligence framework for smart evacuation in industrial disasters. *Applied Intelligence*, *54*(11–12), 7030–7045. DOI: 10.1007/s10489-024-05550-7

Alvarez-Risco, A., & Del-Aguila-Arcentales, S. (2021). A note on changing regulation in International Business: The World Intellectual Property Organization (WIPO) and Artificial Intelligence. Progress in International Business Research, 363–371. DOI: 10.1108/s1745-886220210000015020

Amshi, A. H., & Prasad, R. (2023). Time series analysis and forecasting of cholera disease using discrete wavelet transform and seasonal autoregressive integrated moving average model. *Scientific African*, *20*, e01652.

Anderljung, M., Hazell, J., & von Knebel, M. (2024). Protecting society from AI misuse: When are restrictions on capabilities warranted? *AI & Society*, *40*(5), 3841–3857. DOI: 10.1007/S00146-024-02130-8/FIGURES/2

Andersen, R. (2008). *Governing Agrobiodiversity: Plant Genetics and Developing Countries*. Routledge.

Andersen, R., & Winge, T. (2013). *Realising Farmers' Rights to Crop Genetic Resources: Success Stories and Best Practices*. Earthscan.

Ansari, M. F., Dash, B., Sharma, P., & Yathiraju, N. (2022). The impact and limitations of artificial intelligence in cybersecurity: A literature review. *International Journal of Advanced Research in Computer and Communication Engineering*.

Antony, P. J., Kannan, R., & Professor, A. (2024). Revolutionizing the Tourism Industry through Artificial Intelligence: A Comprehensive Review of AI Integration, Impact on Customer Experience, Operational Efficiency, and Future Trends. In www.chandigarhphilosophers.com *International Journal for Multidimensional Research Perspectives (IJMRP: Vol. ISSN* (Issue 1).

Arya, S. (2024). Harnessing Big Data and Machine Learning for Climate Change Predictions and Mitigation. In *Maintaining a Sustainable World in the Nexus of Environmental Science and AI* (pp. 383–408). IGI Global.

Ashfaq, A., Kamran, M., Rehman, F., Sarfaraz, N., Ilyas, H. U., & Riaz, H. H. (2022, March). Role of artificial intelligence in renewable energy and its scope in future. In *2022 5th International Conference on Energy Conservation and Efficiency (ICECE)* (pp. 1-6). IEEE.

Ashta, A., & Herrmann, H. (2021). Artificial intelligence and fintech: An overview of opportunities and risks for banking, investments, and microfinance. *Strategic Change, 30*(3), 211–222.

Baeza-Yates, R., Fayyad, U. M., & Fayyad, U. (2024). Responsible AI: An Urgent Mandate. *IEEE Intelligent Systems, 39*(1), 12–17. DOI: 10.1109/MIS.2023.3343488

Bahari, N. A. A. B. S., Ahmed, A. N., Chong, K. L., Lai, V., Huang, Y. F., Koo, C. H., Ng, J. L., & El-Shafie, A. (2023). Predicting Sea Level Rise Using Artificial Intelligence: A Review. *Archives of Computational Methods in Engineering, 30*(7), 4045–4062. DOI: 10.1007/s11831-023-09934-9

Bajoria, J. (2016, May 24). *How India's archaic laws have a chilling effect on dissent.* Scroll.in. https://scroll.in/article/808641/how-indias-archaic-laws-have-a-chilling-effect-on-dissent

Bakkum, M. J., Hartjes, M. G., Piët, J. D., Donker, E. M., Likic, R., Sanz, E., de Ponti, F., Verdonk, P., Richir, M. C., van Agtmael, M. A., & Tichelaar, J. (2024). Using artificial intelligence to create diverse and inclusive medical case vignettes for education. *British Journal of Clinical Pharmacology, 90*(3). Advance online publication. DOI: 10.1111/bcp.15977 PMID: 38016816

Ball, J. G. C., Petrova, K., Coomes, D. A., & Flaxman, S. (2022). Using deep convolutional neural networks to forecast spatial patterns of Amazonian deforestation. *Methods in Ecology and Evolution, 13*(11), 2622–2634. DOI: 10.1111/2041-210X.13953

Balogun, A.-L., Marks, D., Sharma, R., Shekhar, H., Balmes, C., Maheng, D., Arshad, A., & Salehi, P. (2020). Assessing the Potentials of Digitalization as a Tool for Climate Change Adaptation and Sustainable Development in Urban Centres. *Sustainable Cities and Society, 53*, 101888. DOI: 10.1016/j.scs.2019.101888

Banasiewicz, A., Moosavi, F., Kotyla, M., Śliwiński, P., Krot, P., Wodecki, J., & Zimroz, R. (2023). Forecasting of NOx emissions of diesel LHD vehicles in underground mines—An ANN-based regression approach. *Applied Sciences (Basel, Switzerland), 13*(17), 9965.

Bangash, S. A., Shah, S. S., Adam, M. A., Khan, M. F. I., & Ahmad, M. (2025). Chatbots in Telemedicine: Exploring Ethical Dimensions of AI in Healthcare. In Duygu, Ç. E., & Atilla, E. (Eds.), *Multifaceted Uses of Cutting-Edge Technologies and Social Concerns* (pp. 33–60). IGI Global Scientific Publishing., DOI: 10.4018/979-8-3693-9591-2.CH002

Banks, J. (2010). Regulating hate speech online. *International Review of Law Computers & Technology*, *24*(3), 233–239. DOI: 10.1080/13600869.2010.522323

Barredo Arrieta, A., Díaz-Rodríguez, N., Del Ser, J., Bennetot, A., Tabik, S., Barbado, A., Garcia, S., Gil-Lopez, S., Molina, D., Benjamins, R., Chatila, R., & Herrera, F. (2020). Explainable artificial intelligence (XAI): Concepts, taxonomies, opportunities and challenges toward responsible AI. *Information Fusion*, *58*, 82–115. DOI: 10.1016/j.inffus.2019.12.012

Bartlett, J., & Krasodomski-Jones, A. (2016). Counter-speech on Facebook. *Demos (Mexico City, Mexico)*.

Batty, M. (2018). Artificial intelligence and smart cities. *Environment and Planning. B, Urban Analytics and City Science*, *45*(1), 3–6.

Bayan, F. M. H. (2024). The Ethics of AI: Navigating the Moral dilemmas of Artificial Intelligence. *Arab Journal for Scientific Publishing (AJSP). ISSN*, *2663*, 5798.

Benbrook, C. M. (2012). Impacts of genetically engineered crops on pesticide use in the U.S.—The first sixteen years. *Environmental Sciences Europe*, *24*(1), 24. DOI: 10.1186/2190-4715-24-24

Berger, A. N., Klapper, L. F., & Turk-Ariss, R. (2017). Bank competition and financial stability. In *Handbook of competition in banking and finance* (pp. 185–204). Edward Elgar Publishing.

Bertot, J. C., Estevez, E., & Janowski, T. (2016). Universal and contextualized public services: Digital public service innovation framework. *Government Information Quarterly*, *33*(2), 211–222.

Bertot, J. C., Jaeger, P. T., & Grimes, J. M. (2010). Using ICTs to create a culture of transparency: E-government and social media as openness and anti-corruption tools for societies. *Government Information Quarterly*, *27*(3), 264–271.

Bewersdorff, A., Zhai, X., Roberts, J., & Nerdel, C. (2023). Myths, mis-and preconceptions of artificial intelligence: A review of the literature. *Computers and Education: Artificial Intelligence*, *4*, 100143.

Beyer, P., Al-Babili, S., Ye, X., Lucca, P., Schaub, P., Welsch, R., & Potrykus, I. (2002). Golden Rice: Introducing the β-carotene biosynthesis pathway into rice endosperm by genetic engineering. *Science*, *287*(5451), 303–305. PMID: 11880581

Bezner Kerr, R., Snapp, S., Chirwa, M., Shumba, L., & Msachi, R. (2019). Participatory, agroecological and gender-sensitive approaches to improved nutrition: A case study from Malawi. *Agriculture & Food Security*, *8*(1), 1–13. DOI: 10.1186/s40066-019-0273-4

Bhatia, S., & Singh, S. P. (2024). Assessing Groundwater Use Efficiency and Productivity across Punjab Agriculture: District and Farm Size Perspectives. *Agriculture*, *14*(8), 1299.

Bibri, S. E., Huang, J., Jagatheesaperumal, S. K., & Krogstie, J. (2024). The synergistic interplay of artificial intelligence and digital twin in environmentally planning sustainable smart cities: A comprehensive systematic review. *Environmental Science and Ecotechnology*, •••, 100433. PMID: 38831974

Biggi, G., Iori, M., Mazzei, J., & Mina, A. (2025). Green Intelligence: The AI content of green technologies. *Eurasian Business Review*, 1-38.

Binns, R. (2018). *Fairness in machine learning: Lessons from political philosophy. Proceedings of the 2018 Conference on Fairness, Accountability, and Transparency*, 149-159.

Boettcher, J. V., & Conrad, R. M. (2021). *The online teaching survival guide: Simple and practical pedagogical tips*. John Wiley & Sons.

Bohr, A., & Memarzadeh, K. (2020). The rise of artificial intelligence in healthcare applications. In Elsevier eBooks (pp. 25–60). https://doi.org/DOI: 10.1016/b978-0-12-818438-7.00002-2

Bonaiuti, R., Zammarchi, L., Giaché, S., Modi, G., Borchi, B., Campolmi, I., Trotta, M., Ravaldi, C., Ornaghi, S., Di Tommaso, M., Bartoloni, A., Costa, P., Lombardi, N., Crescioli, G., Vannacci, A., & Levi, M. (2024). Prevention, diagnosis and pharmacological treatment of infections in pregnancy: The mobile app GAIA! for healthcare providers and patients. *European Journal of Obstetrics, Gynecology, and Reproductive Biology*, *299*, 96–104. DOI: 10.1016/j.ejogrb.2024.05.035 PMID: 38850898

Bose, S., Kumar Dey, S., & Bhattacharjee, S. (2023). Big Data, data analytics and Artificial Intelligence in Accounting: An overview. Handbook of Big Data Research Methods, 32–51. DOI: 10.4337/9781800888555.00007

Botelho, F. H. (2021). Accessibility to digital technology: Virtual barriers, real opportunities. *Assistive Technology, 33*(sup1), 27-34.

Brahmi, P., Saxena, S., & Dhillon, B. S. (2018). Intellectual property rights in agriculture: Implications for food security and farmers' rights. *Journal of Intellectual Property Rights*, *23*(2), 64–71.

Bressane, A., Zwirn, D., Essiptchouk, A., Saraiva, A. C. V., Carvalho, F. L. de C., Formiga, J. K. S., Medeiros, L. C. de C., & Negri, R. G. (2024). Understanding the role of study strategies and learning disabilities on student academic performance to enhance educational approaches: A proposal using artificial intelligence. *Computers and Education: Artificial Intelligence*, *6*. Advance online publication. DOI: 10.1016/j.caeai.2023.100196

Brighouse, H., & McPherson, M. (2022). *Ethics in Higher Education: Promoting equity and inclusion through case-based inquiry*. Harvard Education Press.

Brown-Sica, M., & Beall, J. (1999). Library 2.0 and the Problem of Hate Speech Library 2.0 and the Problem of Hate Speech. *The Electronic Journal of Academic and Special Librarianship Summer, 1*. https://digitalcommons.unl.edu/cgi/viewcontent.cgi?article=1098&context=ejasljournal

Brundage, M., Avin, S., Wang, J., Belfield, H., Krueger, G., Hadfield, G., . . . Anderljung, M. (2018). *The malicious use of artificial intelligence: Forecasting, prevention, and mitigation*. arXiv preprint arXiv:1802.07228.

Brunnermeier, M., Crockett, A., Goodhart, C. A., Persaud, A., & Shin, H. S. (2009). *The fundamental principles of financial regulation* (Vol. 11). ICMB, Internat. Center for Monetary and Banking Studies.

Brush, S. B. (2005). Protecting Traditional Agricultural Knowledge. *Washington University Journal of Law and Policy*, *17*, 59–109.

Bryson, J. R., Castelnovo, W., & Eubanks, V. (2021). *The role of artificial intelligence in education: An overview*. Springer.

Buckley, R. P., Zetzsche, D. A., Arner, D. W., & Tang, B. W. (2021). Regulating artificial intelligence in finance: Putting the human in the loop. *The Sydney Law Review*, *43*(1), 43–81.

Bulutoding, L., Rahmah Sari, N., Yulia, R., & Manoppo, V. P. (2024). Ethical Implications Of Human Resource Development And Application Of Artificial General Intelligence (AGI) In The Context Of Global Business Governance. *International Journal of Humanities, Social Sciences and Business (INJOSS), 3*(1).

Buolamwini, J., & Gebru, T. (2018). Gender shades: Intersectional accuracy disparities in commercial gender classification. *Proceedings of Machine Learning Research*, *81*, 1–15.

Burgstahler, S. (2015). *Universal design in higher education: From principles to practice*. Harvard Education Press.

Burgstahler, S. (2020). Legal and institutional challenges to implementing digital accessibility policies in higher education. *Journal of Postsecondary Education and Disability*, *33*(3), 100–115.

Burgstahler, S., & Cory, R. (2019). Inclusive instruction: Digital literacy for all students. *Journal of Postsecondary Education and Disability*, *32*(2), 125–138.

Cairns, J. E., Hellin, J., Sonder, K., Araus, J. L., MacRobert, J. F., Thierfelder, C., & Prasanna, B. M. (2013). Adapting maize production to climate change in sub-Saharan Africa. *Food Security*, *5*(3), 345–360.

Calo, M. (2020). Scaling Agroecology from the Bottom-Up: Six Domains of Transformation. *Agriculture and Human Values*, *37*, 355–369. DOI: 10.1007/s10460-019-09951-w

Cao, L. (2022). AI in Finance: Challenges, Techniques, and Opportunities. *ACM Computing Surveys*, *55*(3). Advance online publication. DOI: 10.1145/3502289

Cao, Y. (2025). How Ai Is Shaping. *Accounting and Finance*. Advance online publication. DOI: 10.2139/ssrn.5177863

CAST. (2018). *Universal Design for Learning Guidelines version 2.2*. Retrieved from https://www.cast.org/

Causevic, A., Causevic, S., Fielding, M., & Barrott, J. (2024). Artificial intelligence for sustainability: Opportunities and risks of utilizing Earth observation technologies to protect forests. *Discover Conservation*, *1*(1), 2. DOI: 10.1007/s44353-024-00002-2

CBD. (2000). *Cartagena Protocol on Biosafety to the Convention on Biological Diversity*. Secretariat of the Convention on Biological Diversity.

CBD. (2011). *Nagoya Protocol on Access to Genetic Resources and the Fair and Equitable Sharing of Benefits Arising from their Utilization to the Convention on Biological Diversity*. Secretariat of the CBD.

Cecchetti, S. G., Mancini-Griffoli, T., Narita, M., & Sahay, R. (2020). US or domestic monetary policy: Which matters more for financial stability? *IMF Economic Review*, *68*(1), 35–65.

Chakrapani, N. (2025). *Hate Speech Laws in India: Examining Legal and Constitutional Challenges*. The Legal Quorum.

Chambers, D. (2019). Assistive technology to enhance inclusive education. In *Oxford research encyclopedia of education.*

Chandra, R., & Sanjaya, K. (2023). Punishing the Unpunishable: A Liability Framework for Artificial Intelligence Systems. *Springer Nature Link*, 55–64. https://doi.org/DOI: 10.1007/978-3-031-29860-8_6

Chaudhary, G. (2024). Unveiling the Black Box: Bringing Algorithmic Transparency to AI. *Masaryk University Journal of Law and Technology, 18*(1), 93–122. https://www.ceeol.com/search/article-detail?id=1287954

Chaudhary, S., McGregor, A., Houston, D., & Chettri, N. (2018). Reconceptualizing participation in conservation: Towards resilience through engaged political ecology. *Biological Conservation*, *218*, 242–251.

Chauncey, S. A., & McKenna, H. P. (2024). Creativity and Innovation in Civic Spaces Supported by Cognitive Flexibility When Learning with AI Chatbots in Smart Cities. *Urban Science (Basel, Switzerland)*, *8*(1). Advance online publication. DOI: 10.3390/urbansci8010016

Chawla, R. N., & Goyal, P. (2021). Emerging trends in digital transformation: A bibliometric analysis. *Benchmarking*, *29*(4), 1069–1112. DOI: 10.1108/bij-01-2021-0009

Chen, M., DeHaven, M., Kitschelt, I., Lee, S. J., & Sicilian, M. J. (2023). Identifying financial crises using machine learning on textual data. *Journal of Risk and Financial Management*, *16*(3), 1–28.

Chen, W., Men, Y., Fuster, N., Osorio, C., & Juan, A. A. (2024). Artificial intelligence in logistics optimization with sustainable criteria: A review. *Sustainability*, *16*(21), 9145.

Chen, X., Zhang, J., & Yang, C. (2020). Digital accessibility and educational equity: Bridging the gap for students with disabilities. *Journal of Educational Technology*, *38*(4), 115–127.

Chen, Y. C., & Aklikokou, A. K. (2021). Artificial intelligence and public engagement: Enhancing governance through sentiment analysis and predictive analytics. *Government Information Quarterly*, *38*(4), 101590.

Chen, Y. C., & Hsieh, T. C. (2014). Big data and public governance: The innovation and challenges of data-driven governance. *Government Information Quarterly*, *31*(1), 1–7.

Cheong, B. C. (2024). Transparency and accountability in AI systems: Safeguarding wellbeing in the age of algorithmic decision-making. *Frontiers in Human Dynamics*, *6*. Advance online publication. DOI: 10.3389/fhumd.2024.1421273

Chow, J. C. L., Wong, V., Sanders, L., & Li, K. (2023). Developing an AI-Assisted Educational Chatbot for Radiotherapy Using the IBM Watson Assistant Platform. *Healthcare (Switzerland)*, *11*(17). Advance online publication. DOI: 10.3390/healthcare11172417 PMID: 37685452

Citizens for Justice and Peace. (2022, February 1). *Speak up against hate | Safoora Zargar*. YouTube. https://www.youtube.com/watch?v=BjL0itmo0gU

Clayton, C., & Schaab, A. (2022). Multinational banks and financial stability. *The Quarterly Journal of Economics*, *137*(3), 1681–1736.

Cleveland, D. A., Soleri, D., & Smith, S. E. (2000). A biological framework for understanding farmers' plant breeding. *Economic Botany*, *54*(3), 377–394.

Cobanaj, M., Corti, C., Dee, E. C., McCullum, L., Boldrini, L., Schlam, I., Tolaney, S. M., Celi, L. A., Curigliano, G., & Criscitiello, C. (2024). Advancing equitable and personalized cancer care: Novel applications and priorities of artificial intelligence for fairness and inclusivity in the patient care workflow. In *European Journal of Cancer* (Vol. 198). https://doi.org/DOI: 10.1016/j.ejca.2023.113504

Cockcroft, S., & Russell, M. (2018). *Big data opportunities for tax administration*. eJournal of Tax Research, 16(3), 184-201.

Cordella, A., & Gualdi, F. (2024). Algorithmic formalization: Impacts on administrative processes. *Public Administration*. Advance online publication. DOI: 10.1111/padm.13030

Cowls, J., Tsamados, A., Taddeo, M., & Floridi, L. (2023). The AI gambit: Leveraging artificial intelligence to combat climate change—opportunities, challenges, and recommendations. *AI & Society*, •••, 1–25. PMID: 34690449

Cox, A. (2021). AI in education: Ethical concerns and opportunities for students with disabilities. *Journal of Educational Technology*, *58*(2), 127–141.

Crawford, A. D., Slavin, R., Tabar, M., Radhakrishnan, K., Wang, M., Estrada, A., & McGrath, J. M. (2024). Methodological approaches in developing and implementing digital health interventions amongst underserved women. *Public Health Nursing (Boston, Mass.)*. Advance online publication. DOI: 10.1111/phn.13410 PMID: 39221663

Cumming, D., Saurabh, K., Rani, N., & Upadhyay, P. (2024). Towards AI ethics-led sustainability frameworks and toolkits: Review and research agenda. *Journal of Sustainable Finance and Accounting*, *1*, 100003.

Daes, E.-I. A. (2001). *Protection of the heritage of indigenous people: Final report*. UN Sub-Commission on the Promotion and Protection of Human Rights.

Daly, A., Hagendorff, T., Hui, L., Mann, M., Marda, V., Wagner, B., & Wei Wang, W. (2022). AI, Governance and Ethics: Global Perspectives.

Dang, W., Kim, S., Park, S., & Xu, W. (2024). The impact of economic and IoT technologies on air pollution: An AI-based simulation equation model using support vector machines. *Soft Computing*, *28*(4), 3591–3611.

Danielsson, J., Macrae, R., & Uthemann, A. (2022). Artificial intelligence and systemic risk. *Journal of Banking & Finance*, *140*, 106290.

Danish, M. S. S., & Senjyu, T. (2023). Shaping the future of sustainable energy through AI-enabled circular economy policies. *Circular Economy*, *2*(2), 100040.

Das, S., & Das, S. (2021, October 25). *Caste-Based Discrimination Rampant In Higher Educational Institutions, Affirms Study*. Feminism in India. https://feminisminindia.com/2021/10/26/caste-based-discrimination-rampant-in-higher-educational-institutions-affirms-study/

Das, D. (2024). Hate speech in India: Contemporary legal challenges and responses. *LAW&PASS: International Journal of Law. Public Administration and Social Studies*, *1*(2), 250–264.

De Schutter, O. (2009). *Seed policies and the right to food: Enhancing agrobiodiversity and encouraging innovation*. United Nations.

Debata, S., & Elango, S. (2024). Empowering flood forecasting through meteorological and social media data. *International Journal of Information Technology : an Official Journal of Bharati Vidyapeeth's Institute of Computer Applications and Management*, *16*(6), 3757–3770. DOI: 10.1007/s41870-024-01961-4

Delfani, P., Thuraga, V., Banerjee, B., & Chawade, A. (2024). Integrative approaches in modern agriculture: IoT, ML and AI for disease forecasting amidst climate change. *Precision Agriculture*, *25*(5), 2589–2613. DOI: 10.1007/s11119-024-10164-7

Delgado Algarra, E. J., Bernal Bravo, C., Morales Cevallos, M. B., & López Meneses, E. (2024). Pedagogical and Technical Analyses of Massive Open Online Courses on Artificial Intelligence. *Applied Sciences (Switzerland)*, *14*(3). Advance online publication. DOI: 10.3390/app14031051

Department of Higher Education and Training. (2013). *White Paper on Post-School Education and Training*. Pretoria: Department of Higher Education and Training.

Department of Higher Education and Training. (2016). *Disability Framework for Higher Education*. Department of Higher Education and Training.

Department of Telecommunications and Postal Services. (2016). *National Integrated ICT Policy White Paper*. Pretoria: Department of Telecommunications and Postal Services.

Desmarais, M. É. (2023). How to Engage Students with Universal Design for Learning. *Transformative Inclusive Education*, 213.

Desouza, K. C., & Bhagwatwar, A. (2012). Citizen apps to engage with local governments: An empirical investigation. *Government Information Quarterly*, *29*(1), 39–49.

Dhar, S. B. (2023). A comparative study of air quality between pre and post COVID-19 periods in India. *Environment, Development and Sustainability*, •••, 1–25.

Dictionary, C. (2019, December 4). *HATE SPEECH | meaning in the Cambridge English Dictionary*. Cambridge.org. https://dictionary.cambridge.org/dictionary/english/hate-speech

Dirgová Luptáková, I., Pospíchal, J., & Huraj, L. (2024). Beyond Code and Algorithms: Navigating Ethical Complexities in Artificial Intelligence. *Lecture Notes in Networks and Systems, 934 LNNS*. https://doi.org/DOI: 10.1007/978-3-031-54813-0_30

Di, X. (2023). Regulatory leadership in struggling–the US path in robo-advisors governance. *Law and Financial Markets Review*, *17*(2), 116–135. DOI: 10.1080/17521440.2024.2313473

Djarum, D. H., Ahmad, Z., & Zhang, J. (2023). Reduced Bayesian Optimized Stacked Regressor (RBOSR): A highly efficient stacked approach for improved air pollution prediction. *Applied Soft Computing*, *144*, 110466.

Dmytriyev, Y., Carnevale, M., & Giberti, H. (2024). Enhancing flexibility and safety: Collaborative robotics for material handling in end-of-line industrial operations. *Procedia Computer Science*, *232*, 2588–2597. DOI: 10.1016/j.procs.2024.02.077

Doniec, R. J., Piaseczna, N. J., Szymczyk, K. A., Jacennik, B., Sieciński, S., Mocny-Pachońska, K., Duraj, K., Cedro, T., Tkacz, E. J., & Glinkowski, W. M. (2023). Experiences of the Telemedicine and eHealth Conferences in Poland—A Cross-National Overview of Progress in Telemedicine. In *Applied Sciences (Switzerland)* (Vol. 13, Issue 1). https://doi.org/DOI: 10.3390/app13010587

Dutta, S. (2024). Framing the Landscape of Technological Enhancements: Artificial Intelligence, Gender Issues, and Ethical Dilemmas. In *Signals and Communication Technology: Vol. Part F1803*. https://doi.org/DOI: 10.1007/978-3-031-45237-6_10

Dwivedi, Y. K., Hughes, L., Kar, A. K., Baabdullah, A. M., Grover, P., Abbas, R., & Wade, M. (2022). Climate change and COP26: Are digital technologies and information management part of the problem or the solution? An editorial reflection and call to action. *International Journal of Information Management*, *63*, 102456.

Dzuranin, A. C., Jones, J. R., & Olvera, R. M. (2018). Infusing Data Analytics into the accounting curriculum: A Framework and insights from faculty. *Journal of Accounting Education*, *43*, 24–39. DOI: 10.1016/j.jaccedu.2018.03.004

Ebers, M., & Sein, K. (2024). Data-driven Technologies. *Routledge EBooks*, 3–37. https://doi.org/DOI: 10.4324/9781003502791-2

Edenberg, E., & Wood, A. (2023). *Disambiguating Algorithmic Bias: From Neutrality to Justice*. https://doi.org/DOI: 10.1145/3600211.3604695

Edeni, C. A., Adeleye, O. O., & Adeniyi, I. S. (2024). The role of AI-enhanced tools in overcoming socioeconomic barriers in education: A conceptual analysis. *World Journal of Advanced Research and Reviews*, *21*(3). Advance online publication. DOI: 10.30574/wjarr.2024.21.3.0780

Effrosynidis, D., Spiliotis, E., Sylaios, G., & Arampatzis, A. (2023). Time series and regression methods for univariate environmental forecasting: An empirical evaluation. *The Science of the Total Environment*, *875*, 162580. PMID: 36906023

Eggers, W. D., Schatsky, D., & Viechnicki, P. (2017). *AI-augmented government: Using artificial intelligence to improve public sector performance*. Deloitte Insights.

Elegunde, A. F., & Osagie, R. (2020). Artificial intelligence adoption and employee performance in the Nigerian banking industry. *International Journal of Management and Administration*, *4*(8), 189–205.

Elsayed, A. H., Naifar, N., & Nasreen, S. (2023). Financial stability and monetary policy reaction: Evidence from the GCC countries. *The Quarterly Review of Economics and Finance*, *87*, 396–405.

Emon, M. M. H., Khan, T., Rahman, M. A., Hamid, A. B. A., & Yaakub, N. I. (2025). GreenTech Revolution: Navigating Challenges and Seizing Opportunities. In *AI and Green Technology Applications in Society* (pp. 63–90). IGI Global Scientific Publishing. https://doi.org/DOI: 10.4018/979-8-3693-9879-1.ch003

Emon, M. M. H., & Khan, T. (2025). The mediating role of attitude towards the technology in shaping artificial intelligence usage among professionals. *Telematics and Informatics Reports*, *17*, 100188. DOI: 10.1016/j.teler.2025.100188

Engel, C., Linhardt, L., & Schubert, M. (2024). Code is law: How COMPAS affects the way the judiciary handles the risk of recidivism. *Artificial Intelligence and Law*. Advance online publication. DOI: 10.1007/s10506-024-09389-8

Esteva, A., Robicquet, A., Ramsundar, B., Kuleshov, V., DePristo, M., Chou, K., & Dean, J. (2019). A guide to deep learning in healthcare. *Nature Medicine*, *25*(1), 24–29. PMID: 30617335

Eubanks, V. (2018). *Automating inequality: How high-tech tools profile, police, and punish the poor*. St. Martin's Press.

Ewoh, P., & Vartiainen, T. (2024). Vulnerabilities, cyberattacks and Socio-technical Solutions in Healthcare Systems: Systematic Review (Preprint). *Journal of Medical Internet Research*, *26*, e46904. DOI: 10.2196/46904 PMID: 38820579

Express Web Desk. (2017). *What is the not in my name protest?* Indian Express, https://indianexpress.com/article/what-is/what-is-the-not-in-my-name-protest-lynching-junaid-khan-4725668/

Facebook (n.d.). *Community Standards,* Facebook. https://www.facebook.com/communitystandards/hate_speech

Facebook (n.d.). *Facebook Transparency Report | Community Standards*. Transparency.facebook.com. https://transparency.facebook.com/community-standards-enforcement#hate-speech

Fagundes, D. (2025). Genetic property rhetoric and the public domain. Texas A&amp. *M Journal of Property Law*, *11*(1), 1–16. DOI: 10.37419/jpl.v11.i1.1

Fan, B. E., Chow, M., & Winkler, S. (2024). Artificial Intelligence-Generated Facial Images for Medical Education. *Medical Science Educator*, *34*(1). Advance online publication. DOI: 10.1007/s40670-023-01942-5 PMID: 38510393

Fang, B., Yu, J., Chen, Z., Osman, A. I., Farghali, M., Ihara, I., & Yap, P. S. (2023). Artificial intelligence for waste management in smart cities: A review. *Environmental Chemistry Letters*, *21*(4), 1959–1989. PMID: 37362015

FAO. (2009). *International Treaty on Plant Genetic Resources for Food and Agriculture*. Food and Agriculture Organization of the United Nations.

Farina, M., Zhdanov, P., Karimov, A., & Lavazza, A. (2024). AI and society: A virtue ethics approach. *AI & Society, 39*(3), 1127–1140. DOI: 10.1007/S00146-022-01545-5/METRICS

Fazelpour, S., & Danks, D. (2021). Algorithmic bias: Senses, sources, solutions. *Philosophy Compass, 16*(8). Advance online publication. DOI: 10.1111/phc3.12760

FBI. (2022). *FBI Releases 2022 Crime in the Nation Statistics | Federal Bureau of Investigation*. Federal Bureau of Investigation. https://www.fbi.gov/news/press-releases/fbi-releases-2022-crime-in-the-nation-statistics

Ferdaus, M. M., Dam, T., Anavatti, S., & Das, S. (2024). Digital technologies for a net-zero energy future: A comprehensive review. *Renewable & Sustainable Energy Reviews, 202*, 114681. DOI: 10.1016/j.rser.2024.114681

Fiore, P. (2017). How to evaluate mobile health Applications: A scoping review. PubMed, 234, 109–114. https://pubmed.ncbi.nlm.nih.gov/28186025

First Nations Information Governance Centre (2014). Ownership, Control, Access and Possession (OCAP™): The Path to First Nations Information Governance.

Floridi, L., & Cowls, J. (2019). A unified framework of five principles for AI in society. *Harvard Data Science Review, 1*(1).

Fowler, G.A., & Harwell, D. (2018). *2018 was the year of online hate. Meet the people whose lives it changed,* The Washington Post.

Francisco, M., & Linnér, B. O. (2023). AI and the governance of sustainable development. An idea analysis of the European Union, the United Nations, and the World Economic Forum. *Environmental Science & Policy, 150*, 103590.

Free Word Centre. (2018). Responding to 'hate speech' with positive measures: A case study from six EU countries 2018 report. https://www.article19.org/wp-content/uploads/2018/06/Responding-to-%E2%80%98hate-speech%E2%80%99-with-positive-measures-A-case-study-from-six-EU-countries-.pdf

Fundira, M., Edoun, E. I., & Pradhan, A. (2024). Evaluating end-users' digital competencies and ethical perceptions of AI systems in the context of sustainable digital banking. *Sustainable Development*. Advance online publication. DOI: 10.1002/sd.2945

Gagliardone, I., Gal, D., Alves, T., & Martinez, G. (2015). *Countering Online Hate Speech (PDF)*. Paris: UNESCO Publishing. pp. 7–15. ISBN 978-92-3-100105-5. Archived from the original on 13 March 2022. Retrieved 27 March 2025.

Gans, J. (2024). Copyright policy options for generative artificial intelligence. SSRN Electronic Journal. DOI: 10.2139/ssrn.4716669

Gensler, G., & Bailey, L. (2020). "Deep learning and financial stability", *Available at SSRN* 3723132.

George, Dr. A. S. (2024). Bracing for the Coming AI Tsunami: Preparing the Global Workforce for Displacement and Inequality in the Age of Accelerating Technological Advancement. *Partners Universal Innovative Research Publication*, *2*(3), 126–146. DOI: 10.5281/ZENODO.11668571

Ghaffarian, S., Taghikhah, F. R., & Maier, H. R. (2023). Explainable artificial intelligence in disaster risk management: Achievements and prospective futures. *International Journal of Disaster Risk Reduction*, *98*, 104123.

Gillespie, T. (n.d.). *Custodians of the Internet platforms, content moderation, and the hidden decisions that shape social media*. https://tarletongillespie.org/Gillespie_CUSTODIANS_print.pdf

Gipson, S. M. (2024). MITIGATING ALGORITHMIC BIAS. *Scitech Lawyer, 20*(4), 26–32. https://www.proquest.com/docview/3070768938?pq-origsite=gscholar&fromopenview=true&sourcetype=Scholarly%20Journals

Glover, D. (2010). The corporate shaping of GM crops as a technology for the poor. *The Journal of Peasant Studies*, *37*(1), 67–90.

Gnanith, A. (2015). *Shreya Singhal v. Union Of India AIR 2015 SC 1523*. Legal-serviceindia.com. https://www.legalserviceindia.com/legal/article-10124-shreya-singhal-v-union-of-india-air-2015-sc-1523.html

Gomber, P., Kauffman, R. J., Parker, C., & Weber, B. W. (2018). On the Fintech Revolution: Interpreting the forces of innovation, Disruption, and transformation in financial services. *Journal of Management Information Systems*, *35*(1), 220–265. DOI: 10.1080/07421222.2018.1440766

Gondwe, G. (2024). Artificial Intelligence, Journalism, and the Ubuntu Robot in Sub-Saharan Africa: Towards a Normative Framework. *Digital Journalism (Abingdon, England)*. Advance online publication. DOI: 10.1080/21670811.2024.2311258

Gonzalez, C. G. (2020). International economic law and the right to food. In Andreassen, B., & Ulfstein, H. (Eds.), *Research Handbook on Human Rights and Poverty* (pp. 201–220). Edward Elgar.

Goodell, J. W., Kumar, S., Lim, W. M., & Pattnaik, D. (2021). Artificial intelligence and machine learning in finance: Identifying foundations, themes, and research clusters from bibliometric analysis. *Journal of Behavioral and Experimental Finance, 32*, 100577.

Gopinadh Garre, S. S., & Aswathy, V. K. (2024). Examining Rainfall Trends in Guntur District, Andhra Pradesh, India, Amidst the Climate Change Challenge: A Comprehensive Analysis of Global Warming Impacts. In *Climate Change and Human Adaptation in India: Sustainability and Public Policy* (pp. 79–100). Springer Nature Switzerland.

Goralski, M. A., & Tan, T. K. (2020). Artificial intelligence and sustainable development. *International Journal of Management Education, 18*(1), 100330.

Goswami, D., & Verma, B. (2024). The Intersection of Ethics and Big Data. *Advances in Web Technologies and Engineering Book Series*, 269–285. https://doi.org/DOI: 10.4018/979-8-3693-1762-4.ch013

Greif, L., Kimmig, A., El Bobbou, S., Jurisch, P., & Ovtcharova, J. (2024). Strategic view on the current role of AI in advancing environmental sustainability: A SWOT analysis. *Discover Artificial Intelligence, 4*(1), 45.

Gruère, G. P., Mehta-Bhatt, P., & Sengupta, D. (2008). Bt cotton and farmer suicides in India: Reviewing the evidence. *International Food Policy Research Institute (IFPRI) Discussion Paper 00808.*

Gruère, G. P., & Sengupta, D. (2011). Bt cotton and farmer suicides in India: An evidence-based assessment. *The Journal of Development Studies, 47*(2), 316–337. PMID: 21506303

Gundeti, R., Vuppala, K., & Kasireddy, V. (2024). The future of AI and environmental sustainability: Challenges and opportunities. *Exploring Ethical Dimensions of Environmental Sustainability and Use of AI*, 346-371.

Gundeti, R., Vuppala, K., & Kasireddy, V. (2023). *The Future of AI and Environmental Sustainability.*, DOI: 10.4018/979-8-3693-0892-9.ch017

Gunther, H., & Rose, J. (2020). Governing AI: The importance of environmentally sustainable and equitable innovation. *Envtl. L. Rep., 50*, 10888.

Gupta, N., & Gupta, K. (2020). *Do Indian Courts Face A Dilemma in Interpreting Hate Speech?* Economic and Political Weekly. https://www.epw.in/engage/article/do-indian-courts-face-dilemma-interpreting-hate

Gurumoorthy, S., Kokku, A. K., Falkowski-Gilski, P., & Divakarachari, P. B. (2023). Effective air quality prediction using reinforced swarm optimization and bi-directional gated recurrent unit. *Sustainability*, *15*(14), 11454.

Guterres, A. (2019). *UNITED NATIONS STRATEGY AND PLAN OF ACTION ON HATE SPEECH* (pp. 1–5). https://www.un.org/en/genocideprevention/documents/UN%20Strategy%20and%20Plan%20of%20Action%20on%20Hate%20Speech%2

Guttikunda, S. K., Goel, R., & Pant, P. (2014). Nature of air pollution, emission sources, and management in the Indian cities. *Atmospheric Environment*, *95*, 501–510.

Habibipour, A. (2024). Responsible living labs: What can go wrong? *Journal of Information. Communication and Ethics in Society*, *22*(2). Advance online publication. DOI: 10.1108/JICES-11-2023-0137

Haggag, M., Siam, A. S., El-Dakhakhni, W., Coulibaly, P., & Hassini, E. (2021). A deep learning model for predicting climate-induced disasters. *Natural Hazards*, *107*(1), 1009–1034. DOI: 10.1007/s11069-021-04620-0

Hankerson, D. L., & Brown, L. X. (2020). Technology as a civil right and a move toward disability justice: Ensuring digital access for disabled students in the pandemic. *Drexel L. Rev.*, *13*, 869.

Harrast, S. A., Olsen, L., & Sun, Y. (2023). Analyzing eight emerging topics and their importance to career success. *Journal of Emerging Technologies in Accounting*, *20*(1), 289–304. DOI: 10.2308/jeta-2021-047

Hassija, V., Chamola, V., Mahapatra, A., Singal, A., Goel, D., Huang, K., Scardapane, S., Spinelli, I., Mahmud, M., & Hussain, A. (2024). Interpreting Black-Box Models: A Review on Explainable Artificial Intelligence. *Cognitive Computation*, *16*(1), 45–74. DOI: 10.1007/s12559-023-10179-8

Hatano, A. (23 October 2023). Regulating Online Hate Speech through the Prism of Human Rights Law: The Potential of Localised Content Moderation. *The Australian Year Book of International Law Online*. 41 (1):127–156. doi:. ISSN 2666-0229. DOI: 10.1163/26660229-04101017

hate-alert. (2019). *Hate-Speech-Reading-List/README.md at master · hate-alert/Hate-Speech-Reading-List*. GitHub. https://github.com/hate-alert/Hate-Speech-Reading-List/blob/master/README.md

Hawashin, B., Althunibat, A., Kanan, T., AlZu'bi, S., & Sharrab, Y. (2023). Improving Arabic fake news detection using optimized feature selection. *2023 International Conference on Information Technology (ICIT)*, 690–694. DOI: 10.1109/icit58056.2023.10225974

Hayes, C. M. (2023). Generative Artificial Intelligence and copyright: Both sides of the black box. SSRN Electronic Journal. DOI: 10.2139/ssrn.4517799

Herath Pathirannehelage, S., Shrestha, Y. R., & von Krogh, G. (2024). Design principles for artificial intelligence-augmented decision making: An action design research study. *European Journal of Information Systems*. Advance online publication. DOI: 10.1080/0960085X.2024.2330402;PAGE:STRING:ARTICLE/CHAPTER

Herz, M. E., & Molnár, P. (2012). *The content and context of hate speech: rethinking regulation and responses*. Cambridge University Press ; New York.

Hilpisch, Y. (2020). *Artificial Intelligence in Finance*. O'Reilly Media.

Holmes, W., Bialik, M., & Fadel, C. (2019). *Artificial intelligence in education: Promises and implications for teaching and learning*. Center for Curriculum Redesign.

Howard, P. H. (2009). Visualizing consolidation in the global seed industry: 1996–2008. *Sustainability*, *1*(4), 1266–1287.

Howard, P. H. (2015). Intellectual property and consolidation in the seed industry. *Crop Science*, *55*(6), 2489–2495.

Howard, P. H. (2021). *Concentration and Power in the Food System: Who Controls What We Eat?* (2nd ed.). Bloomsbury Publishing.

Hristov, K. (2019). Artificial Intelligence and the copyright survey. SSRN Electronic Journal. DOI: 10.2139/ssrn.3490458

Hsien, K., Chung, Y., Adriaens, P., Han, H., Liu, Z., Wang, X., & Li, S. (2021). Research of the Relations Among Cloud Computing, Internet of Things, Big Data, Artificial Intelligence, Block Chain and Their Application in Maritime Field. *Journal of Physics: Conference Series*, *1927*(1), 012026. DOI: 10.1088/1742-6596/1927/1/012026

Hudson, M., et al. (2020)."Te Ara Tika Guidelines for Māori Research Ethics: A Framework for Researchers and Ethics Committee Members.

Hunt, C. (2016). *"It's just a joke": the subtle effects of offensive language*. The University of Sydney. https://www.sydney.edu.au/news-opinion/news/2016/07/20/_it_s-just-a-joke--the-subtle-effects-of-offensive-language.html

Hyman, T. (2021). *The Harms of Racist Online Hate Speech in the Post-COVID Working World: Expanding Employee Protections – Fordham Law Review*. Fordhamlawreview.org. https://fordhamlawreview.org/issues/the-harms-of-racist-online-hate-speech-in-the-post-covid-world-expanding-employee-protections/

Iacoban, S. R., Piron-Dumitrascu, M., Suciu, I. D., Cretoiu, D., & Suciu, N. (2024). Innovative Models for Integrative Prenatal Care. *BRAIN. Broad Research in Artificial Intelligence and Neuroscience*, *15*(1). Advance online publication. DOI: 10.18662/brain/15.1/532

Imran, M., & Almusharraf, N. (2024). Google Gemini as a next generation AI educational tool: A review of emerging educational technology. *Smart Learning Environments*, *11*(1), 1–8. DOI: 10.1186/S40561-024-00310-Z/METRICS

Ishii, T., & Araki, M. (2016). Consumer acceptance of food crops developed by genome editing. *Plant Cell Reports*, *35*(7), 1507–151. PMID: 27038939

Islam, S. M. R., Kwak, N. D., Kabir, M. H., Hossain, M., & Kwak, N. K. (2015). The Internet of Things for Health Care: A Comprehensive survey. *IEEE Access : Practical Innovations, Open Solutions*, *3*, 678–708. DOI: 10.1109/access.2015.2437951

Issa, A. A., Majed, S., Ameer, S. A., & Al-Jawahry, H. M. (2024). Farming in the digital age: Smart agriculture with ai and iot. In *E3S Web of conferences* (Vol. 477, p. 00081). EDP Sciences.

Iyer, L. S. (2021). AI enabled applications towards intelligent transportation. *Transportation Engineering*, *5*. Advance online publication. DOI: 10.1016/j.treng.2021.100083

Jackson, A. K. (2023). *Closing the Digital Divide: Understanding Organizational Approaches to Digital Accessibility in Higher Education* (Doctoral dissertation, University of South Dakota).

Jain, R., & Jain, D. (2023). Revolutionizing Business Management: An exploration of emerging technologies. SSRN Electronic Journal. *Available at:* DOI: 10.2139/ssrn.4448305

Jain, H., Dhupper, R., Shrivastava, A., Kumar, D., & Kumari, M. (2023). AI-enabled strategies for climate change adaptation: Protecting communities, infrastructure, and businesses from the impacts of climate change. *Computational Urban Science*, *3*(1), 25. DOI: 10.1007/s43762-023-00100-2

Jain, L. R., & Menon, V. (2023). *AI Algorithmic Bias: Understanding its Causes*. Ethical and Social Implications., DOI: 10.1109/ictai59109.2023.00073

Jansen, K. (2020). The debate on public–private partnerships and their implications for agricultural development and food sovereignty. *The Journal of Peasant Studies*, *47*(4), 805–832. DOI: 10.1080/03066150.2020.1743065

Jansma, J. (2018). The ethical imperatives of inclusive digital design in higher education. *Ethics and Education*, *13*(2), 105–118.

Jansma, J. (2020). Improving access for students with disabilities in digital environments: The role of technology and accessibility standards. *International Journal of Inclusive Education*, *24*(7), 709–721.

Janssen, M., & Kuk, G. (2016). The challenges and limits of big data algorithms in technocratic governance. *Government Information Quarterly*, *33*(3), 371–377.

Janssen, M., & van den Berg, R. (2020). Data-driven governance: Creating value through open government data. *Government Information Quarterly*, *37*(3), 101477.

Janssen, M., & van den Hoven, J. (2020). Big data and artificial intelligence for digital transformation in government: The challenges for ethics. *Information Polity*, *25*(3), 267–280.

Jasanoff, S., Hurlbut, J. B., & Saha, K. (2015). CRISPR democracy: Gene editing and the need for inclusive deliberation. *Issues in Science and Technology*, *32*(1), 25–32.

Jinek, M., Chylinski, K., Fonfara, I., Hauer, M., Doudna, J. A., & Charpentier, E. (2012). A programmable dual-RNA–guided DNA endonuclease in adaptive bacterial immunity. *Science*, *337*(6096), 816–821. PMID: 22745249

Ji, R., Wang, C., Cui, A., Jia, M., Liao, S., Wang, W., & Chen, N. (2024). Assessing terrestrial water storage dynamics and multiple factors driving forces in China from 2005 to 2020. *Journal of Environmental Management*, *370*, 122464. PMID: 39265495

Jobin, A., Ienca, M., & Vayena, E. (2019). The global landscape of AI ethics guidelines. *Nature Machine Intelligence*, *1*(9), 389–399.

Johansson, S., Gulliksen, J., & Gustavsson, C. (2021). Disability digital divide: The use of the Internet, smartphones, computers, and tablets among people with disabilities in Sweden. *Universal Access in the Information Society*, *20*(1), 105–120.

Johnson, J., & Olanite Enoch, E. O. (2021). Building Resilient Cloud Ecosystems: The Role of Technological Advances in Data Center Infrastructure.

Jones, M. W., Peters, G. P., Gasser, T., Andrew, R. M., Schwingshackl, C., Gütschow, J., & Le Quéré, C. (2023). National contributions to climate change due to historical emissions of carbon dioxide, methane, and nitrous oxide since 1850. *Scientific Data*, *10*(1), 155. PMID: 36991071

Joseph, S., Ul-Ain, Q., Nosheen, S., Ahmad, M., & Fatima, R. (2024). Navigating the Promise and Perils of Generative AI in Healthcare. In *Revolutionizing the Healthcare Sector with AI* (pp. 91–110). IGI Global.

Júnior, D. S. D. O. S., de Oliveira, J. F., & de Mattos Neto, P. S. (2019). An intelligent hybridization of ARIMA with machine learning models for time series forecasting. *Knowledge-Based Systems*, *175*, 72–86.

Kahrari, P., Khaledi, S., Keikhosravi, G., & Alavi, S. J. (2024). Application of machine learning and deep learning techniques in modeling the associations between air pollution and meteorological parameters in urban areas of tehran metropolis. *Environmental Monitoring and Assessment*, *196*(10), 994. PMID: 39352511

Kajela, D., & Manshahia, M. S. (2017). Optimization of renewable energy systems: A review. *International Journal of Scientific Research in Science and Technology*, *3*(8), 769–795.

Kanalstein, E. (n.d.). *Hate speech and incitement to hatred in the electoral context.* https://www.ohchr.org/sites/default/files/2024-05/information-note-hate-speech-incient-hatred-in-electoral-context.pdf

Kar, A. K., Choudhary, S. K., & Singh, V. K. (2022). How can artificial intelligence impact sustainability: A systematic literature review. *Journal of Cleaner Production*, *376*, 134120.

Kasman, A., & Carvallo, O. (2014). Financial stability, competition and efficiency in Latin American and Caribbean banking. *Journal of Applied Econometrics*, *17*(2), 301–324.

Kaul, R., Ossai, C., Forkan, A. R. M., Jayaraman, P. P., Zelcer, J., Vaughan, S., & Wickramasinghe, N. (2023). The role of AI for developing digital twins in healthcare: The case of cancer care. *Wiley Interdisciplinary Reviews. Data Mining and Knowledge Discovery*, *13*(1). Advance online publication. DOI: 10.1002/widm.1480

Kaur, A., Kaur, H., & Tanwar, A. (2024). *Are Robo-Advisors Revolutionizing Portfolio Management for Enhanced Returns Over Human Advisors?* 165–191. https://doi.org/: Kazu, İ. Y., & Kuvvetli, M. (2025). Digital language learning with Duolingo: assessing its impact on listening, speaking, reading, and writing skills. *Journal of Computers in Education*, 1–27. https://doi.org/DOI: 10.4018/979-8-3693-2185-0.CH008

Kaur, T. (2024). AI Architectures and Technologies for Raising Society 5.0. In *Artificial Intelligence and Society 5.0: Issues, Opportunities, and Challenges*. https://doi.org/DOI: 10.1201/9781003397052-2

Kaur, D., Uslu, S., Rittichier, K. J., & Durresi, A. (2022). Trustworthy artificial intelligence: A review. *ACM Computing Surveys*, *55*(2), 1–38.

Kaur, R., Gabrijelčič, D., & Klobučar, T. (2023). Artificial intelligence for cyber-security: Literature review and future research directions. *Information Fusion*, *97*, 101804.

Kawamleh, S. (2024). *Algorithmic evidence in U.S criminal sentencing*. Springer Nature Link., DOI: 10.1007/s43681-024-00473-y

Keesara, S., Jonas, A., & Schulman, K. (2020). COVID-19 and health care's digital revolution. *The New England Journal of Medicine*, *382*(23), e82. PMID: 32240581

Kelkar, A. H., Hantel, A., Koranteng, E., Cutler, C. S., Hammer, M. J., & Abel, G. A. (2024). Digital Health to Patient-Facing Artificial Intelligence: Ethical Implications and Threats to Dignity for Patients With Cancer. *JCO Oncology Practice*, *20*(3). Advance online publication. DOI: 10.1200/op.23.00412 PMID: 37922435

Khalil, A. S., & Collins, J. J. (2010). Synthetic biology: Applications come of age. *Nature Reviews. Genetics*, *11*(5), 367–379. PMID: 20395970

Khan, M. A., Mittal, S., Roy, R., & Kumar, N. (2020). AI-based energy management for sustainable smart cities: A review. *IEEE Access : Practical Innovations, Open Solutions*, *8*, 206656–206674.

Khan, M. S., Saengon, P., Alganad, A. M. N., Chongcharoen, D., & Farrukh, M. (2020). Consumer green behaviour: An approach towards environmental sustainability. *Sustainable Development*, *28*(5), 1168–1180. DOI: 10.1002/sd.2066

Khan, T., & Emon, M. M. H. (2024). Exploring the Potential of the Blue Economy: A Systematic Review of Strategies for Enhancing International Business in Bangladesh in the context of Indo-Pacific Region. *Review of Business and Economics Studies*, *12*(2), 55–73. DOI: 10.26794/2308-944X-2024-12-2-55-73

Khan, T., Rahman, S. M., & Hasan, M. M. (2020). Barriers to growth of renewable energy technology in Bangladesh: case of solar home system in rural regions. *Proceedings of the International Conference on Computing Advancements*, 1–6.

Kimogol, S. S. (2023). *Accessibility of digital teaching materials. Identifying barriers faced by students with visual impairment in digital teaching materials* (Master's thesis, Oslomet-story universitetet).

Kinney, T.A. (5 June 2008). *Hate Speech and Ethnophaulisms*. The International Encyclopedia of Communication. doi:DOI: 10.1002/9781405186407.wbiech004

Kloppenburg, J. (2010). Impeding dispossession, enabling repossession: Biological open source and the recovery of seed sovereignty. *Journal of Agrarian Change*, *10*(3), 367–388.

Kloppenburg, J. (2014). *First the Seed: The Political Economy of Plant Biotechnology, 1492–2000* (2nd ed.). University of Wisconsin Press.

Klümper, W., & Qaim, M. (2014). A meta-analysis of the impacts of genetically modified crops. *PLoS One*, *9*(11), e111629. DOI: 10.1371/journal.pone.0111629 PMID: 25365303

Kong, F. W., Horsham, C., Ngoo, A., Soyer, H. P., & Janda, M. (2020). Review of smartphone mobile applications for skin cancer detection: What are the changes in availability, functionality, and costs to users over time? *International Journal of Dermatology*, *60*(3), 289–308. DOI: 10.1111/ijd.15132 PMID: 32880938

Kongolo, T. (2024). Intellectual property and artificial intelligence. Intellectual Property and Emerging Technologies, 19–47. DOI: 10.4324/9781003309086-3

Konietzko, J., Das, A., & Bocken, N. (2023). Towards regenerative business models: A necessary shift? *Sustainable Production and Consumption*, *38*, 372–388.

Königstorfer, F., & Thalmann, S. (2020). Applications of Artificial Intelligence in commercial banks–A research agenda for behavioral finance. *Journal of Behavioral and Experimental Finance*, *27*, 100352.

Kordzadeh, N., & Ghasemaghaei, M. (2021). Algorithmic bias: Review, synthesis, and Future Research Directions. *European Journal of Information Systems*, *31*(3), 388–409. DOI: 10.1080/0960085X.2021.1927212

Koshariya, A. K., Kalaiyarasi, D., Jovith, A. A., Sivakami, T., Hasan, D. S., & Boopathi, S. (2023). Ai-enabled iot and wsn-integrated smart agriculture system. In *Artificial Intelligence Tools and Technologies for Smart Farming and Agriculture Practices* (pp. 200–218). IGI global.

Kulal, A., Rahiman, H. U., Suvarna, H., Abhishek, N., & Dinesh, S. (2024). Enhancing public service delivery efficiency: Exploring the impact of AI. *Journal of Open Innovation*, *10*(3), 100329. DOI: 10.1016/J.JOITMC.2024.100329

Kulothungan, V., Ramamoorthy, T., Mohan, R., & Mathur, P. (2024). Assessing progress of India in reduction of premature mortality due to four noncommunicable diseases towards achieving the WHO 25× 25 goal and the sustainable development goals. *Sustainable Development*, *32*(3), 2020–2030.

Kumar, A. B., & Sanjaya, K. (2025). Ethics, Algorithms, and the Rules of Evidence. *Forensic Intelligence and Deep Learning Solutions in Crime Investigation*, 103–124. https://doi.org/DOI: 10.4018/979-8-3693-9405-2.ch006

Kumar, A. B., Sanjaya, K., & Saleem, M. (2025). Justice in the Age of Algorithms. *Advances in Computational Intelligence and Robotics*, •••, 191–210. DOI: 10.4018/979-8-3693-9395-6.ch009

Kumar, N., & Katiyar, A. (2024). *Ompal.* Artificial Intelligence and the Future of Renewable Energy., DOI: 10.4018/979-8-3693-1954-3.ch001

Kyei, A. K. (2023). *Experiences of students with visual impairment in studying Information, Communication and Technology at the University of Education, Winneba* (Doctoral dissertation, University of Education, Winneba).

Kyriazis, N. A. (2021). A survey on volatility fluctuations in the decentralized cryptocurrency financial assets. *Journal of Risk and Financial Management*, *14*(7), 293. DOI: 10.3390/jrfm14070293

Labadze, L., Grigolia, M., & Machaidze, L. (2023). Role of AI chatbots in education: Systematic literature review. *International Journal of Educational Technology in Higher Education*, *20*(1), 56.

Lachman, R., & Joffe, M. (2021). Applications of artificial intelligence in media and entertainment. *Advances in Computational Intelligence and Robotics*, •••, 201–220. DOI: 10.4018/978-1-7998-3499-1.ch012

Lacy, W. B. (2017). The paradox of agricultural biotechnology. In Koushik, K. O. (Ed.), *Agriculture, food and biodiversity* (pp. 141–162). Springer.

Lagan, S., Sandler, L., & Torous, J. (2021). Evaluating evaluation frameworks: A scoping review of frameworks for assessing health apps. *BMJ Open*, *11*(3), e047001. DOI: 10.1136/bmjopen-2020-047001 PMID: 33741674

Lal, N. (2018). *#Notinmyname: Celebrities join protesters in Delhi, Mumbai*, Times of India. https://timesofindia.indiatimes.com/city/delhi/notinmyname-celebrities-join-protesters-in-delhi-mumbai/articleshow/63786171.cms

Lambert, S. R. (2020). Do MOOCs contribute to student equity and social inclusion? A systematic review 2014–18. *Computers & Education*, *145*, 103693.

Laranjo, L., Dunn, A. G., Tong, H. L., Kocaballi, A. B., Chen, J., Bashir, R., Surian, D., Gallego, B., Magrabi, F., Lau, A. Y. S., & Coiera, E. (2018). Conversational agents in healthcare: A systematic review. *Journal of the American Medical Informatics Association : JAMIA*, *25*(9), 1248–1258. PMID: 30010941

Leach, M., Scoones, I., & Stirling, A. (2020). Governing epidemics in an age of science and uncertainty. *Social Studies of Science*, *50*(4), 610–638.

Leape, J., Abbott, M., Sakaguchi, H., Brett, A., Cao, L., Chand, K., Golbuu, Y., Martin, T., Mayorga, J., & Myksvoll, M. S. (2023). Technology, Data and New Models for Sustainably Managing Ocean Resources. In *The Blue Compendium* (pp. 185–211). Springer International Publishing., DOI: 10.1007/978-3-031-16277-0_6

Lee, J., Jin, C., & Bagheri, B. (2018). Cyber-physical systems for predictive maintenance using deep learning techniques. *Journal of Manufacturing Science and Engineering*, *140*(4), 041017.

Lehning, S. (2021). *Hate Speech Laws in Democratic Countries*. JSU Digital Commons. https://digitalcommons.jsu.edu/compass/vol5/iss1/2/

Lepoutre, M. (2017). Hate Speech in Public Discourse. *Social Theory and Practice*, *43*(4), 851–883. DOI: 10.5840/soctheorpract201711125

Leskien, D., & Flitner, M. (1997). *Intellectual property rights and plant genetic resources: Options for a sui generis system*. IPGRI.

Levidow, L., Carr, S., & Wield, D. (2005). European Union regulation of agri-biotechnology: Precautionary links between science, expertise and policy. *Science & Public Policy*, *32*(4), 261–276.

Levin, B. (2002). Cyberhate: A Legal and Historical Analysis of Extremists' Use of Computer Networks in America. *The American Behavioral Scientist*, *45*(6), 958–988. DOI: 10.1177/0002764202045006004

Lewis, J. E. (Sxwpilemaát). (2020). Indigenous Protocol and Artificial Intelligence Position Paper.

Li, C. (2021). "The application of artificial intelligence and machine learning in financial stability", In *The 2020 International Conference on Machine Learning and Big Data Analytics for IoT Security and Privacy: SPIoT-2020*, Vol. 1 (pp. 214-219). Springer International Publishing.

Liew, J. (2024). Translating Vision into Reality for Early Education & Development. *Early Education and Development*, *35*(1). Advance online publication. DOI: 10.1080/10409289.2024.2287684

Lindsay, S. (2020). The legal implications of digital accessibility in higher education. *International Journal of Educational Law*, *38*(1), 33–49.

Lindsay, S., Sussman, T., & Northway, M. (2021). Artificial intelligence and its impact on accessibility in higher education: A critical review. *International Journal of Educational Technology*, *12*(3), 45–59.

Lin, T. C. (2019). Artificial intelligence, finance, and the law. *Fordham Law Review, 88*(2), 531–551.

Liu, G., Dong, X., Kong, Z., & Dong, K. (2021). Does national air quality monitoring reduce local air pollution? The case of PM2.5 for China. *Journal of Environmental Management, 296*, 113232. DOI: 10.1016/j.jenvman.2021.113232 PMID: 34246901

Liu, V., & Yin, Y. (2024). Green AI: Exploring carbon footprints, mitigation strategies, and trade offs in large language model training. *Discover Artificial Intelligence, 4*(1), 49. DOI: 10.1007/s44163-024-00149-w

Li, Z., Pardos, Z. A., & Ren, C. (2024). Aligning open educational resources to new taxonomies: How AI technologies can help and in which scenarios. *Computers & Education, 216*, 105027. DOI: 10.1016/J.COMPEDU.2024.105027

Llansó, E. J. (2020). No Amount of AI in Content Moderation Will Solve Filtering's Prior-Restraint Problem. *Big Data & Society, 7*(1).

Lodhi, S. K., Gill, A. Y., & Hussain, H. K. (2024). Green innovations: Artificial intelligence and sustainable materials in production. *BULLET: Jurnal Multidisiplin Ilmu, 3*(4), 492–507.

Lopes, G. P. (2025). Bias in Adjudication and the Promise of AI: Challenges to Procedural Fairness. *Law. Technology and Humans, 7*(1), 47–67. DOI: 10.5204/lthj.3812

Luckin, R., Holmes, W., Griffiths, M., & Forcier, L. B. (2016). *Intelligence unleashed: An argument for AI in education*. Pearson Education.

Luxton, D. D. (2014). Recommendations for the ethical use and design of artificial intelligent care providers. *Artificial Intelligence in Medicine, 62*(1), 1–10. PMID: 25059820

Lyman, R. (2020). Empowering students with disabilities: The role of assistive technology in higher education. *Assistive Technology Journal, 22*(3), 143–157.

Makanadar, A., Shahane, S., & Patil, U. (2024). Tracing Algorithmic and AI-biased Data. *Economic and Political Weekly, 59*(7).

Makri, V., Tsagkanos, A., & Bellas, A. (2014). Determinants of non-performing loans: The case of Eurozone. *Panoeconomicus, 61*(2), 193–206.

Maleki Varnosfaderani, S., & Forouzanfar, M. (2024). The Role of AI in Hospitals and Clinics: Transforming Healthcare in the 21st Century. *Bioengineering 2024, Vol. 11, Page 337, 11*(4), 337. https://doi.org/DOI: 10.3390/BIOENGINEERING11040337

Mana, A. A., Allouhi, A., Hamrani, A., Rahman, S., el Jamaoui, I., & Jayachandran, K. (2024). Sustainable AI-based production agriculture: Exploring AI applications and implications in agricultural practices. *Smart Agricultural Technology*, *7*. Advance online publication. DOI: 10.1016/j.atech.2024.100416

Mandal, A. K., & Sen, R. (2024). Medium-Term AQI Prediction in Selected Areas of Bangladesh Based on Bidirectional GRU Network Model. *SN Computer Science*, *5*(5), 627.

Manikandan, S., Kaviya, R. S., Shreeharan, D. H., Subbaiya, R., Vickram, S., Karmegam, N., Kim, W., & Govarthanan, M. (2025). Artificial intelligence-driven sustainability: Enhancing carbon capture for sustainable development goals– A review. *Sustainable Development*, *33*(2), 2004–2029. DOI: 10.1002/sd.3222

Mansell, W. L. (2023). Perceptions of Applying Universal Design for Learning to Quaver's Marvelous World of Music to Increase Engagement of Students with Autism.

Maqsood, M., Butt, H. H., Ali, M. A., Chinedu, C. C., Ahmad, M., Maqsood, M., Butt, H. H., Ali, M. A., Chinedu, C. C., & Ahmad, M. (2025). Chatbots as Learning Companions Exploring Ethical Dimensions of AI in Education. In Jean-Éric, P. (Ed.), *Architecting the Digital Future: Platforms, Design, and Application* (pp. 311–348). IGI Global Scientific Publishing., DOI: 10.4018/979-8-3693-2973-3.CH012

Margetts, H., & Dunleavy, P. (2013). *The second wave of digital-era governance: A quasi-paradigm for government on the Web*. Philosophical Transactions of the Royal Society A: Mathematical, Physical and Engineering Sciences, 371(1987), 20120382.

Mason, A. (2020). Digital literacy in the context of students with disabilities. *Journal of Education and Technology*, *15*(3), 152–167.

Matsieli, M., & Mutula, S. (2024). COVID-19 and digital transformation in Higher Education Institutions: Towards inclusive and equitable access to quality education. *Education Sciences*, *14*(8), 819.

Max, R., Kriebitz, A., & Von Websky, C. (2021). "Ethical considerations about the implications of artificial intelligence in finance", *Handbook on ethics in finance*, pp. 577-592.

McMahon, R., & Smith, M. (2021). *Digital Self-Determination and the 'Data Revolution' in Canada's North*. Northern Public Affairs Journal.

Meijer, A. (2019). Public administration and the data revolution: Transparency and data-driven decision-making in the public sector. *Government Information Quarterly*, *36*(4), 100383.

Meijer, A., & Bolívar, M. P. R. (2016). Governing the smart city: A review of the literature on smart urban governance. *International Review of Administrative Sciences*, *82*(2), 392–408.

Mejía-Granda, C. M., Fernández-Alemán, J. L., Carrillo-De-Gea, J. M., & García-Berná, J. A. (2023). Security vulnerabilities in healthcare: An analysis of medical devices and software. *Medical & Biological Engineering & Computing*, *62*(1), 257–273. DOI: 10.1007/s11517-023-02912-0 PMID: 37789249

Memon, F. N., & Memon, S. N. (2025). Digital Divide and Equity in Education: Bridging Gaps to Ensure Inclusive Learning. In Impact of Digitalisation on Education and Social Sustainability (pp. 107-130). IGI Global.

Mennella, C., Maniscalco, U., De Pietro, G., & Esposito, M. (2024). Ethical and regulatory challenges of AI technologies in healthcare: A narrative review. *Heliyon*, *10*(4). PMID: 38384518

Meta. (n.d.). *Hate Speech, Community Standards Enforcement Report*, Meta/com. https://transparency.meta.com/reports/community-standards-enforcement/hate-speech/facebook/

Meyer, K. (2020). Transcribing technology in the classroom: Enhancing accessibility for students with hearing impairments. *Journal of Assistive Technologies*, *22*(1), 56–65.

Mhlanga, D. (2021). "Financial inclusion in emerging economies: The application of machine learning and artificial intelligence in credit risk assessment", *International journal of financial studies*, Vol. *9 No.* 3, pp. 1-17.

Miao, F., & Holmes, W. (2021). *AI and education: A guidance for policymakers*. Unesco Publishing.

Milana, C., & Ashta, A. (2021). Artificial intelligence techniques in finance and financial markets: A survey of the literature. *Strategic Change*, *30*(3), 189–209.

Min, A. (2023). Artifical Intelligence and Bias: Challenges, Implications, and Remedies. *Journal of Social Research*, *2*(11), 3808–3817. DOI: 10.55324/josr.v2i11.1477

Mirchandani, M. (2019, February 12). *The Parliamentary Panel Will Reinforce Bias on Twitter, Not Fix It*. Maya Mirchandani. https://mayamirchandani.com/2019/02/12/the-parliamentary-panel-will-reinforce-bias-on-twitter-not-fix-it/

Mirchandani, M. (n.d.). *Fighting Hate Speech, Balancing Freedoms: A Regulatory Challenge*. Retrieved September 11, 2025, from https://jils.blog/wp-content/uploads/2025/01/maya-mirchandani_9.pdf

Mishra, S. (2024). Classification Based on Ethnicity and Race: A Comprehensive Review. *International Journal for Research in Applied Science and Engineering Technology*, *12*(3). Advance online publication. DOI: 10.22214/ijraset.2024.57989

Mitra, S., Kumar, H., Gupta, M. P., & Bhattacharya, J. (2023). Entrepreneurship in smart cities: Elements of the start-up ecosystem. *Journal of Science and Technology Policy Management*, *14*(3), 592–611.

Mittelstadt, B. D., Allo, P., Taddeo, M., Wachter, S., & Floridi, L. (2016). The ethics of algorithms: Mapping the debate. *Big Data & Society*, *3*(2), 1–21.

Mohamed Hashim, M. A., Tlemsani, I., & Matthews, R. (2022). Higher education strategy in digital transformation. *Education and Information Technologies*, *27*(3), 3171–3195. PMID: 34539217

Mohamed, E., Quteishat, A., Qtaishat, A., & Mohammad, A. (2024). Exploring the Role of AI in Modern Legal Practice: Opportunities, Challenges, and Ethical Implications. *J. Electrical Systems, 20*(6), 3040–3050. https://pdfs.semanticscholar.org/7828/77a8679e1811ad00094d934faee36c23ea1a.pdf

Mohanty, U. C., Sinha, P., Rao, M. N., Swain, D. K., & Singh, K. K. (2020)Climate Risk Management in Agriculture.

Molfino, R., Cepolina, F. E., Cepolina, E., Cepolina, E. M., & Cepolina, S. (2024). Robots trends and megatrends: Artificial intelligence and the society. *The Industrial Robot*, *51*(1), 117–124. DOI: 10.1108/IR-05-2023-0095/FULL/PDF

Monteith, S., Glenn, T., Geddes, J. R., Whybrow, P. C., Achtyes, E., & Bauer, M. (2024). Artificial intelligence and increasing misinformation. *The British Journal of Psychiatry*, *224*(2), 33–35. PMID: 37881016

Morgera, E. (2015). The Need for an International Legal Concept of Fair and Equitable Benefit Sharing. *European Journal of International Law*, *27*(2), 353–383.

Mougdir, S. (2023). *What is in the black box: The ethical implications of algorithms ...: Ingenta Connect*. Ingentaconnect.com; Ingentaconnect. https://www.ingentaconnect.com/content/hsp/airwa/2024/00000003/00000001/art00010

Muheidat, F., Patel, D., Tammisetty, S., Tawalbeh, L. A., & Tawalbeh, M. (2022). Emerging Concepts Using Blockchain and Big Data. *Procedia Computer Science*, *198*, 15–22. DOI: 10.1016/J.PROCS.2021.12.206

Mulla, S., Pande, C. B., & Singh, S. K. (2024). Times Series Forecasting of Monthly Rainfall using Seasonal Auto Regressive Integrated Moving Average with EXogenous Variables (SARIMAX) Model. *Water Resources Management*, *38*(6), 1825–1846.

Müller, K., & Schwarz, C. (2020). Fanning the Flames of Hate: Social Media and Hate Crime. *Journal of the European Economic Association, 19*(4). Advance online publication. DOI: 10.1093/jeea/jvaa045

Munawar, H. S., Mojtahedi, M., Hammad, A. W. A., Kouzani, A., & Mahmud, M. A. P. (2022). Disruptive technologies as a solution for disaster risk management: A review. *The Science of the Total Environment, 806*, 151351. DOI: 10.1016/j.scitotenv.2021.151351 PMID: 34740667

Murikah, W., Nthenge, J. K., & Musyoka, F. M. (2024). Bias and ethics of AI systems applied in auditing-A systematic review. *Scientific African*, •••, 02281.

Murthy, R. V. R. (2020). *Mapping Spatio-Temporal Cropland Changes Due To Water Stress In Krishna River Basin Using Temporal Satellite Data* (Doctoral dissertation, College of Engineering (A), Andhra University, Visakhapatnam).

Muzayyanah, S., Hong, C. Y., Adha, R., & Yang, S. F. (2023). The non-linear relationship between air pollution, labor insurance and productivity: Multivariate adaptive regression splines approach. *Sustainability, 15*(12), 9404.

Mytnyk, B., Tkachyk, O., Shakhovska, N., Fedushko, S., & Syerov, Y. (2023). Application of artificial intelligence for fraudulent banking operations recognition. *Big Data and Cognitive Computing, 7*(2), 93.

Nair, M. M., & Tyagi, A. K. (2023). AI, IoT, blockchain, and cloud computing: The necessity of the future. *Distributed Computing to Blockchain: Architecture, Technology, and Applications*, 189–206. https://doi.org/DOI: 10.1016/B978-0-323-96146-2.00001-2

Narayanan, M. K. (2019, June 25). *The future of parliamentary democracy*. The Hindu. https://www.thehindu.com/opinion/lead/the-future-of-parliamentary-democracy/article28138347.ece

Narendrakumar, N. & Fnu, H. (2023, May 1). *International Journal of Engineering Technology Research & Management from legacy to digital: How AI and cloud computing is changing health insurance*. https://www.researchgate.net/publication/389633691_International_Journal_of_Engineering_Technology_Research_Management_FRO

National Law University Delhi. (2024). *Centre for Communication Governance at NLU Delhi - National Law University Delhi*. National Law University Delhi. https://nludelhi.ac.in/research/centre-for-communication-governance-at-nlu-delhi/

National Planning Commission. (2012). *National Development Plan 2030: Our Future - Make it Work*. National Planning Commission.

Nayak, M. (2025). Analyzing the Integration of Artificial Intelligence in Fostering 21st-Century Competencies and Socio-Emotional Learning in Education: Opportunities and Challenges. *International Journal for Multidisciplinary Research*, *7*(3). Advance online publication. DOI: 10.36948/ijfmr.2025.v07i03.47449

Negi. (2024). The Rise of Hate Speech Around the World. SSRN *Electronic Journal*. https://doi.org/DOI: 10.2139/ssrn.4719266

Nelson, J. P., Biddle, J. B., & Shapira, P. (2023). Applications and societal implications of artificial intelligence in manufacturing: A systematic review. *arXiv preprint arXiv:2308.02025*.

Neville-Neil, G. V. (2017). The chess player who couldn't pass the salt. *Communications of the ACM*, *60*(4), 24–25. DOI: 10.1145/3055277

Ngqunguza, A., Seleke, Z., & Makhoba, T. I. (2024). Digital Transformation in Higher Education: Leadership Strategies for ensuring equity and inclusion in digital learning environments. [JPADA]. *Journal of Public Administration and Development Alternatives*, *9*(2), 101–114.

Nishant, R., Kennedy, M., & Corbett, J. (2020). Artificial intelligence for sustainability: Challenges, opportunities, and a research agenda. *International Journal of Information Management*, *53*, 102104.

Novelli, C., Taddeo, M., & Floridi, L. (2023). Accountability in artificial intelligence: What it is and how it works. *AI & Society*, •••, 1–12.

Nwosu, J. N. (2018). An investigation into the extent of the use of artificial intelligence in nigeria banks. *IAA Journal of Applied Sciences*, *4*(1), 105–111.

O'Neil, C. (2016). *Weapons of math destruction: How big data increases inequality and threatens democracy*. Crown Publishing Group.

Obermeyer, Z., Nissan, R., Stern, M., Eaneff, S., Bembeneck, E., & Mullainathan, S. (2021). Algorithmic Bias Playbook. In *Algorithmic Bias Playbook*. Algorithmic Bias Playbook. https://ic3.center.ufl.edu/wordpress/files/2022/08/algorithmic-bias-playbook.pdf

Obermeyer, Z., & Emanuel, E. J. (2016). Predicting the future—Big data, machine learning, and clinical medicine. *The New England Journal of Medicine*, *375*(13), 1216–1219. PMID: 27682033

Occhipinti, J. A., Prodan, A., Hynes, W., Buchanan, J., Green, R., Burrow, S., Eyre, H. A., Skinner, A., Hickie, I. B., Heffernan, M., Song, Y. J. C., Ujdur, G., & Tanner, M. (2025). Artificial intelligence, recessionary pressures and population health. *Bulletin of the World Health Organization, 103*(2), 155. DOI: 10.2471/BLT.24.291950 PMID: 39882489

Odubo, T. C., & Kosoe, E. A. (2024). Sources of Air Pollutants: Impacts and Solutions.

Ogunwale, A., Smith, A., Fakorede, O., & Ogunlesi, A. O. (2024). Artificial intelligence and forensic mental health in Africa: A narrative review. *International Review of Psychiatry (Abingdon, England), 37*(1), 3–13. DOI: 10.1080/09540261.2024.2405174;WGROUP:STRING:PUBLICATION PMID: 40035373

ÓhÉigeartaigh, S. S., Whittlestone, J., Liu, Y., Zeng, Y., & Liu, Z. (2020). Overcoming Barriers to Cross-cultural Cooperation in AI Ethics and Governance. *Philosophy & Technology, 33*(4), 571–593. DOI: 10.1007/s13347-020-00402-x

Okeleke, P. A., Ajiga, D., Folorunsho, S. O., & Ezeigweneme, C. (2024). Predictive analytics for market trends using AI: A study in consumer behavior. *International Journal of Engineering Research Updates, 7*(1), 36–49.

Olawade, D. B., Wada, O. Z., David-Olawade, A. C., Fapohunda, O., Ige, A. O., & Ling, J. (2024). Artificial intelligence potential for net zero sustainability: Current evidence and prospects. *Next sustainability, 4*, 100041.

Olsen, R., Courtney, L., Warnberg, C., & Samuels, J. (n.d.). *How Prosecutors Are Collecti ng and Using Data for Decisionmaking Findings from the 2018 National Survey of State Prosecutors' Offi ces*. Retrieved September 11, 2025, from https://www.urban.org/sites/default/files/2018/09/25/prosecutor_fact_sheet.pdf

Omar, A., & Hashem, M. E. (2022). An Evaluation of the Automatic Detection of Hate Speech in Social Media Networks. *International Journal of Advanced Computer Science and Applications, 13*(2). Advance online publication. DOI: 10.14569/ijacsa.2022.0130228

Orkin, A. (2020). The importance of digital literacy for students with disabilities in higher education. *Journal of Educational Technology, 58*(2), 215.

Osama, M. (2024). Artificial Intelligence in scientific writing and research publication: A paradigm shift in language inclusivity. In *Journal of Back and Musculoskeletal Rehabilitation* (Vol. 37, Issue 2). https://doi.org/DOI: 10.3233/BMR-245001

Owsley, C. S., & Greenwood, K. (2024). Awareness and perception of artificial intelligence operationalized integration in news media industry and society. *AI & Society*, *39*(1), 417–431. DOI: 10.1007/S00146-022-01386-2/METRICS

Oyedokun, T. T. (2025). Assistive Technology and Accessibility Tools in Enhancing Adaptive Education. In *Advancing Adaptive Education: Technological Innovations for Disability Support* (pp. 125-162). IGI Global Scientific Publishing.

Ozili, P. K. (2024). "Artificial intelligence in central banking: benefits and risks of AI for central banks", In *Industrial Applications of Big Data, AI, and Blockchain* (pp. 70-82). IGI Global.

Ozili, P. K. (2018). Banking stability determinants in Africa. *International Journal of Managerial Finance*, *14*(4), 462–483.

Ozkan, M. (2024). Atmospheric alchemy: The energy and cost dynamics of direct air carbon capture. *MRS Energy & Sustainability : a Review Journal*, *12*(1), 46–61. DOI: 10.1557/s43581-024-00091-5

Papadogeorgou, G., Kioumourtzoglou, M. A., Braun, D., & Zanobetti, A. (2019). Low levels of air pollution and health: Effect estimates, methodological challenges, and future directions. *Current Environmental Health Reports*, *6*, 105–115. PMID: 31090042

Patel, P., Moz-Ruiz, D., Garcia, R., Chatterjee, A., Morreale, P., & Burnett, M. (2024). From Workshops to Classrooms: Faculty Experiences with Implementing Inclusive Design Principles. *SIGCSE 2024 - Proceedings of the 55th ACM Technical Symposium on Computer Science Education, 1*. https://doi.org/DOI: 10.1145/3626252.3630861

Patel, R. (2013). *Stuffed and Starved: The Hidden Battle for the World Food System*. Melville House.

Paterson, J. L., Brown, R., & Walters, M. A. (2018). The Short and Longer Term Impacts of Hate Crimes Experienced Directly, Indirectly, and Through the Media. *Personality and Social Psychology Bulletin*, *45*(7), 994–1010. https://journals.sagepub.com/doi/full/10.1177/0146167218802835 PMID: 30400746

Patterson, L. A. (2006). Agricultural biotechnology and intellectual property: Seeds of change or an uneven playing field? *The Drake Journal of Agricultural Law*, *11*(2), 239–258.

Pawade, A., & Charhate, S. (2024). Assessing environmental influences on radon levels: Analysis of independent variables. *Mathematical Models in Engineering*, *10*(3), 168–192.

Peng, M., Liu, Y., Khan, A., Ahmed, B., Sarker, S. K., Ghadi, Y. Y., Bhatti, U. A., Al-Razgan, M., & Ali, Y. A. (2024). Crop monitoring using remote sensing land use and land change data: Comparative analysis of deep learning methods using pre-trained CNN models. *Big Data Research, 36*, 100448. DOI: 10.1016/j.bdr.2024.100448

Peng, S. (2021). *Blockchain for Big Data : AI, IoT and Cloud Perspectives*. Blockchain for Big Data., DOI: 10.1201/9781003201670

Perc, M., Ozer, M., & Hojnik, J. (2019). Social and juristic challenges of artificial intelligence. *Palgrave Communications*, *5*(1).

Pires, A., Martinho, G., & Chang, N. B. (2019). Solid waste management in smart cities: A review of waste management practices and AI-driven solutions. *Waste Management (New York, N.Y.)*, *91*, 1–14.

Popescu, S. M., Mansoor, S., Wani, O. A., Kumar, S. S., Sharma, V., Sharma, A., & Chung, Y. S. (2024). Artificial intelligence and IoT driven technologies for environmental pollution monitoring and management. *Frontiers in Environmental Science*, *12*, 1336088.

Posey, D. A., & Dutfield, G. (1996). *Beyond Intellectual Property: Toward Traditional Resource Rights for Indigenous Peoples and Local Communities*. IDRC.

Press Trust of India. (2016, March 19). *EC takes up issue of hate speech, provocative ads with parties*. The Indian Express. https://indianexpress.com/article/india/india-news-india/election-commission-nasim-zaidi-hate-speech-provocative-ads/

Putri, T. H., Caraka, R. E., Toharudin, T., Kim, Y., Chen, R. C., Gio, P. U., ... & Pardamean, B. (2024). Fine-Tuning of Predictive Models CNN-LSTM and CONV-LSTM for Nowcasting PM 2.5 Level. *IEEE Access*.

Qaim, M. (2020). *Genetically Modified Crops and Agricultural Development*. Palgrave Macmillan.

Qatawneh, A. M. (2024). The role of artificial intelligence in auditing and fraud detection in accounting information systems: Moderating role of natural language processing. *The International Journal of Organizational Analysis*, *33*(6), 1391–1409. DOI: 10.1108/IJOA-03-2024-4389/FULL/XML

Rahman, M., Ming, T. H., Baigh, T. A., & Sarker, M. (2023). Adoption of artificial intelligence in banking services: An empirical analysis. *International Journal of Emerging Markets*, *18*(10), 4270–4300.

Raihan, A. (2023). Original Research Article Artificial intelligence and machine learning applications in forest management and biodiversity conservation.

Raihan, M. M., Subroto, S., Chowdhury, N., Koch, K., Ruttan, E., & Turin, T. C. (2024). *Dimensions and barriers for digital (in) equity and digital divide: A systematic integrative review*. Digital Transformation and Society.

Rajagopal, B. (2003). *International Law from Below: Development, Social Movements and Third World Resistance*. Cambridge University Press.

Rajesh, R., Mathews, G. V., Rao, N. P., & Begum, S. K. (2024). Groundwater-level prediction in Visakhapatnam district, Andhra Pradesh, India, using Bayesian Neural Networks. *Acta Geophysica*, *72*(4), 2759–2772.

Rajpurkar, P., Chen, E., Banerjee, O., & Topol, E. J. (2022). AI in health and medicine. In *Nature Medicine* (Vol. 28, Issue 1). https://doi.org/DOI: 10.1038/s41591-021-01614-0

Rajput, A. R., Masood, I., Tabassam, A., & Aslam, M. S., ShaoYu, Z., & Rajput, M. A. (2023). Patient's data privacy and security in mHealth applications: A Charles proxy-based recommendation. *Soft Computing*, *27*(23), 18165–18180. DOI: 10.1007/s00500-023-09265-8

Ramadan, M. N., Ali, M. A., Khoo, S. Y., & Alkhedher, M. (2024). AI-powered IoT and UAV systems for real-time detection and prevention of illegal logging. *Results in Engineering*, *24*, 103277.

Raman, R., Pattnaik, D., Lathabai, H. H., Kumar, C., Govindan, K., & Nedungadi, P. (2024). Green and sustainable AI research: An integrated thematic and topic modeling analysis. *Journal of Big Data*, *11*(1), 1–28.

Ramarajan, M., Dinesh, A., Muthuraman, C., Rajini, J., Anand, T., & Segar, B. (2024). AI-Driven Job Displacement and Economic Impacts. 216–238. https://doi.org/: DOI: 10.4018/979-8-3693-2643-5.CH013

Ramaswamy, N. S., & Gulati, A. (2021). *Contract farming in India: Enhancing farmer income. Indian Council for Research on International Economic Relations*. ICRIER.

Rame, R., Purwanto, P., & Sudarno, S. (2024). Industry 5.0 and sustainability: An overview of emerging trends and challenges for a green future. *Innovation and Green Development*, *3*(4), 100173.

Ramirez-Corredores, M. M., Goldwasser, M. R., & Falabella de Sousa Aguiar, E. (2023). Carbon dioxide and climate change. In *Decarbonization as a Route Towards Sustainable Circularity* (pp. 1–14). Springer International Publishing.

Rana, P., Ahmad, M., Stephen, T., & Chemingui, H. (2025). Agricultural Intelligence (AI)'s Impact on Society 5.0 Farming. In Rajiv, P. (Ed.), *Open AI and Computational Intelligence for Society 5.0* (pp. 109–128). IGI Global Scientific Publishing., DOI: 10.4018/979-8-3693-4326-5.CH005

Rane, N., & Choudhary, S. (2024). Role and challenges of ChatGPT and similar generative artificial intelligence in arts and humanities. *Studies in Humanities and Education*, *5*(1). Advance online publication. DOI: 10.48185/she.v5i1.999

Rashid, A. B., & Kausik, A. K. (2024). AI revolutionizing industries worldwide: A comprehensive overview of its diverse applications. *Hybrid Advances*, 100277.

Ravichandra, T., Murugeswari, P., Revathi, M., Senthilkumar, S., Rathore, D. S., & Sudhakar, M. (2024). *The Future of Machine Learning and Robotics in Digital Technology for Hospitality*., DOI: 10.4018/979-8-3693-9586-8.ch014

Rawabdeh, A. (2024). Building a global virtual healthcare system. *Journal of Infrastructure Policy and Development*, *8*(9), 6765. DOI: 10.24294/jipd.v8i9.6765

Ray, S. (2024). Ile constitutional review volume iii and issue i of 2024 code and court: a case study on the impact of algorithmic decisions on legal principles and precedents" best citation -dr sanchita ray, code and court: a case study on the impact of algorithmic decisions on legal principles and precedents". In *Ile Constitutional Review*. Institute of Legal Education. https://cr.iledu.in/wp-content/uploads/2024/08/V3I14.pdf

Rayhan, A. (2023). The role of AI in sustainable development: Opportunities and challenges.

Rehman, A. U., Alamoudi, Y., Khalid, H. M., Morchid, A., Muyeen, S. M., & Abdelaziz, A. Y. (2024). Smart agriculture technology: An integrated framework of renewable energy resources, IoT-based energy management, and precision robotics. *Cleaner Energy Systems*, *9*, 100132.

Reich, J. (2020). Navigating the digital divide: Legal frameworks and barriers to digital accessibility in higher education. *Journal of Digital Education*, *39*(4), 245–259.

Ren, Y., Xie, R., Yu, F. R., Huang, T., & Liu, Y. (2022). Green intelligence networking for connected and autonomous vehicles in smart cities. *IEEE Transactions on Green Communications and Networking*, *6*(3), 1591–1603.

Rezaiy, R., & Shabri, A. (2024). An innovative hybrid W-EEMD-ARIMA model for drought forecasting using the standardized precipitation index. *Natural Hazards*, •••, 1–30.

Riccio, A., & Chianese, E. (2023). Accurate, reliable and high resolution air quality predictions by improving the Copernicus Atmosphere Monitoring Service using machine learning techniques. *EGUsphere*, *2023*, 1–27.

Richard, N. (2018). *Facebook's new Rosetta AI system helps detect hate speech.* CNET. https://www.cnet.com/tech/tech-industry/facebooks-new-rosetta-ai-system-helps-detect-hate-speech/

Richards, R. D., Calvert, C. (2000). Counterspeech 2000: A New Look at the Old Remedy for Bad Speech, *BYU L. Rev*. 585.

Rivera, A., Ponce, P., Mata, O., Molina, A., & Meier, A. (2023). Local weather station design and development for cost-effective environmental monitoring and real-time data sharing. *Sensors (Basel)*, *23*(22), 9060. PMID: 38005448

Robinson, D. F. (2010). *Confronting Biopiracy: Challenges, Cases and International Debates*. Earthscan.

Rodriguez-Rey, D., Guevara, M., Linares, M. P., Casanovas, J., Armengol, J. M., Benavides, J., Soret, A., Jorba, O., Tena, C., & García-Pando, C. P. (2022). To what extent the traffic restriction policies applied in Barcelona city can improve its air quality? *The Science of the Total Environment*, *807*, 150743. DOI: 10.1016/j.scitotenv.2021.150743 PMID: 34634347

Saborío-Taylor, S., & Rojas-Ramírez, F. (2024). Universal Design for Learning and artificial intelligence in the digital era: Fostering inclusion and autonomous learning. *International Journal of Professional Development, Learners and Learning, 6*(2).

Sacchi, R., Bauer, C., Cox, B., & Mutel, C. (2022). When, where and how can the electrification of passenger cars reduce greenhouse gas emissions? *Renewable & Sustainable Energy Reviews*, *162*, 112475. DOI: 10.1016/j.rser.2022.112475

Sachoulidou, A. (2024). Harnessing AI for law enforcement: Solutions and boundaries from the forthcoming AI Act. *New Journal of European Criminal Law*, *15*(2), 117–125. DOI: 10.1177/20322844241260114;PAGEGROUP:STRING:PUBLICATION

Sadok, H., Sakka, F., & El Maknouzi, M. E. H. (2022). Artificial intelligence and bank credit analysis: A review. *Cogent Economics & Finance*, *10*(1), 2023262.

Safdar, N. M., Banja, J. D., & Meltzer, C. C. (2020). Ethical considerations in Artificial Intelligence. *European Journal of Radiology*, *122*, 108768. DOI: 10.1016/j.ejrad.2019.108768 PMID: 31786504

Sahu, D. K., & Rath, G. (2025). Innovative Approaches to Recover Waste in the Textile Sector. In *Nanotechnology-Assisted Recycling of Textile Waste* (pp. 129–169). Wiley., DOI: 10.1002/9781394175017.ch5

Salajan, F. D., Barnes, T. L., & Becker, A. (2024). Comparative regionalism cases of artificial intelligence governance in education: The Caribbean Community and the European Union. *The Round Table*, *113*(1). Advance online publication. DOI: 10.1080/00358533.2024.2307793

Saldanha, A. (2017, December 28). *2017, a year of hate crimes in India: Number of violent incidents related to cows, religion is rising-India News, Firstpost*. Firstpost. https://www.firstpost.com/india/2017-a-year-of-hate-crimes-in-india-number-of -violent-incidents-related-to-cows-religion-is-rising-4278751.html

Salmi, J., & D'Addio, A. (2021). Policies to achieve inclusion in higher education. *Policy Reviews in Higher Education*, *5*(1), 47–72.

Sanchez, T. W., Brenman, M., & Ye, X. (2024). The ethical concerns of artificial intelligence in urban planning. *Journal of the American Planning Association*, •••, 1–14.

Sanderson, N. C., Kessel, S., & Chen, W. (2022). What do faculty members know about universal design and digital accessibility? A qualitative study in computer science and engineering disciplines. *Universal Access in the Information Society*, *21*(2), 351–365. PMID: 35370532

Sanghvi, H., Bhavsar, R., Hundlani, V., Gohil, L., Vyas, T., Nair, A., Desai, S., Jadav, N. K., Tanwar, S., Sharma, R., & Yamsani, N. (2024). MetaHate : AI-based hate speech detection for secured online gaming in metaverse using blockchain. *Security and Privacy*, *7*(2). Advance online publication. DOI: 10.1002/spy2.343

Sarlin, P., & Peltonen, T. A. (2013). Mapping the state of financial stability. *Journal of International Financial Markets, Institutions and Money*, *26*, 46–76.

Sarlon, J., Schneider, E., Brühl, A. B., Ulrich, S., Liwinski, T., Doll, J. P., Muehlauser, M., & Lang, U. E. (2024). Adjunctive use of mindfulness-based mobile application in depression: Randomized controlled study. *European Archives of Psychiatry and Clinical Neuroscience*. Advance online publication. DOI: 10.1007/s00406-024-01884-y PMID: 39230745

Sato, N. N., Condes Moreno, E., Rubio-Zarapuz, A., Dalamitros, A. A., Yaez-Sepulveda, R., Tornero-Aguilera, J. F., & Clemente-Suárez, V. J. (2023). Navigating the new normal: Adapting online and distance learning in the post-pandemic era. *Education Sciences*, *14*(1), 19.

Satpathy, I., Nayak, A., & Jain, V. (2024). *The Green City*., DOI: 10.4018/979-8-3693-6854-1.ch009

Saura, J. R., Ribeiro-Soriano, D., & Palacios-Marqués, D. (2022). Assessing behavioral data science privacy issues in Government Artificial Intelligence Deployment. *Government Information Quarterly*, *39*(4), 101679. DOI: 10.1016/j.giq.2022.101679

Savaşan, Z. (2024). Data Bias and Discrimination in AI: Addressing Social Justice Concerns through Legal Reform. *Mayo Communication Journal, 1*(1), 73–82. https://www.researchcorridor.org/index.php/mcj/article/view/149

Schmitt, M. (2023). Automated machine learning: AI-driven decision making in business analytics. *Intelligent Systems with Applications*, *18*, 200188.

Schroeder, P. (2020). Digital accessibility in higher education: Legal, ethical, and institutional challenges. *Journal of Disability Policy Studies*, *30*(4), 258–273.

Schueffel, P. (2017). Taming the beast: A scientific definition of Fintech. *Journal of Innovation Management*, *4*(4), 32–54. DOI: 10.24840/2183-0606_004.004_0004

Schulze, E. (4 February 2019). *EU says Facebook, Google and Twitter are getting faster at removing hate speech online*. CNBC. Retrieved 25 March 2025.

Scoones, I. (2002). *Science, policy and regulation: Challenges for agricultural biotechnology in developing countries*. IDS Working Paper 147.

Seale, J. (2013). *E-learning and disability in higher education: Accessibility research and practice*. Routledge.

Selimovic, J., Pilav-Velic, A., &Krndzija, L. (2022). Digital Workplace Transformation and innovation in the Financial Service Sector. Lecture Notes in Networks and Systems, 375–396. Available at: DOI: 10.1007/978-3-031-16598-6_16

SELMA Partners. (2019, April 8). *The consequences of online hate speech – a teenager's perspective | SELMA Hacking Hate*. Hackinghate.eu. https://hackinghate.eu/news/the-consequences-of-online-hate-speech-a-teenager-s-perspective/

Servou, E., Behrendt, F., & Horst, M. (2023). Data, AI and governance in MaaS – Leading to sustainable mobility? *Transportation Research Interdisciplinary Perspectives*, *19*, 100806. DOI: 10.1016/j.trip.2023.100806

Seyedan, M., Mafakheri, F., & Wang, C. (2023). Order-up-to-level inventory optimization model using time-series demand forecasting with ensemble deep learning. *Supply Chain Analytics*, *3*, 100024.

Shafik, W. (2024a). An Overview of Computational Modeling and Simulations in Wireless Communication Systems. *Computational Modeling and Simulation of Advanced Wireless Communication Systems*, 8–40.

Shafik, W. (2024f). Factors Affecting Green Purchase Behaviors for Small and Medium Enterprises (SMEs) in Uganda. In *Entrepreneurial Strategies for the Internationalization and Digitalization of SMEs* (pp. 198–224). IGI Global. https://doi.org/DOI: 10.4018/979-8-3693-3518-5.ch009

Shafik, W. (2024g). IoT-Enabled Secure and Intelligent Smart Healthcare: Beyond 5G in Enabling Smart Cities. In *Secure and Intelligent IoT-Enabled Smart Cities* (pp. 308–333). IGI Global.

Shafik, W. (2024i). Mobile Learning and Bring Your Own Device (BYOD): Enhancing Education in the Digital Age. In *Integrating Cutting-Edge Technology Into the Classroom* (pp. 240–267). IGI Global.

Shafik, W. (2024k). Towards Trustworthy and Explainable AI Educational Systems. In *Explainable AI for Education: Recent Trends and Challenges* (pp. 17–41). Springer.

Shafik, W. (2024b). Barriers to Implementing Computational Intelligence-Based Agriculture System. In *Computational Intelligence in Internet of Agricultural Things* (pp. 193–219). Springer., DOI: 10.1007/978-3-031-67450-1_8

Shafik, W. (2024c). Biosensor-Based Drones Anomaly Detection Integration for Sustainable Agriculture Development. In *Achieving Food Security Through Sustainable Agriculture* (pp. 283–316). IGI Global., DOI: 10.4018/979-8-3693-4240-4.ch012

Shafik, W. (2024d). Connected healthcare—the impact of Internet of Things on medical services. In *Artificial Intelligence and Internet of Things based Augmented Trends for Data Driven Systems* (pp. 181–217). CRC Press., DOI: 10.1201/9781003497318-10

Shafik, W. (2024e). Deep Learning Impacts in the Field of Artificial Intelligence. In *Deep Learning Concepts in Operations Research* (pp. 9–26). Auerbach Publications., DOI: 10.1201/9781003433309-2

Shafik, W. (2024h). Machine Learning for Advanced Wireless Communication. In *Microwave Devices and Circuits for Advanced Wireless Communication* (pp. 252–278). CRC Press., DOI: 10.1201/9781032656021-13

Shafik, W. (2024j). The Future of Healthcare: AIoMT—Redefining Healthcare with Advanced Artificial Intelligence and Machine Learning Techniques. In *Artificial Intelligence and Machine Learning in Drug Design and Development* (pp. 605–634). Wiley., DOI: 10.1002/9781394234196.ch19

Shafik, W. (2025a). Machine Learning Techniques for Multicriteria Decision-Making. In *Multi-Criteria Decision-Making and Optimum Design with Machine Learning* (pp. 165–194). CRC Press.

Shafik, W. (2025b). Sustainable Agriculture and Diet for Urban Development. In *Sustainable Smart Cities and the Future of Urban Development* (pp. 165–192). IGI Global Scientific Publishing.

Shafik, W., Kalinaki, K., Fahim, K. E., & Adam, M. (2024). Safeguarding Data Privacy and Security in Federated Learning Systems. In *Federated Deep Learning for Healthcare* (pp. 170–190). CRC Press., DOI: 10.1201/9781032694870-13

Shafik, W., Kalinaki, K., & Zakari, R. Y. (2024). Blockchain's Motivation for IoT-Enabled Smart City. In *Secure and Intelligent IoT-Enabled Smart Cities* (pp. 195–221). IGI Global., DOI: 10.4018/979-8-3693-2373-1.ch010

Shah, N. V., & Patel, Y. S., & DBhangaonkar, P. (2021). Assessing impact of climate change on rainfall patterns of Vadodara District, Gujarat, India. [). IOP Publishing.]. *Journal of Physics: Conference Series, 1714*(1), 012046.

Shan, S., Wang, Y., Xie, X., Fan, T., Xiao, Y., Zhang, K., & Wei, H. (2023). Analysis of regional climate variables by using neural Granger causality. *Neural Computing & Applications, 35*(22), 16381–16402.

Sharada, K., Choudhary, S. L., Harikrishna, T., Dixit, R. S., Suman, S. K., Ayyappa Chakravarthi, M., & Bhagyalakshmi, L. (2025). GeoAgriGuard: AI-Driven Pest and Disease Management with Remote Sensing for Global Food Security. *Remote Sensing in Earth Systems Sciences, 8*(2), 409–422. DOI: 10.1007/s41976-025-00192-w

Sharma, M., Singh, K., Gautam, A. S., & Gautam, S. (2024). Longitudinal Study of Air Pollutants in Indian Metropolises: Seasonal Patterns and Urban Variability. *Aerosol Science and Engineering*, 1-16.

Sharma, G. K., & Ghuge, V. V. (2024). How urban growth dynamics impact the air quality? A case of eight Indian metropolitan cities. *The Science of the Total Environment, 930*, 172399. PMID: 38631640

Sharma, M., & Raskin, S. (2020). The digital divide: Addressing the accessibility gap for students with disabilities in global education. *International Journal of Educational Development, 49*, 57–68.

Sharma, S. (2024). Benefits or concerns of AI: A multistakeholder responsibility. *Futures, 157*, 103328. DOI: 10.1016/J.FUTURES.2024.103328

Shaw, R. (2020). Overcoming barriers to digital accessibility: Strategies for improving compliance and support. *Disability Studies Quarterly*, *40*(2), 85–98.

Shaw, R. (2020). Supporting students with disabilities through digital literacy training: Strategies for success. *Disability Studies Quarterly*, *40*(4), 60–72.

Shi, J. (2022). Research on Optimization of Cross-Border e-Commerce Logistics Distribution Network in the Context of Artificial Intelligence. *Mobile Information Systems*, *2022*, 1–11. DOI: 10.1155/2022/3022280

Shiva, V. (2001). *Protect or Plunder? Understanding Intellectual Property Rights*. Zed Books.

Shiva, V. (2004). The suicide economy of corporate globalization. *The Ecologist*, *32*(6), 28–31.

Shiva, V. (2016). *The Violence of the Green Revolution: Third World Agriculture, Ecology and Politics*. University Press of Kentucky.

Simon, J., Wong, P.-H., & Rieder, G. (2020). Algorithmic bias and the Value Sensitive Design approach. *Internet Policy Review*, *9*(4). Advance online publication. DOI: 10.14763/2020.4.1534

Simpson, R. M. (2012). Dignity, Harm, and Hate Speech. *Law and Philosophy*, *32*(6), 701–728. DOI: 10.1007/s10982-012-9164-z

Singhari, S., & Madheswaran, S. (2016). Social exclusion and caste discrimination in public and private sectors in India: A decomposition analysis. Bangalore: Institute for Social and Economic Change.

Slater, S., Taylor, R., & Green, P. (2020). The impact of AI on personalised learning in higher education. *Educational Research Review*, *15*(2), 189–202.

Smith, L. T. (1999). Decolonizing Methodologies: Research and Indigenous Peoples. Zed Books.

Smith, D. G. (2024). *Diversity's Promise for Higher Education: Making it work*. Jhu Press.

Space, C. (2018). *Self-Regulation and 'Hate Speech' on Social Media Platforms*, ARTICLE 19, https://www.article19.org/resources/self-regulation-hate-speech-social-media-platforms/

Staff, F. P. (2013, September 12). *Muzaffarnagar riots: The inciteful speeches that fanned rioters' fury*. Firstpost. https://www.firstpost.com/politics/muzaffarnagar-riots-the-inciteful-speeches-that-fanned-rioters-fury-1103789.html

Stefancic, J., & Delgado, R. (n.d.). *A Shifting Balance: Freedom of Expression and Hate-Speech Restriction Essay*. The University of Alabama.

Stirling, A. (2008). "Opening up" and "closing down": Power, participation, and pluralism in the social appraisal of technology. *Science, Technology & Human Values*, *33*(2), 262–294.

Stone, G. D. (2011). Field versus farm in Warangal: Bt cotton, higher yields, and larger questions. *World Development*, *39*(3), 387–398.

Storey, V. C., Hevner, A. R., & Yoon, V. Y. (2024). The design of human-artificial intelligence systems in decision sciences: A look back and directions forward. *Decision Support Systems*, *182*, 114230. DOI: 10.1016/J.DSS.2024.114230

Strubell, E., Ganesh, A., & McCallum, A. (2020, April). Energy and policy considerations for modern deep learning research. *Proceedings of the AAAI Conference on Artificial Intelligence*, *34*(09), 13693–13696.

Suarta, I. M., Suwintana, I. K., & Sudiadnyani, I. G. (2022). Technology and information system expertise demand for accounting professionals: A requirements analysis of job advertisements. *Advances in Social Science, Education and Humanities Research*. Advance online publication. DOI: 10.2991/assehr.k.220301.046

Suganya, R., Joseph, L. M. I. L., & Kollem, S. (2025). *Integrating Artificial Intelligence in Electric Vehicles and Optimizing Logistics for Sustainable Transportation.*, DOI: 10.4018/979-8-3693-7483-2.ch014

Suman, D. (2024). Deep Learning Methods for Demand Time Series Forecasting.

Suroor, J. (2012) *You can't read this book*, The Hindu. https://www.thehindu.com/books/you-cant-read-this-book/article2953626.ece

Susskind, R. (2020). *Online courts and the future of justice*. Oxford University Press.

Swanth, B., & Sheela, J. (2024, January). Agricultural Yield Forecasting with the Fusion of Transfer Learning and LSTM Approach. In *2024 2nd International Conference on Intelligent Data Communication Technologies and Internet of Things (IDCIoT)* (pp. 1268-1277). IEEE.

Sweeney, M. E. (2019). Digital assistants.

Szostek, K., Mazur, D., Drałus, G., & Kusznier, J. (2024). Analysis of the Effectiveness of ARIMA, SARIMA, and SVR Models in Time Series Forecasting: A Case Study of Wind Farm Energy Production. *Energies (19961073)*, *17*(19).

Tang, J., Liu, F., Zou, M., & Yang, H. (2020). AI-based dynamic traffic management in smart cities: Trends and applications. *Transportation Research Part C, Emerging Technologies*, *115*, 102622.

Tang, K. H. D. (2024). Implications of Artificial Intelligence for Teaching and Learning. *Acta Pedagogia Asiana*, *3*(2). Advance online publication. DOI: 10.53623/apga.v3i2.404

The Indian Express. (2018). *The mob that hates*. Harsh Mander.

The YouTube Team. (2019). *Our Ongoing Work to Tackle Hate*, Official YouTube Blog, https://youtube.googleblog.com/2019/06/our-ongoing-work-to-tackle-hate.html

Thirumal, S., & Latha, R. (2023). Machine Learning Based Predictive Assessments of Impacts of Influential Climatic Conditions for the Sustainable Productivity of Paddy Crops. *SSRG International Journal of Electronics and Communication Engineering*, *10*(5), 117–128.

ThonseHawaldar, I., Rohit, B., Pinto, P., & T. M., R. (2017). The impact of oil price crisis on financial performance of commercial banks in Bahrain. *Banks and Bank Systems*, *12*(4), 4–16. DOI: 10.21511/bbs.12(4).2017.01

Tohara, A. J. T., Shuhidan, S. M., Bahry, F. D. S., & Nordin, M. N. B. (2021). Exploring digital literacy strategies for students with special educational needs in the digital age. *Turkish Journal of Computer and Mathematics Education*, *12*(9), 3345–3358.

Topol, E. (2019). *Deep medicine: How artificial intelligence can make healthcare human again*. Basic Books.

Treve, M. (2021). What COVID-19 has introduced into education: Challenges facing higher education institutions (HEIs). *Higher Education Pedagogies*, *6*(1), 212–227.

Trocin, C., Mikalef, P., Papamitsiou, Z., & Conboy, K. (2023). Responsible AI for Digital Health: A Synthesis and a Research Agenda. *Information Systems Frontiers*, *25*(6). Advance online publication. DOI: 10.1007/s10796-021-10146-4

Truby, J. (2020). Governing artificial intelligence to benefit the UN sustainable development goals. *Sustainable Development*, *28*(4), 946–959.

Truong, H. M. (2016). Integrating learning styles and adaptive e-learning system: Current developments, problems and opportunities. *Computers in Human Behavior*, *55*, 1185–1193. DOI: 10.1016/j.chb.2015.02.014

Twitter (n.d.). *Hateful Conduct Policy*, Twitter, https://help.twitter.com/en/rules-and-policies/hateful-conduct-policy

U.S. Department of Education. (2020). *Section 508 of the Rehabilitation Act: Accessibility requirements for electronic and information technology*. Retrieved from https://www.ed.gov

U.S. Department of Justice. (2020). *Americans with Disabilities Act (ADA)*. Retrieved from https://www.ada.gov

U.S. Department of Justice. (2023, October 30). *Community Relations Service | 2022 FBI Hate Crimes Statistics*. Www.justice.gov. https://www.justice.gov/crs/highlights/2022-hate-crime-statistics

Ubaydullayeva, A. (2023). Intellectual property in the era of Artificial Intelligence: Challenges and Solutions. *Uzbek Journal of Law and Digital Policy*, *1*(3). Advance online publication. DOI: 10.59022/ujldp.93

UN General Assembly. (1966). *International Covenant on Economic*. Social and Cultural Rights.

UN Human Rights Council. (2018). *United Nations Declaration on the Rights of Peasants and Other People Working in Rural Areas.*

UNESCO. (2006). *Convention on the Rights of Persons with Disabilities (CRPD)*. Retrieved from https://www.un.org/disabilities/convention/conventionfulltext.shtml

Union of India. (1951). *The Representation of the People Act, 1951*. Kanoon.

Union of India. (1973). *The Code of Criminal Procedure, 1973*. Kanoon.

United Nations Office on Drugs and Crime. (2006). *Handbook on Restorative justice programmes*. https://www.unodc.org/pdf/criminal_justice/Handbook_on_Restorative_Justice_Programmes.pdf

van der Vlist, F., Helmond, A., & Ferrari, F. (2024). Big AI: Cloud infrastructure dependence and the industrialisation of artificial intelligence. *Big Data & Society*, *11*(1). Advance online publication. DOI: 10.1177/20539517241232630

Van Dijk, J. A. (2020). *The digital divide*. John Wiley & Sons.

Van Dijk, J. A. G. M. (2020). *The digital divide: The internet and social inequality in international perspective* (3rd ed.). Sage Publications.

Van Woerkom, W., Grossi, D., Prakken, H., & Verheij, B. (2024). A Case-Based-Reasoning Analysis of the COMPAS Dataset. *Frontiers in Artificial Intelligence and Applications*. https://doi.org/DOI: 10.3233/faia241244

VanGessel, F. G., Perry, E., Mohan, S., Barham, O. M., & Cavolowsky, M. (2023). Natural language processing for knowledge discovery and information extraction from energetics corpora. *Propellants, Explosives, Pyrotechnics, 48*(11). Advance online publication. DOI: 10.1002/prep.202300109

Varshney, R. K., Bohra, A., Yu, J., Graner, A., Zhang, Q., & Sorrells, M. E. (2021). Designing future crops: Genomics-assisted breeding comes of age. *Trends in Plant Science, 26*(6), 631–649. PMID: 33893045

Vasileiou, M. V., & Maglogiannis, I. G. (2022). The Health ChatBots in Telemedicine: Intelligent Dialog System for Remote Support. *Journal of Healthcare Engineering, 2022*. Advance online publication. DOI: 10.1155/2022/4876512

Venkataramanan, K. (2022). *Explained | What is "hate speech," and how is it treated in Indian law?* The Hindu. https://www.thehindu.com/news/national/explained-what-is-hate-speech-and-how-is-it-treated-in-indian-law/article64851585.ece

Vergani, M. (2024, January 29). *New Study Explores the Impact of Hate Crimes on Victims - Tackling Hate*. Tackling Hate. https://tacklinghate.org/blogs/new-study-explores-the-impact-of-hate-crimes-on-victims/

Vinuesa, R., Azizpour, H., Leite, I., Balaam, M., Dignum, V., Domisch, S., & Fuso Nerini, F. (2020). The role of artificial intelligence in achieving the Sustainable Development Goals. *Nature Communications, 11*(1), 233. PMID: 31932590

Vis, Y. A. (2020). *Characteristics of a successful public-private-partnership on Artificial Intelligence* (Bachelor's thesis).

von Ingersleben-Seip, N. (2023). Competition and cooperation in artificial intelligence standard setting: Explaining emergent patterns. *The Review of Policy Research, 40*(5), 781–810. DOI: 10.1111/ropr.12538

W3C. (2018). *Web Content Accessibility Guidelines (WCAG) 2.0*. W3C. Retrieved from https://www.w3.org/WAI/WCAG21/

Waldron, J. (2012). The Harm in Hate Speech. In *JSTOR*. Harvard University Press., https://www.jstor.org/stable/j.ctt2jbrjd

Walker, S. (1994). *Hate Speech: The History of an American Controversy*. University of Nebraska Press.

Walter, M., & Suina, M. (2019). Indigenous Data, Indigenous Methodologies and Indigenous Data Sovereignty. International Journal of Social Research Methodology.

Waltersmann, L., Kiemel, S., Stuhlsatz, J., Sauer, A., & Miehe, R. (2021). Artificial Intelligence Applications for Increasing Resource Efficiency in Manufacturing Companies—A Comprehensive Review. *Sustainability*, *13*(12), 6689. DOI: 10.3390/su13126689

Wang'ang'a, A. W. (2024). Consequences of Artificial Intelligence on Teaching and Learning in Higher Education in Kenya: Literature Review. *East African Journal of Education Studies*, *7*(1). Advance online publication. DOI: 10.37284/eajes.7.1.1718

Wang, J., & Azam, W. (2024). Natural resource scarcity, fossil fuel energy consumption, and total greenhouse gas emissions in top emitting countries. *Geoscience Frontiers*, *15*(2), 101757. DOI: 10.1016/j.gsf.2023.101757

Wang, X., Zhang, Y., & Zha, Z. J. (2019). Intelligent surveillance systems: AI-powered video analytics for public safety. *IEEE Transactions on Multimedia*, *21*(9), 2293–2307.

Wardani, A. K., Kristalina, P., Hadi, M. Z. S., & Pratiarso, A. (2024, August). Bi-directional Long Short-Term Memory Method for Weather Prediction in Terms of Evacuation of River Drifting Victims. In *2024 International Electronics Symposium (IES)* (pp. 663-668). IEEE.

Webb, T.J. (2011). *Verbal Poison - Criminalizing Hate Speech: A Comparative Analysis and a Proposal for the American System*. 50 Washburn L.J. 445.

West, S. M. (2019). Data capitalism: Redefining the logics of surveillance and privacy. *Business & Society*, *58*(1), 20–41.

Whitt, L. A. (2009). Science, Colonialism, and Indigenous Peoples: The Cultural Politics of Law and Knowledge. Cambridge University Press.

Williams, D. P., Srinivas, G., Bajpai, A., Ghamande, M. V., Dhyani, B., & Pal, S. (2023, November). Fine Grained Air Quality Monitoring Based on BiGRU and AM Model for Enhanced Public Health. In *2023 7th International Conference on Electronics, Communication and Aerospace Technology (ICECA)* (pp. 235-240). IEEE.

Wilson, C., & Van Der Velden, M. (2022). Sustainable AI: An integrated model to guide public sector decision-making. *Technology in Society*, *68*, 101926.

WIPO. (2009). *Cable Television Networks Rules, 1994 (as amended up to February 27, 2009), India*.int. https://www.wipo.int/wipolex/en/legislation/details/13628

Wirba, A. V. (2023). Corporate Social Responsibility (CSR): The Role of Government in promoting CSR. *Journal of the Knowledge Economy*, *15*(2), 7428–7454. DOI: 10.1007/s13132-023-01185-0 PMID: 40479158

Wirtz, B. W., Weyerer, J. C., & Geyer, C. (2019). Artificial intelligence and the public sector—Applications and challenges. *International Journal of Public Administration*, *42*(7), 596–615.

Wischmeyer, T. (2019). Artificial intelligence and transparency: opening the black box. In *Regulating artificial intelligence* (pp. 75–101). Springer International Publishing.

Wolska, A. (2025). *Bridging the gap: The impact of open banking on traditional banking and Fintech collaboration*. FinTech and AI in Finance., DOI: 10.7190/fintaf.v2i1.414

World Wide Web Consortium. (W3C). (2018). *Web Content Accessibility Guidelines (WCAG) 2.1*. Retrieved from https://www.w3.org/WAI/WCAG21/

WTO. (1994). *Agreement on Trade-Related Aspects of Intellectual Property Rights*. Retrieved from https://www.wto.org/

Xu, M. T., Hu, K., & Das, M. U. S. (2019). *Bank profitability and financial stability*. International Monetary Fund.

Yadav, A. (n.d.). *Countering hate speech in india: Looking for answers beyond the law*. https://ili.ac.in/pdf/csi.pdf

Yadav, A. K. (2024). Challenges facing visually impaired students in inclusive higher education. *Educating for Societal Transitions*, 27.

Yan, B., Hao, F., & Meng, X. (2021). When artificial intelligence meets building energy efficiency, a review focusing on zero energy building. *Artificial Intelligence Review*, *54*(3), 2193–2220. DOI: 10.1007/s10462-020-09902-w

Yang, L., Tian, M., Xin, D., Cheng, Q., & Zheng, J. (2024). AI-driven anonymization: Protecting personal data privacy while leveraging machine learning. *Applied and Computational Engineering*, *67*(1), 273–279. DOI: 10.54254/2755-2721/67/2024MA0053

Yellowhead Institute. (2021). Cash Back: A Yellowhead Institute Red Paper. Toronto Metropolitan University. https://yellowheadinstitute.org

Yigitcanlar, T., Mehmood, R., & Corchado, J. M. (2021). Green Artificial Intelligence: Towards an Efficient, Sustainable and Equitable Technology for Smart Cities and Futures. *Sustainability*, *13*(16), 8952. DOI: 10.3390/su13168952

Yu, Q., & Gu, X. (2022). On the Digital Transformation Path of financial shared services. Lecture Notes on Data Engineering and Communications Technologies, 325–331. Available at: DOI: 10.1007/978-3-030-97874-7_41

Zapata, J., & Deroy, O. (2023). Ordinary citizens are more severe towards verbal than nonverbal hate-motivated incidents with identical consequences. *Scientific Reports, 13*(1). Advance online publication. DOI: 10.1038/s41598-023-33892-8 PMID: 37130915

Zhai, X., Chu, X., Chai, C. S., Jong, M. S. Y., Istenic, A., Spector, M., Liu, J. B., Yuan, J., & Li, Y. (2021). A Review of Artificial Intelligence (AI) in Education from 2010 to 2020. *Complexity, Vol., 2021*(1), 8812542.

Zhang, P., & Kamel Boulos, M. N. (2023). Generative AI in Medicine and Healthcare: Promises, Opportunities and Challenges. In *Future Internet* (Vol. 15, Issue 9). https://doi.org/DOI: 10.3390/fi15090286

Zhang, K., Zhang, L., & Du, M. (2021). Artificial intelligence and smart governance: A systematic literature review. *Government Information Quarterly, 38*(4), 101566.

Zhang, X., Han, L., Wei, H., Tan, X., Zhou, W., Li, W., & Qian, Y. (2022). Linking urbanization and air quality together: A review and a perspective on the future sustainable urban development. *Journal of Cleaner Production, 346*, 130988.

Zhang, Y. (2024). Circular economy innovations: Balancing fossil fuel impact on green economic development. *Heliyon, 10*(18). PMID: 39328564

Zheng, Z., Capra, L., Wolfson, O., & Yang, H. (2016). Urban computing: Concepts, methodologies, and applications. [TIST]. *ACM Transactions on Intelligent Systems and Technology, 7*(3), 1–25.

Zheng, Z., Wu, Z., & Marinello, F. (2023). Response to the letter to the editor "is the z-score standardized RSEI suitable for time-series ecological change detection? Comment on Zheng et al.(2022)". *The Science of the Total Environment, 855*, 1–4. PMID: 36150590

Zheng, Z., Xie, S., Dai, H. N., Chen, X., & Wang, H. (2018). Blockchain challenges and opportunities: A survey. *International Journal of Web and Grid Services, 14*(4), 352. DOI: 10.1504/ijwgs.2018.095647

Zhou, J., Chen, C., Li, L., Zhang, Z., & Zheng, X. (2022). FinBrain 2.0: when finance meets trustworthy AI. In *Frontiers of Information Technology and Electronic Engineering* (Vol. 23, Issue 12). https://doi.org/DOI: 10.1631/FITEE.2200039

Zhu, X., Qiu, T., & Liu, D. (2023). Resisting public monitoring in authoritarian regimes: Evidence from local environmental litigation in China. *Governance: An International Journal of Policy, Administration and Institutions, 36*(2), 459–477. DOI: 10.1111/gove.12675

Zolkafli, A., Mansor, N. S., Omar, M., Ahmad, M., Ibrahim, H., & Yasin, A. (2024). *AI for Smart Disaster Resilience among Communities*., DOI: 10.1007/978-3-031-67317-7_22

Zoran, M. A., Savastru, R. S., Savastru, D. M., & Tautan, M. N. (2020). Assessing the relationship between surface levels of PM2. 5 and PM10 particulate matter impact on COVID-19 in Milan, Italy. *The Science of the Total Environment, 738*, 139825. PMID: 32512362

Zuboff, S. (2019). *The age of surveillance capitalism: The fight for a human future at the new frontier of power*. PublicAffairs.

About the Contributors

Swati Chakraborty is a Visiting faculty (Assistant Professor), at the Institute of Legal Studies and Research, GLA University. Dr. Chakraborty is associated as an Adjunct Faculty with Concordia University, Canada. She is an International Fellow of KAICIID in Lisbon, Portugal. She is the Founder of "Webplatform4Dialogue".

***

Iroda Abdullaeva is a faculty member at the Department of Philosophy at Urgench State University, Urgench, Uzbekistan. She has a background in philosophical sciences and is engaged in teaching and research in areas related to ethics, social philosophy, and cultural studies. Abdullaeva contributes to academic initiatives and conferences, and her research interests include moral philosophy, philosophical traditions in Central Asia, and their relevance to modern society.

Munir Ahmad is a seasoned professional in the realm of Spatial Data Infrastructure (SDI), Geo-Information Productions, Information Systems, and Information Governance, boasting over 25 years of dedicated experience in the field. With a PhD in Computer Science, Dr. Ahmad's expertise spans Spatial Data Production, Management, Processing, Analysis, Visualization, and Quality Control. Throughout his career, Dr. Ahmad has been deeply involved in the development and deployment of SDI systems specially in the context of Pakistan, leveraging his proficiency in Spatial Database Design, Web, Mobile & Desktop GIS, and Geo Web Services Architecture. His contributions to Volunteered Geographic Information (VGI) and Open Source Geoportal & Metadata Portal have significantly enriched the geospatial community. As a trainer and researcher, Dr. Ahmad has authored over 50 publications, advancing the industry's knowledge base and fostering innovation in Geo-Tech, Data Governance, and Information Infrastructure, and Emerging

Technologies. His commitment to Research and Development (R&D) is evident in his role as a dedicated educator and mentor in the field.

Srijani Dasgupta is a Computer Science Engineer with a specialization in Artificial Intelligence and Machine Learning.

Md Mehedi Hasan Emon is a research practitioner in Business and Management, with specialized in Supply Chain Management, Digital Transformation, Marketing, Information Systems, and Educational Technology (Edutech). His work bridges a diverse range of domains including Artificial Intelligence in Business, Human-Computer Interaction, Cognitive Behaviour, E-commerce, and Smart Logistics. His research extensively explores the integration of emerging technologies in business ecosystems focusing on AI-driven innovation, behavioral responses to technology adoption, and digital marketing strategies. He has also contributed significantly to sustainability-focused fields such as GreenTech, Green Finance, Renewable Energy, and Blockchain-enabled financial innovation. Additionally, his work in Smart Cities and IoT adoption emphasizes the importance of user trust, security, and operational efficiency. Emon has authored numerous peer-reviewed publications on topics including AI adoption intention, supply chain visibility, digital learning acceptance, and crisis-resilient supply chains. Many of his studies adopt behavioral and cognitive perspectives to understand how professionals and consumers interact with technology highlighting the psychological and user-centric aspects of digital transformation. He has participated in several research initiatives funded by the University Grants Commission of Bangladesh and the European Union. His work aligns closely with the United Nations Sustainable Development Goals (SDGs), particularly in areas such as poverty reduction, access to quality education, clean and affordable energy, inclusive economic growth, sustainable industrialization, responsible consumption, climate resilience, and ocean sustainability. His work also reflects a commitment to reducing inequalities and fostering international partnerships for sustainable development. In addition to his research contributions, he serves as a peer reviewer for several high-impact academic journals and is widely recognized for promoting academic rigor and ethical scholarship. As a prolific author, he continues to shape the discourse on sustainability, innovation, and digital advancement through his research, writing, and knowledge dissemination.

Noor Hayat is working as Assistant Professor at University of Central Punjab. He completed his doctoral degree from Universiti Sains Malaysia. His research interests are political and international communication, artificial intelligence, media framing and agenda setting and climate change

Kire Jakimoski is an experienced Full Professor with a demonstrated history of working in the higher education industry. Skilled in Computer Networks, Mobile and Wireless Networks, Optical Networks, Cybersecurity. Strong education professional with a D.Sc. in technical sciences from Faculty of Electrical Engineering and Information Techologies, focused in Computer Networks and Cybersecurity.

A.V. Senthil Kumar is working as a Professor and Director, PG and Research Department of Computer Applications, Hindusthan College of Arts & Science, Coimbatore, Tamilnadu. To his credit he has industrial experience for five years and teaching experience of 27 years. He has also received his Doctor of Science (D.Sc in Computer Science). He has to his credit 50 Book Chapters, 225 papers in International and National Journals 64 papers in International Conferences in International and National Conferences, and edited 14 books and 2 Text books. He is as Associate Editor of IEEE Access. He is an Editor-in-Chief for many journals and Key Member for India, Machine Intelligence Research Lab (MIR Labs). He is an Editorial Board Member and Reviewer for various International Journals. He is also a Committee member for various International Conferences.

Maksud A.Madraswale working as an Associate Professor, Department of Management, Presidency University, Bengaluru. For few years he served at Oman and other Arab Countries. To his credit he published five articles in Scopus Indexed journals.

Achyutananda Mishra is a Professor at School of Law, Christ University, Bangalore. He has 25 years of teaching experience. He has his research interests in the areas of Constitutional law, Legal theory, Democracy and Globalization. He has supervised a Postdoctoral research scholar and is currently guiding Ph.D. scholars under his supervision.

Avishek Nath is an enthusiastic scholar specializing in Business and Management as well as Business Administration. His scholarly interests focus on key contemporary areas including Digital Transformation, Entrepreneurial Growth, Innovation Strategies, and Strategic Management. Avishek's expertise extends to Supply Chain Innovation, Digital Entrepreneurship, and Organizational Behavior, with particular emphasis on AI adoption and technology-driven business models. His research also encompasses critical themes such as Operational Efficiency, Strategic Procurement, Business Sustainability, Automation, Data Analytics, and the development of Agile Organizations. With a strong foundation in Project Management and emerging technologies, Avishek investigates how these elements collectively drive business innovation and competitive advantage in rapidly evolving markets. He has more than seven years of industry and market research experience and has numerous research publications. He has also actively participated in international conferences, contributing to global academic discourse in his fields of expertise. Committed to advancing academic knowledge and practical solutions, Avishek's work aims to support sustainable growth and transformative change in today's technology-infused business environment.

Meherun Nisa Nipa is a business research professional with expertise spanning Entrepreneurship Development, Digital Transformation, Strategic Innovation, Strategic Management, Business Ecosystem Sustainability, Innovation Management, Organizational Change, Leadership Development, Knowledge Management, Corporate Governance, Policy and Regulatory Frameworks, Sustainable Business Models, Technology Adoption, Social Entrepreneurship, and Inclusive Economic Growth. Her research sits at the intersection of emerging technologies, organizational strategy, and sustainable development, focusing on how innovation can be systematically aligned with practical business and societal needs. By integrating academic theory with professional practice, Nipa delivers applied research that addresses real-world challenges, driving impact across industries and communities. Her work contributes to shaping the evolving landscape of digital transformation, entrepreneurial ecosystems, and long-term sustainability in the global business arena.

Nitish Ojha is a distinguished scholar, Researcher, and mentor having rich Industrial experience as well as varied experience in Teaching and Research. He has academic experience of over 15 years with renowned universities like American University of Europe, University of Stirling UK, and others where he worked in the capacity of Assistant Professor, also worked as a Core Member of Research and Development in Indian Universities i.e., Chandigarh University, LPU, Amity University. He has worked as a software engineer in Nokia Siemens Network, India. He served in several research projects in different profiles of researchers funded by DST/MCIT/MOHFW Govt. of India having National and International importance at IIT Delhi and in AIIMS.

Ananya Pandey is a Research Scholar in School of Law at Christ University, Bangalore. She has her research interests in the field of Constitutional Law, Environment Law, Human Rights, Food Security, Intellectual Property Law and Jurisprudence.

R. Bhuvaneswari working as an Assistant Professor of English at Dr.Mahalingam College of Engineering and Technology, Pollachi. To her credit she completed 10 NPTEL / SWAYAM and published few articles in Scopus indexed journals.

R. Velmurugan presently working as an Associate Professor in Commerce, Karpagam Academy of Higher Education, Coimbatore. He started his career as a Project Fellow under UGC Sponsored Major Research Project at NGM College, Pollachi. He has 18 years of teaching experience has 15 years of research experience. To his credit he produced 22 Ph.D. Scholars and 5 M.Phil. Scholars. At present 1 scholar submitter his thesis, 6 Ph.D. Scholars are under his guidance. Moreover, to his credit he published 163 articles in various International Journals, of which 56 articles are published in Scopus Indexed Journals and 15 articles in Web of Science and 76 articles in edited volumes. He also participates and presented 27 papers in various International Seminar / Conference and 54 National Seminar / Conference. He acted as an external examiner for various M.Phil. and Ph.D. Viva voce examinations. He acted as a Vice Chancellor nominee for Doctoral Committee Expert at Bharathiar University, Coimbatore and Periyar University, Salem. He acted as a Chairperson at various National Level Conferences. He also acted as an Expert for Syllabus Scrutiny Committee, Question Paper Scrutiny Committee and Expert members for Board of Studies at various reputed Colleges. Considering his meritorious contribution, he received awards like Best Paper Presenter, Best Research Supervisor and Best Faculty Awards from various research foundations and councils. He too acted as a resource person for 27 Guest Lectures, 30 Workshops and 10 faculty development programmes.

Valisher Sapayev is a lecturer at the Department of General Professional Subjects at Mamun University, Khiva, Uzbekistan. He holds an academic background in pedagogical sciences and has been actively involved in higher education teaching and research. He regularly contributes to academic projects at Mamun University, with a focus on modern teaching methodologies, student engagement, and the integration of innovative pedagogical technologies in the learning process. His research interests include pedagogy, educational psychology, curriculum design, and the role of digital and interactive methods in university education.

Snehatit Sett completed BBA-LLB (Hons.) from University of Engineering and Management, Kolkata.

Wasswa Shafik (Member, IEEE) received a Bachelor of Science degree in information technology from Ndejje University, Uganda, a Master of Engineering degree in Information Technology (Computer and Communication Networks) from Yazd University, Iran, and a PhD in Computer Science with the School of Digital Science, Universiti Brunei Darussalam, Brunei Darussalam. He is also the Founder and Research Director of the Dig Connectivity Research Laboratory (DCRLab) after serving as a Research Associate at the Network Interconnectivity Research

Laboratory at Yazd University. Prior to this, he worked as a Community Data Analyst at Population Services International (PSI-Uganda), a Community Data Officer at the Programme for Accessible Health Communication (PACE-Uganda), a Research Assistant at the Socio-Economic Data Centre (SEDC-Uganda), Uganda, an Assistant Data Officer at TechnoServe, Kampala, Uganda, and Asmaah Charity Organization as Cheif Executive Officer. He has hundreds of publications with renowned publishers. His research interests include Artificial Intelligence, Neural Networks, Computer Vision, Smart Agriculture, Digital Health, and Green Computing.

Ravi Thirumalaisamy working as an Assistant Professor, Department of Business and Economics, Modern College of Business and Science. To his credit, he published more than 10 articles in Scopus indexed journals.

Index

A

B

C

D

E

T

U

V

www.ingramcontent.com/pod-product-compliance
Lightning Source LLC
LaVergne TN
LVHW062326300926
849161LV00007B/1594